"The battles we face in life can oftentimes seem insurmountable in the moments of pain from whatever has crossed our path. Whether you're facing a diagnosis of cancer or have survived traumatic events that have led to post-traumatic stress, there is hope and peace available. I have known David since 2019. Even as a seasoned Army Sgt, I shed a few tears as this book moved me! As a medically retired Army combat veteran of the Iraq war, I know just how important it is to have hope, to discover peace within, and ultimately, to overcome my own battles with PTSD. Faith is vital to anyone's healing journey, no matter the diagnosis. I highly encourage everyone to pick up *Grounded and Cured* and don't set it down till you finish! How you fight your battles will be determined by what you believe. So now is the time to grab *Grounded and Cured* and equip yourself with the tools you need to be victorious!

SGT. JASON SAPP USA (RET)
Author of *Fortitude: Rising out of the Trenches of Trauma into a Life Free from Fear, Pain, Shame and Suicidal Thoughts*

· · · · · ·

"Your best chance to win a battle is to have a plan beforehand. David's book could be that edge to give you the perspective and inspiration it takes to win your war with cancer. That battle usually comes as an ambush. An inspirational account of a cancer success story, *Grounded and Cured* is a must-read for anyone who might someday hear those three words, 'You have cancer.'"

BILLY BEST
Cancer Survivor (19 years) & Author of
The Billy Best Story: Killing Cancer with Alternative Medicine

· · · · ·

"LtCol David Trombly is a true example of the fighting spirit displayed by a current-day Warrior. His determination and persistence demonstrate the will to win which is a powerful example for anyone who needs to overcome a major life challenge. You will appreciate the struggle that he experienced and his dramatic recovery. I highly recommend *Grounded and Cured* as an example of great courage and dedicated resilience."

MAJOR GENERAL CARL G. SCHNEIDER, USAF (RET)
Author of *Jet Pioneer: A Fighter Pilot's Memoir*

. . . . . .

"Grounded and Cured is not a book about cancer or fighter pilots. This book is a guide for anyone in a FIGHT! David and Megan tell a story of unwavering focus and determination to WIN! Together with GOD, this awesome couple stood together and beat every odd in an unbelievable situation. This couple walked through that valley of death, they feared no evil, because they were the toughest folks in the Valley, protected and led by GOD. I highly recommend you read this testimonial if you are looking for encouragement and guidance to win your fight."

DR. BRUCE BRIGHT
Head Coach at On Target Leading,
Former Marine Fighter Pilot and Commanding Officer

. . . . . .

"Adversity doesn't schedule itself; it often shows up unannounced. Athletes in every sport experience inevitable highs and lows and without a proper foundation, they can lack peace. T-Bone's story will inspire all readers towards finding peace amidst the storms of life. A must-read for all athletes as this story will both challenge and inspire you towards a stronger and genuine faith or an encounter for the first time with the true and living God"

Don J Liesemer
CEO of Hockey Ministries International

. . . . .

"In *Grounded and Cured,* David's warm, fun, and personal style invites the reader on the journey of empowering healing. David's life is a living parable of how someone faced with one of mankind's greatest physical challenges, perpetually grew an unwavering faith in Christ to radically believe for and receive emotional and physical healing. Upon sitting to read only a few pages before bed, I found myself engulfed by almost 70 pages of the book, excited and intrigued by his testimony! I recommend ordering multiple copies of *Grounded and Cured,* to share with family and friends who may be searching for hope in the midst of life's challenging circumstances."

Papa Joe Bradford
Professional Speaker & Author,
Inspiration behind the movie *Unconditional*

. . . . .

"LtCol David "T-Bone" Trombly, USMC is a living example of how to beat cancer with unshakable faith and natural medicine solutions. He exemplifies the Exceptional Cancer patient described by Dr. Bernie Siegel, MD. He fought cancer and won by pouring all-out effort into his self-care instead of accepting side effects from conventional treatment. Imagine my joy when he reached out 25 years later— not only is he alive and well, but his family is thriving! His journey offers many valuable lessons for everyone fighting illness and seeking wellness."

DR. FELIX LIAO, DDS
Author of *Six-Foot Tiger,*
Three-Foot Cage, Early Sirens, and *Licensed To Thrive*

· · · · ·

"Riveting, raw, Christ-honoring testimony of the dark journey of cancer. David has penned what it feels like to walk through the Valley of the Shadow of Death and come out alive. After being given no chance of survival for a rare bone cancer, he powerfully articulates that there is more than one way to cure disease. It can be done outside the modern medical system. Using plants and God, he and his wife chronicle their incredible story of healing. If you need words of life to hold you through pain, if you need to see that God's plants still heal the human body, and if you need to find your roots in Christ, begin with this book. It teaches worship through suffering. It teaches you how to find God and how to find yourself. *Grounded and Cured* is a soul reset for a world that needs hope. Well done, David. Standing ovation.

SARAH HARNISCH
4-Time Amazon Best-Selling Author of *Gameplan,*
Unstuck, Fearless, and *Ignite;* International Speaker,
Radio Network News Anchor, and Homeschool Mom of 5

· · · · ·

"David Trombly is the real deal. His life is a testimony of God's grace and goodness. He lives to encourage others and make the name of Christ known. David's story is written with great detail and you sense you are on the journey to healing with him. Within the pages of this book you will find inspiration and a challenge to embrace each day with boldness.

Dr. Ted Traylor

Pastor of Olive Baptist Church, Pensacola, FL

. . . . .

"What is our purpose? *Grounded and Cured* as written by my Friend "T-Bone" provides bold insight, a roadmap for those searching for that which they don't know. Have you ever felt like a 'blind man in a dark closet looking for a black hat?' This book will open your mind to fully capture what is possible. Dave and I quickly became friends shortly after he found his cure. I was blessed with Dave's enthusiasm for living a life of what's possible. As an old Army veteran, we often lived by 'pathfinders' logic' which is simply defined as 'Where am I? Where am I going? How am I going to get there?' Everything about T-Bone's journey in life has followed that logic. With great detail, *Grounded and Cured* will guide you through those often-unanswered questions of what we don't know. Dave had absolute conviction that a key element of his cure was to remove those toxic chemicals invading his body from his home's water. Our company AquaOx, Inc was birthed and inspired in 2005 through David's testimony and his concern about our health through what we drink, and more importantly, what we absorb through our skin and into our bodies through bathing."

Michael Corcoran

President of AquaOx, Inc.

. . . . .

"Having known LtCol Trombly for over 4 years, you would never know of his battle with cancer unless he told you. He is a whole man, one who walked through the fire, jumped through the hoops, and led his family through the process. If you are looking for a book that will captivate you from the first page then *Grounded and Cured* is it. Seeing the best of the best, facing his greatest challenge, and doing it through prayer and the natural way God designed our bodies to heal, is nothing short of a miracle. This book is written by a man's man. You will laugh, cry, and get frustrated at times with the situations in this book, but you will always know losing hope was never an option!"

VERICK BURCHFIELD
D Gary Young, Young Living Foundation Board Member

. . . . . .

"T-Bone has managed to effortlessly weave elements of his faith, family, and friends into his true story about overcoming adversity. However, this is not just a story about overcoming cancer, although that's a big part of it. This is a story about facing adversity head-on and overcoming against all odds. For anyone who has hit a rough patch, or deals with depression or PTSD, please take the time to read this book. His actions can serve as a role model for you. All is not lost. Have faith in your God, in yourself, in your friends, and in your family. They are all willing to help you; you just need to look for it like David did... and I am honored and humbled to have played a small part in helping my friend."

COLONEL JAVIER "NERF" BALL, USMC (RET.)
Sr. Manager, GMSS Operations and Military Business
Integration Global Military Sales and Strategy | Bell

. . . . .

"WOW! T-Bone's *Grounded and Cured* is a beautiful piece of art in which the Gospel of Jesus Christ is shared vividly through a powerful, yet personal voice. This book reminds us that we have hope during the darkest days of life. Because of the power of God, 'We are afflicted in every way, but not crushed; perplexed, but not despairing; persecuted, but not abandoned; struck down, but not destroyed; always carrying around in the body the dying of Jesus, so that the life of Jesus may also be revealed in our body.' (2 Corinthians 4: 8-10) *Grounded and Cured* tells the story of a dying man who found abundant life in the miraculous hands of the Savior, Jesus Christ."

DR. LEO DAY
Former Dean of the School of Church Music at Southwestern Baptist Seminary, Fort Worth, TX & Former Music Director of Olive Baptist Church in Pensacola, FL

. . . . .

"*Grounded and Cured* is a must-read for any athlete sidelined from injury as I was. You will be encouraged! T-Bone is a man of God who faithfully supported me and my family when I sustained multiple injuries while playing professional hockey. His intercessory prayers and his counsel were instrumental in my healing. I will always be grateful for T-bone's prayers, wisdom, and compassion."

"BIG JOHN" MCLEAN
Former Goalie with the SPHL Champions Pensacola Ice Flyers

. . . . .

"In a society where standing your ground seems to have been replaced with acceptance, LtCol Trombly brilliantly shows that faithfully fighting for what you feel in your gut to be right is as important as seeking wise counsel. I had the privilege of reading this manuscript as it was finished and know first hand the ability this book has to encourage, bolster, and challenge your perspective on the fight you may be enduring. The only time we are out of the fight is when we give up. T-Bone epitomizes in his book as much as he does in real life: meekness isn't weakness, but strength under control — a character trait we should all strive for.

SCOTT SCHULER D.C.
Author of *Man Up*

. . . . .

"*Grounded and Cured* is a must-read for cancer Warriors. T-Bone shows how undying faith in our LORD coupled with research and prayer guided him through the miracle healing of God he experienced. While this is David's story, the reader will see the impact David makes in the lives of everyone he meets. Little did I know when David came to work for me, that it would forever change my life and my walk with Christ."

DR. BRETT ULANDER
PsyD, Lieutenant Commander, US Navy (retired);
President and Co-Founder of Bluedrop USA

. . . . .

"David is my brother in Christ and a fellow cancer survivor. Only those who have battled cancer can fully grasp the full-scale war it is. While I have never served in the military, he and I share a common attribute: resilience. Quitting is just not in our DNA. David navigates the reader through an inspiring story of how his faith in Christ, his commitment to family, and his military service prepared him to face the greatest battle of his life. Cancer is hard. Life is hard. Choose your hard.

ED RODRIGUEZ
Cancer Survivor

. . . . .

"Whether he is LtCol David Trombly addressing Navy, Marine Corps, or Coast Guard Student Naval Aviators in a classroom; or he is Chaplain T-Bone speaking to professional athletes in a hockey or baseball locker room, his message has always been consistent: Determination, Discipline, Perseverance, and Faith. When faced in situations where the odds are against you, *Grounded and Cured* brings hope to those who choose to overcome!

PASTOR MIKE DIMICK, USAF (Ret.)
Minister, and former Chaplain for the Pensacola Blue Wahoos
Minor League Baseball Team

· · · · ·

"As I did, you, too, will find this engaging and personal story from LtCol Trombly, a story of strong faith and courage in the midst of a very challenging situation in life. Throughout the book there is an evident reliance and assurance of God's providence as revealed in Scripture. Trombly proves himself a faithful and courageous witness to the power of God, a God, in Trombly's words, who 'will deliver a prominent message of peace and hope' for all who walk through personal valleys in life. This is a must-read."

DR. TOM SEALS
Former Professor of Bible and Chaplain to Veterans at Lipscomb University, President/Executive Director of God's Word for Warriors & Author of *God's Word for Warriors: Returning Home Following Deployment*

· · · · ·

"I had the privilege of getting to know T-Bone through a challenge to climb Mt Kilimanjaro in 2019 with a team of 22 people from across the globe. Our purpose was to raise donations for

Hope for Justice to free men, women and children from trafficking (hopeforjustice.org). This was a significant challenge, climbing 5,895m in the midst of punishing winter conditions. T-bone always went the extra mile, and his encouragement helped so many who were struggling to keep going. When it's been raining for 3 days and everything you have is cold and damp, and all you want to do is give up, it was T-bone who continued to lift the team. Reminding each one of us of the 'why' behind the climb and the freedom from slavery we were bringing to so many by our actions. This story will bring hope to so many going through their own fight. I hope that like on the mountain, T-bone encourages you to keep going and never, ever give up! Whatever mountain you are climbing today, T-Bone will remind you of the why and encourage you to keep climbing in Grounded and Cured!

TIM NELSON, Bsc (Hons),
International Development Director and Co-Founder
of Hope for Justice, Manchester England

. . . . .

"I was privileged to meet David Trombly during the latter stages of the writing process. What an amazing journey of knowing the outcome before experiencing the outcome. It's clear to see that at his lowest point where he seemed most defeated, he was also at his strongest level of faith because he was completely dependent on his faith in God for a miracle. God was all he had. David is an example of 'The Working of Miracles!'"

MICHAEL RICKS
Banjo Country Music Artist & Author of *From Cult to Country: An Asthmatic's Search for More Air*

. . . . .

"In the medical profession, we often talk about the art of medicine. There is the data driven scientific side (the medicine side) and then there is the fact that every patient is an individual, and the basic scientific guidelines may not be best suited for that individual patient (the art side). After we met and I had the opportunity to review the medical data available, I also recommended to Dave that he go with conventional therapy (chemotherapy and radiation along with possibly more surgery). I could provide data on treatment side effects and outcomes. I could not provide any data on the treatment plan that Dave had elected to pursue. But it is important to remember that my role as a physician is not to force or coerce patients into my recommended treatment plan, but rather it is to make sure they have available and understand all the information needed to make informed decisions on their treatment. It was clear that Dave knew more about his diagnosis, conventional therapy, and alternative therapy than most physicians (myself included), and that he wished to pursue alternative therapy. At that point, it was my job as his primary physician to support him in any way possible. I know of very few individuals who could have put so much energy, time, determination and true grit into their treatment than Dave, and that was a major part of his success. But ultimately, it was his faith, family, friends, prayer, and his church support that led to God healing him. This was not a medical miracle, but a healing provided by THE great physician."

DR. CARY OSTERGAARD, MD
David's Primary Care Physician while he battled cancer

· · · · ·

"T-Bone's *Grounded and Cured* is an amazing story of God's faithfulness and power to overcome the greatest of challenges while developing an unshakeable faith. David has a skilful pen and is an entertaining host for sure. I count it a privilege to know David as a friend, brother in Christ, and fellow author. I've witnessed first hand his resolve and commitment to his God, family, and country. His book is the ultimate hero's tale everyone loves to read and it's sure to encourage your faith and spirit to overcome all that you face. You are sure to be inspired and blessed as he guides you through his journey.

BRIAN FRIEDL
Author of *Mission Possible: Living A Life That Matters*

. . . . .

"There are very few men I have ever met and even fewer that I get to call 'friend' who have lived as inspiring a life as David 'T-Bone' Trombly. I remember the first time my wife and I ever met David. We were at an event where I was the keynote speaker, and he picked us up to take us to the event. After hearing a quick 20-minute version of his testimony, I remember thinking, This man and I will be friends for life. And then I remember immediately saying, 'When is your book coming out?' This testimony has needed to be written for a long time, because it clearly shows the goodness and faithfulness of God in the lives of the Trombly family. It's an epic testimony and will leave you feeling one thing... HOPE. If this story teaches anything, it's that we can all do hard things when we are trusting in the Lord and allowing Him to guide us every step of the way. There isn't another man alive I respect more than T-Bone Trombly. I know this book and the story contained inside will change your life and leave you completely encouraged."

DR. JIM BOB HAGGERTON, D.C., C.C.W.P

. . . . .

"As a Christian, military colleague, and award-winning author, I can speak with a high level of confidence that this is a miraculous story of the power of human will in God's hands.

JEFF JORGENSON
USAF (RET.) Award-Winning Author of *Open Air: How People Like Yourself Are Changing the Aviation Industry*

. . . . .

"You don't know what you don't know. Think about that for a second. You could be extremely intelligent, advanced, gifted, or just downright lucky. But if you don't know something, it can affect your life in a very profound way. Being a surgeon for the past 21 years has been an incredible journey, filled with many *many* highs and certainly some lows. God has really blessed me with the charge to help improve the lives of my patients, and for that, I am immensely grateful. While I am not an oncologist, I have had many patients who have been diagnosed with cancer. I would always say to them, 'There are only three treatments for cancer: 1) surgery (cut it out), 2) chemotherapy, and 3) radiation. The only one I believe in is surgery.' As a surgeon, I definitely believed in removing cancer, but I had never been a fan of chemotherapy or radiation. Last year, however, I had the incredible experience of meeting David and Megan Trombly and now know that all those years I was WRONG! Surgery, chemotherapy, and radiation are NOT the only treatments for cancer. It took a United States Marine fighter pilot and the power of the Holy Spirit to open my eyes and heart to the other ways that people can slay cancer and instruct the 'body to heal itself.' *Grounded and Cured* is an incredibly powerful and life-changing story. It is a must-read for anyone who has been touched by cancer."

DR. MICHAEL J.COYLE
DO FACOOG, FPMRS, Board Certified Urogynecologist,
and CEO/President Coyle Institute for FPMRS

. . . . .

"Piloting his F/A-18 Hornet, Capt Trombly was instructed to 'immediately turn left off target.' But 'turning left' meant an imminent collision with Mount Fuji. In a split second, he realized the command came from his 12 o'clock, not his 6 o'clock, meaning 'their left' and 'his right'— Trombly turned right. Questioning authority, orders, and science, is an uphill battle. In his battle with bone cancer, again, Trombly chose to 'turn right.' They gave him months to live directing his wife to 'please get your affairs in order.' 'Turn left.' — Negative, Sir. No can do. I have known this guy for 20 years. He was toast and every Doc agreed. Once again, T-Bone 'turned right.' Actually, he turned to his faith in God and self, and in doing so, he punches the face of the food industry, big pharma, and our trusty 3-letter organizations... demanding the answer to why humans are the only mammals on planet earth that develop such widespread disease processes that generate huge profits. God's Intelligent Design provided us incredible, efficient healing mechanisms that thrive undeniably when working with the very tools God gave us in nature... oxygen, hydration, nutrients, and sunlight. His story, his faith, is very hard to believe unless you've known him for 20 years as I have. It is the kind of story that makes you stop and wonder: What powers of healing lie in the human spirit?"

LtCol David "G-Man" Glassman, USMC (Ret)
AHERO Vice President

. . . . .

"If you are looking for help and healing, *Grounded and Cured* is the well from which you need to drink. When you start reading David and Megan Trombly's story, you won't want to put it down.

ERIC HOVIND
President of Creation Today, Executive Producer of the International Award-Winning 3D Film, *GENESIS: Paradise Lost*

GROUNDED
AND CURED

*One Marine Fighter Pilot's Story of Miraculous Healing
from Cancer through Alternative Medicine and
His Unprecedented Return to Flight Status*

LtCol
David "T-Bone" Trombly
USMC (Ret.)

Traitmarker Books | FRANKLIN, TN

Publisher Information
Traitmarker Books
2984 Del Rio Pike
Franklin, TN 37069
traitmarkerbooks.com
traitmarker@gmail.com

Attributions
Interior Title & Text Font: Minion Pro
Editors: Delia McLeod, Sharilyn Grayson
Cover Design & Typesetting: Robbie Grayson III
Cover Photo: Christian Del Rosario, *Attreo Studio Galleries*
Bible References (Versions): New English Translation, New International Version, King James Version, Expanded Bible, New International Version, 1984 Edition]

Paperback ISBN: 978-1-63752-166-3
Hardcover ISBN: 978-1-63752-165-6
Ebook ASIN: B08TKCYC2V

Indexing Categories
1. BIOGRAPHY & AUTOBIOGRAPHY / Military
2. BODY, MIND & SPIRIT / Spiritual / Healing
3. RELIGION / Spiritual Warfare / Healing

Printed in the United States of America.

TABLE OF CONTENTS

PUBLISHER & AUTHOR DISCLAIMER

The publisher and the author are providing this book and its contents on an "as is" basis and make no representations or warranties of any kind with respect to this book or its contents. The publisher and the author disclaim all such representations and warranties, including but not limited to warranties of healthcare for a particular purpose. In addition, the publisher and the author assume no responsibility for errors, inaccuracies, omissions, or any other inconsistencies herein.

Additionally, the publisher and the author make no guarantees concerning the level of success one may experience by following the advice and strategies contained in this book, and one accepts the risk that results will differ for each individual. The testimonials and examples provided in this book show exceptional results, which may not apply to the average reader, and are not intended to represent or guarantee that one will achieve the same or similar results.

The content of this book is for informational purposes only and is not intended to diagnose, treat, cure, or prevent any condition or disease. This book is not intended as a substitute for consultation with a licensed practitioner. Please consult with a physician or healthcare specialist regarding the suggestions and recommendations made in this book. The use of this book implies your acceptance of this disclaimer.

While many names in this true story are revealed, fictitious names have been used in order to protect the individual privacy of some characters.

Doc, I'm not dead yet, and a strong will to win is second only to a deep faith in God. I have both! I will not only beat this disease, but I will fly again!

*I dedicate this book to the most faithful and capable wingman
with whom I have ever gone into battle—my high school sweetheart,
best friend, and the mother of our six amazing children, Megan
Simpson Trombly. Without this trend-setting, paradigm-shattering,
courageous woman of faith, this book could not have been written,
because I would not be alive to write it.*

*I give God, our gracious Abba Father, ALL the glory
for the miracles recorded within these pages!*

*To Megan, I express my endless gratitude for joining me in Combat
Spread Tactical Formation, as we launched through each door God
opened for us. Countless times, my courageous wingman took the
lead in our fight with the unseen enemy as we fought side by side,
one day at a time, until our ultimate victory. I owe you my very life,
my gratitude, my faithfulness, my remaining days!*

I love you, Megan!

FOREWORD

This book is one of courage. Courage in the face of an enemy we can't see and one that has taken the lives of millions . . . cancer. Now I know the author will want me to say that this book is about faith and hope and that God gets ALL the glory, and he'd be right. BUT, I am just astounded at the immense courage in this man. What it takes to be a warrior in today's Marine Corps and the type of people who defend our country and really know how to fight! The need for courage in the face of constant intrusions of the enemy. The courage to pray, the courage to kneel before God, the courage to let someone else fly the plane, the courage to cry, the courage to believe when only your wingman believes with you. Just . . . plain . . . courage! As the author says, "A strong will to win is second only to a strong faith in God. I have both Doc. I will not only beat this disease, but I will fly again."

This incredible act of fighting was amazing. But it's the humility and total understanding that God made this all happen that allows you to read, and learn from this warrior. I love reading the writing of a Marine! It's sharp, crisp, filled with details about Marine pilot life and you know, not the normal stuff you read. Then, to hear how this story unfolds, to learn about the cancer, to see the fight unfold, how conventional medicine is not the only answer . . . it takes your breath away.

One of the most interesting perspectives in the book comes from another source, Megan Trombly, David's wife. Even as you get wrapped up in David's journey, you get another look at this war from a different perspective. One filled with lots of unknowns, but also with HUGE amounts of faith. You begin to understand what

27

having a wingman really means, what a couple!!

"I've got you. You are not alone!" The Holy Spirit fills this book with faith and hope. And trust me, it pours out of the pages into... you! Part documentary, part biography, part drama, this story captures your heart and then takes you on a ride. You are in the fighter jet with the author, as he explains each maneuver he does to fight the enemy. Every lever he pulls in the cockpit and why it's necessary to do at this moment. Fighting cancer becomes a dogfight! And every pilot has to take their own path to victory. David shows us a different path, one not readily flown, but one with a master co-pilot, an incredible wingman, and a belief in healing from sources other than traditional medicine. I'm thankful that it's a ride I can do from my comfy chair and not in the seat behind David as he inverts the plane and dives!

I so enjoyed how David builds his "Success Team." How he talks to each one, rallies them, and encourages them, even though he is the one in trouble. His children and extended family become a part of the team. Others join the fight, some with experience against this enemy, and others just love for him and Megan. There is so much for us to learn from how a warrior battles this enemy, with God anything is possible, and with a team, you can make it!

We all talk about that peace that passes understanding, but David helps to truly grasp why it's so important and how to actually have it, not just talk about it. It's not just prayer, it's also Holy Spirit infused intuition... knowing what is happening and why. It doesn't always happen all at once, it can sometimes take months, maybe even years to play out, but when it does, watch out! The Lord has empowered you to take on an enemy MUCH larger than yourself and to do it with grace in spite of the terrible realities. The story turns from one of fight to one of victory. No, not the medical victory of chemo and radiation, but spiritual victory that David wants to share with you! Most of us have had to deal with death and disease, some closer to home than others. No one escapes death and what better way to face death head-on than with the King of Kings at your side. The author brings that chance to you!

ERIC WALTON | Author and Coach,
President of Building Up Leaders, LLC

INTRODUCTION
A Warrior's Perspective and Gratitude

It has been over nineteen years since God's miracle, manifested in my body, was officially documented in my military medical record by the hematology-oncology department doctors at the National Naval Medical Center in Bethesda, Maryland. It is now 0630, and God awakened me with a message: "Pray a circle around your family's cancer survival testimony! Take a step of faith, write it down, and let Me do what I will with our story."

I realize this is the introduction to a book previously only written on the hearts of myself, my wife, Megan, and my four older children, Alex, Brianna, Brad, and Grace Anne as God's blessings of Noah and Morgan came later. As a Marine Lieutenant Colonel and a fighter pilot, I understand war, but I had a lot to learn about my personal war—a war with cancer.

On October 17, 2000, I was diagnosed with a rare bone cancer and told that my life expectancy was no more than two years if I did nothing and maybe two and a half years with chemo and radiation. At the time, there was not one documented case of anyone beating this rare cancer which could be provided to me.

Our cancer War had begun. Without question, it was the most difficult year our family had endured to date. Many families can relate to a period of time when they, too, walked through their own personal, and sometimes public, valley.

Eleven months after diagnosis in September of 2001, the Bethesda, Maryland oncology doctors announced my cancer-free "All Clear" to my primary care physician at the Pensacola Naval Hospital, reporting that my cancer was gone. They did not, however, report or recognize our 100% biological and naturopathic efforts as the reason for our miraculous success.

31

Cancer is hard. Our battles were tough. But within this terrible war zone, our family experienced the most rewarding and peaceful year we had ever known. We truly lived out the poem, "Footprints in the Sand," as God held us close and carried us.

Footprints
by Carolyn Joyce Carty

One night a man had a dream.
He dreamed he was walking along the beach with the Lord.
Across the sky flashed scenes from his life.
For each scene, he noticed two sets of footprints in the sand;
one belonging to him, and the other to the Lord.
When the last scene of his life flashed before him,
he looked back at the footprints in the sand.
He noticed that many times along the path of his life
there was only one set of footprints.
He also noticed that it happened
at the very lowest and saddest times in his life.
This really bothered him and he questioned the Lord about it.
"Lord, you said that once I decided to follow you,
you'd walk with me all the way.
But I have noticed that during the most troublesome times in my life,
there is only one set of footprints.
I don't understand why when I needed you most you would leave me."
The Lord replied, "My precious, precious child,
I love you and I would never leave you.
During your times of trial and suffering,
when you see only one set of footprints,
it was then that I carried you.

Some read this poem focusing on the author's description of a person who has gone through deep agony and has looked back to ask God, "WHERE WERE YOU?" Many of us, understandably, do the same thing both during and after hard times— such as a terrorist attack, a natural disaster, or a family crisis.

We share this poem as a way to help people understand our

perspective. At the very foundation of our faith is the belief in the need for absolute dependence on the Lord, especially while walking through the valley of the shadow of death, or any other significant low point in life. We have walked this valley. That's why we choose to focus not on the perspective of the man, but rather on the act of God carrying him. That's what God did for us.

We look back now, on the other side of cancer, and see one set of footprints. We know they are the Lord's. We recognized His footprints early in the battle, long before we could look back. Our current vantage point is from a very good place—grateful for God's presence and presents—not doubtful as to where God was during our cancer war.

Agreeing that we had a divine purpose for becoming cancer Warriors, Megan and I have met hundreds of families in similar crises for nearly two decades to share our experiences and to pray for God to bring them hope, peace, and confidence, knowing that God Himself is in charge. We are no longer in the midst of our cancer war but rather commissioned in the fight with so many others who face traumatic circumstances. We won, and now we fight alongside others.

Since then, hundreds of other cancer Warriors and our personal mentors have encouraged Megan and me to write our story. Even one of my military medical doctors encouraged us to pen our journey to encourage others whether they face cancer or a different challenge. Each encouragement has been God's gentle nudge that we must put the journey of His love and amazing peace which we experienced in print.

I suppose that having shared our story as God has given us the opportunity to do so in living rooms and at kitchen tables, cancer support groups, youth hockey camps, and churches, it has given me a better insight of what HIS message truly is. It is far more than a motivational story of a Marine Corps fighter pilot pulling G's and soaring high above the clouds one day, then being grounded with cancer the next.

It is so much more! It is so much bigger than I am! It is about the amazing "God moment" in the doctor's office that first day. The surgeon unequivocally informed me of my deadly diagnosis, a two-year death sentence, one that meant I would never fly again. My reply was firm.

"A strong will to win is second only to a deep faith in God. I have both, Doc. I will not only beat this disease, but I will fly again."

That was the promise I heard loud and clear as God spoke to me on Day One in the oral surgeon's office at the branch medical clinic on Marine Corps Recruit Depot Parris Island, SC. That very day Megan and I stepped out in faith, embracing God's promise which I spontaneously verbalized within the first hour of my diagnosis. We clung to those words and prayed with a belief that God had already given the healing from that day forward, and we never gave up!

This is a story of faith, a faith that was as much a supernatural gift as the healing itself. This is a story of PEACE, a peace that cannot be explained.

I did not understand the power of the prayers we prayed or that were being prayed for us by family and friends around the globe. I do know that we felt, in palpable ways, the strength that came from an army of prayer warriors. We experienced a level of faith like never before. God provided clarity and discernment that kept us making good decisions on a path we had never before traveled and which we had no medical knowledge or life experience to navigate. God carried us down this road, providing all we needed at just the right time to avoid wrong turns on this uncharted path. It all happened in a manner which could give only God the glory.

Here we share our journey, the highs and the lows, in which even our children were used by God as integral members of our "Success Team." God spoke through our oldest son, Alex, only eight years old at the time, on the darkest day of our battle. He spoke life-giving words from Proverbs, and God used him to keep us from making a catastrophic, life-altering decision.

Tim McGraw released a song the year of my diagnosis, "Live

Like You Were Dying." It "stopped me on a dime" the first time I heard it. I get it, Tim! It is a gift to gain such a healthy perspective on life when facing imminent death. It is nothing short of blessings heaped upon blessings to have so many years afterward to enjoy watching my family grow in faith, to climb into airplanes teaching our country's future defenders, to have "church" while inverted in a loop, smiling when the young warrior's maneuver doesn't go so well. It was Kilimanjaro, not the Rockies, that I climbed, but yeah, that song still hits me on an emotional level every time I hear it. Thank you, Tim.

We researched and fought each day as if everything depended on our effort, yet we prayed as if everything depended on God Himself. I did not understand at the time that dynamic which I firmly believed, but I understand now that both are required. "Pray as if it all depends on God, and work as if it all depends on you." We have shared that challenge with many others beside whom we have had the privilege to walk.

Simply, it is a challenge to give God the burden, whatever it is, large or small; disease or a struggling marriage; repaying debt or asking God what career path to take. Let God carry it, and then you work with every ounce of energy and discernment and discipline that God pours into you to do the things He shows you to do. Let God open one door at a time, leading you to the resolution of that situation which He has already prepared a way to accomplish. Simultaneously, have the moral courage to step through the doors and execute the plan which He provides.

Knowing many are fighting a different battle, we pray this story encourages you no matter what you are facing in life. May our story be just one of the ways God opens doors for you should you decide to let Him carry your burdens.

"Cast your cares on the LORD and he will sustain you;
he will never let the righteous be shaken."
—Psalm 55:22 (NIV)

INTRODUCTION

"Cast all your anxiety on Him
because He cares for you."
—1 PETER 5:7

"Come to me, all you who are weary and burdened,
and I will give you rest. Take my yoke upon you
and learn from me, for I am gentle and humble
in heart, and you will find rest for your souls.
For my yoke is easy and my burden is light."
—MATTHEW 11:28-30 (NIV)

God gave us supernatural peace while we were fighting on the front lines. With the fog of War now dissipated, we look back at the entire year and see it in full view. The shock, the unknown, the questions, the sorrow, the tears, the emotions, the decisions, and the prayers were all veiled in God's peace—far beyond our human understanding.

Through our family's full-on engagement with the enemy, God *stretched* us. He *disciplined our willpower*. He strengthened our discernment. He grew our faith.

Some might look on the footprints of our cancer journey, misappropriating the credit for its endgame. Let's dispel that right here in the introduction. Marines are disciplined warriors, but this Marine's M&M'S® and Coca-Cola addiction could never have been traded for a year of raw vegetables in my own strength. No false humility here, just simple honesty.

Megan and I could not have *stayed on the path less-traveled* —but through His merciful leading and divine intervention, God allowed us to stay the course.

The healing was a gift: there is no doubt. The portion of faith we received to walk that path was equally as miraculous a gift. God only called us to take one step at a time. We fully acknowledge that God carried us through a valley that we in no way were prepared or equipped to walk. Megan and I can take no credit. The discernment, the discipline, the courage, the peace, the faith, and the healing were all HIS touch. This battle was HIS battle which HE chose to end in a

36

decisive victory for HIS GLORY alone.

Thank you for reading, and thus traveling with us on our journey. Know that God's miraculous gifts are prepared for you as well, my friend. May you come to know that He will carry you through your valley, too.

Gratefully yours | DAVID & MEGAN TROMBLY

Part One

First Contact
with the Enemy

"What good does it do to be afraid?
It doesn't help anything.
You better try and figure out
what's happening and correct it."

—General Chuck Yeager, (USAF)
First Pilot to Break the Sound Barrier in Level Flight

1 | *Last Flight*

IT was a mid-October afternoon in 2000. My boss, Major Ultimo, call sign *ATOM*, the squadron Operations Officer (OPSO) of *VMFA(AW)-332, the Moonlighters, walked into my office. I'd only been working for him for about seven weeks, but the look on his face made it unmistakably clear he wasn't pleased with the rough draft of the following day's flight schedule I had submitted as his schedule writer.

"*T-BONE*! What the… Why is…" *ATOM* was searching for the words which he eventually found. "Captain Stanley! Seriously? What is his name doing on my flight schedule for 0600 tomorrow?"

"Sir, is there a problem with Captain Stanley flying with us in the morning?" I asked as respectfully as I could.

His quite colorful response confirmed what his body language had already made crystal clear as he turned and headed back to his office. I had a choice either to follow him or to let it go, knowing my inaction would certainly result in that flight being canceled.

I was new to the squadron, having just returned from a Western Pacific (WESTPAC) deployment to Japan. Our Colonel, the Commander of *Marine Aircraft Group Thirty-One (MAG-31), needed pilots to shuffle from each fighter squadron to the other squadrons to help fill a shortage we were encountering. Two of my Marine brothers and fellow captains, call signs *PUDGE* and *GIBBY*, had been chosen to join me in our exit from *VMFA-115 by our Silver Eagle Squadron's Commanding Officer. We were being reassigned to new squadrons as part of the MAG-31 Group Commander's larger pilot-shuffling experiment. This effort was to help stop the loss of so many of us F/A-18 pilots resigning and pursuing civilian airline positions, as the commercial airlines were hiring at a frantic pace.

The Moonlighters' squadron was the fighter squadron I chose to join upon leaving the Silver Eagles. I would soon realize my transfer to the Moonlighters' was a divine appointment, providing what would become an incredibly supportive Command when I needed it most. Additionally, many of the pilots and Weapon System Operators (WSO's) that had been with the Moonlighters the previous two years while I was flying with the Silver Eagles across the flight line, had been flight school compatriots of mine. I had instant rapport upon arrival with a majority of the officers. Equally welcoming to me was the return of my original call sign from flight school—*T-BONE*—as my old friends received me into my new squadron.

What I had learned about the OPSO from my old friends here in my new squadron was that if you ever crossed Major Ultimo and found yourself on his "Naughty List," you never came back. Up to this point, I was one of the few still on his good side. I chose to follow the major to his office to explain to him why I penciled in Captain Stanley's name.

"Major, I put Captain Stanley on the 0700 line of the flight schedule tomorrow because it is important to both the Marine himself and the Corps as a whole. I will be happy to take him up in the morning. Sir, a successful flight tomorrow is required in order to secure his medical clearance for the flight surgeon before he departs MCAS Beaufort. This is the *right* thing to do for the Marine before his deployment."

Captain Stanley had recently gone med-down, unable to fly due to vertigo. In our business when a pilot loses his medical clearance, he is what we call, "Grounded." He is not allowed to fly again until his medical clearance is reinstated. After multiple vertigo episodes in the airplane, Captain Stanley had been grounded and given orders to a desk job in Germany, but not long-term orders.

The flight surgeon had cleared him to do a one-time flight with another pilot at the controls before he departed for Germany. On this flight, Captain Stanley needed to report back to the doctor as to whether his vertigo returned or not; thus determining his future chances of a duty to include flying. That's why I shared with the OPSO that we needed to let him fly and that I would take him if nobody else wanted to.

Brand new F/A-18 Nugget Captains (left to right): PUDGE *Fisk,* T-BONE *Trombly,* FUZZY *Slough,* HARLEY *Davidson, and* COO-COO *Kloch pictured aboard the* USS Abraham Lincoln *during Aircraft Carrier landing qualifications in 1999*

To my great satisfaction, the next morning's flight remained on the schedule, and I had the opportunity to fly Captain Stanley. Taking off out of Marine Corps Air Station (MCAS) Beaufort, South Carolina, we flew down the east coast over Savannah down to Jacksonville, Florida, and continued down to Cape Canaveral. We requested a shuttle approach to runway one five (15) and flew over the Space Shuttle's runway at Cape Canaveral. This is one of the world's longest runways, right at 15,000 feet long, slightly under three miles in length.

We never dropped the landing gear. We only requested to execute a low pass and received clearance from the control tower to overfly the runway no lower than 100' above the ground. We overflew the runway at close to 250 knots. Approaching the end of the runway, we aggressively pulled up into a nearly pure vertical attitude and ignited the afterburners in order to execute an unrestricted climb to over 10,000 feet MSL (Mean Sea Level). What was for me at the controls of my jet an exhilarating experience, was for those who were accustomed to watching tremendously more thunderous shuttle launches likely anticlimactic.

As we reached our assigned working area, we knocked out our tactical checklist. We efficiently executed a series of aerobatic maneuvers pulling G's, and then practiced some defensive maneuvering. These defensive exercises simulate our having a bandit (an enemy fighter) at our six o'clock position (directly behind us) and in very close proximity for a machine gun engagement. The practice of these defensive maneuvers require us to aggressively move out of our current predictable flight path thus quickly confusing and defeating the simulated enemy's gun radar. In actual battles, this is what keeps us alive to fight another day.

During all these maneuvers, my fellow pilot was able to hang in there with no vertigo issues whatsoever. A huge victory for Captain Stanley!

Just as we reached a pure vertical attitude on our last loop, the *Bingo bug warning sounded and our training was over; and therefore, so was the Captain's last flight for the next year due to his brief Med-Down episode. It was time to Knock-It-Off as we passed back through the horizon inverted. I had to apply a little forward pressure on the stick with about half stick deflection for some right aileron, and a little bit of rudder to turn our loop into a Half Cuban Eight. I pointed the nose of the jet right at Beaufort.

Returning to base, we overflew the active runway. Upon reaching the departure end, I aggressively entered the *Break Turn and gave the control stick a good pull, as this was the Captain's last chance to experience G forces on his body for the next year. Rapidly decelerating, I lowered the landing gear and landed the plane uneventfully. We returned home from what was, in our humble fighter pilots' opinions, an almost perfect flight. We both walked away feeling like victors.

Captain Stanley came toward me after our post-flight inspection of the aircraft initiating a motivated high-five smiling from ear to ear.

"Thank you for making this happen, *T-BONE!*"

"It was an honor to take you up on your last flight with the squadron, my brother."

My friend had no idea that this flight almost never happened, and he didn't need to know. We just enjoyed the moment. We reveled being young, healthy, and invincible for another day. We walked across the flight line to unload our flight equipment into our lockers in the paraloft—a walk we had taken many times before. Based on Captain Stanley's great performance physically during the maneuvers, *this was a walk we BOTH thought we would take many more times again.*

Captain Stanley had flown his last flight for at least the next twelve months. For me, it was just another hop, and I was ready to get back to my desk and draft the next day's flight schedule. My career was just taking off—or so I thought.

Captain Trombly receiving salute seconds before initial catapult launch from the deck of the USS Abraham Lincoln *during Aircraft Carrier landing qualifications in 1999*

2| *Ready Room!*
Awaiting Unknown Battles

THE next morning instead of flying, we pilots were all sitting in our ready rooms waiting for an unpleasant All-Officer Meeting (AOM) with the Commanding General (CG) of our Marine Aircraft Wing. Every one of the F/A-18 squadrons' schedules had been scrapped for the entire day. Roughly a hundred plus captains sat in their ready-rooms waiting to hear the Wing Commander share his thoughts on our most recent rash of pilot ejections and aircraft crashes. We had experienced several mishaps that fiscal year, leading to an unusually high number of ejections. While we were sitting there anticipating what the General might have in store for us, the phone rang in my ready-room. I overheard the duty officer say, "Yeah, *T-BONE* is here."

The duty officer called out, "Hey, *T-BONE*, I've got a Captain Morgan on the phone."

Looking at my brothers I commented, "I don't think I know a Captain Morgan."

In the background, one of the Marines said, "Must be Captain Morgan and Coke." I considered the very strong possibility it might be one of my former squadron-mates from down the flight line calling over to have some fun at my expense. We all were bored and passing time awaiting our professional butt chewing from the Commanding General. I inquisitively grabbed the phone and greeted the potential prankster in a proper military manner.

"This is Captain Trombly."

"Hello, Captain. This is Captain Morgan, Parris Island Dental."

At that moment, I was abundantly thankful I had answered professionally because I immediately had full recall of exactly who

Captain Morgan was. This was no mischievous Marine Corps Captain. This was a full-bird Navy Captain, and I was on his radar! The Marine Corps is a combat-arms-focused organization that falls under the Department of the Navy. We rely on "Big Navy" to provide our medical support, and as such, the doctors, nurses, and medical corpsmen who provide our medical services are all Navy. Ask any forward-deployed Marine, and you will quickly learn how valued our Navy medical corpsmen and chaplains are to us.

It was only thirteen days earlier, as a very fit and otherwise healthy 30-year-old with a bright Marine Corps career ahead of me, that I had been sitting in his surgical chair. Captain Morgan had performed a procedure to remove what we all thought was a paradental cyst from my upper right maxillary jawbone. The cyst was something small, no bigger than the size of the tip of my little finger, but nasty just the same. Doc had made a little incision and easily removed the growth. He let me take a look at the hole between the roots of teeth four and five created by this growing threat. A quick rinse, three stitches, and twenty-four hours later, I was back to flying without a second thought about the procedure.

Whenever a military medical department takes anything out of your body, they do a biopsy, and my results were already back. I spoke next after my brain *recaged and I got my bearings as to whom I was speaking.

"Captain Morgan, I thought we had a deal. I wasn't supposed to hear anything from medical for two to three months, and that would be in the form of a letter from Bethesda. Only if it was bad news would I hear from you inside of two weeks. You are calling on day thirteen. Is there something more I need to know?"

This was impressive considering I'm a Marine and rapidly did math in public to determine it had only been thirteen days. Despite having flown fighters and computed angles and intercepts with closure rates over a thousand miles per hour, we Marines tend to jab each other now and then when making simple math calculations in public and in otherwise stress-free situations.

Captain Morgan answered, "Yes. That indeed was the deal. I need you to retrieve your medical record and bring it with you at your earliest convenience, and we can discuss this further in my office."

When you hear this after just having a cyst removed, you immediately think . . . cancer. Standing there in a noisy ready room full of friends, I pressed him, wondering what additional intel I could mine over the phone.

"Captain Morgan, is there anything else you can share with me before I arrive?" I urged, desperate for more intel. I was completely attentive, tuning out all the background conversations, hanging on every word and waiting to hear it . . . waiting for him to say . . . cancer.

"Captain Trombly, grab your medical record, and come on over to Parris Island at your *earliest* convenience."

I pondered if I dare press him again. No, that might come across as disrespectful. There had to be a more tactful way to draw a bit more information from Captain Morgan. I quickly needed to explain the situation our command was in with the General. Perhaps after gaining more knowledge of my situation, Captain Morgan would share something about the gravity of my medical condition.

"Captain Morgan, we have a Two-Star General here this morning who came to corporately chastise the group because one of our Marine brothers recently pulled the ejection handle after running his F/A-18 out of gas. Seeing that the General wants to give us Marine pilots a butt-chewing, I'm thinking maybe I should stick around. But if you are going to tell me what I think you are going to tell me, then that may preclude me from ever having such an experience with the General in the future."

There was silence, and finally Captain Morgan spoke. "Yes, Captain Trombly, I am out-ranked by a Two-Star. Go to your meeting, and hustle over here as soon as it's done."

"Thank you, Captain. Will do, Sir."

Captain David T-BONE Trombly USMC (left) with Rev. Franklin Graham (seated in F/A-18 cockpit) after LeTourneau University Commencement address in 2000 and 2-Ship HORNET flyby two months before receiving Dr. Morgan's call to report to Parris Island for debriefing regarding his biopsy

(From left to right) Joined by his wingman, Captain Eric THE BIG Jakubowski, Captain David T-BONE Trombly discusses 2-Ship HORNET flyby with Rev. Franklin Graham and LeTourneau University President Bud Austin after LeTourneau University Commencement Address in 2000

So did I or didn't I have cancer? His response, though not surprising based on his rank and how I had pushed to stay for the meeting, was in no way helpful in bringing clarity to my situation. In fact, it was less clear now. Had he said "No" and directed me to come straight over, then I had my answer. As he conceded, I was left with just as many questions as I started with. I got to spend the next six hours pondering the cancer question and wondering, "What am I about to hear? How bad is it?" The real question remained, "Do I or don't I have cancer?"

I walked out of the ready room to the back of our squadron spaces where we stored some of our flight planning publications. There, I noticed Captain Stanley, the very Marine that I'd flown with the day before.

Walking up to him, I greeted him. "Hey brother, you know that flight we flew yesterday . . . your last flight?"

"Of course, *T-BONE*. Absolutely. Thanks again for doing that. I truly appreciate you making that happen."

"No worries, brother. I'm glad I did. However, I think God may have a sense of humor because our flight—*your last flight*—may have been *my last flight*, as well."

A couple of my fellow squadron-mates overheard our brief comments. Instantly there were a half dozen Marines huddled around me asking what I meant by that comment. While we waited on the General, I shared my concerns about the forthcoming news regarding the cyst that had been removed from my jaw. I asked a couple of my Marines buddies who I knew to be fellow believers to pray with me about seeing the doc later in the day.

We were eventually summoned to the Commanding General's meeting. As you can imagine, I didn't hear much of the General's opening. In truth, most of it was a blur as the cancer question circled my synapses like a jet circling at altitude in a holding pattern. However, something gradually demanded my attention — the General's growing intensity! It was fiercely palpable as he began thundering away, barking instructions about flight discipline, avia-

49

tors' basic responsibilities, and his stringent expectations for both.

The General's shocking fury unsettled every Marine in the room. While I, too, was shaken by the General's intensity, I was also processing the all-consuming anxiety and fog of a different war. I couldn't help wonder what battle I would be facing in Captain Morgan's office a few hours later. These two juxtaposed, extreme intensities created an incredible tension within me.

The agitated General's troubling meeting finally ended, and I immediately got to a phone to call Parris Island. The date was 17 October 2000, and cell phones weren't something a young Captain with four children could afford. Glancing at my watch, I realized it was well after the close of business. MCAS Beaufort was roughly thirty minutes away from Parris Island, where the Marine Corps trained the next generation of the world's finest Warfighters. Every recruit that enlisted from east of the Mississippi trained at Marine Corps Recruit Depot, Parris Island. This was also where the dental facility for both bases was located.

Hurriedly, I called the doctor's office from my scheduling office desk. The watch stander at the dental facility said that everybody had gone home and to call back in the morning. I asked her to please confirm that *everyone* had gone home, and she placed me on hold. My first thought was, "Great! Obviously, I don't have cancer, since the doctor went on home without meeting with me. I guess it isn't all that serious after all!"

Then the corpsman standing watch shattered my happy thought process.

"Sir, are you Captain Trombly?"

"Yes, this is Captain Trombly," I replied.

"Sir, my apology. I was mistaken. Captain Morgan is still in his office, and he said to tell you that he *does* need you to report here this evening. He will wait for you."

In that short phone call, I experienced yet another aggressive switchback on the emotional up and down roller coaster I had been riding since early that morning. The ride had only just begun. If you or a loved one receives a significant diagnosis, know this paramount truth: Every cancer story does this torturous up-and-down upheaval of emotions—something for which we as participants are admittedly unprepared.

I called Megan, my wife of nine years and the mother of our four children. Our oldest, Alex, had just turned eight. Our next two, Brianna and Brad were five and three respectively. Our youngest, Grace Anne, was only six months old, born shortly after I returned from my first deployment in Japan.

"Honey, I am going to be a little late this afternoon. I have to swing by Parris Island to talk with my oral surgeon from a couple of weeks ago."

"Is everything OK?" she inquired, sensing my tone was not easy-going and optimistic as usual.

"Not quite sure, Babe. Doc called earlier today and asked me to see him *today*. Even though it is now after work hours, he is still there waiting for me. So I anticipate it might be serious news."

"Want me to meet you there, David?"

"Thank you, but I don't want you to have to gather up the children and drive all the way over to Parris Island. I'll just head over and meet up with him one on one. You can stay with the kiddos, and I'll call you back when I know what's going on," I reassured her.

"OK, David. I love you. I'll... I'll be praying from here."

A MOMENT
WITH MEGAN

When a doctor orders a BIOPSY for someone you love, the WAIT from procedure to results is agonizing. Days seem like months, and hours seem like days. After David called to let me know about the sudden, untimely meeting with Captain Morgan, time went into slow motion. I repeatedly asked myself, "Will David call me? If it's really bad, will he just drive home to talk in person? I wish I were there with him!" The WAIT seemed endless.

3| An Unfamiliar Flight Path

THE thirty-minute drive from Beaufort to Parris Island seemed to take hours. I contemplated the impact of the coming news. One more time today, I found myself working through a few more emotional twists on the ride over. I went back in time about a year and a half to when Megan and I visited our families back up north in Boston while on military leave for ten days. I had just completed my training at the Fleet Replacement Squadron in MCAS Miramar, California. I was waiting for my new squadron to return to the States from their exercise in Norway; so we decided to take the children to visit both sets of grandparents.

God's timing was amazing, as that first Tuesday of my visit my mother invited me to join her for her doctor's visit. I was right there with her when she learned of her diagnosis of breast cancer.

I watched my mother get quiet, angry even, and then drift into a stoic state of emotional isolation. She asked me to break the news to my father for her, and I did. That was one of the toughest son-to-father conversations I ever remember having with my dad.

We all spent Wednesday thinking of the worst, hoping for the best, and asking questions inside ourselves that we didn't want to voice to each other. The next tremor to rock our family came the very next day on Thursday. A tumor had been removed from my father's bladder prior to our family visit, and that morning, he was called into his urologist's office. Both Mom and I accompanied Dad to his doctor's appointment.

Having just been shocked by Mom's breast cancer diagnosis, nothing could have prepared any of us for what the doctor was about to tell us only two days later. Dad's test proved to be positive for malignant bladder cancer. I was grateful to be home for both my parents for support as they started on their respective emotional roller coasters.

Now, as I sat driving for over thirty minutes, I began remembering that time and wondering if I was going to respond like Mom and get angry. Or would I respond more like Dad, who was hit with a right hook on Tuesday and an uppercut on Thursday, and go down for the count emotionally? We would soon find out.

Entering Captain Morgan's office, I saw another individual awaiting my arrival. With no introductions, we sat right down and started the conversation. The other older officer sat right up next to me and stared into my left ear as I listened to Captain Morgan begin sharing what I am sure he had rehearsed dozens of times throughout that day. I leaned forward and looked at the collar of the gentlemen to my left to see if he was Medical Corps or a Chaplain. I never got his name. I never asked for it, either. I didn't mince words, and not seeing a cross on his collar, I quickly and politely asked what this officer's purpose was in being there.

Without responding to me, he looked away, quietly stood up,

and looked over to Captain Morgan. In a monotone voice, he flatly stated, "He'll be fine. I'll see you tomorrow." Then he left.

At this point, it was just Captain Morgan and me—one on one.

"Captain Trombly, your biopsy revealed you have Non-Hodgkin's Lymphoma. As an oral surgeon and not an oncologist, all I can share with you at this time is that there exist two broad types of lymphomas: Hodgkin's Lymphoma and Non-Hodgkin's Lymphoma. It would have been better to have Hodgkin's."

"I appreciate your candid report, Sir. So how bad is it?" I asked with the calm confidence a Marine pilot endeavors to exhibit in times of stress, like handling an inflight emergency.

"The gravity of your situation will be better understood after a full set of tests are completed at a larger hospital. I have you scheduled to be medevacked to a small Army hospital not too far away in Georgia tomorrow for staging."

Army?! I was a Marine, Department of the *Navy*. Or as we like to jest around our Navy peers, "The Men's Department of the Navy!" I pushed back—respectfully, of course.

"Sir, as a Marine Captain and part of the United States Navy, would I not rate going to a state-of-the-art Navy medical facility, preferably the National Naval Medical Center (NNMC) in Bethesda, Maryland? If the President gets cancer, or my congressman gets cancer—they're going to Bethesda. Correct?"

Because I had a blood-related cancer, I respectfully but firmly requested that he fight to get me into the Bethesda Hematologic Oncology Department. I figured there couldn't be any better place to go, especially with the National Cancer Institute, a branch of the National Institute of Health, co-located there.

"Captain, I don't think you can begin to understand how challenging it would be to get you into Bethesda with such short notice. There are several hoops to jump through, and I think it is more urgent that we have tests done immediately. I don't want to belabor this point with a bundle of medical details. I just think that

54

with your case, time is of the essence, and Army or Navy—they're all doctors. Our friends in Georgia can begin testing immediately."

"I understand, Doc, but I again respectfully request that you ask for Bethesda orders for me."

Our dialogue on my staging location continued for a few more minutes, but Captain Morgan ultimately assured me he would see what he could do in the morning.

As the doc began to unfold this uncharted and unfamiliar flight path that lay before me, I suddenly realized I had a very important phone call to make. I asked if we could take a brief time out and if I could possibly borrow his phone. The Captain immediately nodded affirmatively and asked if I needed privacy. I replied, "No, Captain, just your phone."

I dialed the number for *ATOM*, the OPSO, and was relieved when he answered the phone.

"Hey, boss, it's *T-BONE*."

"*T-BONE*, what's up?"

"Sir, tomorrow is Friday and I'm on the schedule to fly one of the *Nuggets down to Key West for our Air Combat Maneuvering (ACM) weekend. I'm excited to break in the rookie, but I'm not going to be able to make that flight. Sir, I need you to find a replacement so that we don't lose those sorties."

There was silence for a moment as he paused before asking, "Everything alright? You left abruptly after the General's meeting, and someone said you went to medical. Where are you?"

"Parris Island Dental," I informed him.

ATOM responded with . . . well . . . Considering the direction I want this book to go, I can't put his *exact colorful* response in this manuscript. But let's just say it was colorful enough, and it clearly conveyed in Marine Corps fashion that he was genuinely worried about me.

"Dental?! Well, thank God. For a minute there, you had me thinking you had cancer or some other (blank) like that. The CO and I were just finishing up the flight schedule, and I know you, *T-BONE*, all too well. There is no way in h--- you would give up a great deal like weekend flying over Key West without a truly (blank) good reason."

"Ironically, I do have cancer, *ATOM*. And now that the cat's out of the bag, could you please get me on the schedule with the CO first thing tomorrow morning? And please . . . don't tell any of the guys. I would like to let my brothers know myself when I get to work tomorrow. I just wanted you to be able to find a replacement for that flight in the morning so we don't lose the training."

"You what, *T-BONE*?!"

"I do have cancer, *ATOM*, and we will need to talk more about it in person. But I need to get back with DOC now. Please just find a replacement for tomorrow's mission, Sir, and I'll be in first thing in the morning to update the CO at his convenience."

"You got it, *T-BONE*. I'll inform the CO now."

We hung up. I went back to my seat, and my oral surgeon went back to his desk. Without a doubt, Captain Morgan must have felt I didn't understand what was going on or the gravity of the situation. But I was a pilot, and I did what pilots do. I clearly understood enough that I had immediately gone into problem-solving mode. I didn't want our guys to lose those two days of training events, and therefore, somebody had to take those flights for me. The show must go on, even if I was grounded.

With tomorrow's flights no longer on my mind, Doc and I covered the remaining items we needed to cover, and the conversation wrapped up fairly quickly. The Captain handed me a slip of paper with a couple of pieces of information I needed to know along with my medical record. He stood up, reaching to shake my hand. For the first time, I realized Captain Morgan was visibly upset. I didn't know at the time, but years later when I met a co-worker of his, I learned that my serious cancer diagnosis was the first time he had been saddled with the responsibility of breaking that kind of news to a patient in the twenty-plus years of his military medical career.

He was solemn, apologizing for the bad news he had just shared with me and continually looking down in the direction of my flight boots or the floor.

Recognizing his deep concern, I squeezed his hand good and hard as we shook—not to be disrespectful, but certainly to gain his attention. He looked up questioningly, probably wondering if I had lost my mind. Having quickly gained his full attention, I gave him the best encouragement I could.

"Doc, I'm not dead yet, and a strong will to win is second only to a deep faith in God. I have both! I will not only beat this disease, but I will fly again!"

He smiled and patted my shoulder with his free hand.

"That's good to hear, Marine. You're going to need a positive attitude. I'm glad you have one. I'll get back to you later about Bethesda. I will try to get you an appointment soon. Good evening."

I thanked him and left. The parking lot was empty as sunset approached. It took about two minutes to get to my car, and the entire conversation flashed through my mind on that short walk. I reached my car, and as I started to unlock it, I experienced a strange feeling. Eerily, the lower half of my body just went limp. I leaned against my car, wondering what the sensation was, and as I leaned into the door, a realization hit me.

Friends and supervisors had often accused me of being an eternal optimist. Mentors over the years had also told me that I've been given the spiritual gift of encouragement, an assessment that I believe to be true. While those points were true and fair, the words that I shared with my doctor, Captain Morgan, were not meant for him, despite my best intentions, nor were they purely a gross overreach of optimism.

In that empty parking lot, I realized that I had experienced a God moment. It wasn't me encouraging the doctor; it was the Holy Spirit. It was God, Himself, telling me, "Son, you're not only going to beat this disease, but you will fly again."

Deep in my soul, I knew that God was speaking directly to me the very first hour of the first day of my cancer diagnosis. God spoke to me and through me as I stepped onto a new battlefield, one for which I hadn't been trained.

It would be a long time before I made a correlation between acknowledging that statement, mentally understanding it, and what I had physically experienced in my body while God wrapped His arms around me in that Parris Island parking lot. Many years later, I joined the choir at Olive Baptist Church in Pensacola, Florida. During my first time singing with them on a Sunday morning, the Holy Spirit filled the worship center, and I was immediately transported back to that supernatural moment in the Parris Island parking lot.

As we praised the Lord and led the congregation in worship, I felt that same overcoming power and weak feeling in my legs which I had experienced that day on Parris Island. Never had I experienced worship like that before. That Sunday morning, I made a long-awaited mental correlation. It was the Holy Spirit's presence. It all made perfect sense to me now. It was as I had always known it to be. It was God's Holy Spirit communing with mine, assuring me that He had it all under control and that I would not only beat this plague we call cancer, but I would also fly again.

Gaining my composure, I got into the car and took a deep breath. I had both BAD NEWS and GOOD NEWS to share with Megan when I got home.

A MOMENT
WITH MEGAN

It's hard to hold yourself together in the middle of a stressful situation. But when you have four young children looking to you to know if everything's OK, that's what you have to do. During the long wait following David's afternoon call on October 17, 2000, I finally called my dad. As a kid, you look to your parents to help you solve insurmountable problems. Even now as an adult, I faced something scary and uncertain; so I found myself looking for guidance and support.

As soon as Dad answered, I blurted out, "Dad! I think David has cancer!" My dad broke down in tears. That strong man that I had seen handle so much, now couldn't speak. He and Mom lived with my oldest sister, Sydni, who was also crying and trying to ask questions for which I had no answers yet. The emotional tidal wave the word "cancer" begins extends much farther than the walls of your own home. But I needed their support like never before.

David and I were both problem solvers. But suddenly, there were way too many unknowns to rely on that identity alone. If you've ever been there, I know you can go back to that place and remember what it feels like. This was the first time one word ever scared me. Cancer had taken my grandmother before I was ever born, and in a family of nonmedical people, it had been discussed as insurmountable. I had to close that call admitting that David and I would have to wait for more information before we would have any answers or know what the next step would be.

4| *Weaponless*

A few weeks before the cancer diagnosis, Megan and I had been at our home church, Community Bible Church or CBC, in Beaufort where we were leading our AWANA Group. AWANA is a Christian organization that focuses on the character development of boys and girls through Scripture memorization, Bible study, and team sport competitions.

One of the young men had forgotten to bring his Bible to our AWANA meeting that evening; so I let him borrow mine. Unfortunately, he hadn't returned it at the end of the evening. Three weeks had gone by—three weeks without *my* Bible—the one I had read and marked up all through high school and college, the Bible I took overseas on my first deployment. This was the Bible I would want at a time requiring life-impacting guidance, truth, and comfort. At a time of life or death. At a time of war.

As a Marine, I fully recognized the importance of powerful weapons. As a Christian, I fully acknowledged what Scripture rightly declared as our most powerful weapon—the Bible, our sword. I realized that I did not have mine.

In Ephesians 6, the Apostle Paul described the full armor of God. His explanation communicated the overwhelming sense of urgency I had to re-acquire *my* Bible before leaving town for my first cancer consultation.

"Finally, be strong in the Lord and in his mighty power. Put on the full armor of God, so that you can take your stand against the devil's schemes. For our struggle is not against flesh and blood, but against the rulers, against the authorities, against the powers of this dark world and against the spiritual forces of evil in the heavenly realms. Therefore put on the full armor of God, so that when the day of evil

60

comes, you may be able to stand your ground, and after you have done everything, to stand. Stand firm then, with the belt of truth buckled around your waist, with the breastplate of righteousness in place, and with your feet fitted with the readiness that comes from the gospel of peace. In addition to all this, take up the shield of faith, with which you can extinguish all the flaming arrows of the evil one. Take the helmet of salvation and the sword of the Spirit, which is the word of God. And pray in the Spirit on all occasions with all kinds of prayers and requests. With this in mind, be alert and always keep on praying for all the Lord's people. Pray also for me, that whenever I speak, words may be given me so that I will fearlessly make known the mystery of the gospel, for which I am an ambassador in chains. Pray that I may declare it fearlessly, as I should."
—EPHESIANS 6:10-20 (NIV)

I was going into battle seemingly unarmed, with no knowledge, no plan, and without *my* Bible. This prospect of being weaponless was unacceptable to a Marine, regardless of the shape, location, or type of battlefield. This deficit had to be remedied! Fortunately, I had already been in problem-solving mode ever since the phone call to the OPSO from Captain Morgan's office.

Our church was on my way home; so I stopped. I took a few moments in the sanctuary to gather my thoughts and pray, and then I went to find someone on staff. Finding Mr. Thompson, who worked there and knew me from our working together with the AWANA youth, I shared the news of my diagnosis. Then I asked if he and the other staff would do a quick search to see if they could find my Bible, seeing that I would probably be leaving in the next day or two on my medevac to Bethesda, Maryland.

Yes, I truly believed God would open the door for me to get to Bethesda despite how hard Doc had made it sound. I also believed that God would come through and help someone find my Bible despite searching unsuccessfully for it myself for the past three weeks.

Delayed by the search for my Bible, I realized that I had left Megan in suspense. I needed to call her and at least tell her why I was delayed.

"Megan, it's me. I finished with the surgeon, and I am now over at the church. Would you be able to break away from the children and meet me over here?"

"Is it bad?" she asked.

"It is serious. I swung into the church as I was passing by on my way home to see if anyone had found my Bible. They hadn't. I felt an urgency to find it; so I started searching the sanctuary. I... well I guess... I guess maybe the reality of what Doc said is starting to sink in. Megan, would... would you be able to meet me here, or shall I just head home?"

I obviously wasn't thinking straight, nor was I very considerate of Megan. Based on our prior conversations before I met up with Captain Morgan and with what little I had just shared, I basically dropped the cancer bomb on Megan over the phone. She, of course, grabbed a neighbor to stay with the children and rushed over to the church to meet me. I had left her alone to process the bad news on the drive over while trying to maintain sight of the road through her tears, not even knowing just how bad it really was. I waited for Megan and alternated between quietly praying and frantically searching through the building for my Bible.

When Megan pulled into the church, I stepped outside and met her in the parking lot. As she leaned in to hug me, I could see that she had been crying. We just held each other quietly for a while. Megan held my hand as we stood by the church pond, and I shared with her all the news that Captain Morgan had told me. Then we stepped inside to meet with Pastor Carl Broggi. We used those minutes in his office to begin processing the shocking report. It was a comfort for both of us to have those moments with Pastor. But looking back on it today, I wish that I had handled that moment with more care and discretion. I should have driven straight home and found a quiet place for Megan and me to share the gravity of the moment together first.

A MOMENT WITH MEGAN

FINALLY, *David called me. He had stopped by the church and had called to ask me to pack up the kids and meet him there. That may sound like a demanding task under such disturbing circumstances. But for me, having something to do was easier than just sitting and waiting. The whole way there, I hoped he was NOT going to say what he was going to say. Though the drive seemed to take twice as long as usual, I made it to the church in one piece, and David met me outside.*

For the first few minutes, we just hugged each other . . . then the words spilled out. "Megan, I have non-Hodgkin's lymphoma. We will figure out the next steps together."

I don't know if it was my upbringing or if it was being a Marine Corps wife, but my brain immediately accepted David's words, "We will figure it out together." My mind switched to problem-solving mode. Where we would go, what we would do next, and how we would find answers all filled my thoughts. Yes, grieving would come when things got quiet, but right now we had many problems to start figuring out.

*Trombly family pictured on July 4, 2000 with David's 52
Chevy pickup in front of Beaufort base housing*

After the brief time at church, Megan and I drove home. As we pulled into our neighborhood, we found the normal frenzy of street activity in front of our house. We spent a few minutes sharing with our neighbors the events of the day. When you live in military base housing, that's what you do. The neighbors from across the street, from next door, from two doors down, and from across the way all began gathering. In fact, there were entire families out there as the news spread quickly. I knew immediately that they were all concerned.

I told them I'd be right back as I walked inside. A few moments later, I stepped back out with a Boston Red Sox hat and a Boston Bruins hat. I said, "Well guys, which hat do you think would be best to wear for chemo?" From the beginning, I found that humor worked best for me in dealing with the stress and gravity of it all.

Little did I know what was to come or the path that we would walk. We hugged and talked with most everyone, thanking them for their concern and prayers. It had been a long day. I was done talking. I was overwhelmed and anxious both for a hot shower and for a chance to reflect on the day's unexpected news in quiet. Megan continued talking to our friends and neighbors, accepting their words of comfort and condolences for a few more minutes while I excused myself.

Inside, I headed straight for the shower. Not long after I turned on the hot water and got up a good shampoo lather, the phone rang. When I heard it ring, somehow, I knew instantly that it was the church calling. Megan answered the phone, and while I couldn't hear the conversation, the Holy Spirit began speaking to me,

"I've got you. You are not alone!"

For the first time on this new journey, I began to weep.

Now some might say that was the typical emotional response to being given such a grave diagnosis and to reaching the rapid end of the roller coaster ride which was my day of doubt, fear, and deliberation from the first moment I received that phone call to finally hearing the word cancer spoken in an official capacity in the office. Understandably, no doubt, tears would be a logical emotional response to such bad news. But that was not the case. I was certain of it. As I already shared, it was not the first time I had endured hearing a physician's somber words. It had only been a little over a year since I'd experienced both of my parent's diagnoses in person. But now both Mom and Dad were cancer free. Mom had endured surgery and radiation, but fortunately for her, no chemo. Dad had braved a very impressive yet difficult surgery, one that not only saved his life but improved his quality of life. The doctors had invented a brand-new bladder for him out of a portion of his colon! This innovation was state of the art in 1999. As a result, he was cancer free without the use of chemo or radiation.

Now just over a year later, here I stood in the shower contemplating the cancer news I had heard a little more than an hour ago. *That's* when I started crying. My tears were not for fear or sense of loss, although those emotions were real and certainly warranted. My tears came from an overwhelming and absolute understanding that God had this! God had me in His very hands right there at that moment in my shower. I was not alone!

The phone call I heard in the shower *was indeed* the church saying they had found my Bible, the Bible I wanted with me when I went to Bethesda for my staging. The Bible I wanted with me to find comfort, direction, knowledge, and wisdom as we began to navigate a different, unexpected path—one we would learn that very few people had previously traveled.

Megan opened the shower door to find me not just lathered up in naked perfection, but also in tears. I was completely overcome with the realization that God, my Abba Father, had me wrapped in His loving arms and was not going to send me into battle unarmed.

"David, I . . . " She stopped abruptly as she recognized my emotional condition. Concerned, Megan asked, "David! Are you OK? What's wrong?"

"Nothing's wrong, Honey. That was the church calling to say that they found my Bible, wasn't it?"

"David, how did you know that?!"

I had no words to answer Megan. I couldn't speak as my emotions grew stronger. An even greater rush of gratitude overtook my spirit. What I experienced in those moments alone with God in the shower before Megan opened the door was something I could not adequately explain in this book. All I could tell you was that I was bathed in a wave of peace far beyond human words and logic.

I experienced what the Scripture calls a peace that surpasses all understanding. Twice inside the first couple hours of this journey, God unmistakably made His presence known to me. First, in the doctor's office with the words He gave me to speak to Doc Morgan as I said goodbye, and now a second time right here in the shower.

"And the peace of God, which transcends all understanding, will guard your hearts and your minds in Christ Jesus."
—PHILIPPIANS 4:7 (NIV)

In both instances, I recognized the embrace of God as a Father bringing comfort and peace to His child. I was that child being tossed about in an emotional and physical storm who needed that embrace. Many of you have been there. Some of you will be at some point. My prayer is that this book points you to the Father who is the provider of that unexplainable peace when you walk through your own valley.

The next morning, I went to Community Bible Church to retrieve my Bible before we packed up to head out of town. After that, I headed to the base. There I took some time to talk with my Commanding Officer, explaining the challenges that our family now faced. At the conclusion of our brief visit, I relayed the contents of my conversation with Captain Morgan just prior to my arrival at the hangar. He had called to give me an update on my consult request at Bethesda.

"Captain Trombly, good news. You will be departing on orders to go to Bethesda," Captain Morgan declared victoriously. "I have spoken to your admin department and passed on the information required to get your orders printed. I wish you the best, Marine."

My Commanding Officer, LtCol *SLAM* Amland, was already aware of the situation. My Skipper *(a common yet respectful reference to the Commanding Officer or CO of a flying squadron)* directed me to the admin shop to pick up my orders, graciously instructing me to contact him directly if Megan or I needed any help during my medevac. God had provided me with great leadership in my new squadron. They treated me like family, despite the relatively short time since my arrival in August.

"God Speed, *T-BONE*."

"Thank you, Skipper. I will keep you updated, Sir. Semper Fi!"

5| *Check Six*

I had only been a member of the Skipper's squadron for nine weeks, having transferred over from the Silver Eagles on the thirteenth of August, 2000. Yet I felt as if I had been a part of his team for years. In my twenty-five years of Marine Corps service, I have been blessed with great leaders and great support up through the chain of command—even up to the General. My current Commanding Officer was one of the best, and I was never more grateful to be a member of the VMFA(AW)-332 Moonlighters than I was that morning leaving his office.

After he dismissed me, I walked through most of the squadron spaces, bumping into a number of my fellow Marines. Many of them I had only just met, but like-minded Marines could become fast-friends quickly. We understood each other, just like the Marine I had taken flying only a couple of days earlier. There were others, seemingly life-long friends, with whom I had gone through *The Basic School (TBS) and all the phases of Flight School. And then there were the many WSO's that were my classmates from our time together at the F/A-18 Fleet Replacement Squadron in California.

Several came to greet me. "*T-BONE*, what's up? You're off the flight schedule this morning. Why aren't you going to Key West? What's going on?"

"Guys, unfortunately, after the General's discussion yesterday, I left to meet my oral surgeon and was diagnosed with lymphoma. I have been grounded and am headed out shortly for Bethesda."

Noticeably shocked and upset, they began sharing their concern and emotions as Marines do, only in too colorful a way for me to describe here.

"Wow! That sucks!" was a common response to the news as I made my way around the squadron before departing. God was giving me an opportunity to share my heart with each of them. God allowed me to recognize a particular emotion in my friends that morning that was incredibly rare among fighter pilots—vulnerability.

As young Marines from Parris Island or San Diego or newly pinned Second Lieutenants from Quantico could attest, the Corps bred in us a belief in our own invincibility and in the invincibility of the Marine Corps as well. So you could picture me as a thirty-one-year-old Captain – the picture of health, vitality, and confidence – walking through the squadron saying farewell to my squadron mates the day after receiving a cancer diagnosis.

That news rocked many of my fellow Marines to their core. Yet something incredible was happening. On this day, and again when I returned weeks later, I was able to share my personal conviction of hope and peace with each of them. God had placed me in a very unique and powerful position. Think about this: who was going to ask the Marine who was told he had a shorter expiration date than his peers due to cancer, not to talk about his faith? Significant doors of opportunity were opening, and I was praying for hearts to open as well.

In our own way and in our own language, I was able to encourage my Marines with the truth of Scripture. As I shared these truths, I did not necessarily identify them by chapter and verse but rather in words they could hear and feel. Quoting 2 Timothy or Psalm 91 or 1 Peter in the hangar or on the flight line or at this reunion might have sounded like a Sunday School lesson. I shared these truths metaphorically yet boldly.

"Yes! It does suck, brother, but my God is bigger than cancer. So you guys better keep things in line. I'll see you guys in a few months when we get this cancer thing squared away, and don't forget to Check Six!"

For the non-aviator reading this, Check Six is our way of saying, "Watch your back, brother." It references the six o'clock position on a clock face, and for a pilot it is the area directly behind our aircraft—the place an enemy can approach undetected.

I had a number of conversations like that throughout the morning, and I truly enjoyed those powerful, heartfelt moments visiting with my buddies before leaving to pack up and get on the road. It was truly a privilege to share with these men my faith and the hope I had in Christ as I said my temporary farewell.

God is good. There are many ways He demonstrated His love and perfect timing toward our family and in some ways even His sense of humor in those first few days. One such example of His amazing timing came just days into our journey. I had been out of my first fleet squadron for over two months now. On the very day that we were driving north to Boston to drop off our children before turning back south for Bethesda, Maryland to check into the hospital, my old squadron was having a reunion at MCAS Cherry Point in North Carolina.

The Silver Eagles of VMFA-115 had not only a historic but a heroic pedigree that dated back to our inception in World War II. Major Joe Foss, who was our very first Commanding Officer back in 1943, was the leading Marine Corps Ace in WWII. Major Joe Foss shot down 26 enemy aircraft, matching what only Eddie Rickenbacker had accomplished in WWI. He received the Congressional Medal of Honor for his actions over Guadalcanal against the Japanese. Major Foss later became the youngest governor of South Dakota and retired as a Brigadier General in the Air National Guard. He was the first commissioner of the American Football League and was instrumental in birthing the current NFL out of what was two independent AFL and NFL leagues. We can all thank Joe Foss for the concept of the Super Bowl today.

Joe Foss found the Lord as his personal savior late in life. He was the Silver Eagles' guest speaker in Cherry Point the very day we were passing through. With the family loaded up for an untold number of weeks from home, I took the exit off Interstate 95 and made my way to the reunion. I was not going to miss the opportunity to meet Joe Foss. I made my case to the family that I needed to tell my old squadron mates of my diagnosis in person, and this event was the best opportunity to share.

I received both an autographed copy of Joe's autobiography *A Proud American* and an incredibly warm welcome from my old flying buddies. A group of us Captains, which included some of my best friends, gathered out in the lobby for a heartfelt exchange as I shared the events of the past few weeks from surgery right up through that week's diagnosis. As we spoke, Major *NERF* Ball approached, greeted me, and engaged in our discussion.

NERF and I had been together for the two years I was a Silver Eagle. We had worked together in the hanger as maintenance officers while on our deployment to Japan, and we flew together. He had trained me through a majority of my Combat Wingman Syllabus as a new member of the squadron.

One of my fondest memories of *NERF* involved him as a new Major and our squadron's senior Captain, a gruff Louisiana boy, settling a dispute in a manner that would have made Pappy Boyington and his Black Sheep Squadron Marines proud. Watching the two of them leave the officers club in Iwakuni, Japan to settle their differences the way Marines did back in the last century (a way frowned upon in today's Marine Corps), I followed with a morbid sense of curiosity. Recklessly stepping in between *NERF* and the Captain, I learned that *NERF* knew how to fight. Despite the Captain having a good 8 inches of height and a longer reach, *NERF* dropped the belligerent Captain on the first punch. The Major landed a direct hit with a surgical precision that caught the Captain under the chin immediately as he turned to face *NERF* after stepping out the door. The Captain never had a chance to swing. Suspecting the Captain had it coming, I let *NERF* get in a few more quality blows as his opponent stumbled back and collapsed to the ground. This provided me both entertainment and the ability to break up the scrap from a position of advantage directly behind and from above *NERF*, sparing me a glancing blow or two for my efforts from this fired-up Texan. As quickly as *NERF* directed me to release him, he then barked a second order for me to take my fellow Captain back to his quarters and find him some ice.

I had the privilege of flying with some incredibly talented pilots during my years as a *HORNET* pilot, but few had the skill and situational awareness that *NERF* had. In my short time with the Silver Eagles, those flights with him were the most enjoyable and educational flights of my fleet tour.

On the ground, *NERF* and I frequently had differing opinions and vastly different leadership styles. In time, these personal and professional differences became the foundation of a deep respect for each other as leaders. However, in the air we had a mind meld, and every mission we flew together was a thing of beauty! That evening, *NERF* left our conversation rattled, and his genuine concern for my well-being only further tightened the bond that we had developed in the air.

In God's perfect timing, my orders to Bethesda started on just the right day to be able to drive north and have an opportunity to share with my former squadron mates that my faith was not shaken but resolute. In each conversation throughout the evening, Megan and I clearly delivered the message that we believed God had a plan and the power to execute it. My prayer as I left the Silver Eagle Reunion was that my brothers' recognition that I was not invincible would translate into a similar recognition of their own human frailty. I hoped that sharing my confidence and faith in God's sovereignty in the opening salvos of my new war with cancer might encourage them to look outside themselves for strength in this difficult moment for my family. I wanted to give them a sense of hope and something they could do for us through prayer and seeking God in all of this. I longed for them to remember our time together in the future when they would inevitably face tribulations of their own.

> "In all this you greatly rejoice, though now for a little
> while you may have had to suffer grief in all kinds of trials."
> — 1 PETER 1:6 (NIV)

The evening amazingly lifted my spirits, and I left the reunion blessed with the love and good wishes of my former squadron mates. With the full support of two fighter squadrons and our friends at Community Bible Church, my wife and my four kids and I all together continued north.

This Marine had everything he needed. I could not overstate the blessing of knowing I had the mutual support of my fellow Marines and my family. No longer weaponless, I had my Sword packed, and God's blessing of a robust sense of humor was fully intact. It was now time to cross the line of departure into unknown territories.

The next couple of days were filled with both joy and uncertainty as we traveled up the eastern seaboard to Boston. We had a couple of days to enjoy family and receive their love, prayers, and best wishes as Megan and I braced for the full disclosure of my medical condition at Bethesda.

A MOMENT
WITH MEGAN

At this point in our journey, I was a wife and a mom getting my family packed up for an unknown period of time so that we'd be ready to do what-

ever was necessary to find the answers we needed in order to do whatever came next. "Peaceful" might not have been how I would describe this time in our lives. For me, the focus was on problem-solving, not thinking about the what ifs. My mom instinct took over to take care of my children and get all the facts before I had a chance to run other scenarios through my head.

Shortly after returning from deployment, David and Megan welcome Grace Anne (middle front) to the family, pictured here with her siblings Bradly (left - 3 yrs old) Brianna (middle - 5 yrs old) and Alex (right - 7 yrs old).

Ever since I'd met David at age 15, he was always making the next plan. Life had already been an adventure of jobs, children, moves, and almost always surprises. So in this situation, I was doing what I knew and had conditioned myself to do. David always told me that the next thing we did was going to be the best thing ever, and he had been right so far. Now was the time to pack everything up and head north. But there was a heaviness that weighed on me as we drove away from our home in Beaufort, South Carolina. We were embarking on a whole new journey. All I could do was pray minute by minute that it would be successful—one simply filled with a to-do list that —once checked off—would end in victory. Truly, at this point the HOPE of knowing that God was in control was my biggest comfort.

*Captain David T-BONE Trombly with wife Megan in the background and
their three children, Alex, Bradly, and Brianna, before his departure on first
overseas deployment with the
Silver Eagles of VMFA-115*

6| *The Green Goo and
Second Timothy, Too*

SEVENTY-TWO hours after diagnosis, we were no longer in
Beaufort, South Carolina living out our wonderful daily routine of
getting up early and going late to bed, doing what we loved. Our
daily tasks of homeschooling little ones for Megan and strapping
on a multimillion-dollar jet, pushing both man and machine to
our limits for me, seemed so incredibly far away.

 We were back in New England on the South Shore of Boston,
Massachusetts. Megan and I had grown up just north of Boston

in Andover and Lawrence, respectively. It was like an unplanned vacation that brought us back home to our Northeast roots during our favorite time of the year, autumn. Both sets of our parents, the rest of her sisters, and my brother and sister and their families all lived just north of Boston, but those visits and time to share were on hold for a couple more weeks.

Our first and only stop was to visit with Sarah and Bob, one of Megan's older sisters and her husband, who lived in Abington. Alex, Brianna, and Brad would be staying with Sarah and Bob and their four daughters, Megan, Melissa (who we affectionately called "Sister Baby Lissa"), and Miranda, and Mary, (who we playfully called "Molly.") For the next two weeks, our oldest three would be safe in Boston following the Bruins, Patriots, and Celtics; enjoying evening campfires; and playing in the fallen leaves in the backyard with Uncle Bob. Our Brianna loved their trampoline time.

Alex (8), Brianna (5), and Brad (3) raking leaves on Uncle Bob MacKinnon's trampoline in Boston with their older cousin Mary MacKinnon supervising the clean up

Their vacation was just getting started while we repacked to head back 450 miles south to Bethesda. Megan, myself, and six-month-old Grace Anne, still nursing, would be the only ones traveling to meet the oncology team. Our trip the next morning would not be as fun as Alex, Brianna, and Brad's, as we knew that the gravity of our situation would soon be fully revealed.

That evening, for the first time, we finally slowed down for a moment to share with our children the purpose of our road trip. We sat down with the kids at a picnic table in Bob and Sarah's backyard, just the six of us. I pondered how to explain why Mom and Dad were leaving in the morning.

I started by asking, "Guys, do you remember how Gama and Papa were both diagnosed with cancer last year and how both of them were healed by God?" They nodded that they understood. "Well, this time it's Dad that has cancer. Mom and I have to leave tomorrow morning for two weeks to visit with the doctors and figure out what we're going to do to fix it."

At that time my oldest, Alex, was eight years old. Brianna was almost six, and Brad was three. Of course, Alex, being the oldest, asked questions. "Hey Dad, what's Cancer? That's that green goo in your body, right?"

His question took me by surprise, and I had to look at Megan for an explanation. It was a light-hearted moment. Megan kind of chuckled and said, "In the science homeschooling software the children are using this year, they fly this spaceship around in the body discovering different body systems, organs, and cells. Every once in a while, they shoot from their spaceship trying to kill the 'green goo.' That's the cancer cells!"

So, being the light-hearted moment that it was, I smiled at Megan and then to Alex and affirmed, "Yes, Alex, Dad has the green goo!"

This was a special moment which, to this day, we remember fondly whenever we share our story. We experienced a laugh with Alex and his brother and sisters and also the truth of Proverbs 17:

"A joyful heart is good medicine,
but a broken spirit dries up the bones."
—PROVERBS 17:22 (KJV)

Trying not to make the conversation heavy, I continued.

"Guys, we know that God is bigger than green goo!"

That's the very same thing I had told my squadron mates. That's exactly what Megan and I had believed from day one. That's exactly what we had agreed upon in prayer together during the first few days of this new chapter of our life.

Wanting to protect my children from the heaviness of the burden but also wanting to empower them to be a part of our team, I asked them to help me with just one thing.

"Guys, I need you to do one favor for me while we are gone. I want you to memorize 2 Timothy 1:7. Hey! You don't have any other regular responsibilities during this trip. No homework. No homeschooling assignments. No chores except those that Auntie Sarah needs your help with from time to time. You can have fun with Auntie Sarah and Uncle Bob and your cousins. But I need you to memorize 2 Timothy 1:7. It says, 'For God has not given us a spirit of fear, but of power and of love and of a sound mind.' Will you do that for Dad?"

They nodded and agreed to do it. We ended the conversation shortly after with a prayer and then enjoyed the rest of the evening together with their cousins and Bob and Sarah.

Early the next morning, Megan and I packed up Grace Anne and drove off for Bethesda, Maryland. Knowing that it was a potentially stressful situation for them, Megan and I prayed that our children would handle our two-week separation alright. We knew their aunt and uncle would love them like their own and keep them busy, providing needed distractions while we were away. But despite my comfort in knowing they were safe and loved, I truly hoped and prayed they would drill down, memorize, and capture the richness of the promises within that one verse!

It would be two weeks later when we returned from our trip to Bethesda Medical Center before we would get that answer!

PART TWO
BETHESDA
BATTLEFIELD

"I have nothing to offer but blood, toil, tears and sweat. We have before us an ordeal of the most grievous kind. We have before us many, many long months of struggle and of suffering. You ask, what is our policy? I can say: It is to wage war, by sea, land and air, with all our might and with all the strength that God can give us; to wage war against a monstrous tyranny, never surpassed in the dark, lamentable catalogue of human crime. That is our policy. You ask, what is our aim? I can answer in one word: It is victory, victory at all costs, victory in spite of all terror, victory, however long and hard the road may be."

—SIR WINSTON CHURCHILL

7| *That's Not My Bunk*

WHEN Megan and I finally arrived in Bethesda, we checked into our hotel and then headed for the Bethesda Medical Center. We had Grace Anne with us, and thankfully, she was an easy baby that we could take with us anywhere. We located the Oncology Department and met the attendant, who was expecting us. After receiving my orders and checking us in, Nurse Transtrum escorted us to my room. Megan walked beside me holding Grace Anne in her arms. It was a very serious moment that was not lost on either of us. The weight of it all was like a heavy, damp horse blanket that rested on our shoulders and made each successive step heavier and harder to take.

Though the length of that hallway down to my room was certainly no different than any other typical hospital corridor, it seemed we were walking down an endless passageway. As we moved past each room, I inconspicuously looked to my left and to my right, spying each one of the gravely ill patients lying inside. I was shocked at what I saw. Surely, it must have seemed like I was staring into very personal and painful moments in the lives of individuals and families which I had no business observing.

I felt so out of place! My current condition and physique in no way matched the frail silhouettes I viewed in those solemn quarters. Every one of the patients within that ward seemed so much older than I was, as I had turned thirty-one only two months earlier. Their weak frames seemed so fragile, and many appeared to be at death's door.

As we reached my designated room, I felt like a condemned man assigned to death row, walking to his fateful end. Entering the last door on the right, I felt like the character of Benaiah in Mark Batterson's book, *In the Pit with a Lion on a Snowy Day*. Instantly, something inside me screamed that this oncology ward was not where I needed to be. An overwhelming sense of doom filled my spirit. I realized I could either accept this fate or fight it. Something unplanned, unexpected, and supernatural rose up within me in that next moment.

Nurse Transtrum showed me the bed, the bathroom, and the closet. I looked at her and boldly stated, "Ma'am, I mean no disrespect, but I won't be using that bunk during my stay here."

She gave me an inquisitive glare and reiterated, "But Captain Trombly, this *is* your room, and this *IS* your bed for however long you are with us."

With a calm yet firm resolve I responded, "I understand that, and I'm happy to be here as long as you need me. But I will be staying with my wife in the hotel tonight."

"No, I *don't* think you understand, Sir," Nurse Transtrum stated as she tried to explain to this pilot the Rules Of Engagement (ROE) within her Area Of Responsibility (AOR). "This is where you will be staying during the next couple of weeks," she continued in a more authoritative tone. She now had the bearing and posture of a first-grade teacher tactfully trying to deal with a boy who didn't like the seat assignment she had given him and who was refusing to sit down so the class could begin.

"I'll sit on the bed if you need to take my blood pressure or draw my blood, but otherwise, I'll be sitting in that chair in the corner, standing up, or heading back to the hotel with my wife when the tests are done each day."

This was apparently an atypical response and noticeably a problem for her. So she pulled the military card with an even more forceful tone. "Marine, this *IS* your appointed place of duty."

Seven years a Marine, I could muster up a similar tone.

"That may be so, Ma'am, but as I walked down that hall behind you and looked in every room, I saw people dying. I AM NOT THAT SICK, AND I AM NOT GOING TO DIE. I WILL BE

STAYING IN THE HOTEL WITH MY WIFE AND DAUGHTER TONIGHT."

Well, it didn't take too long after that before the Department Head, Navy Captain Malcus, the doctor who ran the entire HEMONC Ward, entered the room. This was the man who would ultimately be in charge of my care and determine a plan of attack to tackle my cancer. This was also a man, I gathered, we shouldn't have been meeting for several more hours if not days. He introduced himself and got straight to the point. "Good morning Captain Trombly, I'm Captain Malcus, your Attending Physician, and this is my department. I understand you have some concerns. What might those entail, Captain?"

With as much respect as I could muster while shrouded in a resolute conviction that I would not spend a minute in that bed, I replied. "Sir, everyone I see on this hallway looks like they are on death's door. That's not me. I am not in the same condition as the rest of your patients on this ward. I refuse to let this disease get the better of me, and lying in that bed would be like giving in, like surrendering."

"Sir, I will walk across the Bethesda Medical Center Campus at 0400 to be in my appointed place of duty—in the chair in the corner—for whatever testing is required. But when the work here is done for the day, I desire to spend time with my wife and baby in the hotel room rather than with the dying."

Now I was a young Marine Captain (O-3), and he was a Senior Naval Medical Officer, a Navy Captain (O-6). My words were delivered respectfully, but there was an unusual boldness in my voice. I'm not talking about some form of misplaced optimism or the arrogant bravado for which our fighter community is known. I fully recognize the fine line between confidence and arrogance. But occasionally I have had the pleasure of serving with fellow Marine fighter pilots who stepped to the edge of that fine line with a high level of professionalism and managed not to cross it while pushing their bodies and their weapon systems to the absolute edge.

Granted, a few of us have crossed that line into an arrogant bravado that has at times given our community a bad reputation, both within and outside military circles. But today, this was not the case. This was a word of conviction that came from deep within my soul.

> "A good man out of the good treasure of his heart brings forth good; and an evil man out of the evil treasure of his heart brings forth evil: for out of the abundance of the heart his mouth speaks."
> —LUKE 6:45 (NKJV)

Deep within me, I knew I was not to lie in that bunk. It was not for me. It was not going to be my path. My words, both spontaneous and resolute, reflected an inner confidence that I was not going to die. I was not going to give an inch of ground to this enemy, whether it be emotionally, mentally, physically, or spiritually. I certainly didn't know much else at that moment, but I knew I would never lie in that bed!

Understand, I had no intention of pulling a power play in the opening round of this soon-to-develop battle for my life. But there was a tug-of-war ensuing between the medical establishment and what would slowly and providentially, in the weeks to come, present itself as our natural path toward health. I was unaware that there were even options outside of what was presented to us here in Maryland for my type of cancer. I just walked into an environment that was surrounded by death, and something deep within me chose to fight, pushing back in a manner I could never have anticipated before walking down that hallway.

Just as Benaiah came upon that lion in the field and chose to run toward the danger rather than run away from it as anyone else would, from day one, I chased that lion right into that hospital room. I could have "lain down," just as Benaiah could have easily surrendered himself to the beast once in the pit. Benaiah chose to fight! Just moments later, he left that pit, and the lion did not.

I, too, was determined to leave that room!

The character of Benaiah in the Batterson book came from 1 Chronicles 11:22-25. Benaiah was only a teenager, and his willingness to chase down his fear radically changed the entire course of his life. His example made me consider a very important question: What fear are you currently running to face, or have you not yet turned to face that fear?

"And Benaiah the son of Jehoiada was a valiant man of Kabzeel, a doer of great deeds; he smote two ariels of Moab. He also went down and slew a lion in a pit on a day when snow had fallen. And he slew an Egyptian, a man of great stature, five cubits tall. The Egyptian had in his hand a spear like a weaver's beam; but Benaiah went down to him with a staff, and snatched the spear out of the Egyptian's hand, and slew him with his own spear. These things did Benaiah the son of Jehoiada, and won a name beside the three mighty men. He was renowned among the thirty, but did not attain to the three. And David set him over his bodyguard."
—1 CHRONICLES 11:22-25 (RSV)

Dr. Malcus listened to my argument and said nothing more to me. He simply looked at Nurse Transtrum and ordered, "Make that happen." Then he disappeared. I didn't see him again until a few days later, after some of the first tests had been completed.

Granted, what happened in the opening moments of my stay at Bethesda was not something that normally happened, and it certainly fell well outside of protocol. Being a young Marine Captain, no matter how respectfully I asked the question, I was assuredly bucking against the Standard Operating Procedures (SOP) and policies. Nothing said the staff had to concede. Was this concession just a show of generosity that this Navy Captain chose to bestow on a young Marine Officer? Certainly it could have been, but I didn't think so. I believed it was God. It was God who changed the doctor's heart to allow me to spend the evenings outside of the hospital.

Those evenings away were a form of therapy in their own way, and that early victory was the beginning of many victories to come.

We weren't in the adjacent hotel for more than a day or two before the opportunity presented itself to get a room at the Fisher House, a military version of the Ronald McDonald House. This refuge for medical warriors and their families was named after the founders, Zachary and Elizabeth Fisher, who initially donated twenty million in philanthropic funds in 1990 to start the program. That donation has now grown to sponsor more than seventy-five temporary lodging facilities for military families like the one at which Megan and I stayed.

These Fisher Houses provide a haven, allowing military families to stay close to their hospitalized loved ones during long-term illnesses without incurring the tremendous expenses of living in a hotel outside the gates. We were very fortunate to obtain a room and stay there for the next ten days. It afforded us the opportunity to spend time with other families who were also going through challenging situations. This togetherness created an instant sense of community and family away from family.

We met one man who had a football-size tumor behind his sternum. He was staying in our building with his wife and daughter. Another family there shared the heartbreaking story of their child's cancer journey. But somehow, the comfort of being around other cancer Warriors and their families emboldened us, giving each of us a collective sense of hope.

Without a doubt, this group hope proved far greater than the solitary hope we would have embraced staying alone in the hotel. The camaraderie offered a far more positive and joyful environment than the one alone in a hospital room surrounded by reminders of what might be to come.

A MOMENT
WITH MEGAN

The Fisher House was a supportive place for caretakers, where we could all come together to share our stories, concerns, and questions. With all the different medical diagnoses, people, and backgrounds, the many questions ranged far and wide. We sat together discussing what the numbers meant or what the scan results really revealed. We listened to each other's painful realizations of the life-changing moments each was experiencing.

For me, the huge community kitchen with plenty of room to wash veggies was a haven. Grace Anne could sit in her car seat up on the large kitchen island while I put veggies through the juicer. That was such a blessing. I could keep doing my part of this battle plan. I could take an active part in what was happening; I didn't have to sit back and watch.

As the heaviness of the new daily routine of waiting for each procedure, each test result, and each follow-up consult weighed on us, on day three Megan and I went out to a nice restaurant and got something "somewhat" healthy to eat. We didn't know what our future held with regards to how we would fight cancer at this point. We were just making the best decisions we could while living in the Fisher House. Having escaped from our new daily grind, we sat there with our Grace Anne enjoying real food. I looked at Megan and asked a provocative yet sincere question, "Honey, are you scared?"

She paused for only a brief moment, and looking me in the eyes, she answered as sincerely as I had asked, "Not as much as I think I probably should be."

How Megan encouraged me! I did not know what to expect as an answer, but her response resonated within my heart and soul. I echoed her feelings with, "Yes, I feel the same way. There's a sense of peace that I just can't put into words, but I just *know* that we are in God's hands."

We pondered this apparent lack of fear during dinner. Then as we discussed this peace and lack of fear further, it hit me! My mind immediately flashed back to a phone call and a prayer from months earlier that would change my life—literally.

We must travel back two months earlier to Weapons Tactics Instructor School in Yuma, Arizona to understand what led to these next few Supernatural moments. God met us in that restaurant and provided just a little more understanding of what great things He was doing and why!

8| *Be Careful What You Pray*

MAWTS-1 (Marine Aviation and Weapons Tactics Squadron One) is the Weapons Tactics Instructor School in Yuma, Arizona and the Marine's version of *Top Gun*, providing instruction and standardization on Marine Aviation weapons and tactics. Every facet of Marine Aviation and its employment is covered in the training, not just the needed fighter community knowledge.

Multiple times a year, top-performing Marines are selected from *Fleet Marine Force (FMF) squadrons and all types of ground-based aviation units from around the globe to travel to MCAS Yuma to train. These Marines become Weapons Tactics Instructors (WTI) upon graduation and become their unit's training officers when they return. Being selected to go to Yuma serves to distinguish that Marine as one of their squadron's best and brightest.

It is an honor to be chosen by your squadron to go to Yuma. God had given me good favor with my first fighter squadron's Pilot Training Officer (PTO) at VMFA-115. Based on *TROLL*'s recommendation to my current Squadron's PTO and my new boss, the VMFA(AW)-332 Operations Officer, I was set up for success in my new squadron. Needless to say, you don't want to be on the bad side of any of these officers. Thankfully, being on their good side led to my being selected to go to Yuma for a seat in the back of the room for ten days of this outstanding training program. I accepted this assignment in hopes that six months later, I might be one of the top pilots in the squadron and be granted the privilege to go back to Yuma for the full training course.

On the second night of this prestigious schooling, brothers and sisters from the VFW invited our class out for dinner so that they could meet the next generation of Jedi warriors to be trained by the Marine Corps' best instructors at MAWTS-1.

The steaks were burned, and the beer was frosty cold, just the way the Marines like them. So was my ninth Coca-Cola. I didn't drink beer, and soda was my poison of choice, though I certainly didn't think soda was poison at the time.

Our hosts consisted of veteran heroes from the Gulf War, Vietnam, Korea, and even a few from all the way back in World War II. Such is the tradition in Yuma, Arizona. These well-worn officers, Non-Commissioned Officers (NCOs), and Staff Non-Commissioned Officers (SNCOs) of years gone by greeting each new class, doing their "duty" to break in the men and women who were currently carrying the mantle of responsibility in their service's uniform.

They burn the steaks and make sure we rookies are well *dehydrated* for the next morning's classes. The camaraderie, the conversations, and the shared war stories across every generation make the room's synergy more than inspiring for its brotherhood. It was exhilarating to spend the evening with our heroes, and for Nuggets like me, it just didn't get any better than this amazing and humbling experience.

When I was at The Basic School in Quantico, VA, following Officer Candidate School, I had to room with three other Marine Second Lieutenants for our six months of follow-on training. I was one of the married guys; so I was able to go home to my family most nights and come in early each morning with a brown bag lunch. Hence, they called Marines like me "Brown Baggers," a term still used to this day.

Here in Yuma, I managed to reconnect with one of my old TBS roommates, Rob, who after flight school flew Hueys on the west coast. Having not crossed paths in a few years, he and I chose to catch up over a few games of darts. I was especially enjoying the game because most everybody else was getting sloppy drinking beer, while I was just staying highly caffeinated. With the obvious advantage, I was winning more rounds than I lost.

Around 2300 hours, it was time to head back to my room. I had been afforded a rental car on my orders as I was only there for ground school and not the entire program. It was nice to have such flexibility and to leave when I wanted. I asked my old roommate, "Hey Rob, you want a ride home?"

"You bet, *T-BONE*," he answered.

After saying goodbye to a couple of the more memorable veterans we had met that night, we started making our way toward the door. As we walked out, I looked behind me to see nine other F/A-18 pilots staring at me.

"Where ya' goin', *T-BONE*?" one comfortably buzzed Marine warbled.

"I'm heading back to the base," I replied.

"So ya got wheels?"

"I do. I have a rental."

"Great! Can ya give us a ride, too?"

"Happy to do it. I'll make multiple trips back to the base." I was assuming they wanted to get some rest prior to our heavy day of academics.

"Uh, no. How about you take us to 'Mary Jo's . . . ?"

"No thanks, gentlemen, I am just heading back to the *BOQ." BOQ is the Bachelor's Officer Quarters for the civilians reading this.

Mary Jo's (a fictitious name for the strip club downtown which was currently on their radar) was not a destination where I was inclined to go. I'd been around long enough to know that regardless of your age, very little good ever happens after midnight when you're hanging out with your boys.

But as the conversation played out, I realized they were looking for a designated driver. It became apparent that all of them had been drinking. The huddle forming in the parking lot only a few feet away from Rob and me was deliberating as to who had had the *least* amount to drink—clearly not the best plan for determining the safest driver. The Marine Corps has come a long way since 2000, so that far fewer drunken huddles in today's Corps determine who will be driving.

Rob and I looked at each other and in silent agreement and accepted our new mission. "Guess we're not going home, *T-BONE*," Rob spoke first, shaking his head. Rob got in the passenger door, as he, too, had downed a couple of drinks. I asked the current driver to slide to the middle, and I got behind the wheel.

"Hoorah! You're the man! We knew you would be here for us, *T-BONE!*"

The inebriated Marines in the back couldn't hear what I was whispering in the partially sober Marine's ear in the front seat.

"Hey, I'm happy to be your driver, but we're not going to any place named 'Mary Jo's.' We're going to something like a Billy Bob's

Honky Tonk, and since you know this city, you're my navigator," I softly affirmed.

He reluctantly agreed. We decided just to go find someplace where the guys could have a couple more cold drinks and we could make sure everybody got home safely in time for class the next day.

The pilot to my right, currently playing navigator, guided me a few blocks over, and we found your average run-of-the-mill club. I made friends with the bartender and had my 13th, 14th, and 15th Coca-Colas of the night. I talked to some of the other Marines while Rob and I continued to share stories of our experiences in the Corps.

Over the course of the next couple of hours, I just took in the scene. When you're the sober guy, that's what you do. You try to make sure everybody stays safe, that nobody leaves with a strange woman out the side door, or that anything else "bad" happens. In military terms, I was guarding my post.

At this point, I'd been in the Corps for seven years. I had focused my attention on being a good officer and becoming the best pilot that I could be in order to have the most positive influence on the Marines around me. Along the way, I had consciously chosen to volunteer as the designated driver in order to engage my peers and support them while on deployments. Before my first deployment, I had also committed not to visit strip clubs. My commitment to my wife was more important than any temporary enjoyment that could be gained by visiting any strip club.

I had also chosen *to do* some things. I resolved to lead my family and take them to church. I wasn't apologetic about that, but I certainly did not come into the workspace beating anyone over the head with a Bible either. I just wanted to be a good Marine, a good husband, and a good father, and so I had made some commitments to God, asking Him for divine guidance and protection. That's why our van was not parked in "Mary Jo's" parking lot that night.

But now, as I stood in Billy Bob's or whatever the name of this place was, something struck me. It hit me hard. It was absolutely a spiritual sucker punch. As I looked out across the room, I noticed a fellow Marine, Tom Di'Nilbi. We had gone to church together when we first joined the Corps and prepared for flight school. I was not merely observing another fellow Marine fighter pilot, but rather a brother that I knew professed faith in God. Tom claimed to embrace the same faith I did. Though I was not in the same squadron as Tom, I knew that a Marine pilot's reputation followed him throughout our community. It is a *small* gun club. Tom's reputation preceded him, and he was considered one of the best up-and-coming young pilots in our Marine Aircraft Group onboard MCAS Beaufort.

Tonight as I leaned against the bar chasing one soda after another, I realized that Tom had completely swallowed — hook, line, and sinker — the mystique of being a Marine Corps fighter pilot. He was having a great time out on the dance floor — not with his wife, of course. Tom was choosing to go down a treacherous path; one that had consequences.

Yeah, I get it. It was his choice, and we were all grown adults. While all the other Marines were doing their own thing, I had made the choice to do what I thought to be the best thing I could do by keeping watch and making sure we all got home safe. But what struck me that night was a painful and burdensome realization that in my seven years of being a Marine, not one Marine had found faith in Jesus Christ through my witness.

Yeah, maybe some had a sense of respect or a sense of appreciation for how I lived. No doubt others silently dismissed it. However, nothing about me, none of my words, and none of my actions or inactions had driven even one of them to ask me, "What makes you different?" or "What is it that you have that I need to make my life better?" And on this night, I simply served as nothing more than a fire watch and duty driver.

Please don't misunderstand. There had been some discussions among my fellow squadron mates over the years, but none of those talks had ever produced any significant, long-lasting fruit to my knowledge. What hurt so much this night was that I knew this Marine was a believer. It was sobering that in a bar at 0100, my presence, as a man who was trying to live right and set a good example, had no impact on Tom's decisions that evening . . . or so I thought.

When "Last Call" was announced, I started gathering up my Marine brothers to pack them into the van and head back to the BOQ.

Finally, we had nearly everybody together, which is not as easy as it sounds when you are dealing with testosterone-driven, alcohol-drenched males under cover of darkness and far away from home. I did a headcount but couldn't figure out who was missing. Realizing this, we scanned the parking lot. A couple of people had seen one of our Marines hop in a car with a local girl. We pulled out of the lot in pursuit and drove three or four blocks in the opposite direction of the BOQ following her vehicle.

At the first stoplight that caught both vehicles, a handful of Marines jumped out and pulled our wayward Marine out of the car in front of us, forcing the apparently disappointed female driver to travel home alone. We finally got all the men back to base and into their rooms around 0200.

I went back to my own room and found that sleep was not an option. I spent the next hour or more wrestling with God, questioning my purpose. Was the Marine Corps my mission field, or was it my career? Was it even possible for it to be both, or was I serving two masters? What was my priority? What was I doing right, and what was I doing wrong? Was my focus really the Marines around me and their wellbeing or just the furthering of my own career ambitions? If in the service to country I was focused on career ambitions, would that be wrong in and of itself, or wouldn't that also serve to honor God by pursuing excellence?

With an incredibly broken spirit this night, not only did my knees hit the floor, but my entire body lay face-down crying out to God. Then something happened that had only happened one other time in my life, never mind in my career. I asked the Lord to do three things as I laid my personal ambitions at His feet. My prayer was sincere; it was real; it came from deep in my soul; it earnestly poured out of a broken heart.

"Lord, I'm asking You to do whatever it takes to bring me closer to You, to bring my family closer to You, and to bring Marines — these men and women for whose lives and eternal destinies I truly care — to You, God. I beg You to let them see Jesus Christ, Your Son, in my life."

Eventually, sleep overtook me, and I rested a few hours. I got up the next morning not really thinking about that prayer. In fact, other than a brief conversation with Megan about how I was getting too old for staying out all night playing foolish games with my brothers and sharing with her my frustration of feeling I had little impact as a believer with my fellow Marines, it would be nearly two months before I thought about that prayer again.

Back in MAWTS-1 class the next morning, I found myself exhausted by the long night of wrestling with both inebriated Marines and the conviction of the Holy Spirit. With my head and eyelids heavy, I felt something I had never felt prior to that morning. I felt pain in my upper right jaw. It actually felt like sinus pressure, but only when I pushed on my cheek or placed my finger inside my mouth along the right gum line near the roots of my teeth.

As the next few class days passed, the pain increased, and by the end of that ten-day ground school, I could not even sleep through the night. I woke up any time my teeth came together. Something was wrong. Something was drastically wrong. I had to get to dental or medical as soon as this class ended and I returned to MCAS Beaufort....

Now, two months later, Megan and I sat in that Bethesda, Maryland restaurant, our Situation Room, having dinner. We were contemplating the question, "Why aren't we more fearful of this cancer?" Then it hit me. It hit me like a 2000-pound bomb releasing from the *BRU-14/A beneath my *F/A-18. For my non-military pilot friends out there, the BRU-14/A is the bomb rack unit that holds the bomb to the fighter plane before employment—something your civilian Cessna 150 doesn't have.

What I am trying to say is that the realization of what was happening was like a bomb going off in my life spiritually. Rapidly connecting the dots, I understood that both the grave battle we were now fighting and the peace we felt were actually an answer to a prayer breathed two months earlier in Yuma.

I had fallen prostrate on my face in Yuma, surrendering all my Marine Corps' career goals and dreams to whatever God had for me to be an effective servant for Him. I had begged God to do whatever that took! We had peace because though we could not see the path ahead, God was working. He was preparing me for a much greater influence on my fellow Marines. God was preparing me and Megan to impact eternity.

In sharing my testimony, I have rarely ever shared the story you just read about my night in the bar and my middle-of-the-night prayer in the BOQ. Only with my sons and a few groups of trusted men have I ever felt the need and the freedom to share my personal wrestling match with God on that night. I haven't wanted anyone to make a mistake or improper inference about what was happening in my life at this critical moment.

No one anywhere, even for one minute should think that I believed that God gave me cancer!

What I understood in the Maryland restaurant, and understand even more fully today, is the following: Had Rob and I not gone out with our fellow Marines as the designated drivers to ensure that our group of Marines got home safely that night; had I not witnessed those bar scenes; if the Holy Spirit had not moved me to totally dedicate my life purpose to God: I still would have woken up the next morning. I would still have begun enduring horrendous pain in my jaw. I would still have found out a month or so later that I had cancer.

Cancer was coming regardless of my spiritual wrestling as a result of the environment we live in and environmental toxins. But due to God's grace and His divine timing, so was His provision, so was His discernment, and so was His peace. Sharing with you how I found that phenomenal peace and how you can experience it, too, is the very purpose of this book.

Even during that very first week of our family's cancer fight, I was able to clearly see that this was an opportunity to acknowledge God and point my fellow Marines toward Him. This moment was a direct answer to the gut-wrenching cry I had prayed while lying prostrate on the floor that dark and difficult night in Yuma. It was exactly what I had asked God to provide.

I wanted my friends to see Christ through me. It was not for me to dictate how or when, but rather to recognize each challenge as an opportunity to acknowledge God during the crisis. I was definitely not the only Marine that was going to face crushing difficulties. These Marines, my friends, were going to need God at some point in their lives, and now they would be able to observe and one day remember how God kept our family in His full embrace in our most critical time of need.

Only a few days earlier, I was saying goodbye to my brothers and sisters in Beaufort and testifying that my God was bigger than cancer. It had already begun! I just didn't realize I was currently walking out the very answer to the single most powerful prayer I had ever prayed in my life.

I was going to face this cancer trial, whether I had prayed that prayer or not. But because God allowed me to be broken-hearted and broken in spirit that night, He was able to bring me to a place where I was ready to claim the promises of Psalm 91 and acknowledge the truth of 1 Peter. God would receive glory, and these Marines could possibly be the ones to give Him that glory, something for which I continue to pray to this day.

"In all this you greatly rejoice, though now for a little while you may have had to suffer grief in all kinds of trials. These have come so that the proven genuineness of your faith—of greater worth than gold, which perishes even though refined by fire—may result in praise, glory and honor when Jesus Christ is revealed. Though you have not seen him, you love him; and even though you do not see him now, you believe in him and are filled with an inexpressible and glorious joy,"
—1 PETER 1:6-8 (NIV)

Friends, be careful what you pray. And equally as important, if you believe God is working, answering your prayers, stand fast if your world is turned upside-down in order for God to change the world around you! I challenge you today to put down this book for a moment and take some time to ask yourself, "What am I praying for? Will it change the world? Will it change eternity?"

9 | *Fire in My Bones*

AFTER that conversation about my prayer in Yuma, Megan and I left the restaurant with a better understanding of why we were not as fearful as we would have thought we should be. We retired to the Fisher House ready for a restful night's sleep. Stepping out into the cool, late October mornings at 0500 quickly became my new routine as I walked to the hospital each day. Megan and Grace Anne stayed tucked in all cozy and warm for a few more hours. After making my way to my hospital room, I prepared mentally for the day's testing and sat peacefully in my quiet room praying and waiting.

I was filled with gratitude for the revelation of God's peace and answered prayer from our discussion the night before. It was a good morning. I was well-rested and full of fight. Motivated by a knowledge that God had this situation completely under control and having my best friend standing by me through what truly had been one of the most difficult weeks of my life, I had peace.

I waited with anticipation for Megan's return in a few hours after she fed Grace Anne and made herself coffee. Their presence was such an encouragement to me each day. There was nothing I couldn't face that morning. I was prayed up and ready!

The next few days were long, filled with a barrage of tests. Bone scans, Gallium scans, numerous CT scans, a PET scan, and an MRI taxed my body. Plenty of blood work took place, too. Because Bethesda is a teaching hospital, a number of nursing students visited me during my stay. There was this one amazingly skilled, well-seasoned phlebotomist who could take my blood without me ever feeling the needle penetrate the skin. Mrs. Jones was friendly and warm. Giving blood was never easier than when she was taking it.

Mrs. Jones asked me, "Captain Trombly, would you mind if some of my nursing students practiced on you? You have nice, sturdy veins, sir. Most of our patients on this oncology floor are a lot older than you. And their veins, well, they're kinda like biceps. They sort of shrink as we get on in years. Many of them are also much more seriously ill. All that makes it a lot harder for these young nursing students to find a vein."

"Roger, Mrs. Jones. These students have to learn on someone, and it might as well be me for a while."

Yes, I was happy to oblige for the first few days. But after a number of needles found their way all the way through my veins, I started "firing" some of the rookies. More than once, when one particular male student walked in, he immediately heard my reprehension.

"Don't even think about it, Stud! Go get Mrs. Jones to take my blood." I was tactful and playful, yet he knew I wasn't joking.

As the long, slow days dragged by, Megan and I continued to read books on alternative medicine and natural health. We swapped books and pointed out stories and articles to each other. Together we found and focused on some amazing stories about folks who had fought cancer in unique and non-conventional ways. Equally as important to us was WHY they did it.

It was absolutely the best use of our downtime between appointments and tests. Ultimately, that time spent reading empowered us, allowing us to feel productive and a part of the solution. We didn't know that what we were reading would become a major part of our future efforts, though that reality was about to settle in on us within days.

At best, we thought we might be learning about options to support my body through the chemotherapy and radiation treatments and then to rebuild the immune system after the cancer was gone. We were using our time to learn all we could in order to do our part. Simultaneously, we were dutifully walking through every test and procedure directed by the doctors. We even had an intern tell us that the staff regarded me as a model patient. We anticipated executing whatever plan Dr. Malcus, the lead oncologist, presented as we continued waiting on test results and a plan from my military doctors.

One of the last tests performed, and certainly the most challenging test of all, was the bone marrow biopsy. My doctors performed this test at a time when Megan happened to be at the hospital with Grace Anne; so they both saw me off as the nurses came to get me. I wasn't looking forward to this procedure, but I knew it was just part of the process and it had to be done. Our anxiety level was higher than normal that morning, as we had heard that this test is one of the most painful procedures anyone can experience in this life.

As the marrow is being pulled from the bone, it reduces the volume in the bone. The subsequent movement of the remaining bone marrow to fill the vacancy created in the procedure initiates an intense, burning sensation deep inside the bone throughout its length. This sensation doesn't last long, only for the brief duration of the marrow movement. But the pain level is off the charts! Time stands still for those few seconds.

Captain David Trombly with his new friend and now fellow aviator who just received his Wings of Gold from T-BONE *during his visit to the children's cancer hospital in Brisbane, Australia while on deployment*

This painful ordeal basically consists of having a fairly large needle inserted into the pelvic bone until it penetrated all the way through the bone and into the soft marrow inside. Marrow is drawn out of bone in order to be tested.

After the first sample of marrow is removed, the technician pushes farther through the marrow to the other side and into the inner wall of the pelvis to pull off a bone chip. Both the needled specimen of marrow and the removed bone chip are sent to the lab to determine if the cancer has advanced to a level that it now invaded the bones.

The nurses dutifully put me in a wheelchair and took me down to the procedure room where the biopsy would be done. I had told the nurses when they came for me that I wouldn't need a wheelchair. I planned to walk back to my room when the test was finished. The hospital staff insisted that it was protocol to use a wheelchair following a bone marrow biopsy. I had already broken one procedural precedent by sleeping in the Fisher House instead of my hospital room. I decided it probably wouldn't be prudent to push the envelope today. This time, I would be immensely grateful I listened to them and had the wheelchair for the trip back upstairs. I would soon realize that walking back to my room would not have been an option immediately after this test!

The attendant dropped me off for my bone marrow procedure, and I hopped up on the table. After a brief discussion with the technician, he explained what he would do and what I could expect. Following the application of lidocaine to numb the area, he would slip another larger needle through the skin and into the bone. He assured me that all I would feel was essentially a pin stick and then what would initially be equal to a bee sting worth of pain with the lidocaine. This would numb everything to the point he would be able to insert another larger needle, which looked to be the size of a soda straw, through the bone to pull out the marrow. I should only feel pressure on my hip as he inserted this pipe and pushed it through the thick bone.

I prayed for strength and bit my pillow, something the doc recommended that I do. I held my breath and bit down as he worked to push that pipe through the bone. I could feel the pressure, but not much pain. The lidocaine was working. Somehow, the doc could tell when he broke through the bone and had entered the softer material to draw out the bone marrow samples. This was accomplished through a smaller tube that was inside the larger soda-straw- sized pipe.

He warned me, "Captain, I'll let you know when I am about to draw the marrow so you can brace yourself. This will feel like *a fire in your bones."*

Sure enough, when the doc gave me the signal, it felt like the fires of hell for a few seconds. The pain subsided rather quickly, but if that is what fire feels like, then I'm glad it only lasted a few seconds and that I know where I'm going when I reach eternity. He fed me a tremendous amount of praise. "Marine, I've never had anyone in all my years ever go through that without as much as a whimper, cry, or a moan; and you didn't make a sound."

I was starting to feel pretty good about myself. All my peers were back in Beaufort flying and doing great things. I missed that, but my job today–my duty–was to climb this hill, my one battle to win for today. It was done! With a sudden sense of satisfaction and pride in being the Marine that I had just demonstrated myself to be, I began to relax. Too soon... I shuddered at the doc's next words.

"Again, Marine, I am very impressed. You did great on that first procedure. Let's see how you do this time."

"This time?" I tried to say with as calm and cool a pilot voice as I could muster, that voice we use as pilots when our only engine is out of gas over northeast Texas around midnight, and the only place to land is in a field full of cows you can't see, and you have under 90 seconds to get out your mayday call.

"Yes, Marine. It is time to do the other side."

"No problem. Let's do this!" I lied, but I sounded confident.

I would rather have been breaking the ice on the "Quigley" back in Quantico that morning. The Quigley is a water and barbed wire obstacle course with drainage tubes just big enough to squeeze through with our rifles. Every Marine officer candidate has had to negotiate this challenge during OCS for nearly fifty years. As long as you are not claustrophobic, the Quigley is actually a motivating challenge to tackle with minimal anxiety in the summertime.

But I went through OCS in January twenty-five years ago. Our drill instructors had to break the ice so we could enter the water and negotiate the obstacle. Up until this biopsy, the Quigley had topped my list of the most uncomfortable and challenging experiences I had endured. I distinctly remember my body voting never to revisit the Quigley. Today, this biopsy replaced the Quigley at the top of my personal list of things never to do again. Yet here I was about to do it a second time in only a matter of minutes.

It was time to quickly break out every resource available to me. Mental toughness exercises? Negative. No time for that; the lidocaine was already being injected.

How about a positive affirmation? OK, here goes. "This is great, Marine! You have the privilege of taking a second hill today!" That was definitely not going to work, as all my emotional and mental energy had been fully exhausted during the first assault.

There was nothing left within me, no mental energy to make it up another hill. Realizing I wasn't going to do this one on my own power, I began quoting my college fraternity house verse in my mind as the pressure of the larger needle was introduced to the opposite cheek. I prayed through this Scripture, believing what I repeated as I worked through the verse multiple times.

"But they that wait upon the Lord shall renew their strength; they shall mount up with wings as eagles; they shall run, and not be weary; and they shall walk, and not faint."
—Isaiah 40:31 (KJV)

My college soccer coach, Dave Diehl, had shared a story about this verse with our team when I was a freshman. I never forgot it. His college soccer team had been accidentally scheduled for two soccer games at two different colleges on the same day. They played both and gave everything they had both games. His team was exhausted, but as they stepped onto the field for the second game, he prayed this verse. Coach trusted God to lift him and carry him through. Coach Diehl shared with us that he went on and played one of the best games of his college career.

That next semester, I pledged Lambda Alpha Sigma, the aviation society at LeTourneau University. As a rite of passage to join, we had to memorize the house Bible verse, which also happened to be Isaiah 40:31. It was quickly becoming one of my favorite verses, as well as the most impactful verse of my college years and the one I relied upon most often.

One of the greatest memories I have from college was the bonding with my fraternity brothers in LAS. The society required new members to memorize Isaiah 40:31 and the entire third chapter of James before initiation. All these years later, it has been great to reconnect with my brothers and share how those verses impacted our lives both during and after college. It was a great tradition. Those verses helped shape us as believers and as future leaders.

With the power of prayer and Isaiah 40:31, the second procedure went about as smoothly and quickly as the first with no whimper and again, no cry. A second victory! I could not take credit for it either, as God certainly carried me through the second biopsy. The immediate sense of relief after the second procedure ended was much greater than the first. Now I knew I could completely relax. I was coming down after my full-on adrenaline rush from my dog fight with a large needle. Finally, rest was coming. At least that was what I thought.

10| *Ambushed!*

I looked forward to a much less stressful afternoon. That was not going to be the case, unfortunately. I was wheeled back to my room, where I would spend the next day and a half rubbing my butt cheeks subconsciously.

I arrived back at my room prepared to get some well-deserved praise for my heroics and sympathy for my throbbing glutes. I was hoping to have my ego massaged with the same high praise from Megan as I did from the technician as I proudly shared my story of accomplishing this maneuver with the moral courage and tenacity of a tough, battle-hardened Marine! Instead, I was greeted with Megan's tears as she sat holding Grace, sobbing in our room.

There was no great storytelling experience to be had as all I could do was ask, "Megan, what's going on?"

Waiting until the attendants left with the wheelchair and certainly, beyond earshot, Megan began to share. I had already popped out of the wheelchair and had sat on the bed beside her, positioning myself to provide comfort while not sharing with her the pain I was feeling.

"They are gone, Honey. What happened?"

"You hadn't been gone two minutes…" She paused to compose herself. "Two minutes!" she said emphatically while wiping the tears away from the top of her cheeks with the back of her hand. She finally looked up at me with her beautiful tear-filled blue eyes glistening.

I stood up as Megan continued to compose herself and waddled out into the middle of the hallway, looking for no one specific and anyone within arm's reach. Nobody was in the hall. What was I going to do, anyway? I was angry, and I didn't even know why yet.

I returned to Megan's side and grabbed her hand. "What did they do? What happened, honey?"

Better composed after taking a deep breath and blowing it out, I started to see the fighter in my wife rising to the surface. Her tone became stronger and bolder.

"You hadn't been gone two minutes before a couple of the doctors walked in and proceeded to tell me that you were going to die and that they wanted me to convince you to follow their protocol to the letter. Then they had the audacity to ask me…" She stopped and looked down once again, and her body convulsed as she struggled to repeat their words.

"Megan, what did they ask?" I queried with as tender a voice as I could muster while the anger boiled within me.

They asked me, "How many children do you have, Mrs. Trombly? Are you prepared to take care of all those children emotionally and financially?"

"What?!"

"David, I was so angry that I told those doctors that they had no idea who I was or what I was capable of doing. People don't just walk up to family members of a person diagnosed with a terminal illness and ask them what they are going to do when their loved one dies. David, they were bullying me to try to convince you to do anything they said."

As Megan fought to compose herself, I took a breath and processed not only the moment but what we had experienced together the past few days. Based on all that had begun to unfold rapidly in the previous hours and days, Megan and I very quickly did the math and calculated why the doctors had come to Megan that day to speak to her alone, while we were separated by multiple floors. During the previous few days, both of us had been asking all the normal questions that any cancer Warrior would ask. "How serious is it? Have you found any more tumors? How much time do I have? What should we do? Are there any other *ALTERNATIVE* procedures? Are there any special studies or trials that we can become a part of?"

Frankly, Megan and I learned quickly that we were asking too many questions. Not necessarily the wrong questions, just asking them in the wrong place and to the wrong audience. We were innocently asking everything we could without realizing we were placing a target on ourselves. Many of our questions started to indicate to our lead oncologist and his team that we weren't keen on the chemo and the radiation.

Rightly so, considering we had just received word from the doctors prior to doing the bone marrow biopsy that I was considered to be "Stage One." They had found only one tumor, and that was the one that had been removed from my jaw by Captain Morgan at Parris Island Dental only three weeks earlier.

With no tumors present, we had asked the simple question, "Why do chemo if there is no other tumor? If there's no tumor, then there's no cancer, right?"

But the doctors' response had surprised us.

"Captain Trombly, there *is* cancer," they argued. "There is cancer; it just hasn't been detected in any of the tests up until now. That's why we want to do a bone marrow biopsy as one of the final tests before starting chemo shortly after the results come back."

On biopsy day, while I was literally tied up undergoing the gruesome procedure, Megan was alone. She was stressed and completely unprepared to be bombarded by the coming blitz of questioning, doom, and gloom to be shot her way from our own team of doctors. They had come to dissuade us from our current line of research, study, reasoning, and decision making due to our most recent line of questioning.

The many alternative medicine books we had been reading had been lying around our room for days in full sight of the doctors and nurses. I quickly went from being considered a model patient to being handled as a non-compliant potential problem for the medical team. That change led to some attention from the senior medical staff in the oncology department. We had a number of doctors who in mid-conversation would just abruptly close down any further discussion regarding alternative anything when we would bring it up.

Our frustration grew as there was very little opportunity while in the hospital to get any answers regarding the alternative medicine options we had been researching. Any time we pushed back from conventional medical advice and asked about what might be available outside of chemo and radiation, we were quickly shot down, and the doctors would just as abruptly shut down and disengage from further discussion. Frustration naturally built to anger as Megan and I were both very ignorant of the significant cultural differences between the two schools of thought. We couldn't understand the hostile responses or lack of responses we were receiving.

One of the most memorable conversations late in our stay was with the lead doctor. When pressed on the subject of alternative medicine, he said that due to the Hippocratic Oath, he had sworn to do no harm. So to him, that oath meant that he was not even allowed to discuss anything outside the AMA and conventional medical academia. I could understand not being able *to recommend* methods not yet approved by the FDA or sanctioned by the AMA or the governing establishment of any hospital. That was reasonable. But not to be able *to discuss* alternatives seemed cowardly.

I've taken the time to read the oath and understand its origin and purpose. To use the oath as a shield to avoid difficult conversations with a patient was disingenuous at best. Citing the oath to mask a lack of understanding and to hide one's ignorance of the knowledge and wisdom existing outside one's realm of expertise or culture seems (please excuse the pun) hypocritical.

As I waited for Megan to continue, all I could do was look into her eyes, filled with hurt and hold her. Her frustration and sadness brought me to a dark place. Feeling helpless to console her, I sensed the frustration of not only that moment, but also of all the previous fruitless conversations with our doctors regarding alternative options compounding, and a fire began to rage inside me.

Megan looked up as my Warrior wife again fought to power through the tears. "They said to me, 'Mrs. Trombly, your husband is surely going to lose this fight with cancer if you both keep considering this path of alternative options and do not start the chemotherapy immediately.'"

"Cowards!" I was back in the hallway looking for someone to

engage once again. No one was there. Ghost town. It was as if they just knew. They were playing a game with my wife's emotions, and it was a costly gamble on their part.

Back in the room and pacing through the soreness radiating from both glutes, I asked, "What else did they say?" I wasn't asking my wife in an effort to hear her or comfort her anymore. I was looking for ammunition for the coming fight. I was preparing to blast who-ever came into the door next. I was going to skip the missiles and go directly to guns! Secretly, I was hoping it would be the senior doctor himself, but he never visited. No one did.

Megan knew why I was asking and gave me exactly what I want-ed. It hurt to receive the insult, even if it was second hand.

"David, they said, 'It is surprising that a young man with such intelligence would make such a foolish decision and throw his life away by not doing the chemotherapy.'"

The doctors added insult to injury by encouraging Megan to journal everything, absolutely everything, and to share it with them. They wanted to climb into our minds and see what decisions we made as we battled through alternative therapy questions they felt would lead to my ultimate demise.

Ironically, we did just that and offered the journal to them almost a year later. Oddly enough, they were no longer interested in what we thought or what we did without the morbid climax they were predicting.

It all seemed like . . . well . . . I'll just call it what it was—an AM-BUSH—going after my wife while I was going through the most difficult procedure of all the procedures I endured during staging! If there was a moment of vulnerability for either or both of us, these two doctors knew it and perfectly timed their effort to ex-ploit it. This ambush must have been a tried and true tactic from the conventional playbook to employ when a cancer Warrior dared to start thinking outside of their "scientific" box.

Megan was momentarily shell shocked by the heavy arm twisting as the medical team was trying to get her to pressure me into conforming to whatever modality they presented us in the coming days. My two doctors double-teamed and preyed on a young mother of four's fear of becoming a widow. Megan was so caught off guard and angry she couldn't respond. I was so angry that I no longer required rest or recovery time. I was instantly ready to fight again!

Megan and I didn't fully grasp what these doctors were doing or why! They sure knew how to hit us low when we were already down on that difficult biopsy day. At the time, we naively hoped that they just had bad timing and a lack of proper bedside manner. We quickly came to realize the doctors had visited that day deliberately and strategically to soften up the beachhead with heavy artillery prior to dropping the big news about my staging results and the modality selected for me. This difficult news was inbound and quickly approaching.

This ambush started opening our eyes to a great chasm between two distinctly different schools of thought. We were not going to find all our answers here. Only conventional consultation was at our disposal when discussing options with our Bethesda team. What had been a serious point of frustration had been made perfectly clear after this ambush on Megan. Our education had begun. There was a methodology we would need to embrace if we were to gain all the information from every source we could. We had to know our audience. We had to play the game.

As day drifted into late afternoon, my frustration dissipated very little. We didn't see either of those two doctors again that day. I had no chance to run them down and share my displeasure with them regarding how they had treated my wife. Feeling like a caged animal in that room, I very badly needed a pressure relief valve, and one was about to present itself.

I received a phone call from my squadron ready room. A half a dozen Marines from my squadron VMFA(AW)-332 and one other friend were talking about my situation. They just decided to call the hospital and find me. A pleasant distraction from the day's events, the call came directly to my room. I enjoyed every minute of small talk. Then, searching for the true gravity of my situation, they asked about my week so far. Our day had been heavy enough; so I spared them the details and instead took advantage of a priceless moment.

There it was: my opportunity to go for the kill. I finally had a chance to get some well-deserved praise for my heroics while at the same time providing some comic relief for my friends, whose deep concern was evident in their tone.

"Gentlemen, is *ATOM* there?"

"Just down the hall finishing up the flight schedule for tomorrow. Uhhh, do you want us to get him?" they asked sheepishly, as most of the Marines were sideways with my boss. Though they were not sure what I was doing or where I was going with the conversation, they got him nonetheless.

"*T-BONE*."

"Sir."

"How are you doing?" he asked genuinely.

"Things are going well, Sir. I have been undergoing many tests. Sir, am I on speaker?"

"Yes, *T-BONE*, you are on speaker."

I almost thought twice about what I was going to do next, but it was a once-in-a-lifetime opportunity that I could not pass up. I felt compelled to take advantage of it. The tension-breaking that would come of my next anecdote would be therapeutic both for me and maybe even more so for my squadron mates.

"Thank you, Sir." I started. I shared the word picture as best I could about the challenge of undergoing the bone marrow biopsy. I could only imagine a dozen or more Marines now huddled around the duty phone in the ready room with my current boss closest to the desk. I could see the look in their eyes and even picture a few of them shifting uncomfortably in their stance. Maybe one or two were subconsciously rubbing their backsides through their flight suits only to catch themselves and see if any of the other pilots caught them in the act.

I was enjoying telling this story because I knew something they didn't. There was a "gun's kill" shot opportunity coming. That is the moment in an aerial dog fight when one pilot has the upper hand and the key advantage through aerial positioning of their aircraft to quickly maneuver their fighter into position to fire a kill shot from our 20 millimeter M61 cannon and win the day. In combat, we would first seek to acquire a kill from a safe distance with a missile shot to knock our adversary from the sky. But secretly, our inner fighter pilot and glory-seeking persona strives for a glorious up close and personal "gun's kill" as if engaged in a knife fight in a phone booth. This represents the very type of fighting and flying for which our World War II and Korean War fighter pilot predecessors, like my grandfather, became legends.

There are times when two skilled airmen can work themselves close aboard to each other's aircraft, what we refer to as a "merge," and have to fight in close. At this range, the outcome of the battle will most likely be determined with a gunshot versus a missile launch. Whichever pilot most skillfully flies his weapon system and best managed his energy will win the day.

I had been drawing *ATOM* in close as I told my story. I was preparing to take my shot. I was going for the kill. My fellow Marines listened attentively, also unaware of my intentions.

I concluded my story. "As the needle drew out that specimen of bone marrow, the fires of hell shot through my bones! It was truly the most excruciating pain I ever felt! *ATOM*, when they said it was going to be the ultimate pain in the ass, they weren't kidding, Sir. And for those brief moments, all I could think of was you."

"Trigger down, SNAP!" I had fired that shot, and it landed squarely on my target, our difficult-to-work-with Operations Officer—my boss. I heard the laughter through the phone and knew my peers appreciated my target choice. I felt pretty good about the kill myself, and my tension significantly subsided as I, too, laughed right along with them.

I was uniquely positioned to take that shot, considering I was sitting over five hundred miles away in the oncology ward. I was untouchable. The guys loved it, and to his credit, *ATOM* played along and allowed me my small victory, graciously playing it off as me using my sense of humor as a fighter pilot to cope with the challenges I now faced. I had done it. I had crossed the line, no doubt, to join the rest of my peers on his "naughty list." It would end up never being an issue during my career, as I was about to learn I wasn't likely to have *ATOM* as my boss for very long.

11 | *Intel Report:*
Outlook Uncertain

TWO weeks since diagnosis, hundreds of miles from home, and what seemed like months away from my comfortable world of aviation, I found a friend in one of the doctors on our medical team. This threesome consisted of the Attending Physician, Captain Malcus, who ran the ward, and his resident, Dr. Nachamer—both of whom Megan got to know quite well the day before when I was out of the room enduring my bone marrow biopsy.

The third and most welcomed doctor on our team was the intern, LCDR *FENDER* Gavriel. Fortunately for me, he was a former Naval Flight Officer *(NFO) who could speak my language, and we spoke to each other with ease. We addressed each other daily not by name, but by call sign. *FENDER* was the doctor who just days earlier had shared with me that my tests, so far, looked fairly promising. Today, unfortunately, his demeanor was significantly sullen. He came to my room and closed the door.

"*T-BONE*, I've got both good news and bad news. Let's sit down."

When a former aviator uses the words, "Bad news," it gets your attention. I sat beside Megan, not sure if I was going to need to brace her or have her there to brace me. *FENDER* began to lay things out for us.

"The good news is we have found only one tumor after all the tests, the one that was originally removed by your oral surgeon. This included the bone marrow biopsy results, which are complete, and they found nothing!"

Could there be any better news at that moment than that? Only one tumor which had already been removed weeks ago sounded like the best possible outcome from over a week of testing.

"The bad news," continued *FENDER*, "is your cancer started in your bone, which makes this an extremely rare primary lymphoma of the bone as opposed to a more common Non-Hodgkin's lymphoma."

Military trained individuals like to get to the point quickly. I wanted the *BLUF (Bottom Line Up Front), and so I interrupted him and asked for just that.

"Can you give me the BLUF, *FENDER*?" I asked in a more serious tone than in previous discussions. He obliged and got straight to the point by talking numbers, a pilot's dream. We love numbers. Quantifiable, determinant, helpful in allowing us to make quick and accurate decisions while moving at over four hundred knots at only five hundred feet above the ground. Well, here came the numbers, and they were not encouraging.

"*T-BONE*, that means that instead of having a stage one Non-Hodgkin's Lymphoma with an approximate success rate of 75 to 85 percent with chemo, you probably have closer to a success rate of around 20 percent. This number is much lower due to your tumor presenting itself in your jawbone. These lymphomas that start in the head or neck area are far more difficult to treat due to the differences in vascularity. Unfortunately, anywhere else in the body would have been better for treatment purposes."

Being the eternal optimist, I re-engaged my former flying friend with, "At least it's not zero, *FENDER*." Looking him square in the eye, I also challenged him while maintaining an upbeat, yet serious tone.

"And don't come back into my airspace again saying you got BAD news when it's really not BAD news. You had me worried there for a minute, brother. The way I hear it, 20% is OTHER news, not BAD news, and we can turn that into a victory. *FENDER*, remember, in our aviation world there are GOOD'S, then there are BAD'S, and finally, there are what we affectionately refer to as OTHER'S. And OTHER means we still have something to work with here.

"BAD'S are those 'Safety of Flight' issues that need to get fixed and need to get fixed quickly, or well, you get the idea. BAD is when you're flying across the Pacific and your wingman tears the refueling basket off the KC-135 in bad weather, forcing everybody to divert to some island in the middle of nowhere with minimal fuel. Now that is BAD!

"But taking two dozen stabs at that fueling basket on the drogue because you're just not settling into it to start the flow of fuel, with seven of your fellow Marines watching you, pulling for you, trying to calm you down with a joke while secretly praying that you don't rip the basket off on one of your wishful stabs with your extended refueling probe . . .. well, that is an OTHER. That is where we find ourselves today. We are somewhere in the clouds over the Pacific, running low on fuel and patience, but still just moments away from success. No, we haven't quite reached the level of BAD yet."

I wasn't sure if I was saying this to encourage him or calm Megan's anxiety, knowing that she had just heard the same percentages I had from *FENDER*. In fact, I wasn't sure that I wasn't trying to convince myself. Regardless, it sounded good, and I held onto that position for the next couple days until we found a reason to revisit it or scrap it.

The way I saw it, *FENDER* had given me a GOOD as I only had one tumor, which was removed three weeks ago and was already out of my body. And he gave me an OTHER, as there was a small but hopeful chance I'd still beat this with chemotherapy or alternative measures once we made a decision. Even more encouraging was that I knew who my God was, and I believed He was in control and had a plan.

Well, being a fighter pilot and not a doctor, I wanted supporting documents. I wanted more of those definitive numbers and studies to support them. Megan and I needed information that would help us make our decision about what to do, about which path we should go down.

"*FENDER*, in light of these diminishing odds, can you get us some studies with the actual numbers of how many people have beat this primary lymphoma of bone?" We wrapped up our discussion as he agreed to find any supporting data he could on the success of conventional modalities with this type of rare bone cancer.

As Bethesda is so closely located near and linked to both the National Cancer Institute (NCI) and the National Institutes of Health (NIH), my oncologists would certainly have the best information available as to the past success of their recommended modalities. Surprisingly, the data was scarce, and it took some time to research the numbers.

In the meantime, the oncology team continued with their testing and reviewed all my results at their modality board. I spent time getting "mapped" for radiation to my head should that be one of the protocols selected. That approach was still being debated by the board, but their mapping allowed them to keep me busy and not able to read my alternative medicine books.

I even spent an afternoon debating with the radiation team that it made no logical sense to radiate a part of my body that was to be surgically removed! You read that right. The maxillofacial surgeon told me he was going to remove a significant portion of my upper right maxilla (the top right portion of my jawbone with at least five or six teeth included.) I was essentially going to lose the right half of my upper jaw and wear a prosthetic. Once fitted with the prosthetic, I was going to undergo radiation of the same area that was now nothing but a gaping hole covered by a piece of plastic shaped to keep food out of my sinus cavity. It seemed to me we should be doing one or the other, but certainly not both.

Megan and I were still just waiting for the medical team's final game plan, sitting in a holding pattern. Now any good pilot flying on instruments and cleared to fly a racetrack orbit in a holding pattern somewhere between their departure airport and their destination will stay busy and work to keep their situational awareness high. As a pilot, I always wanted to get myself mentally and procedurally well out in front of my aircraft, always planning for the next clearance from the air traffic controllers.

Megan and I took that same approach while we were waiting for the doctor's final determination of my condition and our new way forward. We used that time to get ahead of the disease with research and worked to develop our own plan just in case the doctors came back with actual BAD news.

We were rapidly realizing we would become the team that had to find our own flight path. We had each other, and that was a tremendous encouragement to me! Unfortunately, we were about to find out that we were going to have to figure this one out all on our own. We had no idea who else would be on our team, but it was becoming clear that Bethesda was not going to be the lead in our efforts to beat this.

We kept reading and researching anything we could find. We also got smarter and stopped leaving those alternative medicine books out in plain sight.

A couple of days later, *FENDER* came back with the information we had requested and brought his boss with him. We were pretty confident this conversation was going to be a decisive, course-altering one, and it was.

"We've got some research results for you, *T-BONE*. We found two published studies. This one comes straight from the National Cancer Institute right here in Bethesda, and this one is from Johns Hopkins University in Baltimore," relayed *FENDER*.

"You can review these for yourself, Trombly," continued Captain Malcus, taking over the conversation. "Fifty patients' cases are documented in these two studies."

"May I take a look at those?" I inquired.

Captain Malcus handed me the studies, and I began to scan the pages as both doctors looked on and silently gave me a moment to take in what I was reviewing. I was no doctor, but I had seen enough tactical manuals and aircraft performance charts to make sense of data in whatever form it was presented.

Once I was able to cage my brain around the formatting, I realized we were about to get the "BAD" news. What I saw was not only eye-opening, but it was going to become truly liberating from a cultural perspective in the coming weeks and months. When deciding how to battle a significant illness, we all consciously or subconsciously wrestle with cultural norms, the expectations of family, and the looming financial pressures.

There were no names on this list, only vital statistics like age, gender, timeline, etc. I could see that no one had reached the five-year remission milestone.

Reaching five years clean is a sign of a successful conventional modality for Non-Hodgkin's Lymphoma. No one, not one conventionally treated cancer patient, had reached five years of being cancer free according to these two studies.

We saw what the military doctors at Bethesda had to offer us as we looked at this staggering empirical data they presented. I asked them one final question. It was a leading question for which I already knew the answer, because I was holding the answer in my right hand.

"So, your basis for determining 'success' when dealing with lymphoma is maintaining a five to seven-year remission following the prescribed conventional treatments. And of these 50 people in the only two studies you could find to support your plan for me, not one of the 50 survived five years past the chemo and radiation. Based on this fact, the *real* 'success' rate for conventional medicine is zero percent for my Primary Lymphoma of Bone. Is that not correct?"

There was a pause. There was a deafening silence. *FENDER* and his boss both looked down and then back at each other briefly. Then my closest ally on the medical team, *FENDER*, truthfully yet solemnly finally conceded in the form of a whisper, "Affirmative."

I then asked an unfair question of my doctors. This is a question that they have no way of knowing, yet almost every cancer Warrior facing a grave diagnosis can't help but ask. I'd seen the numbers which I'd anticipated would rock our world, and they did. I believed the doctors in front of me had been anticipating the next question and even knew where I might go next as their response communicated not only their original serious tone but also a previously absent palpable urgency. "How much time do I have, Doc?"

"Captain Trombly, if you do nothing, you will be dead inside of two years." Captain Malcus was doing all the talking now. "If you start the chemo immediately, there is a chance, although smaller than we had hoped, that we could extend your longevity six months or more."

FENDER knew what I was thinking, as we had already had a similar conversation regarding the CHOP protocol. Most often, the treatment for Non-Hodgkin's is a chemotherapy regimen of four drugs known as CHOP (cyclophosphamide, doxorubicin, vincristine, and prednisone), plus the monoclonal antibody rituximab (Rituxan). *FENDER* was the only one on my Bethesda medical team willing to listen to our ideas and questions about natural

119

medicine, or at least humor us. I was sure he had felt sympathy toward me as a fellow aviator, especially as we had talked through a number of the side effects from one of the main chemical meds in the CHOP protocol, Adriamycin, also known as doxorubicin.

I had asked *FENDER* about the side effects and the chances of getting to fly again earlier in the week. I was concerned about the chance of incurring some heart muscle damage or other second-ary cancers from the chemo. Even eye problems during and after chemo, like cataracts, were a concern. All these side effects were known and listed by the drug companies, and any one of them was a showstopper if I were to try to fly again.

The Captain continued, "You are an otherwise healthy, strong, young Marine who could be the first to make it five years."

There was a chance he was right. But was I willing to be the next person to follow this conventional modality blindly, when it had not worked for anyone else according to their own medical re-cords? Was I willing to surrender full control to the doctors and take my position in the passenger's seat for this painful ride? No, I was not. These doctors had no answers for me at the moment, and neither did I.

Megan and I found ourselves in much the same place as we had on the first day of the diagnosis. This week had been emotional-ly and physically demanding. We were running low on emotional fuel and could only do one thing as we closed out this final day of staging. Pray.

"Come to me, all you who are weary and burdened,
and I will give you rest. Take my yoke upon you and learn
from me, for I am gentle and humble in heart, and you will
find rest for your souls. For my yoke is easy
and my burden is light."
—MATTHEW 11:28-30 (NIV)

12 | *Tumbling Gyros Recaged in an Instant*

NIGHT had fallen. This day had been the culmination of more than a week of testing. The results were back, and today's news of my two-year death sentence weighed heavily on both Megan and me as we made our way back to our little room in the Fisher House. Megan fed Grace Anne and laid her in our bed to sleep. I prepared for bed but felt drawn to sit and read a passage or two of Scripture as I kept seeking God's peace, which had been slowly eroding throughout the day.

We knew that back in Beaufort as we accepted the love and hugs of our military friends standing in front of our home at 263 Beech Street, we were taking our first steps down into the deep valley of the shadow of death as a couple, as a family. The doctors, on this day, had given us a "glimpse" of how long that journey through the valley might be. It was appropriate that I started reading Psalm 23, considering where we were walking.

> "The Lord is my shepherd; I shall not want.
> He makes me to lie down in green pastures:
> he leads me beside the still waters.
> He restores my soul:
> he leads me in the paths of righteousness
> for his name's sake.
> Yea, though I walk through the valley of the shadow of death,
> I will fear no evil: for you art with me;
> your rod and your staff they comfort me.
> You prepare a table before me in the presence of my enemies:
> you anoint my head with oil; my cup runs over.
> Surely goodness and mercy shall follow me all the days of my life:

and I will dwell in the house of the Lord forever."
—PSALM 23:1-6 (NKJV)

This psalm was one of the first passages I had memorized as a young child, and tonight it brought me great comfort. I don't remember what I read next, as the reading turned quickly into a conversation with God.

It's not every day that you look two years into the future and imagine how the final chapter of your life will read. At thirty-one, I considered myself to be invincible, not imagining that my expiration date could be so close. But tonight, I did just that. I sat at the little desk decorated with a small lamp. It was the only light breaking the darkness of the room, as Megan had extinguished the room lights and joined Grace Anne.

The table stood just under our lone window, overlooking the parking lot. Megan and I had been enjoying the crisp air and the beauty of the fall foliage these last two weeks of travel. We were now in the last days of October before the first snow, and the trees on this night appeared to have started fading past their brilliant peak. Nature's annual reminder that life is short and death must come was never more poignant.

Approaching midnight, I was still observing the autumn leaves covering the ground and gently blowing across the parking lot. A state of prayerful negotiation was unfolding within my soul. I processed the view from the window as well as the view from a deeper place within the valley. We had come through a number of switchbacks and roundabouts the past few days, and for a brief moment I had reached a place of higher ground where God momentarily allowed me to see the far end of the valley.

It was as if God was showing me my future. An internal calm had quieted my formerly restless spirit in these quiet moments, and it was as if I already had one foot in Heaven. I desperately wanted to take that next step, right then and there, and plant both feet firmly in glory with my Heavenly Father. No wait. No fight. No chemo. No pain. No struggle. *Home* was waiting at the end of the valley; a place of eternal peace, joy, comfort, unconditional acceptance, and unearned love awaited.

Looking on a calendar to see where the finish line of life might be is not a normal human experience. But as I stopped and pondered such a sobering possibility, my deepest beliefs about life and death rose to the surface. My faith became incredibly important and the ultimate source of peace. Conversely, I knew that where there was no faith, a vacuum existed — a void that would leave someone desperately searching for hope.

As a young six-year-old attending VBS (Vacation Bible School), I had heard the story of Jesus Christ, about how he died and shed His blood in order to be the Savior of the world. At six, that story became personal as I learned that He did that even for me.

"David," my VBS teacher asked, "do you believe that Jesus died for you? Do you want to ask Him to forgive your sins and to trust Him as your Lord and Savior?"

"Yes, I do, Mrs. Town," I replied.

That day, I prayed and trusted Christ with a short, simple, honest prayer void of heavy or controversial theological concerns. It was just me, as a young boy, recognizing that I was a sinner and accepting by faith alone God's gracious gift of Jesus' perfectly lived life and His ultimate death on a cross. I believed that Jesus rose to life again. He conquered sin and death — once and for all for everybody — three days later, just like they taught us in that class using a 1970s era felt board.

That summer day, I accepted what Jesus claimed about Himself in the Gospel of John when He said,

"I am the Way, the Truth, and the Life.
No one comes to the Father except through me."
—JOHN 14:6 (NKJV)

I was OK with that. I easily accepted the biblical truth that I could never earn salvation, and I put my complete, childlike faith and trust in Jesus, whom I had never seen.

It wasn't hard for me as a six-year-old to think back to the one and only thing I had ever done wrong. I think I was four that one time when Mom told me not to sneak any cookies before dinner, but I did. Or wait, maybe it was that time my lima beans found their way under my plate, and I lied about having eaten them. The only problem was that I left the table to play with my Matchbox cars, forgetting to dispose of the evidence of my transgression. That was a long night!

Yep, I was guilty, and I knew it. I'd had no time yet for sex, drugs, or rock and roll. I was only six and still hadn't even purchased my first rock and roll album. When I did, I got Journey's *Escape* album from 1981. I knew the words to every song on both sides of the LP. And yes, in this age of digital technology, I've kept the cassette though I have nothing to play it with.

My grandmother brought me to her church. Regularly I turned to her to talk about the things of God. I asked her questions, and she took the time to answer them.

"Nana, do you 'member when I prayed that special prayer at Vacation Bible School? I do bad stuff sometimes, and I can't be good all the time. But I believe Jesus died for me, and I asked Him to forgive me and be my Savior. So Nana, am I *saved*? Will Jesus take me to Heaven *for sure*?"

The BLUF is that there is nothing any of us can do to earn salvation. We only know we are Heaven bound by trusting the sacrifice Christ made on the cross as payment for our sins. Those are the basics of the Christian faith. I knew this truth, but I wrestled with doubt, the weapon the enemy uses repeatedly to take me and other believers off course, to yield us ineffective in the service of the High King.

Reflecting on my youthful doubts, I concluded that it was probably during those periods of my life when I was rebellious, distracted, or just dealing with issues of life and its complexities that I questioned my relationship with my Heavenly Father. By the time I was a teen, I owned all the Journey cassettes and CDs.

But on this night of nights, something intimately special happened. There was no wishing that my grandmother was still alive to go back and ask her again, "Nana, am I truly saved? Is that all I had to do was truly mean that prayer I prayed? Is there really nothing else I need to do? Is confessing to God that I am a sinner, and asking Him to forgive me because of what Jesus did for me, and telling Him that I put my eternal destiny in His hands actually enough?"

Though Nana Trombly would certainly, one more time, have patiently reassured me that these truths from God's Word were true if she had been there, I didn't need her tender, "Yes, David, that's right," on this night.

No. All of those questions and doubts fell away like scales from a blind man's eyes. Sitting in that small chair at the little desk spying out the window at the leaves illuminated by the sulfur lights outside, something supernatural happened. At that moment, something eternally important, deep inside my soul—in a place only God can touch—was cemented forever. God gave me absolute confidence, knowledge, assurance, a KNOWING that my eternal destiny was sealed forever. Doubt would never again be a concern like it had been in my early teens and twenties. I had approached and faced the giant of my pending death eye to eye.

At that moment I searched my soul, considered my childhood beliefs, reflected on how I had lived, contemplated the beliefs and truths by which I was leading my family, and weighed what I considered to be fact or fiction. I did not blink, and at that moment spiritual victory was mine. God saved my soul at six years old; of that event there was no doubt. But the enemy of us all continues to rage against all believers, seeking to steal the only thing he can, our peace. Our soul is forever secure in that moment of faith, but our peace can often be trashed, trampled, and stolen, as mine had been throughout my childhood.

"Be sober, be vigilant; because your adversary the devil, as a roaring lion, walks about, seeking whom he may devour. Resist him, standing firm in the faith, because you know that the family of believers throughout the world is undergoing the same kind of sufferings."
—1 Peter 5:8-9 (NKJV)

I knew beyond a shadow of a doubt that if I were to lose this battle within two years, I would stand in the presence of Jesus Christ, who sits by the right hand of the Father interceding for me and for all those who trust in Him. There was no uncertainty. There was no wavering. Instead, there was a sense of peace that filled me and filled that room—so much so that I reached the point of *yearning* for my eternal home.

That's when it happened. I wanted to take that second step into Heaven and finish this amazing conversation in person, face to face with God. No longer did I only embrace a complete assurance of Heaven with my Savior and with my loved ones to come, but I began genuinely *longing* for this cancer journey to be over quickly so that I could get there even sooner. The assurance was in place, and my pleading with God began in earnest.

"Why two years, Lord? Why not now? Why wait? The victory is at hand. My salvation is sure!"

As I reveled in that special moment, with my deepest gratitude I thanked God for His mercy and His grace, for Christ's saving work on the cross. Every cell in my body, every fiber of my being, and the completeness of my soul and spirit knew that I had won the ultimate victory. Complete and unexplainable peace was mine.

Then, as I leaned back in the chair and looked to my left, my gaze fell on Megan and Grace Anne sleeping. It was almost as if that glance *jerked* me out of Heaven and back to the reality of where I was, of what I was about to face.

My brain immediately caged like an old-fashioned tumbling attitude gyro in my old fighter. Gyros are prone to tumble and spin during *sudden*, excessive pitch and roll maneuvers. Once a gyro has tumbled, it's indications of actual aircraft pitch and roll become *untrue*. However, when the pilot pull the knob labeled "pull to cage" at the bottom of the instrument, the gyro immediately reset and cease to tumble. Once "caged," it once again provides *true* representations of the aircraft's actual situation.

Seeing my Grace Anne peacefully sleeping beside my beautiful bride instantly re-caged my focus from things heavenly and eternal back to my family and the immediate task in front of us. It was like the "Pull to Cage" knob on my brain had been pulled, and my family came into clear focus, as did my mission.

My one-on-one training flight with the Creator of the Universe was not yet over. No doubt pleased that His student had a spiritual light bulb going off, God doubled down His efforts and hit me hard with His next truth, as my lesson wasn't over quite yet. Suddenly, a second Scripture truth charged to the forefront of my mind. Another childhood verse learned in my formative years meant more to me than it ever had before in my previous three decades.

As I gazed at my devoted wife and daughter, I understood anew what Paul meant when he wrote to the Christians in Philippi:

"For I fully expect and hope that I will never be ashamed, but that I will continue to be bold for Christ, as I have been in the past. And I trust that my life will bring honor to Christ, whether I live or die. For to me, living means living for Christ, and dying is even better. But if I live, I can do more fruitful work for Christ. So I really don't know which is better. I'm torn between two desires: I long to go and be with Christ, which would be far better for me. But for your sakes, it is

better that I continue to live."
—PHILIPPIANS 1:21-25 (NLT)

I had first read these verses as a child in my King James Version of the Bible, which read like this: "For me to live is Christ, and to die is gain." . . . Oh, to give in to this disease, to step away from the mortal cares and the battle that was to come, to step into heaven— that would have been gain. . .

"But to live is Christ." To live. . . to fight on. . . to man up and step up. . . to pursue and persist. . . to refuse to give in until Christ said it was time to come home. . . to turn away from exiting the scene early by my choice. . . to keep my hand from pulling the ejection handle before all other options were exhausted. . . to stay in the battle as a faithful husband and father. . . —*that is living for Christ!* I needed to fight until God said I had crossed the finish line. The *when* was up to God not a man, not me, not the doctors, BUT GOD!

Until then, I had to do all that I could to beat this disease! I needed to stand in the gap for my family, be the man God intended me to be, and do the work He intended me to do! Right now, there was no retreat. I had to fight!

13| *The Heroic Gift*

IF you're fighting cancer and you have that same faith in Christ, let me encourage you, my fellow cancer Warrior, you have already won! Your victory is sure — whether that's healing in this physical body in the coming months or years or reaching Heaven soon to enjoy your sanctified and perfect body free from pain for all of eternity.

Maybe you don't have the peace I experienced that evening. If you have been diagnosed with a disease; if you've been given a death sentence; if you are facing a difficult timeline based on man's conventional wisdom; then I first encourage you to consider that only God knows how much time we have. Do not accept anyone else's timeline.

My German doctor, whom I look forward to introducing to you shortly, had a hopeful word that he used to tell me in his strong German accent: "Captain, if you are breathing, there is still hope."

A dear friend shares a similar word of encouragement that he received from his pastor, "If you are not dead, God is not done." This is true for everybody.

If you or someone you love is looking imminent death squarely in the eye, contemplating what's on the other side of life's final breath, you will want to have the answers to a few questions: Will I go to Heaven? How do I get there? What can I do? Can I do anything? What are God's Rules of Engagement?

The Bible, God's perfect and inspired Word, has the answers. The Bible, is the ultimate reference. It is the tactical manual of all tactical manuals with all the techniques and procedures to defeat the enemy on this side of eternity. Fortunately for us, this tactical manual is not classified as TOP SECRET like the one I studied for countless hours during those years I was blessed to be a young fighter pilot.

You will find more peace and truth from Scriptures than you could ever receive from this Marine's humble testimony. For a moment, let's look at what the Bible has to say on the subject of eternity.

The Bible is clear on God's one requirement—perfect holiness. That's where God sets the bar. That means never sinning, never breaking any of God's commandments. "What?" you say. "Perfection is the standard? So then no one can earn it?" Affirmative.

"For all have sinned and fall short of the glory of God."
—ROMANS 3:23 (NIV)

I don't believe for one minute that any readers of this book need convincing that they are not perfect. Just look at the Ten Commandments. Have you ever lied? Have you ever stolen something? Have you ever taken God's name in vain? Lima beans? Need I say more? Yes, truly we're all guilty, and we will never reach the benchmark of perfection that God, our Creator, requires.

But God loves us so much that He provided a way for us when He sent His only Son, Jesus Christ, to die in our place—something God did for us while we were still His enemies. Jesus is the sacrifice Who takes our punishment in order to pay the debt our sins created.

Because He lived a sinless and perfect life by God's standards, only Jesus successfully meets God's standard of holiness. Only Jesus can say that He lived a sinless life and then willingly paid our penalty in our place by selflessly laying down His life through the torturous punishment of the day — crucifixion. He shows His perfect love in the fact that He did this while we were still his enemies and He did it for all who would believe.

"But God demonstrates his own love for us in this:
While we were still sinners, Christ died for us."
—ROMANS 5:8 (NIV)

There are plenty of history books and current works written by individuals far more talented in the art of Christian apologetics than I if you are debating the historical existence of Jesus Christ. It is not my goal to convince you but to encourage you. If you are still weighing the veracity of Christ's existence and His claims in Scripture, I recommend Josh McDowell's book *The New Evidence that Demands a Verdict.*

With the presupposition that you accept Jesus was and is real and that He is who He says He is, let us take the next logical step in the human experience. Let's consider what all people must determine on a personal level when faced with the evidence of His life, death, and subsequent return to life three days later. What does all of this mean for you?

You may be asking a question that plagues many good people who work hard to pay their bills, earn an honest wage, and live as good citizens. You may be thinking, "OK. Jesus was perfect, and He died on a cross. But what gives? How many good things do I have to do in order for Jesus Christ to accept me or cover all my sins? Do I not have a role or responsibility here to earn my salvation on some level?"

This next truth is almost unfathomable. The God of the universe loves YOU so much, that He fully accepts Christ's substitutionary death as full payment for your unholy life for… Wait for it… FREE! It is His *gift* to all who will receive it.

> "For the wages of sin is death, but the free gift of God
> is eternal life in Christ Jesus our Lord."
> —ROMANS 6:23 (NKJV)

You can't earn this gift. You can't buy this gift. You can't do enough good things to merit this gift. You only have to receive it. Allow the following example of an ice hockey championship ring to serve as a humble example of what I am trying to explain about this special gift God offers us.

On April 14th, 2013, the Pensacola Ice Flyers beat the Huntsville Havoc 2-0 in game three of their series to clinch their first of three Southern Professional Hockey League Presidents Cup Championships. They would go on to win a total of three cups in four years. Yes, like the Stanley Cup, only smaller and less well known, but nonetheless a championship. The team has lifted this cup three times to toast a championship in their locker room after the hard-fought victories and long drawn out seasons full of triumph and challenges, injuries, and obstacles.

Following that first championship, the coach and players presented me with a championship ring. It was a gift. It was symbolic of the relationship we had one with another, as I had been their team chaplain since their inception in 2009.

You cannot buy one of these rings. It must be earned. Who earned it? Obviously, the goalie who flashed the leather and sacrificed his body between the pipes, shutting out the Havoc in game three, earned it. The defense man with the bone-crushing hit in the corner forcing the opposing offense to lose the puck on his offensive drive deep into our defensive end earned it. The centerman masterfully winning face-off after face-off earned it. The winger who found the gaps between the goalie and the pipes to score the game-winning goal earned it.

The trainer who, with dedicated care and expertise, skillfully glued and stitched players back together earned it. The equipment manager who burned the midnight oil sharpening skates, ordering sticks and supplies, and sewing names on jerseys minutes before game time due to last-minute trades earned it. The coach with the leadership skills and the system along with the owner with the financial resources earned it.

I knew who earned that ring and what it took to achieve the championship, yet here it was being presented to me as a gift during a chapel the following season in the team locker room. I had a choice. I could accept or reject the gift. I could have easily, in my pride, rejected the gift, saying that I in no way earned the ring, and simply thanked the team for the gesture.

Did I reject the gift? Seriously? It was a championship ring, my friend. No way did I reject it. I could not pass on such a special gift that came at such a cost. I understood what sacrifice and effort had gone into earning it, as I knew each one of the men who laced up their skates and took to the ice all season long. Had I said, "No thank you," what would the implications have been? How would that rejection have impacted my relationship with the team, the coach, or the owner?

Instead, I quickly got past my own pride, knowing that I had not earned that ring with even a single minute of ice time, and I respectfully accepted the gift with incredible joy and a sense of awe. I did not accept the gift based on personal merit or effort. I humbly accepted the championship ring based purely on the basis of my relationship with the team, a gesture for which I will forever be grateful.

This personal illustration of the championship ring is a simple one. It is but a humble example of a gift in comparison to the greatest gift ever offered in all of history—the gift of salvation, spending eternity with the forgiving and loving Heavenly Father, God Almighty in Heaven.

As I had the invitation to accept or reject that championship hockey ring, so each of us has a far more important choice, and our eternal destiny depends on our decision. God is seeking a relationship with you, my friend.

If you are ready for that relationship, if you seek that resolution for your soul, then do what God's Word asks you to do. Pray. That's talking to the God of the universe. Just have the conversation that He longs to have with you. Trust that He is right there with you as your Creator who knows your heart and your intentions. Because He made you who you are, the way you are, with special gifts and talents and passions, He already knows and loves you despite your not knowing Him. Trust Him, and just share your heart.

Take a moment and do what may be the hardest thing you have ever done and yet the most liberating at the same time. Admit to God that you are a sinner, and then seek forgiveness. You must admit you need this gift, or there would be no purpose for this gift.

Dr. Luke, one of the authors of the four Gospels in the New Testament, writes in chapter thirteen of his Gospel:

> "I tell you, no! But unless you repent,
> you too will all perish."
> —LUKE 13:3 (NIV)

Tell the Lord that you believe Him and trust Him as your Savior, your only way into Heaven.

> "Very truly I tell you, whoever hears my word and believes him who sent me has eternal life and will not be judged but has crossed over from death to life."
> —JOHN 5:24 (NIV)

If you have already told God you recognize you are a sinner, asked for forgiveness on the merits of Christ's saving blood that He shed for you, and openly declared that you trust in Jesus, God's Son, as your Savior, you are what the Bible declares as "saved." You are no longer condemned as unholy, but rather you are a son of God, a new creation in Christ Jesus.

> "Therefore if any man be in Christ, he is a new creature: old things are passed away; behold, all things are become new."
> —2 CORINTHIANS 5:17 (KJV)

You are now what Jesus explained to Nicodemus as being "born again" in John's Gospel account of Jesus' life. This is not a physical birth but a spiritual birth experienced by simply accepting God's free gift. It is miraculously accomplished through God's Holy Spirit bringing spiritual life to you when you completely trust Him.

"There was a man of the Pharisees, named Nicodemus, a ruler of the Jews: The same came to Jesus by night, and said unto him, Rabbi, we know that thou art a teacher come from God: for no man can do these miracles that thou doest, except God be with him.
Jesus answered and said unto him, Verily, verily, I say unto thee, Except a man be born again, he cannot see the kingdom of God.
Nicodemus saith unto him, How can a man be born when he is old? Can he enter the second time into his mother's womb, and be born?
Jesus answered, Verily, verily, I say unto thee, Except a man be born of water and of the Spirit, he cannot enter into the kingdom of God. That which is born of the flesh is flesh; and that which is born of the Spirit is spirit. Marvel not that I said unto thee, Ye must be born again."
—JOHN 3:1-7 (KJV)

You are now a child of God, and He will never forsake you. And you can trust that promise because God keeps His promises. The Apostle John writes,

"Yet to all who did receive him, to those who believed in his name, he gave the right to become children of God."
—JOHN 1:12 (NIV)

Accepting this free gift is the resolution to your unrest, the answer to your questions about eternity. If you seek peace, real peace that passes all human understanding, then the first step is knowing your eternal destiny is secure once and for all. That's right. God is the ultimate judge, and if you have His forgiveness, you have eternal security. You are in God's hands, and nothing can remove you from this place of confidence in your relationship with God Himself.

"I give them eternal life, and they shall never perish; no one will snatch them out of my hand. My Father, who has given them to me, is greater than all; no one can snatch them out of my Father's hand. I

and the Father are one."
—JOHN 10:28-30 (NIV)

Paul shares this promise from God in his book to the Roman Christians:

> "No, in all these things we are more than conquerors through him who loved us. For I am convinced that neither death nor life, neither angels nor demons, neither the present nor the future, nor any powers, neither height nor depth, nor anything else in all creation, will be able to separate us from the love of God that is in Christ Jesus our Lord."
> —ROMANS 8:37-39 (NIV)

Please consider taking that step of faith today. There can be nothing more important to capture from the pages of this book than what I have shared with you in this chapter from God's book.

Maybe you already have that resolution. If your spirit is resonating with these words and you have experienced God yourself; if you know beyond a shadow of a doubt that your victory is sure; then walk in God's peace through your current valley, my fellow Warrior. That's the most important word any of us could ever share with others if given the privilege to walk alongside them through their valley for a time. War on, Warrior! Walk through the doors God opens for you to walk out your faith in Him.

With the Apostle Paul, we say, "Thanks be unto God for his indescribable gift!"

Megan and I were still very much in the valley at this point in our family's story. We had just hit the highest point in our valley only three weeks into our journey. There are lower, darker corners we must still traverse. To continue the journey to reach ultimate victory, we must take the next step off this elevated and holy ground we have enjoyed. We must experience not only the coming victories and moments of love, family, and clear vision, but also the darkness, loneliness, confusion, and all the rest of the human emotions through the remaining challenges and turns that lay ahead.

Well, almost all of them. Fear suffered a death blow that evening as I sat and prayed by the window. Death no longer had any sting, as the assurance of my salvation protected my thoughts and mind like a helmet— a helmet not unlike the one I wore in my aircraft or when I stepped onto the ice to play hockey. That protection bred confidence and alleviated fear. Fear had been replaced with God's inexplicable peace.

> "Take the helmet of salvation and the sword of the Spirit,
> which is the word of God."
> — EPHESIANS 6:17 (NIV)

> "And the peace of God, which transcends all understanding,
> will guard your hearts and your minds in Christ Jesus."
> —PHILIPPIANS 4:7 (NIV)

A fighter pilot must know when to engage and fight or when to extend and exit the engagement in order to live to fight another day. The same principle would prove to be true in the coming days as we learned what the conventional realm had to offer. The battle space in which we would choose to fight was to be equally as important as the intensity with which we planned to fight. A decision point lay ahead.

Part Three
The Fork
in the Road

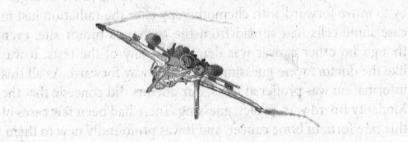

"If you are on the wrong road, progress means doing
an about-turn and walking back to the right road;
and in that case, the man who turns back soonest
is the most progressive."

— C.S. Lewis, Author of *Mere Christianity*

14| *Reconnaissance Mission*

WITH the Cancer Modality Board now completed and their results presented to us, the ball was in our court. The pressure to decide grew steadily. Megan and I both felt an instant loss of peace when presented with the conventional recommendations to remove a significant portion of my jaw, then radiate the very location that had been removed.

Additionally, we were pressured with a relentless sense of urgency to move forward with chemotherapy after the radiation just in case some cells had spread from the jawbone's tumor site, even though no other cancer was detected by any of the tests. It was like the doctors were guessing at the best way forward. As all this information was proffered to us, our doctors did concede that the Modality Board was, in fact, guessing. There had been few cases of this rare form of bone cancer, and it was profoundly new to them, too.

Our peace had been slowly waning ever since *FENDER* had shared forthrightly that there was actually far less than a 20% probability of success following Bethesda's recommended treatment. The medical community's empirical data served as a harbinger of my most likely fate using their conventional methods which had produced zero survivors.

Megan and my waning peace had become no peace at all. We had no confidence or peace to follow Bethesda's treatment protocol and no assurance within our spirits that we should move forward with the conventional options presented thus far. Our confidence that we would find any answers here was completely gone. The zero percent survival rate meant that we had hit a dead-end in Maryland. Bethesda had nothing for us. The time had come for a reconnaissance mission, a military operation outside an area occupied by friendly forces to gain information.

In civilian terms, it was time for a second opinion outside the military establishment. At the end of that final meeting, Megan and I respectfully requested that the Captain modify my orders to coordinate a second opinion from a civilian hospital close to our families up north.

According to the "Patient's Bill of Rights," we were all entitled to information regarding potential alternatives. Taking advantage of those rights, we wanted to meet a civilian oncologist for that second opinion.

It was almost time to pack up and head back to Boston. We had at least another night or two in the Fisher House while we waited for modified orders. Because I was still on active duty, my orders had to reflect my leaving Bethesda to travel back to Boston. Thankfully, Bethesda was able to get an appointment set up quickly. I had asked to go to Boston's Dana Farber Cancer Institute, and quite honestly, it was because that was the only one I could remember.

How did I even know Dana Farber existed? I grew up a Boston Red Sox fan. The Red Sox organization supported a charitable program known as the Jimmy Fund, which raised money for Dana Farber's cancer research. For years we had heard our favorite Red Sox color commentators, like Jerry Remy, make announcements for the Jimmy Fund during their radio and television broadcasts; so it was an obvious choice for us.

After my appointment was scheduled by the Bethesda staff, I called Dana Farber myself and requested to be rescheduled ten days later. They kindly obliged. I needed time to process what was happening. After more than a week of test upon test, Megan and I needed time to wrap our minds around the devastating news we had just been told.

Yes, it was going to take some time to recover from the emotional blow of a two-year death sentence, but there was more. We needed time to research. We needed time to learn about non-conventional options. We needed to slow down the clock so that we could find the info and do the praying required to make informed decisions before blindly choosing a course of action. This wasn't a carefree game, like a preschooler playing pin the tail on the donkey or swinging at a birthday piñata. This choice was a high stakes game of chance. It was a gamble either way, and we were going to have to go all in one way or the other with all our chips on the table. We had to make the most informed decision possible.

Now years later, whenever Megan and I have had the absolute honor of sharing our testimony with fellow cancer Warriors, in addition to sharing 2 Timothy 1:7, we have made a practice of asking them if they have had a second opinion. We've asked everyone. There were a couple of reasons, and the first was obvious. What if they were misdiagnosed? While that was rare, it was still a good reason for everyone to get a second opinion.

The main reason Megan and I encourage absolutely everyone to get a second opinion is so they could slow down the decision-making timeline, to take time to physically breathe. Warriors need to take the time not only to breathe, but also to emotionally and spiritually process the information they have been given.

In the early days and weeks following such a shocking diagnosis, the patient and the spouse or parents are typically inundated with information from doctors, friends, family, and all types of well-meaning individuals and even some unscrupulous opportunists. I still remember receiving packages of information in the mail from people I didn't even know. It was as if Megan and I had been placed on some "recently diagnosed cancer patient database" for anyone who had something to sell to reach out to us.

We have seen that all cancer Warriors need time to find wise counsel in order to make a well-informed decision. The Bible speaks of the need for wise counsel when making key decisions.

"Plans fail for lack of counsel,
but with many advisers they succeed."
—PROVERBS 15:22 (NIV)

Megan and I would soon be building a team of advisors from
both conventional and alternative medical circles and from both
secular and spiritual mentors. This team would consist almost
completely of people we had never met before starting this journey.

It was this ability to develop a network and to build bridges between conventional and alternative coalition partners that worked
well for us. We sought to foster a spirit of cooperation between the
allopathic and naturopathic circles of influence for the benefit of
ourselves and others.

"For lack of guidance a nation falls,
but victory is won through many advisors."
—PROVERBS 11:14 (NIV)

The wise prevail through great power, and those who have
knowledge muster their strength. Surely you need guidance
to wage war; and victory is won through many advisors."
—PROVERBS 24:5-6 (NIV)

Proverbs 24:6 applies not only to military strategists but also to
medical associations and federal organizations designed to provide protection and oversight. Our medical establishment has
been waging war on cancer for decades. Megan and I felt that if we
could link the amazing advances of conventional medicine using
state of the art diagnostics with the millennia-old, tried-and-true
therapies provided through alternative medicine, we might win
this war.

Nations wage war, but so do individuals. The authors of the sage
Proverbs above speak directly to us, as well as to empires. This

truth applies to anyone or any group engaged in a conflict. You may be personally conscripted to battle in this war on cancer at any time. Why limit the number of resources you use to fight your personal war against cancer or any major illness? I would never encourage anyone to disregard conventional diagnostics. It is wise to take full advantage of thorough staging upon diagnosis.

In the same way, I would encourage all who find themselves in such dire need to consider every option available to them in this country or overseas, both conventional and alternative. We are not all the same. We should not all receive the same standard treatment. Far better it would be for all cancer Warriors to have a personalized, focused, protocol specifically tailored for their very unique condition and body makeup, as I would do in the coming weeks.

If you are reading this book and have been recently given a serious health-related diagnosis and have not yet scheduled a second opinion, I gently yet earnestly encourage you to put down this book and schedule that second opinion *now.* Make that call—then pick the book back up. I waited over nineteen years to print this story. What is another fifteen-minute delay in your reading it to make that call in the grand scheme of things?

Such a precaution could save your life, and that statement is by no means an overreach. Please buy yourself that time which is otherwise so hard to carve out of the fast-paced initial tsunami of appointments, tests, and pre-op or pre-chemo appointments. Before you know it, the decision will have been made *for you* without your having had a chance to consider all the options available to you. I urge you to be a thoroughly engaged member of the decision-making process and not just submissively lie on the conveyor belt blindfolded through the conventional process. "Eyes and mind wide open" is my prayer for you.

You are afforded the right to choose which path you take. Do your own research. Please take the time to do your homework by learning everything about your particular disease, condition, and treatment as is possible. Be empowered, and then go down whichever path you choose with a sense of confidence that it is exactly what you should be doing. Be sure you have a peace about it. That peace comes from taking the time to process the news and then turning over every stone and considering every option before you get started, not afterward. You have access to GOOGLE.com, SCHOLAR.GOOGLE.com, WebMD.com, and PUBMED.gov along with so many more online resources than I had in late 2000. Many of the resources we found and share with fellow cancer Warriors are located on our www.groundedandcured.com page for your investigation. I respectfully encourage you to employ all these websites!

Many fellow cancer Warriors have shared with us their similar experience of an urgent call to action with minimal time to process all the information required. We have had friends go from diagnosis on Tuesday to chemo on Friday before even completing the full staging process. Sadly, many of us have found ourselves making life's most crucial decisions while under serious emotional stress, which actually keeps us off-balance, unable to focus and make sound decisions.

Please understand that when sharing our story with fellow cancer Warriors, we never try to influence or urge anyone to follow the same cancer treatment path that we did. Rather, we hope to FREE Warriors to take what they need from our testimony and other sources of information and wisdom, that they might purposefully choose *their own* path for *their* journey. Our heart's desire is to share, encourage, empower, and most importantly, point our new friends toward God and help them find *His peace* regardless of the path they take. How others attack their disease is not our decision to make. That is between them and God and those they choose to place on the cancer war council.

Megan and I polled the audience and phoned our friends. We

used every lifeline available, doing our research like we were on a high-stakes modern-day game show. The prize was not sixty-four thousand dollars nor one million. It was my life. We searched for every possible option and took as long as we needed to develop our final battle plan. In the end, God led us to our plan, and His peace kept us. Our war room deliberation took almost three months, but once we had peace about our plan of attack, we stuck to it.

A MOMENT WITH MEGAN

People tend to look at one scenario, like the miraculous peace we felt, and think it is the result of a momentary, isolated decision. But the peace we felt after hearing the diagnosis, doing our due-diligence in research, and prayerfully finding the path we felt God had for us was the aftereffect of a lifelong relationship trusting God through the unknown.

I had watched God move through the unknown and take care of me time after time. I knew that His relationship with me was all about trust. I knew my heavenly Father was there through my difficult childhood when I needed him, and I had watched God take David through major changes in his life already. To me, this was another part of the amazing story God was writing in our lives. I learned that you don't have to know the outcome before you can trust God's path forward for you.

At times it felt as though Megan and I had only God and each other, as our final treatment decision was certainly controversial.

We felt the push back from doctors, family, friends, and even one of my childhood pastors and his deacon board. But that resistance was OK. We had God's peace. We had confidence that God had shown us our path, and we were walking it out by faith.

Ecclesiastes 4 speaks to the strength of having a three-way bond. God, Megan, and I formed our strand of three. If you and your spouse are on a path God set you on Himself, you have an unbreakable cord, an unshakable faith. Nothing can break your confidence in that chosen path, no matter how hard the winds blow and how big the storm rages around you. If you do not have that peace, then you may be traveling down the wrong path. The storm will tear through your sails, and doubts and fears will pour in like floodwaters incessantly. Moments like these encompass us even if we're on the path God has directed. However, God's peace will always be present for us, even when we walk through doubt. The strand of three offers help in time of need!

> "Two are better than one,
> because they have a good return for their labor:
> If either of them falls down,
> one can help the other up.
> But pity anyone who falls
> and has no one to help them up.
> Also, if two lie down together, they will keep warm.
> But how can one keep warm alone?
> Though one may be overpowered,
> two can defend themselves.
> A cord of three strands is not quickly broken."
> —ECCLESIASTES 4:9-12 (NIV)

If you find yourself navigating a storm similar to ours, your path back to health may be completely conventional. Your path may be completely alternative. Your path may start conventional and then go alternative, as it has for so many others once their cancer was gone, and they took the needed years to rebuild their body's immune system back to full strength. If you are already on a conventional path, we would be honored to assist you in rebuilding and recapturing your vitality once you're cancer free. If the conventional comes up short, let me encourage you that many others have found success on another road when the conventional path led to a dead end.

Regardless of the path you choose, our goal is to help you find God's peace in the storm; the kind of peace we experienced during our walk through the valley; peace mentioned below in Philippians 4:7. From early in the fight, a huge component of your peace is knowing you are on the right path for *you*, not for me, not for your doctor, not for the insurance company, your friends, co-workers, or in-laws. You will have peace when you know you are on the path God intended for you, rather than one that was forced upon you by the culture, your finances, or indecision.

If you afford yourself the time to:

Catch your breath physically, emotionally, and spiritually

Gather as much intelligence as is available to you

Take that information into your War Room Council of Advisors

Deliberate your battle plan in prayer

Then peace will come. God will show you your path, and God's peace will settle it. He will guard you and guide you one day at a time. This holy trust, my friend, brings peace beyond human understanding, just as our Abba Father promised.

> "Do not be anxious about anything, but in every situation,
> by prayer and petition, with thanksgiving, present your requests to
> God. And the peace of God, which transcends all understanding,
> will guard your hearts and your minds in Christ Jesus."
> —PHILIPPIANS 4:6-7 (NIV)

15 | *Diverting to Our Alternate*

*INSTRUMENT Flight Rules (Federal Aviation Administration [FAA] published guidelines) dictate that every flight crew must file for an alternate airport when forecasted weather is expected to be below the prescribed minimum ceiling or visibility at their filed destination airfield. If the weather is good, this diversion is not required. However, if the weather is so bad that the crew cannot break out of the clouds on their instrument approach at their destination, they must have a backup plan.

Here we were at our chosen Bethesda destination, the one where Captain Morgan had fought to send me, but a destination that we now found ourselves questioning. We were much like a pilot desperately trying to land his aircraft in a raging storm, unable to see the runway obscured from view. The pilot finally reaches his "decision height," or furthest point of continuance, at a published minimum descent altitude.

This decision height is the altitude or published mileage from the landing runway for precision and non-precision approaches respectively at which he must decide to attempt to land with the runway clearly in sight, or to add power, rapidly climbing away from the ground if the runway is not in sight. Once safely climbing away from the ground, the pilot requests clearance from air traffic control to his weather alternate. Based on all his information, training, and experience, the pilot must quickly assess the situation and choose his path.

By requesting our military doctor for an orders modification to visit the civilian doctors in Boston, I had effectively just requested my clearance to our cancer battle plan alternate.

During our ten-day stay in Bethesda, we were blessed by one

149

incredible act of friendship. My best friend from my first fighter squadron, Captain Mike *PUDGE* Fisk and his wife, Cara, drove up from Beaufort to visit Megan and me. *PUDGE* was one of the Captains who had been shuffled out of our first squadron VM-FA-115with me to our new squadrons during our first tour. The result of that shuffle was that I ended up in VMFA(AW)-332, and he ended up a few hangars down the flight line flying with VM-FA(AW)-533.

The previous couple of weeks, *PUDGE* had been on orders away from MCAS Beaufort on a training detachment. He had called me to let me know that he had just learned of my diagnosis. He offered to take leave so that he and Cara could come to visit us at the hospital upon his return to MCAS Beaufort.

Captain PUDGE Fisk holding Grace Anne in Bethesda, Maryland

PUDGE and Cara came bearing gifts. Cara was able to give Megan a brief respite and care for Grace Anne. This time was an amazing gift after days of holding a six-month-old in a hospital room. We were only a couple of weeks into this ordeal, but the vast amount of reading we had done in that short time had already impacted our decision making and started us on a path toward health.

One of the common themes each cancer survivor shared in the stories we were reading was stopping their intake of sugar immediately. Megan and I had already committed to eliminating sugar by the time *PUDGE* arrived with a surprise he had collected from the Marines back in Beaufort. I had a notorious sweet tooth, regularly grabbing a couple of candy bars between flights and drinking soda like it was water during my work hours in the squadron.

And wow! *PUDGE* brought the best gift I could have ever wanted ... had it been three weeks earlier.

"*T-BONE*, the guys sent a little gift for you. Now you'll KNOW they are thinking of you, Bro!"

"What?! Three pounds of the BEST candy in the world? Plain M&M's! Chocolate heaven!"

"Yeah, we knew you'd have the first bag wiped out before midnight."

As I held that three pounds of melt-in-your-mouth joy, my fighter pilot mind triggered back to the words Megan and I had been seeing over and over—no sweets, zero sugar, nada $C_6H_{12}O_6$.

But my mouth could almost taste these beauties! There weren't even any peanuts in the center to reduce the total amount of chocolate sugar goodness. Adding to the difficulty of saying no was the fact I was just coming off my addiction, and M&Ms may as well have been my personal version of candy crack. I had been experiencing withdrawals from no caffeine or sugar for days, and these colored candies were calling out to me!

Plus, how could I decline this incredibly well-thought-out gesture from a dear friend? This Marine who took leave to come to deliver them and spend time with Megan and me in a dark place should not be rejected. I truly did not want to come across as ungrateful.

"*PUDGE*, you probably are gonna think you went to the wrong bunk, but I have to say thanks, but ... no thanks. Megan and I have been taking a crash course in health education, and we've committed to no sugar during this cancer battle."

I reluctantly handed them back to *PUDGE*. "Tell the guys to enjoy these in my honor when you get back to the squadron."

"We'll do that, *T-BONE*," whispered my understanding friend.

Bolstered by a great visit from great friends, we packed our things, checked out of the Fisher House, and grabbed my orders. We were executing our climb out with clearance to our alternate in hand. The trip to Boston took almost ten hours. It was a little longer than the trip *PUDGE* and I had made flying at Flight Level TWO-NINE-ZERO, twenty-nine thousand feet, less than a year earlier from Andrews Air Force Base right here near Washington D.C. up to Hanscom Air Force Base outside Boston. We flew that flight the first weekend after he and I both had passed our check-rides, graduating from the Section Leader training syllabus.

As the Silver Eagle's two newest section leaders, we were no longer relegated to flying solely on the wing of a more senior flight leader, usually one of the Majors (O-4). We had joined the squadron around the same time, six to nine months before our first deployment to Japan. Due to the large turnover of pilots, there were nine new Captains (O-3) in our squadron of eighteen pilots. It took us a significant amount of time to get all of us "Nuggets" through our initial Combat Wingman training syllabus just to be eligible to fly as a wingman into combat with the basic qualifications.

As a result of a pending U.S.-led air campaign against Serbia's President Slobodan Milosevic and his forces, our squadron was sent on a deployment to Japan six months early. Our task was to support the Marine Corps' Unit Deployment Program defending the Korean Peninsula and Japan, while another squadron flew to Europe for some action. Our training toward section leader was delayed during our seven-month deployment. It would be over a year before we were eligible to lead a two-*HORNET* flight on a mission.

With brand new Section Leader qualifications, *PUDGE* and I took two Silver Eagle jets and flew up the eastern seaboard, dropping in and out of military airspace. On each flight moving north toward New England, we were practicing our Basic Fighter Maneuvering (BFM) skills. *BFM skills applied strategically to the way my cancer battle dynamic unfolded on its darkest day.

David's parents, Megan's parents, and extended family and friends with Captain Trombly in front of our jets on the Hanscom AFB flight line

I vividly remember our short flight from Andrews up to Boston, though I do not remember whose turn it was to lead that flight. *PUDGE* would lead one hop, and I would lead the next. We quickly climbed up and out of Washington's airspace and were up at our cruising altitude. We flew with one-mile separation off each other's wing in a formation referred to as combat spread. This tactical positioning allowed us the ability to maneuver freely, employ our weapon systems, and yet provide mutual support to effectively defend our wingman in a combat scenario. This mutually supportive positioning is indispensable in the event one of us was attacked from a ground-based weapon system or an airborne bandit.

Facing no threats on this night's flight other than a 737 descending out of thirty-three thousand feet, our spacing allowed us the freedom to enjoy the incredible view while maintaining our sec-

153

tion integrity. As I looked left at *PUDGE*, I could see the sun setting between cloud layers. As *PUDGE* looked right past my F/A-18, he could see a full moon rising over the Atlantic, also breaking between thin cloud layers.

This flight is one of my fondest memories from my days flying the *HORNET.* My friend and I were young, invincible pilots flying fast jets and seeing God's splendor in a way that most people never dream of seeing from those altitudes. Man, we were blessed, and we knew it.

We were completing our third and final flight of the day, no BFM, just a straight flight from base to base before our crew day expired. Looking to make our best time to Boston, we pushed the throttles up and flew at .98 MACH. We were flying as fast as we could without breaking the sound barrier. Fighters are prohibited from breaking the speed of sound over the continental United States except in certain training areas out west. We are restricted to flying at those high speeds out over the ocean in order to prevent breaking windows and rattling dishes in people's homes below. With a favorable tailwind and a warm dinner waiting, we made it to Boston in just under an hour.

Megan's and my ten-hour trip from D.C. back up to Abington, Massachusetts to Bob and Sarah's was not nearly as fast as that amazing flight earlier in the year. Our reunion with our children, along with the week together that followed, however, were certainly as memorable.

Better than any sunset or moonrise that I had experienced with *PUDGE* on our descent into Boston's airspace, our reception upon arrival back in Boston started with Brad, our three-year-old, running up to me rocking my world emotionally and spiritually. Brad persistently tugged on my pant leg like a typical toddler, desperately working for my attention. "Dad, Dad... Dad... *Dad!*"

*(Kids left to right): Brianna, Grace Anne, Bradly, and Alex
experienced God's PEACE, while Megan and David enjoyed their smiles day
and night.*

"Yes, Bradly Bear?" He had my full attention now, and he hit me with something so powerful that it instantly impacted my outlook on what this next year or so was going to be about. It wasn't going to be about cancer, but rather about family and faith! Cancer was simply the obstacle, the challenge. God had something much bigger in store for that year than only a walk through the valley.

"Dad, Por Gawd, has not giben us a spirit a fear, but ub power and wub, and a thound mind." There it was... 2 Timothy 1:7!

> "For God has not given us a spirit of fear, but of power,
> and love, and a sound mind."
> —2 TIMOTHY 1:7 (KJV)

My youngest son recited that reassurance from memory with an adorable lisp. Bradly had confidence in his eyes that drew me right in! He sounded like a child, yet that confident child-like faith knocked the breath from my chest. It was as if God had said it Himself to me right there in my sister-in-law's kitchen. In that moment, I knew that God had not just me but my entire family in His

155

embrace. Beautiful joy and peace took hold of my spirit in that special moment between a father and a son.

We had just returned with some really tough news, but before we could share it, our first encounter was a GOD encounter as He sent Bradly like an angel, as a harbinger of good news!

At that moment, I once again stood resolute and empowered. I stood there with my Bradly knowing that God was with us as confidently as I had the first day when God had given me that word of promise that I would beat this disease and fly again, the words I had spoken in Captain Morgan's office on Parris Island.

God would use 2 Timothy 1:7 mightily in the days ahead in ways Megan and I could never imagine!

16| *A New Base of Operations*

MEGAN and I ran down leads, read more books, and called nutritionists. I personally spent hours in the local library on the internet researching Lymphomas and alternative medicine during the week we had in Boston before my consultation with the hematology-oncology team at Dana Farber. Sarah's and Bob's kitchen table became our new Base of Operations, and we had a week to set up shop, research, and implement what we could before I would see the civilian doctors, make another key decision, and then return back to base in Beaufort to brief my plan of attack to my Commanding Officer.

We thought our divert from our preplanned destination of conventional military medicine in Bethesda was to be up and over to the conventional civilian doctors in Boston. Our landing was at Sarah's and Bob's kitchen table. The alternate to which we diverted was actually an alternative medicine path!

Megan and David with their four children outside Bob and Sarah MacK-
innon's house, having returned from Bethesda Hospital in time for Halloween
2000 Trick or Treating

Why is it that healing methods that are thousands of years old, or products that are non-pharmaceutical are labeled alternative? Why are medical practices only decades-old labeled convention-al? These and other thought-provoking questions were going to be asked and researched by Megan and me in the coming weeks and months.

One of the books Megan reread and I read for the first time the previous week in Bethesda was written by an American nutrition-ist named Dr. Ted. His was the first book I read in the realm of health and wellness. It would not be my last. We listened to the enclosed audio recordings, read the handbook, and even made a phone call to speak with him directly.

Dr. Ted was approachable and friendly and shared our common faith. We worked through a number of topics in his book. Megan and I were like sponges soaking up all his great advice and knowl-edge quickly. Within a couple consultations, he had encouraged us to seek out biological medicine experts who focused on cancer, as we had exhausted his resources.

It was this phone call with Dr. Ted that gave us our first tangible offensive tool to implement in our alternative battle plan—colonics! This intestinal cleansing is a key component to complete health. He encouraged us to consider that disease is often caused by excessive toxins building up within us, especially in the colon and liver.

His audio recording of Dr. V. E. Irons (widely considered to be the pioneer of the modern intestinal detox) explaining his seven-day colon cleanse provided our first steps. From my hospital room in Bethesda, Maryland, I ordered the "7-Day Cleanse" through Dr. Ted. This package was already waiting for us when we arrived at Bob's and Sarah's. The cleansing agents, supplements, bucket, tubing, and colonic board were all there waiting to be used. Knowing that there was a seven-day cleansing program waiting in Boston and wanting enough time to complete it, I decided to push my second opinion consultation out ten days from my departure from Bethesda.

My first full day back, I started my "7-Day Cleanse." This would be the first of seven cleanses I would execute over the coming year, averaging a seven-day fasting cleanse with colonics every seven weeks.

At the time of this writing, I have done over forty cleanses. Following my successful victory over cancer, I have completed two cleanses per year for nearly two decades. I am only a few years and a handful of colonics away from having skipped an entire year of meals doing these colon and liver cleanses. I have certainly become a believer in the power of cleansing.

The Greek physician Hippocrates has been called the Father of Medicine. The phrase "Death begins in the colon," was first attributed to him. His theory from over two thousand years ago was simple. He believed, as have so many others since him, that maintaining a clean colon is critical to our overall health and wellbeing.

If a clean colon is paramount to overall health, then it is logical to conclude that cleaning it out regularly is important. Doing so could even reverse degenerative diseases. Dr. V. E. Irons shared Hippocrates' strongly held beliefs that clean health is closely tied to a clean colon. Dr. Irons shared the story of a farmer who came to him with what his doctors had labeled as incurable cancer. This farmer was told by his doctors that he had a short time to live and that there were no viable options for him.

The farmer sought out Dr. Irons, who took the farmer through a series of colonics which helped in reversing his disease. This testimony alone was enough to influence me to order the program and have it waiting for me in Boston. I share this farmer's story with fellow cancer Warriors to encourage them to consider colon hydrotherapy as an option on their journey back to health.

During this week of detox, I fasted from all food and only ingested the supplements that were included with the program. My only food source was the ten ounces of apple juice and four ounces of water with psyllium hulls and bentonite clay in the five detox drinks. I drank five required drinks every three hours each day from 0700 to 1900. The evening of the first day and then in the morning and evening of the remaining six days, I performed a five-gallon colonic.

Each colonic took about forty-five minutes, followed by fifteen minutes to clean up, grab a shower, and put all the equipment away. These two very effective hours every day for a full week pulled poisons directly out of my body. Using only gravity, it is a very gentle cleanse. These cleanses are usually very comfortable, but there are moments that can be a little uncomfortable when a large portion of the waste and sludge breaks free and makes its way through the colon to exit.

Despite the occasional moments of discomfort, the program as a whole is incredibly empowering. Seeing what had left my body in the toilet gave me a sense of confidence that each colonic was moving me forward to my ultimate goal.

Once family and friends caught on to what I was doing, I would jokingly say that I had to go sledding and slip away to knock out my colonic. If that led to further questioning, I would explain things in a little greater detail. I would just tell them I was going to grab a garden hose and proceed to describe its very specific placement and purpose in as colorful a manner as the audience would allow.

This program is designed to allow you to do the cleanse from the comfort of your own home. As I was not at home, I set up the colonic board (the sled as our family likes to call it) and a five-gallon bucket in my sister-in-law's downstairs bathroom just off her kitchen. So much for being discreet.

To avoid being overheard, I attempted to work the colonics board after dinner for the family's sake while they were in the living room watching a movie. If dinner was late, I would try to play the radio loudly, as I was only on the other side of a thin door. Fortunately, I could get a Boston Bruins' hockey game on the radio most nights at colonic time and muffle the colonic activity sounds. Even with only gravity pressuring the five gallons of water, coffee, and bentonite clay from the bucket, through me, and into the commode, the procedure made for an awkward waterfall sound heard through the walls. The children never had to ask where daddy was.

During my very first week of cleansing, I dropped thirteen pounds. Once I started eating food again, I put back on four pounds. Though Marines are not known for being good at math in public, I have told the story enough times that the math has become fairly easy for me. Nine pounds. Nine pounds of sludge left my body that week. I could be more colorful in my description here, but I will stay clinical for the squeamish.

What left me was not fecal matter. I did not have nine pounds of meals exit my body. There were no meals. This was nine pounds of toxic sludge that had built up on the inside of my intestinal wall over the previous thirty-one years. The minimal amount coming into the body in those five drinks a day could not congeal and equate to the vast amounts of material that was coming out of my body during that time frame.

If you have never had a colonic or heard of a colonic before, think of an enema. Most of us are familiar with the small red rubber bag which can hold about a liter of water with a two or three-foot-long hose and a rounded tip for insertion into the rectum. These can usually be found at grandma's house or any local pharmacy. This small bag is typically filled with an enema product, also sold over the counter at the pharmacy, or with distilled water, coffee, or pure olive oil.

The purpose of an enema is to assist in the elimination of fecal matter that may be impacted in the sigmoid colon, which is the last thirteen to fifteen inches of the colon. This serves as a very effective tool for assisting an individual to eliminate when constipated. It is not, however, a detoxing treatment.

To detox, the entire colon, which is approximately five feet long, must be addressed, not just the last foot of it. A colonic is to your colon what a garden hose would be to your trash barrel. Every week the trash is "eliminated" from the barrel when the garbage truck makes a visit. Over the weeks, months, and years, the barrel itself will become filled with a film of sludge and dirt, despite never missing a regularly scheduled visit from the garbage truck. Trash elimination takes place, yet residue and filth remain behind and build over time in your barrel.

Taking a garden hose once a year to your trash barrel eliminates the sludge left behind even after the trash is gone. In the same way, a colonic removes the sludge left behind after the fecal matter has been eliminated through normal regularity. Homeowners clean their trash barrels, yet people rarely clean their colons. Now you have the knowledge and the power. So grab a garden hose, and let's clean out that colon!

A colonic is much like an enema in that the detoxifying agents (such as coffee and water, bentonite clay, or olive oil) are also inserted rectally, but a colonic will then irrigate the entire large intestine. This includes, in reverse order of normal fecal flow, the descending, transverse, and ascending colon, which is the exact direction of flow of the colonic itself.

The liquid from the colonic bucket travels down through a tube purely by gravity; so there is no excessive pressure on the recipient when done at home. Once in the colon, these agents work their way backward deeper into the colon, providing the detoxing and flushing action desired through gentle massage. The individual receiving the colonic will usually self-massage if at home or will be massaged by a technician if done in a professional setting.

As the fluid moves up and through the entire colon, fecal debris is eliminated, but more importantly, toxic sludge which is not fecal matter is also eliminated. This sludge is a highly concentrated semi-solid mass of stored toxins, which over time poisons our blood supply. During our daily digestive process, we consume foods and chemicals in our foods that our body immediately recognizes as foreign invaders. The body floods the gut with white blood cells, and mucus forms to encase the dangerous invaders safely, but oftentimes these encased toxins are not eliminated, creating "sludge." This sludge then sticks to the wall of the colon, storing the poisons within our bodies for years, even decades. This toxic layer hardens, and over time, bowels fill up and distend. As we age, our waistlines get wider as our colons fill with this unremoved toxic trash.

Equally as devastating to our overall health is the inevitable overcoating of the intestine's epithelial wall, which provides gut maintenance and nutritional absorption. Over time, this epithelial wall is overwhelmed by this toxic sludge. The sludge barrier prevents food nutrition from being absorbed into the bloodstream. Obviously, this degrades proper nutrition and leads to long term health challenges.

Now that you have a better understanding of colonics, take a moment and Google the words "colonics images." What will appear on the screen will be a number of pictures of the sludge that leaves the body and the shapes it takes while forming itself to the sides of the intestinal wall. There are entire sections from a few inches to a couple of feet in length that can release during the colonic. These sections might even startle an individual upon the first release. It is slimy and rubbery, unlike fecal matter. This material does not easily leave the body, requiring the mechanical action of psyllium hulls to scrape and chisel at the bulky deposit. The irrigation of the colonic itself assists in flushing the waste quicker than the natural peristalsis, which would eventually push it out on its own if colonic irrigation were not available.

With my first colon cleansing week complete and some positive energy flowing from feeling like we were moving in the right direction, Megan and I rolled up to Boston for my second opinion at the Dana Farber Cancer Institute. Being thirteen pounds lighter, I moved pretty quick. I felt clean and energetic and ready to face whatever news they had for us.

Not long after our arrival, we started receiving information. The pathologist quickly confirmed that I indeed was properly diagnosed with a rare Diffuse Large B-Cell Primary Non-Hodgkin's Lymphoma of the Bone. Well, there went any hope of misdiagnosis or of enjoying a large Snickers® or M&M'S® Blizzard® with extra candy from Dairy Queen® on the way back to the house.

Interestingly, the oncologists in Boston did not want to remove the upper portion of my jaw surgically. In fact, they did not want to use radiation, either. They came up with a plan to double chemotherapy alone.

Hearing about the possibility of doing chemotherapy alone brought us some mixed emotions. I was glad to learn of a course of action in which my jawbone and teeth could remain in place. The thought of radiation made no sense with the jawbone gone, yet even if radiation remained a part of the plan, I was very worried about it scattering into vital parts of my brain and doing collateral damage. So removing radiation, too, seemed like great news.

I had a large number of metal fillings from my time drinking soda since joining the Corps. On each of my CT scans, there were "Starbursts" where a beam of radiation would catch the edge of a filling and shoot off in a random deflection, leaving a line on the scan image. I raised this concern with both the radiologists and oncologists in Bethesda. They had said it would not be an issue with the bone removed as the teeth would go with it.

Had Dana Farber wanted to do radiation without surgery, I'd be right back to this serious concern. With radiation not on their list of modalities for me, this starburst effect was no longer a concern, and two of my three biggest issues were immediately resolved. I was preparing myself mentally for a single-pronged attack on this disease that would be chemotherapy alone received right here in Boston.

It was time to talk about chemo. I could see myself rolling into Boston for the next few months doing chemo, living in or around Boston, and watching the Bruins every night, at least until the opening day at Fenway. Maybe I could score some seven-dollar, standing-room-only tickets at Fenway with my little guys. I was certainly not thrilled with the idea of chemo, but at least I was going to be home with family and childhood friends. This thought came and went in a flash.

"Mr. Trombly, we would like to do twice the chemotherapy than had been recommended by your team in Bethesda."

"Twice the chemo?" I paused there and let this new thought twist and turn for a moment. This could not be good. They continued to explain their reasoning for the greater dosage, speaking to the lack of vascularity in the bone structure, etc.

"Doc, I don't think double chemo is going to work for me, as I have Gilbert's Syndrome."

This condition is not life-threatening, and I found it on an annual flight physical doing my normal blood work. While in flight school in Kingsville, my flight surgeon had diagnosed me with it and asked if I drank alcohol. I said no, and he told me not to worry about it then. He did tell me that if I started drinking after flight school to expect a longer recovery time than my peers to work through a buzz or a hangover.

I remembered his warning to me and shared with the oncologist, "Sir, if my liver processes less effectively than others, causing me to have longer recovery times if I were to drink alcohol, wouldn't doing double chemo have far greater endgame toxicity and organ damage?" The doctor's desire to do double chemo ended when he heard "Gilbert's" about as abruptly as my thoughts of getting Fenway tickets vanished when I heard "double."

The doctor told me he would have to get back with the modality board to discuss this concern and would give me a call as soon as he could convene a second board. Megan and I thanked him for his time and departed south back to the children. Our conversation immediately after that appointment quickly centered around how Dana Farber could have missed something so significant in my medical record as my having Gilbert's Disease. This condition was something that would determine my eligibility for chemo or double chemo, yet the board missed it, leaving me, the "patient" to point it out.

"Patient." I hate that word and will not use it to describe myself. To this day, I just won't use it when I refer to my friends fighting cancer. It carries an air of vulnerability and passivity. No, I was not going to be a cancer patient, but a cancer WARRIOR!

Sitting in the sidecar without any control while the oncologist or radiologist had the controls of the motorcycle was not how I wanted to go through this fight. That moment of me raising my concerns as my own best advocate regarding my liver condition was the moment that I completely removed my cancer protocol from the hands of the conventional doctors. Megan and I knew

165

we were going 100% natural that day; we just didn't know exactly what that meant quite yet.

17| *The Birth of Our War Plan*

WHILE Megan and I waited a few more days to hear back from Dana Farber for the results of their second cancer Modality Board involving my case, we reviewed all we had researched over the past few weeks. Though leaning toward the all-natural methods we had been researching, we were struggling. We were holding out for one last phone consultation.

Our first call after we were given my grave diagnosis was to Miss Barbara, a naturopath that Megan's sister had been seeing for years with her young girls. A Bostonian, Miss Barbara had already launched Megan on a natural path four years earlier when our first daughter, Brianna, had been referred to an Ear Nose and Throat (ENT) surgeon to have her tonsils and adenoids removed.

Brianna had multiple infections and visits to the pharmacy for antibiotics during her first three years. It was so commonplace that even she as a toddler referred to her medicine as either her "pink stuff" or her "white stuff." Miss Barbara was instrumental in saving Brianna from that surgery by directing Megan to take our children off dairy and to use homeopathic remedies. That experience was our first call, our first attempt to reach outside of our own knowledge and experience for assistance. It would not be our last.

Miss Barbara was able to share both sympathy and empathy with us, as her family had recently lost a loved one to cancer. She had learned of a German doctor who worked with cancer Warriors using alternative methods. In addition to several homeopathic remedies for Megan's elevated stress, Miss Barbara gave us Dr. Schildwaechter's contact information. God had supplied our first and best lead that would soon become the central hub of our natural and biological approach. Faces forward with a new battle strategy, we set up a consult with Dr. Schildwaechter and would soon have our biological doctor, or as you could call him, our alternative General, in place.

My sister-in-law, Sarah, had also learned of a local family whose miraculous cancer survival story had aired on Boston's local FOX News station. After we contacted this family, they invited us over. Megan and I sat at their kitchen table and were inspired as they unpacked the details of their journey down an alternative path fighting their son's cancer.

That's how we met the "BEST" family. William and Susan were pretty amazing people to open their home and give of their time, for sure. But no kidding, *Best* was their last name. The mom, Sue Best, shared most of the story as we listened intently.

"Billy was only seventeen," Sue started. "He was still a minor when he was diagnosed with Hodgkins Lymphoma and went to Dana Farber for his first chemo treatment. He struggled with that first treatment, and he refused any further treatments. He begged us not to take him back, and when we agreed, that is when we learned the hard realities of caring for a minor with a grave illness in this country."

Megan and I shuddered at the thought of one of our children going through a similar experience and us having to fight the state and federal authorities to choose the path our child would take to regain health. We were so fortunate it was me and that I only had to push back when pressured by my military doctors or request maneuver space by seeking a second opinion with civilian doctors. We sat in awe as we listened to Sue Best unpack their story. This courageous family not only had to battle cancer but had to fight for the opportunity to battle the way that Billy, himself, believed best, as well as they, themselves as parents believed was best for their son.

"David, Megan, as adults, anyone over the age of eighteen is protected by the 'Patient's Bill of Rights,' and are thus able to choose their treatments. Minors are not afforded that right. As parents choosing a path that was inconsistent with conventional wisdom, we faced possible criminal charges for neglect. We could even have lost custody of Billy to the foster care system, where another family would have taken him in and ensured that Billy made it to all the doctor's prescribed treatments."

Sitting there listening to the heart of a mother, even years after Billy had found his cure naturally, I heard the pain and frustration in her voice. We could see it in her body language. It seemed Orwellian to me that the government could determine what was best for a child, trumping a parent's rights in a free society.

Sue continued to unfold their story like a tapestry.

"Billy had 'run away from home' via a Greyhound bus ticket all the way to Texas to avoid taking chemotherapy at Dana Farber. We were threatened with losing custody and possibly going to jail, but his act of 'running away' saved us from that hardship. Billy made it to Texas on his own, but the nationwide search prevented him from reaching California where he had lived as a child and intended to die. Billy spent a few months hiding out in Texas. Eventually, he returned home months later by his own choice, not by force or apprehension. These two decisions by Billy demonstrated that he had the ability to make his own decisions at seventeen. Therefore, the court determined to treat him as an adult, which allowed him to make his own choices moving forward. He was cancer free not long after his return home, and by the grace of God, he has remained cancer free."

Sue continued to share how the state did not actually pursue charges against them and allowed Billy to finish his natural treatments. He traveled to Canada with his father and learned how to administer 714X to himself. In addition to a number of natural therapies, Billy included Essiac Tea, which Sue shared with us. We immediately purchased a few boxes of Essiac Tea and brewed my first cup as soon as we returned back to Sarah's and Bob's house. I continued using Essiac Tea through the early months of my battle before starting my raw diet.

Billy Best wasn't the first person to find a natural cure or healing approach to cancer. There were others that we had read about while down in Bethesda. Megan had been reading stories of people who had beat cancer alternatively for the past few years in her studies. The Best family, however, was the first family that we were blessed to meet in person.

It would be hard for me to put into words the impact that meeting this family had on us and how that gift of time and love boosted our confidence in our decision at this point to go completely natural. This amazing family stepped out of their busy schedule to share both spiritual encouragement and life-saving information with us in our health crisis.

We took a moment to thank a number of key supporters in the acknowledgment section, but we must, right now, take a moment to thank this family.

"William and Susan Best, thank you for the time, love, faith, knowledge, and generosity you invested in us! When we were at the crossroads of our war with cancer, you stood with us, not ordering us, but giving us the option of an alternate battle plan. Your emotional support cleared our minds to evaluate both roads.

"Billy Best, thank you for having the courage of an experienced soldier, though only seventeen, to stand for what you believed in, for fighting for your life, and for sharing your story with us and others.

"You inspired me, Billy! When this fighter pilot felt sorry for himself and was having a 'bad day,' I just thought back to your story and told myself: 'Suck it up! If Billy can wage this war as a teenager, how dare I, as a Marine, give an inch of ground up to the enemy?' Billy, I am confident you would agree with me that God is the source of our strength, but I want you to know

169

that it didn't hurt to have your teen-testimony there to kick me in the prover-bial gluteus maximus on the days I needed it most!"

We finally heard back from Dana Farber. The battle plan Dana Farber shared did more to dissuade us from considering some portion of conventional treatments than it did to invoke any sense of confidence in their belief that they could help me. We had been leaning away from the chemotherapy ever since our in-person hospital visit with them, but this new plan cemented the decision for us.

Dana Farber proposed doing half the chemotherapy dosage but for four times as long as opposed to their original battle plan for double chemotherapy. We were convinced that the civilian doctors, just like the military doctors in Maryland, were guessing. To their credit, they were certainly trying to determine a way forward, but with so few cases, it was as if they were starting at square one with me. Following their guesswork felt too risky, and Megan and I were not willing to have me be the fifty-first human test subject on an unproven theoretical protocol.

This was the week we would learn that there were no convention-al options offered by the civilian doctors at Dana Farber which we could consider viable, either. This was the week God would open one door followed by another and then another for us to learn and execute an alternative cancer battle plan.

Megan and I used this week of cleansing and research to finally link up with the rest of our family. We had made it north of Bos-ton, where I was able to sit down with my parents, both of whom were recently cancer free themselves. Mom had successfully beat breast cancer with surgery to remove a single tumor followed by radiation.

My father had been given a clean bill of health after having sur-gery to remove his bladder. The urologist not only completely re-moved his bladder, but then built Dad a new one with a portion of his intestine which was removed, cleaned, reshaped, and relocated. Dad had some new plumbing, but otherwise, he was free of cancer and blessed not to have to wear a bag on the outside of his body.

Both my parents beat cancer conventionally, though neither was required to undergo chemotherapy. Mom enjoyed another ten years cancer free before dealing with a second and different form of breast cancer. Being the fighter that she was, Mom subsequently beat breast cancer a second time the same way, also without chemotherapy. Dad lived another seventeen years without dealing with cancer again. It was comforting to have both parents cancer free and not to have to carry that concern and stress for them through my own cancer journey.

My parents had been diagnosed with different cancers, and therefore, they saw two different oncologists. It was like having a couple of bonus oncologists as part of our core advisory group. During those early weeks, Mom and Dad shared my diagnosis and what both Bethesda and Dana Farber were recommending, and of course, they got their doctors' advice to share with us. When I was finally able to share that Megan and I were going to forego the surgery, chemo, and radiation recommended by Bethesda, as well as the chemo plan from Dana Farber, to seek out 100% alternative options, you can bet we heard from Mom's and Dad's oncologists. We heard through my parents, of course, who had shared their concerns with their doctors and then relayed the warnings of such a risky decision back to us.

It helped that this feedback was tempered by my parents' understanding that Megan and I were stepping out on a faith-walk and were not going to be easily swayed or pressured. This common ground allowed my parents to share their concerns while voicing them as if they spoke purely of their oncologists' concern versus their own. This verbal distance freed my parents to express their apprehension in a far less threatening manner, to have peace, and to then let it go—fully supporting our efforts.

Not having to wrestle daily or weekly with family about our cancer-fighting decisions blessed us immensely. Sadly, the majority of cancer Warriors must add constant family arguments to their already maxed out stress levels. While fighting the disease, they must also fight pressures from family, friends, and even physicians for pursuing an alternative path. Effectively, this tension turns an already difficult conflict into a two-front war. Don't misunderstand. We faced our share of opposition, but both sets of our parents fell into our camp of supporters pretty quickly. That unity strengthened our weapons of warfare, something Megan and I gravely needed.

As a matter of fact, as we wrapped up our trip to Boston, the family came together for one final group visit. We had traveled to New Hampshire and met at Syd's house, Megan's oldest sister. Everybody came. My parents, Megan's parents, all Megan's sisters, and each brother-in-law were there. My brother and sister came, too. What support we garnered from this uncommon gathering!

Before we wrapped up the night, the entire family gathered around me as I sat on a kitchen chair in the middle of the driveway. The early November evening was cool at sunset. My sister-in-law, Vicky, anointed my head with oil while many family members prayed over me, asking God for my healing just as Scripture directs us in the New Testament book of James.

> "Is anyone among you sick? Let them call the elders of the church
> to pray over them and anoint them with oil in the name of the Lord.
> And the prayer offered in faith will make the sick person well; the
> Lord will raise them up."
> —JAMES 5:14 - 15 (NIV)

18 | *You're Fired*

BACK on I-95 South, Megan and I moved our natural battle plan forward. The signs for Bethesda came and went as we traveled from Boston to South Carolina. It was empowering to be driving right on past versus pulling in to start treatments. We had a developing strategy, and it did not include chemotherapy or radiation along the nation's beltway. Beaufort was our destination, and we neared it by the hour.

On the day after we returned, we were warmly welcomed by our neighbors, and to my great pleasure, by my Commanding Officer, LtCol *SLAM* Amland. I made an appointment to debrief the Skipper regarding my past few weeks of testing and appointments at both hospitals. When I shared my desire to stay in the squadron and continue to fly, he was receptive. With my tumor removed, no sign of cancer on the tests, and our plan to fight any cancer that might be left in my body naturally, there would be no medical downing treatments or side effects— no vomiting, no vertigo, no loss of hair or fingernails, and no other negative results.

"Skipper, as part of our alternative cancer war plan, I'm going on a raw diet. I believe I'm gonna be in better shape and healthier than the rest of this command. I want to stay in the squadron and fly for you, Sir."

"*T-BONE*, you'll have to see our flight surgeon, Commander Briggends. He's the only one that can ensure you are eligible to stay in the cockpit on that diet."

"Roger that, Skipper. I'll make that appointment right away. Thank you for your time and consideration."

Immediately, I stepped directly to medical to seek yet another unscheduled appointment, this time with our unit's doctor. I was engaged and feeling empowered. I was ready to begin executing my rudimentary plan. All I needed was just one doctor to sign off on it, or so I thought.

The flight surgeon serves as an aviator's primary care manager and is responsible for all the pilots in the squadron. Once a year, all pilots undergo a complete physical from this physician to ensure they are healthy enough to maintain their flight status. If an acute ailment arises, such as a sinus infection or migraines, the doc will temporarily ground the affected pilots, provide them with the required medication, and schedule a re-check. After a healthy status is confirmed at the post-visit, he subsequently returns the healthy pilots to flight status. This new order rescinds the previous memo grounding us with what we call an *"Up Chit."

When something more significant (like a heart murmur, diabetes, or cancer) is diagnosed, the ability to grant our flight status becomes more complicated. In order to get that pilot back into the air, the flight surgeon has to submit a request for a waiver from *NAMI (Naval Aerospace Medical Institute). I knew that I was not able to fly following the serious diagnoses from a month earlier, but I actually had yet to speak with our squadron's assigned flight surgeon. Today would be the day.

I had only been in my new squadron for a few months. So Commander Briggends and I had no prior connection, no relationship like the one I had with my last squadron's Flight Doc, who had deployed with me to Japan. I gathered it made things rather simple and surgical for the Commander when I arrived with a request that he could not possibly approve. I shared with him my desire to return to flight status and made my argument. He considered my request to be foolhardy at best due to well-established medical guidelines. However, these guidelines were unknown to me, and I boldly charged forward ignorant of the rules.

When I entered his office, we made our introductions. Without hesitation, I forthrightly asked for the impossible.

"Commander Briggends, I am Captain Trombly, and a few weeks ago I was diagnosed with a rare Primary Lymphoma of Bone. It is a Diffuse Large B-cell Non-Hodgkin's Lymphoma, to be specific." Without taking much of a breath, I continued. "Both Bethesda and Dana Farber confirmed the pathology and consider it a two-year death sentence. The two hospitals offered vastly different treatment plans, and I decided against both in order to pursue a holistic plan without chemo. This would allow me to continue flying and..."

"Captain," the flight surgeon abruptly interrupted, "I don't know if you've been hit in the head by the canopy climbing out of your cockpit or if you are just living in a fairytale. But make no mistake about it: you are not flying anything in this squadron until you fly your ass back up to Bethesda and get this thing medically treated and taken care of!"

His strong, condescending tone was one that I had never done well receiving, not since I was a teenager. The entire conversation started off on the wrong foot and never found the right one. Commander Briggends immediately got to the bottom line, which normally I would have been grateful to hear. Today, I wasn't as appreciative, as his delivery was as blunt as a sledgehammer to the back of the skull.

"Captain, you are going to die trying to beat cancer with your holistic alternative approach. It is a foolish plan, and even if you somehow did survive, you will never fly for the Marine Corps again. Your flying days are over."

In the past few weeks, Megan and I had focused mainly on staging and determining how to get healed. I had not yet seriously considered that I may have flown my last military flight, or any flight, for that matter. I planned to go fight cancer, beat it, and climb back into the cockpit. After determining to fight this cancer battle 100% naturally and biologically, I envisioned flying and fighting concurrently. Commander Briggends, the medical authority who controlled whether I could fly or not, had just taken the keys to the jet away from me—indefinitely!

That crushing blow delivered more than enough collateral damage to send me away forlorn, but Commander Briggends was just getting warmed up.

"There is a waiver guide that determines flight status eligibility, Captain. According to the regulations, even if you survived using your dietary approach—which YOU WON'T—you would not be permitted to fly because you refused to do the prescribed treatments to reach remission to be eligible for a waiver!"

Commander Briggends' rant proved true, but it was all news to me. I never had any need for special waivers in my early career; so I had never considered the regulations. I simply went in every year, gave blood, had my eyes and hearing examined, and on occasion turned my head and coughed.

Minutes later, I would be walking back to my squadron with my annual medical clearance secured and a piece of paper saying I was "good to go." That "golden permission slip" is placed in my NATOPS jacket. That is the folder every pilot has which remains locked away in the squadron's filing cabinet containing every important document pertinent to our flying career. Every year, we swap out our medical "UP CHITS" during our birth month.

To his credit, the doctor was telling me the truth to the letter regarding the regulations. To my frustration, he was talking down to me like I was an oblivious child. Commander Briggends was bewildered by my ignorance of the waiver system. He opened the waiver guide to Lymphomas and showed me in black and white where it said I had to have followed the doctor's prescribed modality and have been cancer free for two years before I could fly again. It was then that I decided I wasn't going back to work that afternoon. I did not want to tell the Skipper I had failed in my mission.

When Commander Briggends closed the regulations, I thought our meeting was over, but he wasn't through as he took the gloves off without pulling any punches in his coming rant.

"Captain, you are a coward for not wanting to do chemotherapy! You're a selfish fool to try this stunt in order to avoid the side effects that will keep you grounded. Furthermore, you're an undependable Marine and an unloving husband and father to be so short-sighted as to prioritize your love of flying over your desire to live!"

I stood up, stepped back, and stared him down—not something a junior officer does to a senior ranking officer. But Commander Briggends was not in my chain of command, and at that moment I didn't recognize him as a Navy Commander but a schoolyard bully. I realized what he was doing, and I was not going to be bullied on my own base! I hadn't allowed myself to be pressured into unwanted treatments in the hallways of Bethesda, and no disrespectful medical braggadocio was going to bully me into taking a zero-survival-rate path today either.

With significant frustration and anger quickly percolating to a boiling point, I had to get to my point fast before I broke down. I leaned in and stated, "My priority is beating this disease first, Commander *Br-r-r-i-i-iggens*. Flying has been a secondary concern from the beginning; so please give me more credit than that. Don't confuse my desire to fly while doing alternative medicine as me prioritizing flying over getting well. Rather, know that I want to fly because I am using a better approach that might actually work, as Bethesda's own medical records demonstrate theirs hasn't ever worked."

The building emotions launched my argument up to the next level. I crossed over the threshold into direct antagonism as I continued my rebuttal.

"If anyone is misguided, it is YOU thinking you can use my love for flying as a way to manipulate me into doing your 'prescribed protocol' just so you'll sign that waiver for me to get back into a jet one day!"

I barked that last line at him and choked down the frustration and anger that had my chest on the brink of exploding. I was furious at his accusation and was already standing at this point. Quietly, without response, he just leaned back in his desk chair staring me down.

I opened the door and stepped back into the hallway. I swapped hands on the door handle, and rather than the customary departing words of "Good afternoon, Sir," I snapped "Commander Briggends, you're fired!"

I slammed the door behind me, startling the rest of the branch medical staff as the hallway echoed with the sound. It was not my proudest moment, but my message was delivered loud and clear.

Turning and walking to the end of the hall, I was greeted by my old flight surgeon from VMFA-115, my friend Lieutenant Reynolds.

"*T-BONE*, come in my office," he invited reassuringly. "Was that you that just shook every wall in this building?" he asked softly.

He afforded me the needed opportunity to vent. I moved erratically around his office as the emotional eruption spewed like an overwhelming lava flow.

"Can you believe the nerve of that guy? Who the heck does he think he is? That is the most self-righteous jerk I've ever met—civilian or military! How dare he accuse me of being irresponsible or call me an unloving husband, an uncaring father, and a foolish idiot who selfishly wants to fly more than he wants to live!"

No doubt, other choice adjectives were tossed about liberally, as I vented for a significant period of time. My blood was boiling at the Commander's attempt to manipulate me with my passion for flying. My anger for his lack of respect and bullying was still coursing through my veins.

LT Reynolds invited me to have a seat once my blood pressure started to come down. He began to explain the realities of any future flying. But he did so with a level of respect and a reasonable demeanor that was more agreeable to my overly stimulated ego at the moment.

"*T-BONE*, I agree that the Commander has no bedside manner. Truthfully, we all try to avoid him whenever possible. But, as much as I hate to tell you this, he is right."

I stopped fuming and started to allow myself to listen and take in what my friend was now sharing. He calmly explained, "The waiver guide is the regulation that we must follow to submit the paperwork for waivers of any kind. We don't make the rules; we just work inside them. And this rule is pretty clear. You must show yourself to be cancer free for two years before we can submit a waiver. When we do, we have to show that you followed the military doctor's recommendations."

The Lieutenant continued, assuring me that he knew I had my priorities right, that he recognized I was more concerned with beating this than trying to get back into the cockpit at the expense of my longevity. I was rapidly coming down from my heightened state of agitation as he spoke. Total exasperation was giving way to a deep sense of loss. The anger drained from my body; a deep aching filled the void it left behind.

"Don't worry about the waiver, *T-BONE*. Right now, focus on the more important task of beating the disease. There is a process in place to argue for a waiver, and so long as you are cancer free, we can exercise the waiver-granting process at that time."

Hearing this sound advice, LT Reynolds and I shifted gears and focused on a way forward from within the military medical system. I was going to fight the disease naturally, but I still had to be followed by a military primary care manager for as long as I was on active duty.

"Here is the contact information for Doctor Cary Ostergaard. He's the *Officer In Charge (OIC) of one of the family practice teams at the Pensacola Naval Hospital down in Pensacola, Florida. If at all possible, get to Pensacola. Dr. Ostergaard is the best doctor you could have. He is the complete package. When we served together, LCDR Ostergaard was not only the top of his class, but he also had a personality." The LT joked on, "You know that the really smart docs don't usually have a dynamic personality or good looks. But I'm darn jealous that Doctor O has it all! I guess I have to settle for just the good looks." We laughed, and he sincerely wished me the best with my endeavor.

We shook hands, and heading for the door, I looked back and asked, "Door open or closed, Doc?"

Smiling he said, "You better leave it open, *T-BONE*. I'll take care of it."

I trekked out to my 52 Chevy and climbed in hastily but did not fire it up. I sat for a moment processing both discussions. Two doctors giving me the same information regarding my chances of ever flying again. One angered me to a point I had not reached since the ambush on Megan weeks earlier. The other one provided hope and a course of action. This would not be the first time I would experience a dichotomy of bedside manners as I walked this out in the coming year.

I turned toward base housing rather than the squadron. The aching deep within was growing, and I could not walk back into the squadron that afternoon and face anyone. I wanted to avoid any conversation or contact with my friends or superiors. I needed time to work through this revelation.

As I pulled into the driveway of my house, I could hear a flight of four F/A-18s approaching. Base housing was right under the flight path for aircraft returning from the training areas. It was commonplace for neighborhood children and the pilots to look up and try to see the tail flash, the art on the aircraft rudder identifying to which squadron the aircraft belonged. Families could look up and see the jets overfly and then guess how long it would be until Mom or Dad came home for dinner.

Some things never get old. To this day, I still look up when I hear any aircraft fly over, whether it is a jet or not. I suspect I always will. So it was not unusual for me to be looking up at the sky as a flight of *HORNETs* flew by. What was unusual today was that I found myself stuck in that position even after they passed by.

Bradly, Brianna, and Alex on bicycles outside the Trombly's kitchen window of their Beaufort base housing home

I sat there holding my head up, looking toward the sky, trying to keep the tears that had started to fill my eyes from rolling down my cheeks. I was holding my eyes as wide open as I could, hoping that the tears would roll back into their ducts before anyone saw me. Too late. Megan had been looking out the tiny kitchen window as I pulled up to the house, and when my entry was delayed, she came and joined me on the front lawn.

Megan, recognizing my posture was off, knew something was wrong. She leaned into me with her arms around me and just waited for me to compose myself. She didn't have to ask. She knew.

Finally, with some composure, I confessed, "Megan, I may never get to fly my jet again."

The reality of the challenge was beginning to set in, and hearing those words come out of my own mouth made the possibility seem that much more daunting. It was going to be a fight on two fronts after all. Beat the cancer . . . then beat the system.

181

19| *Unexpected Orders*

OUR time living and serving on MCAS Beaufort was going to end abruptly now that I was officially grounded. The *Skipper *(a common yet respectful reference to the Commanding Officer or CO of a flying squadron)* would not be able to hire another Captain to replace me in the cockpit as long as I was in the squadron taking up space on his roster. The Moonlighters needed pilots, which is why I had been transferred there three months earlier. My inability to fly was a liability that needed a quick resolution. My Skipper and I worked together to formulate a plan as we both recognized that leaving was the best option for the command and for me.

With no option to fly anywhere else due to being grounded, I had to come up with a quick, career-saving plan. Whatever I came up with had to allow me to fight my cancer my way, naturally, yet also allow me to have a daily sense of pride, significance, and accomplishment in my Marine Corps duties. Being able to take pride in my work each day was a form of medicine in and of itself. I was not a victim of this disease, and I never felt like a victim.

Planning to do natural treatments and detoxing, I would now be able to go to work almost every day. Once a month, I had to go in for monthly blood work and check-ups for an hour or two. Every six months, I would need a half-day to get a CT or PET scan. No special treatment, handling, or coddling was required. I was going to pull my weight and then some in whatever job I was assigned.

To this day, I am convinced that working while fighting cancer gave me a mental edge over the disease. This call to duty to country each day and my inner sense of purpose to win and live for Christ as a husband and father gave me an advantage in the fight. This edge, this purpose, allowed me to win most of the daily skirmishes and firefights with the enemy as he regularly and repetitively tossed grenades of doubt and frustration into my mental and emotional tent. These attacks often came from within my own mind but were, most days, quickly defeated through prayer and this sense of purpose and belief that God had already promised me the victory that first day in Captain Morgan's office.

The initial plan proposed by my Skipper was for me to transfer out of the unit, move across the base, and become the Executive Officer of the Base Headquarters and Headquarters Squadron. This leadership position was vital to the support of the personnel on the base and a position usually held by a Major. I was a rank junior as a Captain but was offered the opportunity anyway by the Group Commander, a full Colonel. This job offer was an indication that I had the trust and confidence not only of my boss but of his boss as well.

I demonstrated gratitude for the vote of confidence yet tactfully turned down the offer. I then respectfully but resolutely told my CO, "Skipper, I need to leave Beaufort. Staying and hearing these jets fly all day and all night while grounded would kill me before this cancer could."

I needed a job that I could do each day, knowing I was having a direct impact on Marine aviation. I did not just want to fill a random billet outside of my personal strengths and skill sets on some corner of my current base collecting a paycheck while the Corps waited for me to die and then replace me. No, I wanted to teach in the classroom. I desired to keep talking with my hands, a skill we pilots like to show off at work and at parties. If I could not fly, I wanted to train the next generation of pilots coming up behind me until I could again.

My Skipper supported my desire, and I immediately went to work. I called Headquarters Marine Corps back in Quantico and spoke to the Marine in charge of providing orders for Marines of my rank and specialty. This position was known as the "Fixed

Wing Captain's Monitor."

Captain Gabriel, the Marine I spoke with, the one who had control of my destiny when it came to what orders I would receive, was a fellow Captain. He was a C-130 pilot, and we hit it off immediately. He was a blessing, and as a headquarters' monitor, he supported me well beyond the call of duty. He explained up front that what I was asking was non-standard.

When a pilot is grounded for a significant issue, as I had been, that pilot does not rate a new set of orders. Those orders cost money because we move our entire families with us, and frankly, the uncertainty of our fate presents too much risk for headquarters to invest in transfer orders. The situation dictates that the pilot stays put and gets well before getting new orders. The normal procedure is simply to transfer out of the squadron and stay on base, as my Skipper had initially offered with the Beaufort Executive Officer billet, or medevac to the hospital, as that becomes the Marine's new appointed place of duty while undergoing treatments.

Captain Gabriel, my monitor and new best friend, took the time to plead my case with his boss, the Colonel in charge of the monitor branch. Having recently lost his grandfather to cancer, Captain Gabriel was tremendously sympathetic to my request. We spoke about our two families' cancer battles. There was no coaxing or pleading required, as he completely supported my request to be transferred down to NAS Pensacola as a classroom instructor for my own sanity and sense of purpose. However, he needed the Colonel to sign off on the order's request.

Departing and being in Pensacola would uplift my heavy heart, which was burdened with the daily reminder of what had been taken from me by my grounding chit. Captain Gabriel strategized a way to make wise planning decisions for the good of the Marine Corps while granting this Marine's request to stay relevant.

After pitching his non-standard plan to issue me flight orders despite being grounded, he was pleasantly surprised by Colonel

Cortez's response.

"Colonel Cortez, we have a fighter here who wants to maintain his credibility, and that says something about a man's character," began Captain Gabriel. "He is a leader, and we must afford him the ability to lead. I believe he would be a great asset as a Flight Instructor."

The Colonel smiled at the Captain with full knowledge that I could not be a flight instructor until being reinstated to flight status, and that was exactly his strategy.

"Captain, issue orders for Captain Trombly to be transferred to MATSG-21 at NAS Pensacola as a flight instructor for two years," dictated the seasoned Colonel. "Include that the two-year orders are to follow the completion of his training syllabus at the Fixed-Wing Instructor Training Unit. Since Captain Trombly cannot fly while he is medically grounded, that will give him essentially open-ended orders, within reason, to NAS Pensacola. He needs to focus on fighting that damn cancer, not beating the clock."

"Colonel Cortez, if Captain Trombly does beat this godforsaken illness, then these orders would need to be *DIFOP, correct?" (Duty Involving Flying–Operational)

"Affirmative," acknowledged Colonel Cortez, nodding in approval.

So the Captain, with Colonel Cortez's blessing, did one more very special thing that set me up for incredible success in my post-cancer career. Rather than issuing me a set of *DIFDEN orders (non-flying orders), which is what I rated as a pilot who was not medically qualified to fly, he issued me DIFOP orders. These DIFOP orders meant that I had one less administrative obstacle preventing me from flying once I beat my cancer. It was a personal and professional way of conveying a message to me that these gentlemen believed I would be successful in my cancer fight, and they valued my leadership ability in the Marine Corp.

Captain Gabriel was a great American who took care of a brother. He was also humble and gave all the credit to his Colonel as he shared with me over the phone how his conversation with Colonel Cortez fleshed out.

Colonel Cortez continued looking out the window, still in somber contemplation. "Captain Gabriel, only one of two things can happen. If Captain Trombly does beat the odds against him, he will be in a position to fight for his flight status clearance right there in Pensacola, as the doctors located there represent the needed signatories to grant that man his waiver to fly again."

"And if he doesn't beat the cancer, Colonel?" quietly asked Captain Gabriel.

"Then the Marine Corp granted a dying Marine his last wish. Good work, Captain. Dismissed."

Orders back to Naval Air Station Pensacola were mine, where I had been only six years earlier as a new student pilot. *MATSG-21 (Marine Aviation Training Support Group Twenty-One) was to be my future command. This one set of orders would be instrumental in sending my career on a trajectory I could not have imagined or even considered important at the time. I was too fixated on just beating my diagnosis, not thinking of the logistics of winning my cockpit seat back in those early weeks of the fight. What a gracious gift to one who only rated a dreaded transfer across base!

This set of orders was just one example of the extraordinary leadership that I have witnessed during my twenty-five-year career. This wise stalwart wielded his position and influence to take care of both his command and his Marines, thinking outside the black and white print in the regulations to make appropriate exceptions in exceptional circumstances.

In this case, I was the recipient of the visionary leadership of the Colonel and my fellow Captain in the fixed-wing monitor's office. Their foresight and prudence provided a crucial link in the chain of events essential to our successful cancer war. God went before me, granting me favor and support from military leaders, both those with whom I had served and others whom I did not know and who did not know me.

20 | *My Grandad- My Hero*

THIS work change would not be the first time I would have military leadership go beyond the call of duty to support me through my personal and professional challenge. This gift of outstanding leadership followed me from my days at VMFA(AW)-332 at MCAS Beaufort, South Carolina right through my three-year fight to get back into the cockpit. Too many doors opened for me not to realize the multiple, miraculous details God provided during this journey. Only God can get the glory, but both my Creator and my superiors get my gratitude for the unlimited and undeserved favor they afforded me. I remain forever grateful.

My Navy Chaplain in Beaufort, Chaplain Johnson, proved to be another senior officer God used to influence me shortly after my diagnosis. When I returned from my first deployment in Japan, Chaplain Johnson visited and dropped off a stack of bookmarks at the squadron duty officer's desk in our ready room.

I was impressed by the Chaplain's gesture, reaching out to us in our own pilot ready room, a pilots' sacred place, our inner sanctum. This harbor, meant only for pilots is filled with the same briefing chairs found onboard aircraft carriers' ready rooms. This room is where pilot training sessions and weekly meetings with the Commanding Officer are held.

Learning well from his example, I both appreciated and internalized Chaplain Johnson's esteem for us as Marines and as pilots and his respect for our ready room. If ever placed in his shoes, I wanted to be ready to influence others in their ready rooms. Little did I know at the time that I would indeed wear those chaplain shoes sooner than later.

A few years after my cancer fight, I shared my miraculous testimony with the campers at a Hockey Ministries International (HMI) hockey camp. The HMI founder's son, Don Lismer, Jr., approached me as the chapel service ended. Mr. Lismer invited me to serve as the Chaplain for my hometown's professional hockey team, the Pensacola Ice Pilots. I served in that capacity for one season, and then four years later I returned as their Chaplain once again. The original team had gone bankrupt and closed down, no longer a part of the East Coast Hockey League (ECHL). When one of the previously successful owners returned to reconstitute the team, he did so as a part of the new Southern Professional Hockey League (SPHL) and took on a new name, the Pensacola Ice Flyers. At the beginning of each Pensacola Ice Flyers professional hockey season, I would introduce myself to the new players as their Hockey Ministries International Team Chaplain. It was important that they heard me say the following as we built our relationship:

"Gentlemen, it's a privilege for me, as your Chaplain, to be invited into your locker room each week. I recognize this is your sacred territory, and I sincerely honor that. As a fighter pilot, it indeed reminds me of our squadron's ready room. That is our sacred inner sanctum, as well.

"If our Skipper needs to chew us out, just as your head coach might do between periods of a hockey game, then it happens right there. When we promote one of our own to the next rank, it happens there. If the Captains at our pay grade have a point of contention that needs to be worked out without the Majors or the Lieutenant Colonels present, yep... it happens there. It is a place only for those who have earned the right to be there. We as pilots absolutely take it as seriously as you take your locker room as professional athletes."

This declaration sets the tone for our year's relationship of mutual respect for each other. As the Ice Flyers make trades and players come and go, I drop reminders of our bilateral esteem and share my thanks for the privilege to be in their inner sanctum. One such privileged entry into the Ice Flyers' sacred space will always be one of my favorite memories. The season had just ended with the Ice Flyers winning the championship. The players invited me back to celebrate and called me out to raise their trophy—the President's Cup right there in the locker room. What a thrill! What a special honor!

That day back in Beaufort when Chaplain Johnson visited our ready room, I doubt he had any idea of the special mission God had sent him on. The gift he left for each of us would soon be more impactful than he could have imagined. His faithfulness in following God's prompting to deliver those gifts was going to play a huge part in my battle's success.

Chaplain Johnson had joined us on our Trans-PAC flights from South Carolina over the Pacific Ocean to Iwakuni, Japan. I had an opportunity to get to know him pretty well during our time overseas. My first personal experience with him occurred within the first few days into our travels. We had flown from the east coast to Hawaii behind two U.S. Air Force KC-10 tankers in two days. Having crossed that many time zones in forty-eight hours, we were required to spend an extra day on the ground. This non-flying day would allow our circadian rhythm to catch up with us somewhat before we continued flying the next two days over to Japan, with a one-night stop on Wake Island.

This was my first time in Hawaii, and on my day off, I made a special request of the Skipper.

"Skipper, I respectfully request permission to take one of the duty vehicles for a couple of hours. I'd like to drive up to the Punchbowl Cemetery, the National Memorial Cemetery of the Pacific, to pay my respects to my personal hero, one of the greatest influencers of my life."

"And who might that be, Captain?" inquired the Skipper.

"I request the honor of visiting my grandfather's grave for the first time, Colonel, U.S. Army Air Corpsman Major Carleton Charles Dutton, my mother's father. He was a fellow fighter pilot and flew the P-38 Lightning. Unfortunately, I never met him as he died in China on a special mission just before the end of World War II. His service and sacrifice left an indelible impression on me. Today is my opportunity to say thank you."

"Permission granted, Captain."

When *CHAPS (an endearing nickname we Marines afford to all the Chaplains we come to know and respect)* heard what I was doing, he asked if he could tag along. I agreed, and we spent the afternoon together. I especially appreciated how he stayed back and allowed me some personal time to process my own experience. Right before we departed, I called the Chaplain up to join me at my grandfather's headstone.

Though tainted with a deep sense of loss over not having ever met my grandfather, a swelling pride swept over me as I shared the few stories I knew. I smiled as I spoke of his time in the P-38 flying anti-submarine missions in the Atlantic during the opening months of World War II. I proudly shared how he had earned an Air Medal for those patrol missions, had achieved the rank of Major, and had been selected for a special project in the Pacific. Pausing, I pointed out the date on his headstone and explained how in early 1945 he died in China at the age of 28, right before the end of the war.

Having *CHAPS* along for the ride up and back gave the two of us some time to connect. This was time well spent as I would, as a junior officer, come to rely on the Chaplain while we were deployed. On more than one occasion, I was able to refer one of the Marines in my shop to *CHAPS* when their families back home were going through a crisis. Little did I know that I, too, would need his moral support in the months to come.

The gift that *CHAPS* delivered to our squadron ready room that day was a handsome bookmark. It was thin and long with Psalm 91 printed on the front. Being a man of faith, I appreciated the gift, and I happily requisitioned one from the stack *CHAPS* had left behind on the Duty Officer's post.

During those first two years in the squadron, my non-military reading was limited, with four children at home to help rear. My reading focused purely on tactical manuals and technical pubs related to the F/A-18 and how best to employ it as a weapons system. These books were locked in my squadron safe, not sitting on our living room coffee table with a bookmark holding my last page while I stepped away to throw a football in the backyard.

My pleasure reading from the "Marine Corps Commandant's Professional Reading List" had dropped significantly while working on my early pilot qualifications and passing those critical check rides up through my section leader check flight. As a result, I place the gifted bookmark in the only other book I was reading at that time, my personal Bible.

In the days and weeks after my diagnosis, Megan and I had received an amazing outpouring of love, good wishes, Scripture passages, prayers, and information. One friend had encouraged me to read Psalm 91. I did not recognize the reference at first. Psalm 23 had been a go-to passage since my childhood when referencing God's love, provision, and control. But eventually, I took a moment to read Psalm 91 and was immediately enthralled by God's powerful promises of protection!

Psalm 91 has become my life's Scripture passage. This passage has had more impact on my life than any other. Before executing my orders leaving MCAS Beaufort, I would once again find *CHAPS'* gift in my Bible. There was no way I could understand the depth of strength this short Psalm, recommended by a friend and printed on *CHAPS'* bookmark, would provide in the coming months. I read and reread that passage every day that difficult year, praying the verses, celebrating them, and most importantly, believing them.

21| *"The Plague That Destroys at Midday"*

My close friend, Jack Siler, is the author of a book entitled *GOD of WONDERS*. Its pages contain a single chapter dedicated to every one of the 66 books of the Holy Bible. Each chapter comes from the heart and the pen of a different author whom Jack personally invited to co-author with him. There are chapters written by our pastor, our minister of music, other pastors, fellow choir members, convicted felons, and even a former secret service agent cleverly disguised and embedded in our choir as a mild-mannered church member. Jack asked me to write on Psalms.

Before I share my personalized poem and prayer of gratitude to the Lord, I ask that you read Psalm 91 from the New International Version of the Bible printed below. These are the words I read every single day during the year I fought my cancer. The promises in this passage still give me hope and peace daily, providing instruction and direction.

The message of this Psalm encourages me to acknowledge God on the good days and the "other" days, as well, a practice I endeavor to continue every day. The powerful influence of this one very personal Scripture passage is life-changing for me. It remains the cornerstone of any presentation or testimony of what God had done and continues to do for our family as a result of that most difficult journey. If you have never read Psalm 91 before, then it is my honor to share this dynamic Scripture with you now.

> "Whoever dwells in the shelter of the Most High
> will rest in the shadow of the Almighty.
> I will say of the Lord, 'He is my refuge and my fortress,

my God, in whom I trust.'
Surely he will save you
from the fowler's snare
and from the deadly pestilence.
He will cover you with his feathers,
and under his wings you will find refuge;
his faithfulness will be your shield and rampart.
You will not fear the terror of night,
nor the arrow that flies by day,
nor the pestilence that stalks in the darkness,
nor the plague that destroys at midday.
A thousand may fall at your side,
ten thousand at your right hand,
but it will not come near you.
You will only observe with your eyes
and see the punishment of the wicked.
If you say, 'The Lord is my refuge,'
and you make the Most High your dwelling,
no harm will overtake you,
no disaster will come near your tent.
For he will command his angels concerning you
to guard you in all your ways;
they will lift you up in their hands,
so that you will not strike your foot against a stone.
You will tread on the lion and the cobra;
you will trample the great lion and the serpent.
'Because he loves me,' says the Lord, 'I will rescue him;
I will protect him, for he acknowledges my name.
He will call on me, and I will answer him;
I will be with him in trouble, I will deliver him and honor him.
With long life, I will satisfy him and show him my salvation.'"

—PSALM 91: 1-16 (NIV)

As I read this passage each day seeking only strength for the day
at hand, I picture the plague spoken of in verse six to be cancer

itself. Is cancer not a modern-day plague in our world? Do we not all know at least one person in our own family with it: a grand-parent, mom or dad, a brother or sister, cousin, or even what is so heartbreaking and far too prevalent today, a child?

I consider the prayer list that comes around every Wednesday at choir practice. On it are prayer requests for family members going in for surgery, loved ones deployed overseas, etc. And then there's the list of friends and family with cancer. Is it not always the larg-est list on the prayer page in any church? Cancer is a plague. It is an epidemic! Yet as verse six cries out to us to know and consider, "whoever dwells in the shelter of the Most High (God) will not fear the plague that destroys at midday." My God is bigger than this plague!

My heart cried out in praise, "You gave that year a healing and message that now must be sent!"

Here is what I submitted to Jack to publish in *God of Wonders:*

> "At thirty-one as a Marine Captain and F/A-18 fighter pilot, I thought at the time that I was an invincible force until the day I was told my flying was over and I had two years to live due to a rare primary lymphoma of the bone in my jaw. Shortly after diagnosis, I was given Psalm 91 and it became a passage I would read every day during the battle. It has since become my life's passage and my salutation to letters and emails."

Below I have written a poem to share Psalm 91 with you. It is Psalm 91 in the form of a prayer to my Lord as I reflect on how God's promises within this passage applied to our cancer war and our future.

Psalm 91 verse one sets the framework for the promises in verses fourteen through sixteen.

"He who dwells in the shelter of the Most High..."
Let me ask you, where do you "dwell"
as you read this Psalm and poem?
If you are dwelling in God, saved and free from sin, and walking with
your Lord you and I can hold tight to the following promises:
"Because he loves me," says the Lord, "I will rescue him;
I will protect him, for he acknowledges my name.
He will call on me, and I will answer him;
I will be with him in trouble, I will deliver him and honor him.
With long life, I will satisfy him and show him my salvation."
—PSALM 91:14-16 (NIV)

If you are not dwelling with God, I would encourage you to ask yourself why. What could be so appealing and so drawing to keep us from dwelling and experiencing the peace and promise of a relationship with the Most High. There is none more powerful, yet so tender as the God we serve. He seeks to dwell with even us. He knows and responds to our love. He gives us, in the last verse, the great promise of long life and salvation for those who acknowledge Him.

When we are in Christ, VICTORY comes in many forms. As you read this you may be weeks away from victory over cancer yourself... or... you may be days away from "LONG LIFE AND SALVATION" in the very presence of God as He fulfills His promise with a safe and glorious passage HOME to Heaven to spend eternity with Him and with Jesus Christ your personal Savior. I chose to thank God for my healing and acknowledge that for me to Live is Christ, but to die one day is gain!

PSALM 91
A Poem of Praise from One "Grounded and Cured"

I was high and lifted up;
A man of thirty-one with an overflowing cup.
My wings could take me high, and I praised you when I would soar.
Yet, how could I know that your wings would do ever so much more?
For three years I lay my wings of gold down;
dwelt under your wings as I stayed on the ground.
Never before did I reach so high, as I did those years I could not fly.
You told me that very first day, I would beat my disease and fly away.
We faced the plague that destroys at midday
while your wings deflected the arrows that flew by day.
My bride did not fear the terror of night,
For YOU gave us peace and we all slept tight.
The feathers of your wings were our shelter and
No disaster fell upon our tent.
You gave that year a healing,
And message that now must be sent!
Your faithfulness IS our shield;
My faithfulness IS how we yield.
You commanded your angels to guard our ways;
You gave three gifts:
PEACE, discernment, and discipline those difficult days.
We cannot know how the battle will turn,
But if we Acknowledge YOU, there is so much we can learn.
More challenges to face,
And inevitable scorn;
But may Your unexplainable PEACE remain,
as we seek all the more your will to discern.
Grant us audience with many
who need to see your face;
Help us faithfully acknowledge your unending Grace.

Yes, once again God had divinely used extraordinary military leadership to pave the way for me through my squadron chaplain. I am sure he had no idea when he gave us fighter pilots a book-mark imprinted with the words of Psalm 91 just how instrumental it would be to our family. How could he know that one of those pilots would be walking through the valley and leaning on the truths of those promises over the coming year every day? Thanks, *CHAPS!*

Part Four
Building
the Armory

"One mark of a great soldier is that
he fights on his own terms or fights not at all."
"Security against defeat implies defensive tactics;
ability to defeat the enemy means taking the offensive.
...Hence the skillful fighter puts himself into a position
which makes defeat impossible, and does not miss the
moment for defeating the enemy."

—Sun Tzu,
Chinese Tactician, and Author of The Art of War

22| *Reporting as Ordered*

AS we all drove around the corner, I asked Megan and the children to close their eyes. Soon we would be pulling into the driveway of our very first non-base housing home since I had started flight school years earlier. We had enjoyed the benefits of living in each base housing community, including Lubbock and Kingsville, Texas; Meridian, Mississippi; Milton, Florida; Irvine, California; and finally Beaufort, South Carolina. We had benefited financially with affordable rent and no utility bills. We developed great friendships with like-minded military families, as well.

The strength of such a community was exactly that, community. We all had each other's backs, especially when a family member was deployed. Because our family had grown to include four children in Beaufort, base housing was getting tougher to acquire. With the waiting list for a four-bedroom house unreasonable onboard NAS Pensacola, Megan trusted me to find our first mortgaged home on my own.

Castle Realty of Pensacola was working at the volunteer information desk the day that I was seeking assistance at the base housing office. I met Ken, a retired Navy Chief, and his wife, Thelma, with her amazing British accent, the kind made for movies. This wonderful couple helped me find the perfect home just a few blocks from Naval Hospital Pensacola. It had four bedrooms, a great back yard, and the perfect location only a few minutes from the base. The short commute allowed me to maximize my time on the job and with my family.

As I would soon learn, sleep is vitally instrumental in the success of any battle plan to regain one's health. There would be long days busily doing what needed to be done to get healthy, yet sleep remained absolutely essential. My seven-minute drive to the front gate afforded me that rest. I anticipated frequent follow-up appointments at the hospital; so being in the neighborhood just behind the hospital was a plus. Of course, raising four young children tends to lend itself to an occasional ER visit as well.

Megan was impressed when she opened her eyes. Well, at least she never said anything negative about my choice. So either I married a saint, or I had done well selecting our first home without her input.

The children entered the house and immediately found their bedrooms, where I had staged some surprises—a giant stuffed animal for each on their floor. My oldest daughter, Brianna, loved horses, and she received her first stuffed one that day. It was so large it made it difficult for any other stuffed animals to sit on her bed. Grace Anne, still less than one-year-old, received a giant tiger which, of course, she hated because it was four times bigger than her. Alex and Brad shared the last room down the hall and received a turtle and an alligator respectively, the same size as each boy in height.

We spent the weekend unpacking the moving truck. Laughter spilled out as we explored our new home, backyard, and the wooded green belt that abutted our back property line. For our little guys, this stand of trees was a vast forest where we patrolled and built forts. Megan took great pleasure in setting up the home-school room, replacing a dining room in the front of the house.

I took great pride in finding a home that sat directly under the approach corridor for runway ONE NINE at Naval Air Station Pensacola. On Sunday when the Blue Angels came home from their weekend air shows, if the wind dictated using Runway 19, we could run outside and see their smoke as they flew overhead. While I recognized that being around fast jets every day could have been agonizing, seeing the Blue Angels once or twice a week was a healthy reminder of where I wanted to be when my health returned.

The children were happy. Grace Anne was quickly capturing tree frogs in the backyard. The boys were building forts, and Brianna was Megan's number one helper, setting up the house the way Mom wanted it. But something was missing from our huge backyard, and I knew exactly what it needed. Having recently read about the power of an animal's love in giving hope to folks with terminal diseases, I made my case. Seriously, who was going to argue with the guy who had cancer and wanted a puppy? I really didn't need to play that card as Megan and the children were all about it.

We went to the Pensacola pound and rescued a sweet little puppy with big paws. "Daddy, look at this one." Brianna captured my attention with her exuberance. "He is so pretty and has awesome colors!" she continued.

"Excuse me, Ma'am," I interrupted, vying for the attention of the volunteer at the rescue shelter. "May we hold this little guy here with the big paws?"

"Oh, that is a very sweet puppy. The ladies named him Thor when he came in with his sister last week. Those huge paws have us all thinking he will be a very large dog."

"What kind of dog is he?" Megan asked.

"We have no way of knowing. He and his sister were found in a box and dropped off; so we have no idea what kind of dogs the parents were. With those large paws, we are all guessing that he is a Husky or an Alaskan Malamute."

"Glad we have a big yard for this little guy to grow into," I said, picking the puppy up and enjoying his head dropping into my chest. He captured my heart and the children's excitement.

We tossed around names on the short ride home. We played with him for hours in the living room as he sought the attention of each child. We finally settled on the name "Thumper," as he was supposed to be a large dog. He was friendly and funny, reminding me of one of my Beaufort squadron mates who had the call sign

THUMPER. And so it was. Little Thumper brought a joyful distraction to our family, something we desperately needed during this challenging year.

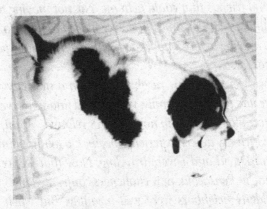

David's cancer battle puppy, THUMPER!

Thumper turned out to be a mutt, not a Husky, and he was by far the most loved and loving puppy ever. That little guy truly was *my dog*. Thumper and I were inseparable whenever I was home. There really is something to the study that says there is a connection between dogs and our inner needs.

A MOMENT WITH MEGAN

While I deeply appreciated David working so hard to provide a house close to the hospital for us, honestly, I was stressed. I was just supposed to return to normal living, but nothing about our new

normal was normal. I was dealing with some of the top stressors of life: a husband with a terminal illness diagnosis, parenting young children, and now moving raised the bar! No, not moving close to family and friends that could help me. No, not moving to an area I was familiar with or that I had ever longed to live. No. We were actually moving to a neighborhood with several elderly people and no support systems.

Here we were in a new neighborhood, in a new city, in a new state. We had no church family, very limited finances, a very uncertain cancer plan, and again no friends or relatives. At this moment is where I felt my desert experience begin. Up to this point, life was busy, and David and I were traveling. Now that we were in our new home in Pensacola, new challenges confronted me.

Our elderly neighbors were well-meaning. But when the man next door began pulling weeds from our yard because he said we didn't keep our yard tidy enough for the neighborhood, I just chose not to interact much. I suddenly felt so alone.

It was time to check in to my new Command and meet the boss. My orders were to Naval Aviation Schools Command (NASC) in Building 633 onboard NAS Pensacola. This is the schoolhouse where all future Naval Aviators, including Navy, Marine, and Coast Guard, start the process of becoming a pilot or navigator after they are commissioned through their respective Officer Candidate Schools.

Every aspiring pilot must walk these hallways and graduate from the initial six-week classroom training known as *API (Aviation Preflight Indoctrination) before obtaining orders to one of the Training Wings to start flying. Seven years earlier when I'd first arrived as a student, the military had brought multiple branches of the Armed Forces together to work under one Command, making this program a Joint training program. This effort included bringing in Air Force students and instructors.

Pilot training had gone Joint back in the early 1990s in an effort to convince Congress to spend money on a joint venture to get both the Air Force and Naval Aviation a new primary training aircraft. The Air Force T-37 operated on 1950s technology, and the Navy's T-34 was pushing the limits of its useful lifespan as well. The new aircraft would be designated the T-6A Texan II after the WWII-era trainer by the same name.

As a result, the schoolhouse where I was working was a melting pot of every service except the Army. The Army was helicopter heavy, and their pilots could start flying immediately after high school as Warrant Officers. As such, they employed a different training style and location in Alabama.

I rolled in hot with my full-Service Alpha uniform and a fresh haircut, as would any squared-away Marine. First impressions are everything, and I needed to let these newbies know that, cancer or not, they were about to meet their top instructor. The Admin Department took my paperwork and sent me to find the Senior Marine officer down the hallway. I met a Marine that to this day I call a friend. Walking into Major *DOC* Knell's office space, I introduced myself.

"Good morning, Major. I'm Captain David Trombly, your new join from Beaufort."

"Good morning, Captain. Welcome back to NAS Pensacola," greeted Major Knell. "Beaufort? F/A-18 pilot?" he asked as he smiled deviously and shook my hand.

"Yes, sir."

The major asked me a few questions in an effort to determine the best shop for me to instruct. Schools Command taught everything from meteorology, aerodynamics, and engines to basic flight rules and regulations, all of which any designated Naval Aviator was qualified to instruct. *DOC* was looking for something to help him determine the best use of my Fleet experience; so I gave it to him.

"Captain, in your F/A-18 flying, have you had any experience in

205

a two-seat squadron?" he queried.

"Affirmative, Major, my last squadron was an F/A-18D squadron with WSOs," I immediately answered without the slightest hesitation, praying that he would not ask how long that experience had been. I had just come from VMFA(AW)-332, which was an F/A-18D squadron with a Weapon Systems Officer (WSO) in the back seat on every flight.

"Excellent. I am looking for a Marine jet pilot to go teach upstairs. I need a *CRM (Crew Resource Management) expert to fill a gap in the CRM Department of the schoolhouse."

Stealing a line from *Tombstone*, I looked *DOC* square in the eye and said, "I'm your Huckleberry, Major."

DOC seemed satisfied with my answer; so I did not volunteer that I had only flown three flights in a two-seat model of the *HORNET* in my short time in the squadron before I was medically grounded and had left my two-seat squadron in Beaufort for Pensacola.

Major Knell welcomed me aboard and sent me upstairs to a quiet and secluded wing of the building, far from the hustle and bustle of the first floor's many classrooms, to meet my new OIC (Officer In Charge) Navy Commander (CDR) Harry *HARRY* Heatley. The Commander was a Navy helicopter pilot, but his claim to fame was being the brother of Navy CDR Charles *HEATER* Heatley. *HEATER* was one of the Navy's F-14 pilots who had flown in numerous scenes for the filming of *Top Gun* back in 1986.

I gathered that my being a pointy-nosed jet guy warranted my knowing that family connection on my first day. I also gathered the Commander and his brother had a good relationship, as he and I got along just fine for the few weeks he had remaining in the job. Shortly after my arrival CDR Heatley turned over his responsibilities to a new OIC, Navy Lieutenant Commander (LCDR) Brett Ulander. Brett and I would work together for nearly two years before his retirement, during which time we became the best of friends.

The CRM Department of the schoolhouse was a relatively new creation. It was developed to train and certify new CRM Instructors to go back out to their fleet flying squadrons to share newly developed CRM principles with their fellow pilots and crew members. The CRM program was replacing the Navy's *ACT (Air Crew Training) program and aligning itself with the U.S. Air Force and civilian airlines.

Our school was placed in Pensacola inside the Naval Aviation Schools Command, allowing us as the Navy and Marine Corps' CRM experts to be in a position to bring these vital skills to the newest generation of Naval Aviators in their first few weeks of training. Our mission was to foster increased mission effectiveness in every cockpit with proper crew skills in communication, leadership, mission analysis, situational awareness, assertiveness, adaptability, flexibility, and decision-making. It was my privilege to develop and teach the introductory CRM class to nearly every new class of aviators weekly for the next three years.

Lieutenant Commander Ulander took over the department not long after I had arrived. He was an effective delegator and a great leader, earning our small team's respect quickly. The department was undergoing a major overhaul with a contracting firm that was to rework all our courseware. LCDR Ulander had a way of balancing the office dynamic that was masterful. He kept us off the Command's radar and had us, as military subject-matter experts, fix everything the defense contracting firm sent to us that was erroneous or broken.

We had a great team of experts, and we essentially rewrote the curriculum ourselves, sending our rough drafts back to the civilian firm. This method allowed us to get exactly what we needed in order to have quality classroom material. Brett found a way to make the system work not just to satisfy Big Navy, but for us as instructors to succeed in our mission as well. Successfully educating the instructors who taught the men and women actually using our military defense systems was critical to our mission's success. Brett understood this and gave us the green light to develop our classes the way we knew they needed to be taught.

Our work was a resounding success. We effectively rewrote the Navy's CRM program in-house. It was empowering to be a part of a team once again. This job fulfilled the innate human need to have a purpose and to be impactful during my non-flying years.

The location of this school and the opportunity to work at NAS Pensacola proved a godsend for me. Due to its shoehorned placement into this command structure, the CRM department was nearly autonomous and ran efficiently so long as the Commanding Officer of NASC had full trust and confidence in the CRM OIC (Officers In Charge). Thankfully, during my three years in that job, we earned and enjoyed that trust and confidence.

As a result, I had a job with more flexibility than I had ever before enjoyed in the military. So long as the job was completed, I had max maneuver space to focus and to do whatever I needed to do to get healthy. Indeed, God had me right where I needed to be. Only by God's sovereign plan could all of the puzzle pieces have fit together enabling me to sit in that second-floor office. In this room, I would wage war against cancer, day in and day out. Rolling in early in the morning and rolling out late afternoon, having done the Corps' work, I swallowed every enzyme, every capsule, and every ounce of juice Megan sent to work with me. Effectively, this office would be my personal fighting hole to wage war against cancer every Monday through Friday.

Once cancer free, that flexibility allowed me an incredible amount of time to rebuild my body and get back to flying fitness, ready to experience and sustain excessive G forces as I had in the past. God was divinely orchestrating the events which placed me in this strategic location. My office was walking distance from the very organization I would have to win over to get back in a cockpit one day!

As adaptability and flexibility often prove to be key factors in successful endeavors, developing those life skills early in my career allowed me to excel not only as an instructor but also as a cancer Warrior. These crucial character traits would soon be tested—tried with fire—in the days and weeks to come.

Looking back on my first day reporting as ordered to NAS Pensacola, I've seen how God orchestrated a myriad of details for my benefit. This included June 1, 2000 when I left my single-seat squadron for my two-seat squadron, which made this CRM job a possibility. It just wasn't even humanly possible to know what all we needed to engage in this battle fully. But God knew I needed to be in Pensacola working in the CRM schoolhouse during my cancer-fighting year and the two following years while I fought to climb back into my cockpit. I've thanked God many times for *SLAM*, my VMFA(AW)-332 CO, who fought to get me there. I've been equally grateful for LCDR Brett Ulander and for the tight relationship, the trust, and the confidence we fostered. This incredible working relationship afforded me flexibility and support unlikely to be found in a more cookie-cutter, cog-in-the-wheel kind of production job that would have required my presence every day doing the same task over and over.

After checking in at NASC that first day, I made a split-second decision, one born from inner confidence in God's promise to me that He and I were going to win this physical battle and that I would fly in uniform again. I wasn't being nostalgic. I was on a mission.

Climbing back in my 52 Chevy 3100 pickup, I drove over to the flight line on the other side of the base. I had a bold announcement to make. Still in full uniform as a new check-in, I seized the perfect time to walk into the Commanding Officer's office at *TRARON Eighty-Six (VT-86) across the base on Sherman Field. Because the CO was out flying, I was introduced to the Executive Officer (XO), Lieutenant Colonel *BONEY* Orabona. The XO was a Marine F/A-18 WSO. Perfect!

209

"Good afternoon, Colonel," I started as I walked into his office.

He was surprised to see a Marine in Service Alphas, not expecting any new joins that week. He invited me in, and I got straight to the point.

"Colonel, I do not have orders to your squadron, but I wanted to introduce myself to you. I am the Marine who was transferred down here from MCAS Beaufort this week. I have been diagnosed with extremely rare bone cancer, and the docs up in Bethesda say I have two years to live. Colonel, I intend to beat this cancer, and I have every desire to fly for you and VT-86 as soon as I return to flight status. I thought you might want to put a face with the name, because you will be hearing about me in the near future, Sir."

The XO received my confident declaration with a robust Marine Corps, "Sierra Hotel, Marine. I look forward to that day." It was a brief meeting, as I didn't wish to waste any of his time. Unknown to me then, this cancer war and the subsequent flight status battles would necessitate three more visits to his office, one for each victory required to return to my Marine cockpit calling. Only God knew what path to that destination lay ahead.

23| *Our Defense's Critical Vulnerability*

ON a cool, crisp Friday in January 2001, the Trombly squad pulled into Pensacola with our household goods in the moving truck. Two days later, Megan and I packed up the children and hopped into the Suburban to go find a church. We had been given a great lead from some military families at Community Bible Church back in Beaufort to check out Olive Baptist. They bragged that Pastor Ted Traylor's expository preaching style was similar to that of Carl Broggi, our pastor at CBC, taking us through complete books of the Bible in context. Serious about finding a new church home and encouraged to know that Pastor Traylor taught solid biblical truth, not watered-down opinion, we headed out to visit Olive Baptist Church.

Traveling up the main thoroughfare from our neighborhood on Fairfield Drive, I nearly took out a pedestrian standing in the road! But it wasn't a pedestrian at all; it was a newspaper salesperson peddling the Sunday paper. I wasn't used to that type of activity in busy intersections; so the salesman totally caught me off guard. The light turned red, and in the awkwardness of the moment, I purchased a paper from him. It seemed the least I could do.

Our family did find the church, and we enjoyed the service. In fact, we ended up attending Olive for the next four years.

Megan carried in the paper when we returned home. It had been over six years since we had been in Pensacola for flight school; so we thumbed through the paper re-familiarizing ourselves with the community. Once again, timing was everything, and we found ourselves sitting in our new home absolutely dumbfounded by what we were reading.

That Sunday, the *Pensacola News Journal* released the first of a five-part series on how toxic Northwest Florida water was. For five straight Sundays from January into February, the front section of the newspaper heralded article after article declaring the overwhelming number of environmental toxins and poisonous hazards that surrounded our family in our water supply.

Many times during those first few weeks in Pensacola, Megan and I honestly prayed, "God, really? We believe You are going to bring miraculous, natural healing, but why put us here, Lord?" I asked that question more than once, but in the end, if God was going to bring healing, did it matter where? Why not Pensacola? Maybe God would receive that much more glory for His victory!

Megan and I immediately suspended our research on Non-Hodgkin's Lymphoma, natural cures, alternative medicine, or anything else. We had a new mission. We shifted our most precious resource—our time—toward the newest and greatest threat to our entire family—toxic bathing water. Maximum effort went into researching how to defeat our greatest threat to my recovery.

We recognized early on that if we were going to fight this enemy, this disease, through detoxing and natural methods, we had to close the flood gate of toxins rushing into our own home. Otherwise, all our efforts would actually be one step forward followed by two steps backward each and every time we jumped into the shower.

Never before had we even thought about the risks posed by chemicals such as the chlorine used to disinfect our water. We soon received an education about CBPs (Chlorination By-Products) that are created when chlorine is combined with organic material in the water. We found and read a fifth edition copy of the book *Coronaries Cholesterol Chlorine* by Dr Joseph M. Price, which was published back in 1977.[1] Even back then Dr. Price theorized that heart disease was linked to the deadly poison chlorine in our water rather than the cholesterol in our food.

Diligently researching this insidious threat, we saw one of the key eye-opening reports demonstrating the ratio of toxin absorption by comparing ingestion and skin absorption. We learned that a person has to drink contaminated water for approximately FIVE YEARS to absorb as many cancer-causing toxins as our skin (the body's largest organ) absorbs in ONE MONTH of showers or baths. As early as the late 1990s, research from the EPA, American Chemical Society, the American Heart Association, American Journal of Public Health, and others all documented the mammoth role skin absorption played in toxic contamination. This information had not been recognized or well documented previously by those who provide or consume municipal water.

Living in the Panhandle of Florida, we are surrounded by die-hard college football fans. It is hard not to get drawn into the culture when you live in SEC country. If you ask fans who the best team is, you never find agreement. If you ask them what wins championships, however, you find almost immediate consensus. Everyone seems to know that defense wins championships!

To protect our family, Megan and I needed to build a virtual wall of defensive measures to block the toxins coming into our home. The defensive plan became our one and only focus for the next few critical weeks as we learned how to build an impenetrable perimeter around our home. We had to solve the problem of toxic water if we were going to have a fighting chance at beating my cancer using natural methods. Natural approaches would take time, and every toxin removed from our water, food, and air allowed the offensive weapons we would use against the disease more efficacy. In strategic terms, every toxin we could successfully remove brought us one step closer to victory.

> "Industrial toxins are now routinely found in new-born babies, in mother's milk, in the food chain, in domestic drinking water worldwide. They have been detected from the peak of Mt Everest (where the snow is so polluted it doesn't meet drinking water standards) to the depths of the oceans, from the hearts of our cities to the remotest islands."[2]
> —Julian Cribb, Author of *Surviving the 21st Century*

Our new mission entailed learning everything we could about whole-house water purification. For weeks, we scrolled websites, read books, studied peer-reviewed published reports, and made phone calls. Several companies came over and made sales pitches. Sales representative after sales representative came and went. We figured out very quickly that most of them only knew their companies' marketing material. Most were ignorant of the true nature of water and the great threat posed by skin absorption, and they were shockingly unaware of the threats we faced in our own backyard, despite those threats being recently published in the local paper.

As far back as May of 1984, *The American Journal of Public Health* published an article authored by Halina Szeinwald Brown, Ph.D. titled "The role of skin absorption as a route of exposure for volatile organic compounds (VOCs) in drinking water." The article published the findings of exposure to multiple toxic compounds and stated,

> "We found that skin absorption contributed from 29-91 percent of the total dose, averaging 64 percent . . . We conclude that skin absorption of contaminants in drinking water has been underestimated and that ingestion may not constitute the sole or even primary route of exposure."[3]
>
> —*The American Journal of Public Health*

Fortunately, in our research we found the book, *Healthy Water for a Longer Life* by Dr. Martin Fox, which drove us to ask questions about skin absorption of these toxic chemicals when bathing:

> "An adult who takes a 15 minute bath typically absorbs almost twice as much water — and chemicals dissolved in it — as he or she gets in a day's drinking water."[4]

The water filtration industry's complete lack of knowledge as to how our body absorbs our water's high toxicity through our skin and its overwhelming threat to our health became most apparent when a young salesman came over to sell us a high-end Reverse Osmosis (RO) system, an overpriced three-stage system. We gave him our time but not our money. Once he finished his pitch, I asked him what his company offered for the rest of our water now that he had solved our drinking water issue. He was at a loss. They didn't have anything more than a salt softener, and he said that was all we needed.

This salesman did not understand that water softeners do not purify water, which is what we were seeking. We explained to him that softeners only condition the water by removing the inorganic mineral content; they do not remove the hundreds of chemicals that threatened all of us.

To his credit, he didn't try to oversell his system, as our water here in the Florida Panhandle didn't contain a lot of minerals or heavy metals. But though we didn't have hard water, we did have two major industrial complexes. For decades, these two plants had been dumping toxic waste hundreds of feet deep into the earth. Toxins injected into the ground could only go one direction once in the earth's crust—UP and back into our local sand aquifer!

Because sales reps for drinking water products were ignorant of the real threat, we stopped reaching out to companies that only serviced drinking water needs. How was it that I had lived in the area for only a few weeks and had learned more about our toxic water than these water professionals? Because my life depended on it, not my paycheck. My skin was absorbing approximately sixty times as many toxins through contact with our water as my intestines were absorbing by drinking it.

Day after day, Megan and I drilled deeper and deeper into the subject. Sunday after Sunday, the *Pensacola News Journal* published their articles on the Superfund sites in our local area and the elevated cancer rates along the Gulf Coast from Jacksonville, Florida all the way to the mouth of the Mississippi River in New Orleans. The sordid evidence was stacking up.

One article we stumbled upon from October 1998, in *USA Today* stated,

> "Every year, eighteen billion pounds of new pollutants and chemicals are released by industry into the atmosphere, soil, and groundwater."

That same article had a few more bombshells that staggered us.

> "The number of new and different contaminants released into our water systems has grown faster than the ability of science, government, or citizen groups to keep up with. ... [Tests concluded that in 1998,] twenty-five million people had water with significant [toxic pollution] violations posing serious threats to public health."

They also reported that, "Fifty-eight million people got water last year that violated testing and purity standards."

One interesting statistic I read in Lono Kupua's article entitled, "Don't Drink the Water," shared the following. [5]

> "In 1987, the *Journal of the National Cancer Institute*[6] reported a study showing that drinking chlorinated water increases one's risk of developing bladder cancer by 80%."

This stat rocked my world. Knowledge was power, and I immediately shared this data with my parents. My father had bladder cancer. Yet, for over twenty years prior to his diagnosis, my family thought our home was safe and protected. My parents had installed a distillation unit for our three-story multi-family home when I was around eight years old. Distilled water was pumped from the basement to our kitchen sink, and we drank pure water for the majority of my childhood. Dad took five-gallon jugs of distilled water to work every few days. Yet Mom, Dad, and I all got cancer.

We would think that in light of these eye-opening statistics from 2000, great strides have been made in our nation's water quality. Unfortunately, that is not what my research has indicated during two decades of continued study. Below are quotes from a *USA Today* 19 SEP 2019 article titled "Can you get cancer from tap water? New study says even 'safe' drinking water poses risk."

216

"A new report from an environmental advocacy watchdog group cautions that carcinogenic products in tap water may altogether increase cancer risk for thousands of U.S. residents over a lifetime.

In a peer-reviewed study published in the journal *Heliyon*[8] Thursday, the Environmental Working Group (EWG) found that 22 carcinogens commonly found in tap water – including arsenic, byproducts of water disinfectants and radionuclides such as uranium and radium – could cumulatively result in over 100,000 cancer cases over the span of a lifetime.

Although most tap water meets legal standards set by the federal government, EWG researchers found that contaminants present in tap water create a measurable risk for cancer.

The vast majority of community water systems meet legal standards," said Olga Naidenko, the vice president for science investigations at EWG, in a statement. "Yet the latest research shows that contaminants present in the water at those concentrations – perfectly legal – can still harm human health."

Drinking water contains complex mixtures of contaminants, yet government agencies currently assess the health hazards of tap water pollutants one by one," said Sydney Evans, the lead author of the paper, in a statement. "In the real world, people are exposed to combinations of chemicals, so it is important that we start to assess health impacts by looking at the combined effects of multiple pollutants."

This 2019 *USA Today* article goes on to point out our current significant challenges in aging systems nationwide:

"In recent years, multiple crises, from Newark, New Jersey, to Flint, Michigan, have revealed the complications and failures in

217

the management of public water systems, from the different water sources used by municipalities to the pipes that deliver water to homes."

Our research and my own family history were clearly demonstrating that clean drinking water comprised only a very small part of establishing a toxin-free solution. The far greater threat was unmistakable—the water we used for bathing. My parents and I were proof of that connection. The evidence was irrefutable. This reality was slowly becoming clear to Megan and me, but only after weeks of research, as this information is not common knowledge.

The water filtration company and purification product we would ultimately choose to establish our defensive perimeter had to have an answer for the shower water, too. Any company who didn't have the solution for this threat was going home empty-handed. The price tag to use either RO or distillation to purify all our water in our home—not just the drinking water—in order to prevent absorption of toxins through our skin was astronomically cost prohibitive. Thus, Reverse Osmosis (RO) and distillation options were immediately removed from the equation. But there was another problem with Reverse Osmosis and Distillation processes.

Unknown to us before our water research was that RO and distillation not only removed everything bad from the water, but these methods also removed everything good. Our bodies desperately need the good minerals; so this problem, too, took RO and distillation off the table.

We discovered that even if you only have a small amount of minerals in your local area, you want them to remain in your water and that a quality, layered-media, whole-house filter allows for that retention. This asset wasn't merely a bonus feature. It was an absolute mandatory element of our water weaponry. We found that when water is stripped of its natural mineral content, it becomes aggressive, leaching those very necessary minerals from the body when consumed. The challenge presented is less about the bioavailability of the minerals in the water than it is about the nature of the water itself once the minerals are removed.

Additionally, this "dead water" tends to have a lower PH, increasing the acidic level of the body. The goal is to alkalize the body to get it out of an acidic state, as cancer grows only in an acidic environment. Therefore, both the RO and distillation drinking water purification methods are counterproductive to our PH needs, as well as missing the far more serious threat—skin absorption of carcinogens.

After enduring the exhausting list of unhelpful water system salespeople, we finally settled on a local company that offered a whole-house purification system, not a softener. Their multi-stage filter combined two variants of high-quality Carbon and KDF (Kinetic Degradation Fluxion). The KDF media composed of copper and zinc remove heavy metals and render the water bacteriostatic to prevent any possible build-up of algae, in which carbon is prone to grow over time.

One of the greatest selling points of their design was its maintenance-free feature. Every three days, the unit would backwash itself at midnight, regenerating the media and providing for its longevity. It was equipped with a timer, allowing us to determine the best time for its automated maintenance. Providing the clock was set accurately, our unit would backwash at night while we were sleeping. I wanted a system that after installation would not require additional regular costs or man-hours to maintain, and at long last, we had found it!

Finally, our research and perseverance produced an impenetrable perimeter to prevent the greatest source of toxins from entering our home. As any veteran knows, setting up a perimeter of protection around your Area Of Responsibility (AOR) is paramount to a successful operation. Now that our defense was in place and secure, we could start focusing on our offensive game plan to knock out this cancer once and for all.

24| *Lethal or Life-Giving*

URGENCY compels me to leave the storyline for a moment and spend this chapter offering you an action step, a solution you can implement today to move you toward better health.

Before I do, and because I love living in Pensacola, and God willing I will never move from this Emerald Coast paradise, I'd like to share three thoughts. I present these as three arguments as to why, in spite of its toxic water, I chose to live here; and to encourage you no matter where you live to know you, too, can have pure water.

First, actions speak louder than words. Case in point, despite the fact that Pensacola routinely gets identified in the national media for some of the county's worst water, I still think well enough of it to have moved back here when I left my active duty Marine Corps position up in New England in 2008 to fly as a Marine reservist and initiate my civilian career.

Second, I can testify that God healed my cancer while living in this toxic-water-sourced city. I do not live in fear of our water supply or any water supply. Granted, I make a practice of installing a whole-house water system on every home where my family has lived since we purchased our first one in 2000, and I will NEVER live without one in any city. With our defensive perimeter set, I am confident that we could live in any city in the country, even Flint, Michigan, which has also had its share of bad press.

Third, the reality is that planet earth operates with a closed water system. The world's water supply is all connected. As a result, pretty much every community's water in industrialized nations is loaded with hundreds, actually thousands, of toxins. Think that your small mountain community at the top of the nation's watershed is safe from this liquid poison? Then how is it that ice core samples from the North Pole have trace levels of mercury as well as pesticides, like DDT for example, which have been banned for decades? These toxins are also found by testing in other remote places.

> "Pollutants that were never produced or used in the Arctic are now showing up in this remote region [the Arctic Circle] of the world, sometimes in higher concentrations than in the countries where they were made and used. Air, river, and ocean currents, drifting sea ice, and migrating wildlife species carry industrial and agricultural chemicals from distant sites of production and use to the polar environment. In many cases, transport of chemicals to the Arctic from sources in Europe, Asia, or North America can occur in just a matter of days."[9]
> —*The tip of the iceberg: Chemical contamination in the Arctic, Executive Summary, WWF International Arctic Programme*

To make the idea simple, the water here in my city of Pensacola evaporates, taking impurities airborne and redistributing them wherever the air currents take them. The same thing happens with what is dumped in rivers and streams, making its way to the ocean, reaching currents to traverse the globe. This cycle continues and perpetuates itself all the way up to the Arctic Circle. In the southern hemisphere, a similar phenomenon exists to a lesser extent, yet still significant, as these toxins are also found in the Antarctic.

I will not live in fear of any city's water system. That said, even the people responsible for our municipal systems understand that astronomical costs prohibit perfecting the water coming to your home. Even if government agencies could disinfect the water to one hundred percent purity, the municipality would still have to add chlorine back into the water to avoid bacteria and dysentery outbreaks. Providing safe water, as in water free of bacterial contamination, is the government's job. Providing healthy water, as in water filled with life-giving properties for our family, is our job.

If you are dealing with a health concern or are just interested in prevention versus finding a cure, let me share what has been a significant part of our cancer ministry efforts for the past two decades. Whether a cancer Warrior chooses to battle with conventional (allopathic) or alternative (biological) medicine, we believe that utilizing water purification is the most important defensive weapon to incorporate in any health battle, regardless of the battle plan executed.

As a result, I continue to study water and the water industry. I repeatedly confirm that a layered carbon media filtration powerfully supported by KDF media is the most effective way to remove over ninety-nine percent of toxins. Whether sourcing from a well or a municipal water supply, make your defense sure. You must purify all your water supply for your entire house.

Megan and I have established that RO and distillation only purify drinking water, not the whole home's water supply, and that water softeners do little more than remove the minerals and many of the heavy metals. Most of the man-made chemicals—hundreds of them—remain behind.

While the requirement for chlorine is necessary to sanitize the water and pipes in the municipal system, most municipalities add fluoride, which is not a necessity. And fluoride's harmful effects have been documented repeatedly. For example, according to a 1999 Dartmouth College study, there is a direct correlation with fluoridated communities and higher concentrations of lead in children's blood work. The study included more than 280,000 Massachusetts children. [10]

While more difficult to remove than chlorine, fluoride can be filtered out a number of different ways. Our family is at peace knowing we no longer have the fluoride risk in our home's water. Let me give you a quick explanation of what most of us in this country are dealing with when it comes to our local water supply and the fluoride. Most communities that add fluoride to the water are actually adding one of the most corrosive chemical agents in existence, known as hydrofluosilicic acid. This substance is a byproduct of the manufacturing of phosphoric acid, the phosphate fertilizer industry, and the aluminum industry as well. The composition of this toxic waste contains, among other things, mercury, arsenic, and lead.

This Dartmouth College scientific study identifies fluoride by name as a causal factor for osteosarcomas in adolescent males residing in fluoridated water communities. This contaminant should be banned in every community, because it should never have been added to our water in the first place. The solution is for your community to vote to ban its local municipality from continuing its fluoridation process. However, if your municipality fluoridates your water supply, there are definitive ways to remove fluoride completely, no matter where you live or the source of your water.

While I continued to serve in the military for nearly two decades after my grave diagnosis and continued to learn of these toxic water threats, I also followed my passion to educate families along the way. As Megan and I began helping hundreds of families clean up their water as a part of their efforts either to battle a current disease or, in many cases, to prevent disease based on knowledge from their own education, we faced a looming dilemma.

The cancer Warriors Megan and I were privileged to walk beside struggled with the quality filtration systems pricing which had surged over the years. I reached out to a national company with a challenge. I asked the company for a better-designed filter at a lower price. This national company did just that, providing a superior system at a fraction of the next best competitor's cost. It would be an honor to connect you to them. If protecting your family from toxic water is a step that you believe is as critical to good health as we do, you can learn more about toxic water threats and water purification solutions under the supplemental information page on our website at www.groundedandcured.com

Megan and I had a lot more to learn about life-giving water's precedence to health. As we studied, it drove home why God uses water to speak of spiritual life throughout Scripture. Pure water as God created it cleanses and heals the body. The words of Scripture cleanse and heal the soul. Without water, we die physically. Without the Word, we die spiritually.

> Jesus answered her, "If you knew the gift of God and who it is that asks you for a drink, you would have asked him and he would have given you living water."
> "Sir," the woman said, "you have nothing to draw with and the well is deep. Where can you get this living water? Are you greater than our father Jacob, who gave us the well and drank from it himself, as did also his sons and his livestock?"
> Jesus answered, "Everyone who drinks this water will be thirsty again, but whoever drinks the water I give them will never thirst. Indeed, the water I give them will become in them a spring of water welling up to eternal life."
> —JOHN 4:10-14 (NIV)

Confident that this brief dissertation on how the quality of your water affects your health gives you enough information to research the subject further; and having offered you a roadmap for implementation of the highest-quality, first-defense system of which I am aware; I leave the responsibility in your hands to make an educated decision as to whether the H2O your family uses will be lethal or life-giving.

With our family's defensive perimeter of life-giving water firmly in place, we were ready to execute the offensive Blitzkrieg we had been researching and stockpiling to begin!

25 | *Biological Blitzkrieg*

THREE months of testing and meetings with military and civilian doctors had passed since that unforgettable deadly diagnosis day on Parris Island. The conventional options realistically only proffered a possible two-year life span for me. Megan and I had made some very calculated decisions, certainly risky, but decisions which had placed us in Pensacola for close to three weeks so far. From diagnosis to relocating the family to Pensacola took a total of three months.

Our decision process was actually very simple. If conventional medical options had recorded a zero percent successful survival rate according to the reports provided by my Bethesda team, why rush into those therapies? We chose to take a few months to research every option available, and then pick the best one and run with it. Simple yet risky, but for my military mind, our approach was perfectly logical.

We had made some quick gains in those three months. To recap, we removed chemo and radiation from the options list, eliminating those two modalities and their significant negative side effects to threaten my immune system. With my liver condition, the chemo probably would have killed me; so we dodged that bullet.

We had relocated to Pensacola, a decision which had both positives and negatives. The positives were two-fold: I had found a job I could pour myself into and capture the mental edge I needed for emotional stability and positivity. Second, I had found an ally in my cancer fight in my new boss. He would be instrumental in my success in ways I had yet to discover.

The most significant negative from relocating was the toxicity of our new environment, but that had been quickly mitigated by our whole house water purification system. Our baths and showers, the food we cooked, and the clothes, vegetables, and dishes we washed were all done with pure water.

We had established our defensive perimeter. The enemy's toxicity weaponry was going to be held at bay. It was time to go on the offensive. Settled into our new normal of mom homeschooling children and dad heading to the base from 0800-1600 daily, we had our base of operations established. It was time to unleash the big guns. Megan was ready, but was I?

It was time for a biological *blitzkrieg! In German, the term blitzkrieg literally means "lightning war," a word representing a multi-pronged military tactic calculated to create psychological shock and resultant disorganization in enemy forces through the employment of surprise, speed, and superiority in presence and firepower.

The time had come to break out big gun number one. Megan and I knew that we are what we eat. We have all heard this saying, but how many of us have acted as if we believe it? I was about to live it. Sugar is to cancer what gasoline is to fire: pure fuel exploding cancer's growth. Sugar in the form of candy, ice cream, and soda had been eliminated on week one, but sugar in the form of processed food and hidden sugars remained. Megan and I determined that during our transition from Beaufort to Pensacola, I would eat a fairly normal diet until we got our household set up and could aggressively prepare a completely raw diet.

With our household set up, including our water filtration system, there was no reason to wait. The day after the filter went in, not only did our defensive mindset change to an offensive one, but my diet changed radically. Just like adjustments made by a team after the halftime inspirational monologue with the coach, my second-half adjustments were ready to go. They came at a cyclic rate.

Miss Barbara, Megan's naturopathic friend in Boston, had recommended Dr. Schildwaechter, a wise, experienced oncologist in his seventies. Dr. Schildwaechter had attended medical schools in both Germany and in the United States and studied both conventional and biological medicine. He supported the American military, mainly the Army, early in his career in Germany, where he eventually became an oncologist, working out of a hospital in Pennsylvania. As an oncologist in his fifties, he had become disenchanted with the concept of standard conventional practices. He felt that his profession was losing the war on cancer in North America and returned to Germany where he visited some of his biological medicine fellows and revisited his roots.

After developing a wealth of knowledge over the next decade, Dr. Schildwaechter returned to the United States to begin helping people beat cancer naturally and biologically versus conventionally. So when I learned of him, he was no longer a doctor practicing medicine, but rather a doctor doing consulting. Not long before we met him, his Alexandria, Virginia office had been raided and his files confiscated.

Through God's providence, the gracious Dr. S. became my alternative and biological medicine consultant. He would be my coach in the locker room making halftime adjustments. Megan and I had reached out to Dr. Schildwaechter while at Bob's and Sarah's home near Boston. Dr. S had directed us to contact his daughter, Kerstin, for enzyme support and monthly blood work to determine the strength of my immune system. Kerstin took out monthly orders for enzymes and blood tests. These German tests required my blood work to be mailed to Germany every month. Fortunately, since our relocation to Pensacola, I no longer had to go find a lab that would accept my German paperwork and then require me to pay to have my blood drawn as I had during the first month in Boston. The Naval Hospital Lab in Pensacola drew my blood without question, and I simply sent it off like clockwork each month via FedEx to Dr. S and Kerstin.

The test checked some normal cancer markers, but what was

unique was that it screened for DHEA sulfate, which is a precursor to testosterone and estrogen. American labs tested DHEA levels, but DHEA-sulfate testing was not common in the U.S. Dr. Schildwaechter used the DHEA-S testing to monitor the progress of our alternative efforts.

With our blood work and enzyme therapy in place, Dr. S. and Kerstin encouraged me to contact a Canadian nutritionist. He took us down an extreme path of nothing but raw foods. My diet, free from overt sugars, might have seemed well-balanced for a thirty-year-old, but our nutritionist took me to a whole new extreme. With no idea what I was in for, I was all in. He very intentionally removed everything cooked, all meats, all store-bought foods, everything but what was in a salad, or processed through juicers or blenders.

My nutritionist graciously offered to work me into this war regiment gradually, but I was motivated and wanted to pull the trigger overnight. I took aim and fired all my motivation, eliminating every off-limit food at once. I chose the first day after the water filter went in to begin. It was the best time to start, forming an immediate deadline without room for procrastination or excuses.

When dealing with major life changes in the middle of a war zone, I know that mental toughness plays a huge part. To execute a major offensive attack like I was about to do requires inertia. The momentum of the big win from installing the water filter filled my sails granting that inertia needed to build consistency.

Yes, it all seems to be a mind game, but Scripture instructs Warriors to find strength by renewing their minds in Romans 12:1-2. That is what mental toughness is, fighting the enemy with a renewed mind. You have to know yourself and know the enemy (2 Corinthians 2:11).

I know me, and I have always been able to take a small victory and get great mileage out of it. I also know the enemy, and if I waited even one day, the enemy would continue to help me find excuses not to start. Truth be known, beginning the raw diet for me was now, or I am ashamed to say it, very possibly never.

A MOMENT WITH MEGAN

I had been prepared to walk the strict nutritional part of David's journey just as I had in previous years when my children had needed to revamp their diet due to diet-related health issues. In 1996, I had started switching my children's entire nutrition plan and watching what they ate to keep the toxic foods out of their diet. Though we had found great success, David was supportive but not on board himself.

So changing to a healthier lifestyle was harder for David than for the kids and me. David had not grown up with a healthy diet and was heavily addicted to sugar. He loved the Standard American Diet minus all vegetables. But David was ready to do what it took. I wasn't as strict on my kids when we were on the road or at an aunt and uncle's house; so the big change for me was carrying all of David's vegetables and fruits in Rubbermaid tubs in the back of the car wherever we went. Our juicer was always packed as well so that no matter where we stayed, David could stay on course. His nutrition plan was simple for me as the limitations made making his daily food easy. The hard part was watching him have to remain disciplined enough to drink and eat the strict diet with absolutely no cheats. For him, it was life or death.

So the day after the water filtration system was installed, my diet went 100% raw. My morning consisted of a thirty-two-ounce fruit smoothie. I followed that with a small salad without dressing other than olive oil or flax oil for the next year, as dressings have all kinds of preservatives and sugars.

Now, the diet got aggressive after lunch. The afternoon consisted of, wait for it… ninety-six ounces of fresh, organic, juiced vegetables of every kind. The veggies had to be juiced that morning, not the night before and left in the fridge. That's right; I essentially had a liquid diet of nothing but pure nutrition. Fruit pulverized and combined with flax seeds and soaked almonds for breakfast and 96 ounces of juice for the second half of the day.

To put the prep work required into perspective, Megan and I would fill up our double sink with vegetables to soak overnight in food-grade hydrogen peroxide. We would have to rinse all those veggies and juice them around 0530 in order to gain their most potent nutrition, not allowing for any of the oxidation that would destroy nutrients if we prepared the juice ahead of time.

When I say, "we," you may have already guessed that I mean Megan. My 0530 routine included immune-boosting 714-X injections, a controversial Canadian natural immune-boosting weapon I'll unveil in the next chapters. I also added an inhaler treatment of 714-X in an ultrasonic nebulizer after 21 days of injections. For both Megan and me, our morning started with prayer together, gathering and organizing the myriad of enzymes and vitamins for the day, and Megan making my fruit smoothie breakfast and vegetable juice lunch to take to work. While my skin was slowly turning orange from all the beta-carotene in the carrots over the next few months, Megan's fingers and wardrobe were turning purple from the beet juice.

A Moment with Megan

This cancer war required a regimented routine. My day began at 5:30am, sorting and washing 7 to 9 fruits to make David's smoothie for his breakfast. For the next hour, I sorted through the veggies, hoping I had not let any spoil in the never-ending task of purchasing and rotating fresh, organic vegetables. After the proper soaking and scrubbing that these require was completed, I needed to juice the produce until I acquired the 96 oz of veggie juice David had to drink every day. I put this high-powered liquid nutrition in Ball glass canning jars before David left for work.

As I worked, I prayed for David and prayed that the kids would sleep a little longer so that I would have an opportunity to breathe. Next came preparing the kids' food, usually cereal with almond milk because usually, that's all we could afford. Though many days we didn't have the finances to feed them more than cereal, God was always faithful to provide something.

My veggie juice went into glass, only glass, gallon containers that sat in my office fridge so that I could grab an eight-ounce glass every thirty to sixty minutes throughout the day. The frequency of my drinks depended on whether I had desk work or was teaching on the classroom podium.

During weeks when I was in the classroom all day, I would knock back two glasses every fifty-five minutes while students were on break.

I was literally never hungry on this diet. I left the house with a gallon bottle three-fourths full and brought it home empty almost every night. If it did not come home empty, that was supper. If it was empty, I got a bonus second salad of the day. Something I could actually chew!

Megan and the children were still eating a normal diet, yet with some very healthy modifications. The family benefited from my need for a crazy regimen. Megan even started grinding her own wheat kernels and making incredible homemade bread sweetened with honey, and the children loved it. But grains were off-limits for me. No bread, not even Megan's homemade bread!

God had supplied a gift. He had granted me a level of discipline I had never possessed before or since that time. In the months that followed, I was blessed with a desire to win and an ability to stay the course. Until I heard the "all clear," I was able to carry out our dietary offensive attack, finishing the juice nearly every day. Even on the rough days, and I had more than I want to admit, I would stay up later than planned in order to choke it down. The bread I desired so strongly never touched my lips that year, and no sugar or meat did, either.

This one hundred percent, all-in approach, I believe, was as instrumental in my success as the food I was actually consuming. That mental edge of knowing that I had done all I could do to stand that day, was paramount ammunition in the battle mentally. I was speaking life, not beating myself up over failures.

I have had other successes in life since cancer, but none that required such extreme and rigid execution as that year's raw diet. I could not and would not take credit for that—not as a man, as a competitor, as a Marine, or even as a cancer Warrior. That discipline was not of me, not in me, not from me; it was not me. God gave me the gift of discipline that year, and I give Him all the glory and gratitude for it.

If that discipline came from God, what did I have in me? What did I bring to the fight? Along with a strong desire to win to be there for my family and the belief that God was going to bring the cure, I brought my own human nature and a full arsenal of personal, emotional baggage, just like we all have.

I include here one brief example of my temptation, lest you think I'm claiming to be Superman. I'm not. Before I had gone completely raw, Megan had started making her homemade healthy bread. I fell in love with this bread and enjoyed it for a few months before I had to leave it behind for my raw program. Warm and fresh from the oven, it would often send me into an internal rage when I smelled it. Inside, I became the little boy wanting a piece of bread as if it were a giant piece of birthday cake that I couldn't have. That volatile child often came out to play, and I would lose it right in front of my family.

To this day, my oldest daughter, Brianna, reminds me of the time my fruit smoothie erupted like a volcano and ended up on the kitchen ceiling. I shamefully had lost control, wanting to take a small cheat that day.

"Homemade honey wheat bread? You are killing me!" I snarled as I reached for the bread.

"It is for the children." Megan cautioned and pulled it away from me.

"It's just one piece of bread! It's homemade and healthy!" I argued. Continuing I barked, "I just want something warm to eat. You try eating but frozen fruit and cold veggies every day!"

I violently slammed my thirty-two-ounce cup of blueberry, blackberry, and raspberry rich fruit smoothie on the counter, and Newton's third law of motion unleashed. For every action, there is an equal and opposite reaction. In other words, the force released by my emotional outburst as I slammed my giant cup downward on the kitchen counter led to an equal, upward force sending the berry smoothie contents stretching upward and reaching our eight-foot white ceiling, leaving a permanent purple stain.

This embarrassing, permanent stain became a visual reminder to me that I was not capable of doing this work alone, but with Megan, my children, and God's peace, this emotional child could be tamed, trained, and controlled. There were other moments of personal emotional outburst, but for the most part, by God's grace and my wife's wisdom, I made it through with only a few more infamous trophies to display like the one on the kitchen ceiling. On the bright side, as a homeschooling family, our children had opportunities to learn about Newton's laws of motion as a result of the occasionally demonstrated volatility.

Yes, there was also the closet door that didn't survive a later outburst as well as other examples I could supply, complete with the physics to explain my embarrassing behavior scientifically. But I have unveiled my feet of clay for you to fully understand that there were low points on the path to victory.

We had launched our biological blitzkrieg, but we still needed more in our armory. Megan and I realized early in our battle for my life that we were going to need some natural weapons, if conventional options were not used. We also knew we were going to need some supernatural ones, too. Each day as we awoke, sometimes together and other times separately, we prayed for our day. Each day we asked the Lord for three things, and God liberally granted us those three gifts. We prayed for them believing that God was not only listening but yearning to bless his children bountifully. And He did.

> "Which of you, if your son asks for bread, will give him a stone?
> Or if he asks for a fish, will give him a snake? If you, then,
> though you are evil, know how to give good gifts to
> your children, how much more will your Father in heaven
> give good gifts to those who ask him!
> —MATTHEW 7:9-11 (NIV)

We needed strong weapons for this biological blitzkrieg, and together we asked first for a shield of supernatural PEACE—not for the war but for the battle at hand. Not for the year ahead, but solely for the day we were facing. Megan and I did not dare look at the entire battlefield and take in the gravity of our situation. We looked only as far as the day was long, executing that day's battle plan. Megan had her action items, and I had my orders to eat whatever she gave me. Just as wars demand a level of strategic planning, finding answers, and adjusting the strategy, our war demanded constant vigilance. Daily, we kept our heads down and tactically executed our individual and complimentary missions. One day at a time, one battle at a time.

If a young infantry Marine in a fighting hole hears his Corporal directing him, "Shoot any enemy that enters your field of fire from the top of the far left hill to the far right lateral limit of the shed's side!" then that Marine can be an effective force in the fight. What would happen if that same young Marine is distracted by the enemy tanks rolling through another Marine's area of responsibility or the flying mud and sand from exploding mortar rounds just feet away? What if that young Marine looks away from his field of fire to take in the full view of the rest of the battlefield, which is actually the General's responsibility, not his own? The Marine will become, at best, ineffective and allow the enemy to gain ground within his limited area of responsibility. At worst, he will become overwhelmed and incapacitated by fear.

If, however, the Marine keeps his head down and protects his field of fire, then that single avenue of approach will be properly protected, making victory possible. Megan and I knew that our job each day was to focus on that single day, not the entire year. Lifting our heads up and out of our daily foxhole would have allowed fear to creep in and set us up for failure. We purposefully asked for peace for the day and asked again the next day. That's how Jesus instructed his disciples to pray, too. "Give us this day, our daily bread," Matthew 6:11. That's how He instructed his followers in Luke 9:23—to take up their cross daily.

Warrior, focus on the present day's battle, and don't be overwhelmed by the long war. Give all you have within you, and leave nothing in reserve at the end of each day. Ask God for today's portion of peace. When engaged in the fight, every day is the first day!

> "Therefore do not worry about tomorrow, for tomorrow
> will worry about itself. Each day has enough trouble of its own."
> —MATTHEW 6:34 (NIV)

God grants a peace that again, neither Megan nor I can possibly put into words. It is truly indescribable, and it feels incredible. Often we would step out of our busy daily battle to discuss the amazing peace we enjoyed in our home. To sit in our living room after a day of battle with the enzymes, injections, juice, cod liver oil, etc. and to feel at peace knowing we did all we could do that day gives great victory. Those victories stack up. They create momentum.

Those last minutes of the day before I went to bed with our new puppy, Thumper, or my cozy Brianna up on my lap, provided priceless joy, the kind worth fighting for. I would bask in God's provision of peace, enjoying my family before breaking out my next effective, essential weapon—sleep.

Together, Megan and I witnessed peace in our children's hearts. They did not go around fearing their father's pending death but played merrily in the living room. We saw peace in their eyes when they spoke to us about childhood things and school and tree frogs. We felt and heard their joy. God had allowed peace to settle over us like a heavy blanket in winter. It felt safe; it felt right; it felt like God was holding us daily in His embrace because He was. As Psalm 91 had promised, "no disaster will come near your tent."

Secondly, on days when we had to make more strategic, trajectory-altering, long-range decisions, we prayed for the supernatural resource of smart weapons of DISCERNMENT to choose wisely, along with our daily refreshment of peace to stay the course. We needed to know which way to go when we came to the forks in the road, and there were many.

We had to trust that God was guiding us. Because much of what we were doing represented a counter-cultural approach, it drew much-undesired criticism. It would have been easy to justify not following what we believed God was leading us to do in order to avoid the painfully condescending opinions of a number of the military doctors who were providing some of our care and oversight—and sadly, also from some of those we loved. This constant negative reaction to our naturopathic war plan added even more pressure to the challenge of each decision.

Yes, we desperately needed discernment weaponry! And God supplied it, just as He promised in the book of James:

> "If any of you lacks wisdom, you should ask God, who gives generously to all without finding fault, and it will be given to you."
> —JAMES 1:5 (NIV)

Third, we prayed for a never-ending logistical supply chain of supernatural discipline. We needed an unlimited supply of missiles with which to assail the enemy, and God faithfully granted that in ways that made us stand in awe of Him. We could reach down deep for the daily discipline in much the same way a noob video gamer can access an endless supply of bullets while practicing with a bottomless clip on the firing range before competing with the other gamers online.

It was truly all God. The will to execute the plan of the day that was designed to save my life demanded a level of discipline I did not possess on my own. God freely supplied this gift so necessary during the battle.

Without a doubt, the greater the stakes of the war, the greater the challenge of the discipline required. Fighting cancer required a deep level of discipline that was not of me or within me—one I had to ask God to give me. He granted it daily, for which I can only give Him the glory. The discipline of that year came supernaturally. Yes, God supernaturally supplied the shield of peace, the smart weapons of discernment, and the unlimited supply of disciplinary missiles DAILY to fight a war where the stakes were my very life. This war demanded both a full-on biological blitzkrieg and a well-stocked supernatural armory!

26| *A Controversial Canadian Weapon!*

GROWING up in Boston, I loved listening to Rene Rancourt sing the Canadian and American national anthems before Boston Bruins' hockey games. Those songs have stuck with me to the point that I find myself whistling or singing the Canadian anthem while buzzing with a chainsaw or working my land, times when I am most relaxed. It became my happy song. Don't mock me, we all have one. If you hear me singing it, I am as stress-free as I get.

Recently, I sang it at the start of an Ice Flyers' hockey game here in Pensacola. It took me forty-eight years to muster the moral courage, but this Ice Flyers Chaplain finally sang the Canadian anthem as a way to honor the Canadian players on our team. It also served as chapel material for the following week's locker room talk as I spoke about chasing lions and chasing fears. Though I may love to speak in public, singing a solo ranks up there with harvesting honey from a beehive naked.

"Gentlemen, great games this weekend. Congrats on your victories." I started chapel the following Tuesday morning on a positive note because our team had won after I had sung the anthem at the Ice Flyers' Faith and Family night the previous Saturday.

"Great job with the anthem Saturday, *T-BONE*," one of the Flyers shouted out. "When's your audition for *American Idol*?" quipped another.

"So you talk as much trash in the locker room as you do on the ice, eh?" I responded. "All joking aside, you know I consider you all modern-day gladiators on ice. Today, I am going to share the story of a real-life mighty man of God whose exploits in battle have been documented for all of history."

I shared the Old Testament story of teenager Benaiah chasing and killing a lion, found in 2 Samuel 23. And yes, I encouraged them all to get a copy of Pastor Batterson's book, *Chase The Lion*.

"We all have lions to chase. We all have fears to face. It was truly a privilege to sing the Canadian anthem Saturday and to honor our Canadian players in doing so. What you don't know is that I have my own personal fear of singing a solo in public and forgetting the lines halfway through. Today's subject is more personal for me, as I recognized this lifelong fear and chose to face it publicly, chase it boldly, and conquer it with your support on Saturday evening."

"Gentlemen, there are fears that cannot be avoided. Cancer was not a challenge I could ignore or run from. I had to face it head on and fight every day until it was defeated and I achieved my victory–the cure. I could have avoided singing at center ice, and no one in this life would have been the wiser to my natural fear of singing solo in public."

Then came the point I wanted to drive home. "But I would take to my grave the knowledge that I had backed down from a fight. I cowered to a fear that gripped me for all of my life. Or I could conquer it in a single 75-second act of boldness and courage, chase that lion, and defeat it."

"Men, you all have fears. Some you cannot avoid; others you can hide from everyone but yourself. What are you going to do with those roaring lions roaming around holding you back? I challenge you to identify those fears and chase them down. Enjoy having no regrets at the end of this life."

I have long possessed a strong affinity toward Canada and Canadians. I have been privileged to befriend many Canadian hockey players as they come and go through our locker room in Pensacola. I flew with a couple of Canadian Exchange F/A-18 pilots in my squadron back in Beaufort. One of the smartest pilots I ever met flew with us for over a year on an exchange tour. He had been an engineer before joining the Canadian military, and he knew more about our radar system than I had the capacity to comprehend. I have maintained tremendous respect for the Canadian culture and for each of the Canadians I have served with or played hockey with who have represented their country so well.

I look back and smile as I think about this connection I've had throughout my life. With the last name, Trombly, our French-Canadian heritage came through forefathers who traveled down from Canada hundreds of years ago. I sometimes wish they hadn't, as having an extra vowel in my name might have afforded me a fighting chance at making it to the National Hockey League. (Hey! I may be fifty now, but there is still a chance I can make the pros, now that I'm retired from the Corps.)

In addition to our Canadian nutritionist, Dr. Schildwaechter directed me to another wonderful couple north of the border who had an immune-boosting biological medication. Dr. Gaston Naessens and his wife, Jacinte, joined our cancer-fighting coalition.

Dr. Naessens only spoke French; so his wife Jacinte interpreted when we called to speak with them. Years later in a Boston hotel, we met personally and captured our cherished exchange on video. Megan and I shared our cancer Warrior testimony and our deep gratitude for this couple. Their dedication and perseverance allowed for the development of the 714X amazing immune-boosting treatments. (You can view the entire 2008 interview with Megan and me and Dr. Naessens and his wife, Jacinte, on YouTube by searching Trombly714X, located at this link: https://www.youtube.

com/watch?v=qUO4AzCMo7k.)

While you are scrolling the internet for that 2008 interview, you should take the time to peruse the other links that appear. You will find plenty of positive and negative reporting on Dr. Naessens and 714-X. Welcome to the vortex!

Travel back in time with me to my original diagnosis and imagine trying to make life and death decisions while reading Quakwatch. org and balancing that with Dr. Naessens' CERBE company website. Both read as presenting the truth. I have seen decision making paralysis set in often with cancer Warriors because of these mixed messages. I had no time for that stalling, and fortunately our answered prayer for discernment granted by the Holy Spirit offensively pressed Megan and me forward. Each day remained a faith walk.

We were no experts on biochemistry like Dr. Naessens, and we were not sure who was behind Quakwatch.org or what their agenda was. Years later, we have developed a far better understanding of both, but in that critical and vulnerable period, we had to trust someone. We had to rely on God's peace to quiet us and settle the decisions we had to make.

Both military and civilian doctors told us we were foolish to waste our energy and limited time on alternative medicine. The Quakwatch site further bolstered our doubts as we tried to balance our research with both sides of the arguments. But we had something that many others in that critical decision-making process did not necessarily have.

We had the testimony of Billy Best and the Best family further supporting the claims from my real-life biological doctor, Dr. Schildwaechter. We had his daughter, Kerstin, telling us that 714-X did work and could work for me. What a blessing to have a network of alternatively minded families and doctors there to help educate and guide us! We did not have this network of support initially. We had to build that coalition over time, and fortunately, we took that time despite the overwhelming pressure to act hastily.

The product that Dr. Naessens had invented, called 714X, was essentially nitrogen in a camphor base. The 714X compound is injected paranodularly (next to the lymph nodes rather than directly into them) in the lower right portion of the abdomen, which aids in rapid absorption into clogged lymph nodes. This placement allows the lymph nodes to liquefy and release their toxins over time. According to Wikipedia,[11] "714X also referred to as 'trimethylbicyclonitramineoheptane chloride,' is a mixture of substances manufactured by CERBE Distribution Inc. and sold as an alternative medical treatment which is claimed to cure cancer, multiple sclerosis, fibromyalgia, and other diseases. There is no scientific evidence that 714-X is effective in treating any kind of cancer, and its marketing is considered health fraud in the US."

Though I have no reason to doubt the validity of Wikipedia's quote, I do, however, know that Dana Farber started a blind study of 714-X years before I used it. According to Dr. Naessens, it was producing success. The scientists eagerly looked to determine what medication had apparently been successful, and when they realized it was the alternative from Canada, they pulled the plug on the study. Oh, Canada!

Having read and researched all I could online, both positive and negative, and having held conversations with the Best's and the Schildwaechter's, I called CERBE in Canada and placed my first order to ship to our new address in Pensacola. It arrived a few days after I started my raw diet.

The daily 714-X injections followed a 21-day cycle. After taking two days off, I immediately started the second cycle and adhered to this routine for a total of ten cycles. I took a one-month break only once while out of the country. If the treatment was frowned upon in the U.S., I figured it best not to pack it in my suitcase for a trip across the Atlantic. When I started my second cycle, Dr. Schildwaechter and Dr. Naessens recommended I double-dose by taking an inhalable version through an ultrasonic nebulizer, which I faithfully did for the remaining nine cycles. I had fully employed a controversial, offensive weapon from Canada in the fight!

27 | *Breach in the Perimeter*

I was packing the rental truck for our DIY (Do It Yourself) move from Beaufort down to Florida in early January when I ran my tongue over the surgery site where the stitches had been. The sutures had healed up nicely, and the bone that had been eaten away had left a prominent indentation that I could roll my tongue over and into. It was a nervous habit that was certainly understandable. It was as if I was subconsciously looking over my shoulder, wondering if and when the tumor might come back. While believing and praying for the best, I was yet checking with the tongue for the worst.

I knew in my heart that I was not actually doing anything truly alternative yet to fight my cancer. My focus since returning in early November had been on the logistics of getting orders to Pensacola, traveling down for a week to find a home near the hospital, and packing our household goods. Additionally, I was making a deliberate attempt to get through the holidays with some semblance of normalcy for the children's sake before packing our household goods the week after Christmas.

These next couple of months were an extension of our timeline for researching and formulating a plan. In the meantime, I focused on not doing things that would lower my immune system. I had stopped lifting weights and running—a conscious decision not to break down muscle tissue and create more free radicals during the cancer fight.

Many other cancer Warriors I studied used strenuous workouts as a way to keep their mental edge. Although I get that strategy, but my mental edge came from working; so I saved the free radicals and went for three-mile walks every day. I employed deep, concentrated breathing walking around our Beaufort base housing complex and later our new Pensacola neighborhood after we moved. The walks were intentional, as walking exercises muscles which in turn forces lymphatic fluid to pump through the body and remove toxins. Pushing toxins out was the goal. The full-focused inhalations and thorough exhalations were to fill and subsequently fully empty the lungs in order to hyper oxygenate the blood. I would almost hyperventilate at times, producing a sort-of natural high. Colors got brighter, and my attitude got positive.

As you can imagine, the enemy at the gates did not rest while I was avoiding candy bars and taking walks in the woods. Cancer did not wait for me to make my next move on the chessboard. It just silently, slowly, and insidiously grew as time ticked by. I knew this, and I checked the pit in my jawbone probably hourly.

When it started to grow back and fill in, I was concerned and held that information back from everyone—even Megan for a few days. Telling the doctors would only add fuel to the fire and increase the number of calls that I was receiving from Bethesda to return for chemotherapy. This was my secret, and I wasn't sharing it with anyone but Megan until I had a doctor in Pensacola I could establish a relationship with. That day finally came.

I met Dr. Ostergaard, and he did not disappoint. He was exactly what my flight surgeon had built him up to be and more. We selected him as our primary care manager for Megan and all four children also. After our meeting with him, I asked him if he would take me on as a patient. He responded that pilots have flight surgeons and that his treating me would be highly unusual.

Dr. O appreciated hearing how his friend had recommended him. He listened intently as I explained that, according to Bethesda's research, no one had beat my cancer to this point, at least not out to a full five-year remission, and that we were taking a different approach. When he realized I was not going to go back to Bethesda, I believe he recognized I would be unmonitored. Dealing with the Naval Aviation Schools Command (NASC) flight surgeon, who was my assigned doctor, was not going to happen until I was cancer free and ready to fight to get my flight status back. The flight surgeon's hands were tied. He could not recommend or do anything for me outside of grounding me, which had already happened back in Beaufort, South Carolina.

Considering my most trusted flight surgeon had recommended him, Dr. O took me on as his patient. Dr. Ostergaard became my official Primary Care Manager. Doc O had his stipulations, and they included monthly blood work, which I needed for Germany anyway. He also wanted a monthly appointment with me to palpate all my lymph nodes and to feel the tumor site in my jaw.

I made my first appointment with Dr. Ostergaard, who possessed an amazing bedside manner. I shared the whole story from toothache to oral surgery, from Bethesda to Dana Farber, to the week I first felt the tumor growing back, which had been about a month prior to that appointment. Doc O was concerned about that development, and he shared his heart. I was ready to receive whatever he had for me.

"David, I respect your faith. I am a believer, too. I believe in prayer and anointing by the elders of the church. I am one, and I do that on Sundays at my church on Blue Angel Highway. But I am also a scientist, and I feel it is my duty to recommend you go back to Bethesda for chemotherapy."

I accepted his warning, and we had a healthy discourse. It was refreshing, because it was one of the most *respectful* conversations I had had with anyone in the medical field since my diagnosis. When I had convinced him that this course of action was truly a faith walk and that we were convinced beyond any doubt that God had us on this path of only natural and biological medicine, he conceded.

All I had to do to maintain him as my PCM was to honor his request to be seen monthly and to give blood. If he wanted a CT scan, I accepted and made the appointment. Dr. Ostergaard and I developed a mutual respect for each other, and we worked incredibly well together. I looked forward to every visit.

Because I had not been seen by anyone in my last couple of months in Beaufort, Doc O did ask me to make an appointment to visit the ENT on the other side of the hospital. We were concerned that if the tumor grew too fast for my natural methods to keep up, I might lose my teeth or worse. My plans were to ask the ENT to consider doing a second surgery to remove the new tumor just like the first one had been removed. I set the appointment.

My visit to the Ear, Nose, and Throat Surgeon, Dr. Bose, proved colorful, to be mild. He sat me in the chair, looked and felt the tumor, and very quickly started his sharp dissertation.

"Why the hell aren't you in Bethesda?" he demanded. "You are a fool!"

I'd heard that before. Had he been talking with my doctors in Bethesda prior to my visit?

"Captain, we need to go for a walk," Captain Bose ordered

We made our way down to the cafeteria area. It was late in the afternoon, and no one was there, just empty chairs and candy machines. He asked me to wait and went to speak with

Dr. Ostergaard. Doc O was not in his office, and Dr. Bose returned shortly.

Dr. Bose moved with a possessive posture, a bearing unlike any other. Though I'd spent less time with this man than any other doctor I met that year, he left one of the strongest impressions. He had only heard a brief portion of my story and had taken only a quick look at my record. I did not know who he may have spoken with other than possibly Dr. Ostergaard. I could not have anticipated what I was about to hear next as he and I sat alone in the cafeteria.

"Captain, you are making a terrible mistake not doing what you have been told by the experts, and I believe you are going to die. I will not do the surgery you are requesting. While it may buy you a little more time, in the end, it will come back and spread everywhere. You seem like a determined, strong-willed, stubborn man. I think you will just keep trying to find doctors to do what you want them to do, and with your charismatic personality, you may be able to manipulate some other ENT to do your surgery. But eventually, you will be so riddled with cancer you will come back and beg us to give you chemotherapy. Because we are the Navy, we will do it, but it won't work. You will die. Frankly, I think the Navy should Med Board you out now and spare the expense of treating you!"

The chemistry from the moment we met was prickly, but I did not expect these words to come from any doctor's lips. I sat there processing his blunt delivery of such a cutting message. Silently glaring through the man with the professional stare I had developed in the Corps, I could only imagine what my glaring, unblinking eyeballs were communicating to him. I was not going to speak. I couldn't speak. I was still processing his last sentence. Had he really said I was not worth the Navy's money to save? Was this the God-complex I had heard that some doctors possess? If so, it was my first exposure.

The silence was deafening. There was no quick-witted Bostonian smart-ass response I could muster. There was no NERF-like "let's take this outside and see who the last Marine standing will be" flare-up inside my spirit. I just stared him down. Dr. Bose had crossed a line, not just professionally but as a human being, one creation of God to another, man to man. He had placed a dollar value on my life, and it was less than the price of a few cycles of chemo. The silence, the loathsome silence remained. Dr. Bose had to speak first, or we were never going home.

He did speak first, and I knew instantly I was going to get the last word. There was going to be an opportunity for the Bostonian in me to get my shot in after all, I thought briefly, but it didn't happen. God had grabbed my tongue, because He wanted me to speak life was going to be spoken.

Dr. Bose realized he had crossed a line which he could not easily work his way back across. He was a phone call away from some serious backlash, and he was trying to back paddle. This situation was actually a little humorous to experience, as the God-complex took a back seat to a man hoping to salvage his military career. His next words were epic (and if you are reading this aloud to your children, STOP)! Dr. Bose broke the awkward silence and in a far more subdued tone of voice, almost as if we were friends, said,

"Captain, you know, maybe you will beat this, and I hope you do. If that happens, you will probably send me a postcard that says, 'Hey Asshole, I beat it'. How about we just agree right now that I should not be your doctor and you should not be my patient?"

I had an opportunity there that few people would ever pass up. I could literally say anything to this man and get away with it. That only happens to an enlisted member every four years when their enlistment expires and they relish that brief moment to speak their mind prior to re-enlisting. Even then, they have to be somewhat tactful as after they lambaste their direct supervisor, they swear their reenlistment oath and go back to work for the same boss, only to get sent out to clean the latrines.

It was open mic night, and here is what God laid on my heart, "Dr. Bose, if today was ten years from now, I might say those exact words. But ten years is a long time, and when that day comes, what I hope you hear from me is this, 'Dr. Bose, my belief that God would come through proved correct, and He worked His miracle in me.'"

No one said anything else. We didn't shake hands. He just left, and I sat back down alone in the empty cafeteria area to process. Absolutely, God was with me. He held my tongue. He gave me those words because they needed to be spoken. I don't know who needed to hear them, me or Dr. Bose. Both of us, I guess. Either way, heated, emotional Marine conversation just doesn't happen like that! But God!

I wanted to give Megan a quick call. I had to find a desk in one of the shops. I called to tell her what happened and to continue processing it for myself. Megan hit the roof! Her righteous indignation was coming through the phone loud and clear. The sailor behind the counter must have heard what sounded like Charlie Brown's mom coming through the earpiece.

What I heard was the same hurt and anger I had felt the day those two doctors ambushed Megan while I was getting my bone marrow biopsy. Megan wanted me to head straight to the Navy Hospital Commanding Officer's office and report Dr. Bose for malpractice or some form of inhumane treatment. I let her vent, but I had learned something over the past few months since that Bethesda ambush.

I realized that while we cannot control the environment we are in; we can control how we react to that environment. Even more impactful was the reality that we could not afford to waste any emotional strength on negative energy.

If I had taken the time to march up to the CO's office, the trip upstairs would have only reinforced the negative experience I had just endured and created even more negative energy. It would have been a waste of the emotional capital and spiritual resources I needed in order to heal. No, all I needed to do was come home and be with my family. Someone was waiting for Hubby and Daddy to come home, and that was good medicine.

I have not retained the memory of that doctor's face. I have not searched through my medical records to look him up, especially since, unlike most Marines who only have one or two medical volumes after twenty-five years of service, I have *four*! The incident that day in the cafeteria was forgiven but not forgotten. I tucked it away as a reminder of the power of a prideful human ego and how impactful words can be. I saw how we can speak life or death with the tongue.

> "Likewise, the tongue is a small part of the body, but it makes great boasts. Consider what a great forest is set on fire by a small spark. The tongue also is a fire, a world of evil among the parts of the body. It corrupts the whole body, sets the whole course of one's life on fire, and is itself set on fire by hell. All kinds of animals, birds, reptiles and sea creatures are being tamed and have been tamed by mankind, but no human being can tame the tongue. It is a restless evil, full of deadly poison. With the tongue we praise our Lord and Father, and with it we curse human beings, who have been made in God's likeness. Out of the same mouth come praise and cursing. My brothers and sisters, this should not be."
> —James 3:5-10 (NIV)

> "Death and life are in the power of the tongue:
> —Proverbs 18:21 (KJV)

I hope that I get to meet that doctor one day. I want to shake his hand, and in case he didn't recognize it, I want to tell him I forgave him that day. I want him to know that God did pull out a miracle, and that miracle gives me the privilege to share the truth of God's peace in this book with anyone who will receive it. May God grant me that divine appointment.

28| *Operation Mercury*

I had been in Pensacola for close to six months. The natural therapies were working, and each day I fought the good fight drinking all my juice and popping all my supplements while at work. Up in the CRM Department, I had quickly established myself as a reliable member of the CRM team. The study came naturally to me as

I prepared to teach my few assigned classes for the CRM instructor course.

The limited number of courses I was responsible to teach quickly led to restlessness and boredom; so I sought out some additional responsibilities downstairs with the new student population. Teaching ground school is actually designed to be more of a collateral duty. The idea is to become a subject matter expert quickly and streamline your efforts so you can get out of the classroom and office a couple days a week or so to go fly with students on the other side of the base. Because I was grounded, I soon went looking for other classes to teach.

I rapidly made friends downstairs when I asked a couple of instructors if I could take their classes once a month so they could go fly. These classes were usually only three to five-day courses, and fellow instructors gladly handed me their work and tore up the sky. Flight Rules and Regulations was a quick class to conquer, and I routinely stepped in to teach for the primary instructors over the next three years so they could spread their wings. If I were a person who drank beer, I would have never had to buy one on a Friday at the Officer's Club during that tour. Unfortunately, they don't serve beet, kale, and carrot juice at the Mustin Beach Officer's Club; so I was out of luck.

The two-hour Introductory CRM course for all our eager young flight students downstairs needed to be refreshed as well. This had been a fairly painful, dry course that did not have a test at the end, making it a sleeper for these future pilots. I had asked to rebuild it and was given the green light from LCDR Ulander. I loaded the updated version with funny videos and changed the entire flow and structure, saving a rocking, key leadership section for the end. The poignant lesson on how quickly lives can be lost if good leaders fail to do their job left an impression. I enjoyed building the course and had even more fun teaching it. It surprised me how quickly I fell in love with the classroom environment. It was a joy passing on the important and the mundane through a combination of standup comedy, motivational speaking, and inspirational storytelling.

Everything was going incredibly well with my new job, and Megan and I had settled into a rhythm. I was also finding support in our new church home. Despite its incredible size and the ease with which we could get lost in the sea of faces, we enjoyed the preaching here. I quickly found a friend in our Sunday school teacher, Todd Leonard. Despite being a West Point grad with an Army pedigree, he appreciated my Marine sense of humor. While he couldn't respond as I knew he would like, my occasional smart-ass comments, strategically placed at the most inappropriate times for a Sunday school class, put a smile on his face.

We grew to love this small group at Olive Baptist where we felt the bond of family and friendship in the hour of Bible study and fellowship. Multiple times over the next year, Megan and I would share a heavy request prior to a scan or even a trip for a medical procedure. This group prayed and prayed hard. While there was great prayer support, there was also an interesting tension in the room as we routinely shared our completely natural cancer battle plan requirements. One class member was a conventional doctor who came to class every Sunday morning with his Diet Coke in hand as I entered with a large glass of vegetable juice. It was an interesting dichotomy of worldviews regarding health and wellness approaches that was not lost on the class members in the room. Despite our differing opinions and ideas on health and how to attain or maintain it, the class bonded and prayerfully supported us in our year of need.

A MOMENT
WITH MEGAN

David and I had enjoyed church homes in which our friends were as close as family. Moving to Pensacola and leaving this precious support behind was incredibly difficult for me. I was stressed emotionally and financially, and accepting help from total strangers was overwhelmingly difficult for me. But GOD was always with us, and during this time He reinforced in my heart that it was my Heavenly Father in whom I needed to put my trust—not man.

I have seen that God sometimes strips us of everything and puts us in a desert experience where we must look for the pillar of clouds by day and the pillar of fire by night. Pensacola was my desert! The outcome was great, but the battle was bitter.

At this time, the staff from our new church hadn't visited us. However, as we grew closer to those in our small group and its leaders, we began sharing our needs. Still, it was humbling when our teacher and his wife stopped by to give us food and money donations from others in the group.

God also provided for us through the churches we had attended in our youth. Others learned of our needs through my sister Sarah. But how embarrassing this public knowledge of our need was for me! Imagine standing in front of a church with your children, one where everyone had known you since childhood, and expressing deep, basic needs. Can you visualize the reaction as we explained that we weren't going with conventional medicine because there was no hope, there were no survivors, in that scenario? Humbling!

Yes, the Lord provided every step of the way. The 10pm deep cries of this worn-out wife and mother were met with an overflow of peace so that I could sleep and rest for the next day of doing my best for my family. God had checks in the mail and food at the door in the most timely instances. He helped my kids find friends in the neighborhood, and God even helped our little 8-year-old boy, struggling to read, speak life into his parents on our darkest day. So if you find yourself alone, afraid, without financial support, and struggling to do it all . . . the Lord is faithful . . . one day at a time . . . faithful!

My monthly visits with LCDR Ostergaard had been very exciting over the past couple of months. While the first visit had been very positive, it was not without great concern because that tumor had grown back significantly in the two months since Christmas. It took about seven weeks after we had gone on the offensive for my tumor to start shrinking. It was encouraging to experience the body functioning well, receiving the nutrition and the tools that God had provided. My body was responding to the nutrition, the enzymes, the cleansing, and the rest of our battle plan.

My third month's visit with Dr. Ostergaard brought some cautious optimism from Doc.

"Good morning, David," Doc greeted as he stepped into the Family Practice Department's examination room on the second floor of Naval Hospital Pensacola. "I have some good news this morning."

"Good morning, Commander, Let's hear it, Sir."

"Blood work is looking good for the third month in a row. That is very positive," he exclaimed. "Have you noticed any activity with your lymph nodes?"

"Commander, as you can certainly appreciate, I can't help but check them every day. So far, I have noticed no enlargement or soreness of any kind in my groin or neck, but I do have a small, very hard lymph node under my left arm."

"Very good. Just relax your arms, and I am going to lift and check them myself. I'll be pushing pretty hard; so power through and let me know if you feel anything as I push." After a brief search under both arms and around the front and back of the neck down to the collarbone, he finished with the nodes by the groin.

"Well, I do not feel anything significant. There was a small lymph node under the left arm that seemed a little larger and harder than on your previous examination. Have you had a cold or been feeling under the weather at all?"

"Negative, Sir. Feeling really strong, and no colds or allergies to report."

"Let's just keep an eye on that area, and you let me know if you notice any changes over the next month," he directed. "Any changes along the jawbone?" he asked.

"Actually, Commander, I think we have had a breakthrough. Granted, I am checking this growth with my tongue nonstop every hour of every day between our monthly visits, but as I place my finger on it, the protrusion seems to be receding. I think the tumor is shrinking."

"OK. Let me in there, and let's see what we can feel."

He smiled, lifted my lip, and instinctively placed his finger exactly where the tumor was located behind my cheek. Dr. O was quiet and looked me in the eye with his calming, relaxed demeanor as he started palpating the gum tissue and rolling his finger across the jawbone. He then looked away for a few moments before looking back intently at my cheek as he thoroughly felt around the outside and inside of my upper right jawbone. After about a minute or so, I looked back at him to notice his eyes were closed as if in deep concentration.

He paused to pull up a stool beside me before he spoke, nodding in silent agreement. Finally, he spoke.

"Captain, I would have to agree with you that the growth does appear to be smaller than on previous examinations. I believe that we may have made some progress, but I must caution you that we cannot know for sure without another CT scan. Let's wait another month or two, and if it feels even smaller, I will request a CT scan of the head and neck to confirm our theory."

I nodded in full agreement, too excited to find words.

Without my interruption, he continued, "Keep up with all you have been doing with your natural program, and don't be afraid to come back sooner if anything changes for the worse. Please get yourself an appointment with Miss Lilly on your way out for the first of next month, and we will go from there, Marine."

"YES, SIR! I won't leave here without one. Thank you for your time, and you have a great week, Doc!"

Dr. Ostergaard actually waited two more months and two more examinations for a total of five months of evaluations before ordering the CT scan. In each of these visits, Dr. O and I shared a growing confidence that the tumor did feel like it was shrinking. Finally, with the CT scan ordered, we impatiently waited for the results.

I greatly appreciated his mutual faith and understanding of our family's faith walk. Immeasurable respect developed from his approach as a conventional doctor willing to seek out and use all resources at his disposal to stay ahead of this disease.

The results were finally made available! In early June, I met with Dr. O one more time to discuss my CT scan from late May. While we both acknowledged the tumor was still visible in the image, we agreed that it had been shrinking over the past few months. Continuing with monthly follow-ups and blood work was the mutually accepted plan going into the summer.

I was making progress. My blood reports from Germany showed a significant increase in my DHEA-S levels, confirming that I no longer had the immune system of an eighty-year-old man, but closer to a guy in his late forties. Even though I was only thirty-one years of age, that report represented a huge step in the right direction.

Nine months after diagnosis and a solid five months into our natural battle plan, it was time for our next campaign, another big step. As Megan and I continued researching, we were unwilling to rest on what we considered to be a very significant milestone— a shrinking tumor. We were looking for the next piece of the puzzle and asking God daily for discernment as to what was next.

In our research, we learned about the hazards of mercury amalgam fillings, and we believed there was evidence pointing to mercury as a causal factor for Non-Hodgkin's Lymphoma. We also learned that the rubber material in a root canal has the same negative effect on our body systems as a rubber cap does on an electrical outlet. Both prevent the flow of energy.

From our early research, we already knew the importance of pure water, as our bodies are mostly water. We knew of our vital need for minerals, which is why we avoided Reverse Osmosis filtration systems and water softeners. Now the electrochemical nature of the body became a subject of study for us. If we do not have the proper hydration or the proper level of minerals and electrolytes, then homeostasis is disrupted.

Equally important, but not as well-known are the energy channels, known as meridians, that run throughout the entire body, including the organs. You can learn more about these energy channels by researching reflexology or visiting an acupuncturist, who can give you an incredible education. What was eye-opening for Megan and me was the newfound knowledge that every single meridian runs through the jawbone!

Having cancer in my jaw made us concerned about what meridians ran through the area of teeth number four and five and what we should be looking out for. It was simply amazing once we found a meridian chart and saw what parts of the body were connected with that section of my jaw! Just another affirmation from the book of Psalms.

"I praise you because I am fearfully and wonderfully made;
your works are wonderful; I know that full well."
—Psalm 139:14 (NIV)

When you have a root canal or a dead tooth, you have essentially placed a rubber baby outlet protector in a major body system. While I was fortunate not to have any root canals to block the electrical energy currents, I did have many metal fillings. There was just too much evidence between that mercury and Non-Hodgkin's Lymphoma to ignore. It was time for the mercury to come out.

Dr. Schildwaechter came through once again, as he had a friend in Providence, Rhode Island he wanted me to go see, Dr. Felix Liao. He was a renowned biological dentist. Megan and I set an appointment for a couple of weeks out, and I put in for three weeks of leave. We took advantage of the vacation days to spend time with our family in Boston while also having all my mercury amalgam fillings removed. Not your typical summer vacation!

(For additional information on biological dentistry and Dr. Felix Liao, visit our website www.groundedandcured.com)

29| *Confidence or Bravado*

WE were heading north on I-95 to Boston for three weeks of military leave so that the family could have a vacation with the cousins and grandparents. This was our first visit back to New England since receiving my "second opinion" from the Dana Farber civilian doctors eight months ago. The main purpose of our trip was to have all of my metal fillings removed by a biological dentist, Dr. Felix Liao, in Providence.

As we sped past the interstate exits for Quantico in northern Virginia, powerful memories from six years ago came flooding back. With my shoulders rolled back, I sat taller in my seat. I was in great spirits, executing an effective holistic battle plan, and my confidence was building.

Quantico, which is home to the Marine Corps Combat Development Command (MCCDC), is affectionately referred to as the "Crossroads of the Marine Corps," where all Marine Corps officers get their start at *Officer Candidate School (OCS). Graduation brings the coveted commissioning as a Second Lieutenant of Marines.

Following OCS, a young officer receives another set of orders across the base for their six months at The Basic School (TBS). Just one of the many facets of Marine Corps training, TBS sets Marines apart from all the other service branches. In those six months, we learn a little about every aspect of the Marine Corps, from administrative documents to the complete structure of its active and reserve components. We train with every weapon system our Marines employ, including mortars and the plastic explosives our combat engineers use to clear obstacles on the battlefield. Before it's over, we acquire a healthy appreciation for the entire Marine Air-Ground Task Force team.

While other services go directly from their commissioning source of OCS or respective service academy to their Mission Occupation Specialty School (MOS) school, Marine Officers do not. We go directly to TBS. It is instilled in all young, enlisted Marines —methodically broken down and rebuilt hard at either Marine Corps Recruit Depot Parris Island or San Diego — that they are infantry Marines first. Whether they are to serve as a cook, aviation supply clerk, artillery Marine, or a helicopter mechanic, they master infantry skills first because "Every Marine is a rifleman!" The same is true of the Corps' officers. Every Marine Officer is an Infantry Officer first.

Here at The Basic School, I came to understand that every mission specialty, every job in the Marine Corps, exists to support the Marine Infantry Officer and his Marines on the ground. This methodology of young officer maturation allows us to recognize quickly and humbly that the opportunity before us is not self-serving, but a privilege to serve others. You learn real quick that it is not about you.

As Coach Herb Brooks shared rather poignantly with the 1980 USA Olympic hockey team during a grueling post-game skate, "You better think of something else, each and every one of you. When you pull on that jersey you represent yourself *and* every one of your teammates, and the name on the front is a hell of a lot more important than the one on the back!"[12]

Coach Brooks was referring to the large USA on the front of the team jersey. The players' last names were stitched on the back, like most of today's college and professional teams. One notable exception is the Army's West Point, which has "ARMY" in place of the players' names, which further exemplifies the team mindset.

In 1980 under Coach Herb Brooks' leadership, the USA Olympic hockey team faced the Russian Army's Olympic hockey team. That year, like most years, the Russian world hockey superpower was expected to win it all. Not so for 1980! That year the American team pulled off an unprecedented Olympic upset which to this day people call the "Miracle on Ice." For those who understand leadership in any area of life, this unlikely victory and the incredible leadership Herb Brooks provided is inspirational.

In my mind, Coach Herb Brooks represents the virtual Chesty Puller of athletic coaches. Lieutenant General Lewis "Chesty" Puller, every Marine's personal hero and role model, is the highest-decorated Marine in the Corps' history. He sharpened his warring skills as a young Marine engaging in combat operations in Haiti and Nicaragua and later served in both World War II and Korea. He is best known for leading the Marines of the First Marine Regiment into hell and back, landing in the port of Inchon,

South Korea in the Korean conflict of the 1950s.

As Chesty Puller did with his Marines, Coach Brooks knew how to break a handful of cocky college athletes down to parade rest and build them into something bigger than themselves. Chesty would have been proud. The extraordinary Olympic victory would never have been achieved without each team member fully embracing a particular role and responsibility. The Marine Corps OCS and TBS training processes execute with a very similar endgame in mind.

The goal is to train their young officers so they become something greater than they could be on their own. This training instills in each an understanding that the Corps' primary function is to win wars. And there is no question that this message sinks into the hearts and minds of eighteen, nineteen, and twenty-year-old Marine Privates and Lance Corporals in boots on the ground.

As officers, our responsibility is to excel in our given MOS, each of which is designed to support that young Marine rifleman. While this process is a humbling transition at the start, it ultimately instills a level of confidence that few other training programs or occupations do. You cannot leave Quantico without a deeply held belief in the Marine Corps' core values of honor, courage, and commitment. You also leave with a level of confidence and an air of invincibility that is not easily shaken. This character trait carries over into every other area of a Marine's life—truly a worthy asset in most circumstances. It can, however, present itself in unhealthy ways if unbalanced.

Those memories of training, esprit-de-corps, and pride had me bursting with confidence as my family and I continued to roll north. At that moment, I longed to experience once again the thrill of flight and to lead Marines. Reflecting on why I had joined and the fulfillment it brought, I pondered deeper emotions.

I was living my dream flying for the Corps, yet even more valuable to me was the privilege to have led Marines down in the "barn."

We affectionately referred to the hangar spaces where our aircraft were maintained as the barn. My two years in *Marine Fighter Attack Squadron One Fifteen (VMFA-115), the Silver Eagles, leading both the Airframes Division and the Quality Assurance Division Marines as their OIC (Officer In Charge) were the best of my active service.

Those Marines took care of me, and I took care of them. Those opportunities are often short-lived, only months to a year at a time in any one leadership billet. I was living for the day I could lead Marines like them again, fighting to go back to MCAS Beaufort.

You may have heard that the only people who are impressed by fighter pilots are children and other fighter pilots. That is somewhat true. But what absolutely holds true for all of us who like to fly upside down and push the limits of the laws of physics is that we are notorious for our intense level of confidence. This on occasion reaches an unhealthy level of overconfidence—a bravado—that gets us in trouble.

Without exception, every time I have put myself in harm's way in the air or on the ground in my professional or personal life and felt the backlash, I had allowed my overconfidence to take me to a place I should not have been. On this day as the Tromblys traveled up the interstate, the Marine fighter pilot in me found a boldness that had been mildly tempered having been benched for eight months, since 17 October 2000.

But today, driving past Quantico, my chest began to swell with the unhealthy bravado for which Marines are sometimes known. Remembering my proud days in Quantico training and preening with confidence that we as cancer Warriors were doing all we could do, I started brewing a perfect storm of overconfidence and invincibility in my soul that I had not felt in many months. My fighter pilot alter-ego was emboldened, and I decided to make an unannounced appearance at the Hematology-Oncology Department at Bethesda.

I was only a few exits down the interstate from making a very rash decision, based completely on misplaced confidence. I guess the positive energy of knowing I had a shrinking tumor and a great plan to remove my metal fillings in the coming days made me think that flying jets again might happen sooner rather than later. I had a fresh shave and a boldness that was daring me to take an unplanned exit.

As we hit the I-495 loop around D.C., I hit a literal fork in the road. We could go east toward Baltimore and New Jersey as planned, or we could go north and west toward Bethesda, Maryland. The sign must have said Bethesda, because I made a split-second decision, something I had been paid to do for years while flying at three to four hundred knots in the air.

But today, I was on the ground traveling at 70 mph. Without consulting my wife, I took that Bethesda exit. Employing a boldness that caught Megan off guard, I informed her, "We are going to make an unannounced visit to the Bethesda Oncology department." And we did, on a Friday afternoon without an appointment.

I was boastfully eager to let the Bethesda doctors know just how well I was doing on the all-natural program we had put together. But I had no idea the aerial battle the day held for me. Neither did my wife or children.

You know this is not going to turn out well already, don't you?

PART FIVE

THE FOG
OF WAR

"It is not the critic who counts; not the man who points out how the strong man stumbles, or where the doer of deeds could have done them better. The credit belongs to the man who is actually in the arena, whose face is marred by dust and sweat and blood; who strives valiantly; who errs, who comes short again and again, because there is no effort without error and shortcoming; but who does actually strive to do the deeds; who knows great enthusiasms, the great devotions; who spends himself in a worthy cause; who at the best knows in the end the triumph of high achievement, and who at the worst, if he fails, at least fails while daring greatly, so that his place shall never be with those cold and timid souls who neither know victory nor defeat."

— THEODORE ROOSEVELT
26th President of the United States of America

30| *Thirty Days from Certain Defeat*

SOMETIMES we look back at our bad decisions with regrets and wish we could go back and revisit that momentary lapse of reason to set in motion a different course. I admit making some of those decisions, as have all who are truly honest with themselves. Some may be minor regrets; some may be life-changing.

This may come as a surprise, but this incredibly poor decision to take the Bethesda exit on what would soon become the Darkest Day of our journey has since become a source of inspiration for me, my family, and for hundreds of families with whom Megan and I have shared our story.

A little over an hour after we traveled past Quantico, we parked our suburban in the National Naval Medical Center parking garage. We made our way down the familiar hallways toward the Hematology-Oncology department. I was bursting with overconfidence, eager to share the images from my most recent CT scan and get the well-deserved "Attaboy!" from Dr. Malcus, the leading oncology physician. He had been faithfully pursuing me with the greatest urgency for the past eight months via phone calls to come back north and start chemotherapy treatments.

Here we were—totally unannounced—for our first face-to-face contact with these doctors in months. To say that Dr. Malcus and his team were surprised to see us would be greatly understating the moment. Surprised is far too mild a word, considering the lightning-quick speed at which activities began to unfold. Remember, I had no scheduled appointment, and it was already afternoon on a Friday at a shore-based military facility.

My children were neatly tucked into a waiting area with a TV and coloring books and a window to the outside world. I was immediately escorted to another floor to visit with Navy Commander Perry, the oral surgeon, and let him inspect my jawbone from which the original tumor had been removed and the new tumor had since grown back and replaced. In the meantime, the oncologists were on a different floor looking at my scans with the radiologist. I briefly visited with the oral surgeon and then reported back to Dr. Malcus, who now had in tow two other senior officers, both doctors.

Megan and I walked down the hallway following these three doctors with our children still left alone in the waiting room. I overheard my doctor say to the other two, whom I did not recognize from our previous ten-day visit back in October, "I have looked at his scans, and they are impressive."

Looking over at Megan, who was holding our youngest daughter, Grace Anne, now just over one-year-old, I repeated the doctor's word with a raised brow and a near eruption of my brewing overconfidence, "IMPRESSIVE!" For those of you who have a medical background, you are probably already laughing at my naivety or swallowing hard knowing I am about to fly into the side of a mountain when the door closes behind me. Megan and I had no idea these doctors were about to perform a flanking maneuver on us that would knock us back on our heels.

When the evening news reports the catastrophic collision of an aircraft into the side of a mountain, you can rest assured that in most cases, the pilots never saw the mountain. Possibly it's obscured by cloud layers or smoke or volcanic ash. But under most circumstances, a mountain is a large enough obstacle for a pilot to see and fly around or over it. A cow in the middle of a field on a dark night is something altogether more difficult to avoid, and you will have to read my next book to learn more about that Texas-style cow-tipping exercise from my college days.

Most pilots fly into mountains they can't see. On my first deployment overseas, I flew a training mission supporting *U.S. Army Forward Air Controllers (FACs). The Army controller would call us in on a simulated target strike in his AOR (Area of Responsibility). This training mission had us simulating air-to-ground weapon releases on a weapons range at the base of Mount Fuji, Japan.

On one of my last bombing runs, the FAC on the other end of the radio called for an abort to the run and directed me to come off target and break left. Fortunately, it was a perfectly clear day, and just off to my left was the unmistakable shape of the immovable Mount Fuji. I chose to break right. Depending on the orientation of the FAC making the radio call, it may have appeared that I did indeed break to *his left*, but had I broken to *my left*, I would not be sharing this story today. In our profession, words are vitally important, and misunderstanding a radio transmission and making a wrong turn can be catastrophic.

I remember well the picture hanging in our fraternity house at LeTourneau University. It made an indelible impression on me as a young student pilot. The frame contained an image of a light fabric WWI-era military aircraft in which a pilot had crashed into a tree. The caption on the picture said,

> "Aviation in itself is not inherently dangerous, but to an even greater degree than the sea, it is terribly unforgiving of any carelessness, incapacity, or neglect."
> —ALFRED GILMER LAMPLUGH

It would have taken more than the FAC directing me to turn the wrong direction that day for me to actually fly into the mountain. However, had there been a few more distractions, such as poor visibility from smoke or clouds, or had I been excessively fatigued, it very easily could have been my last flight. I easily dodged the mountain that day, but the obstacle in my flight path I was about to encounter today was going to be far harder to maneuver around.

The day started with a clear sky and what seemed to be a clear path to victory after months of progress. But storm clouds were building, and the clarity of which path to take was about to reach Zero-Zero conditions. For the non-aviator, think blizzard. Zero-Zero means the cloud ceiling has dropped to ground level, and the visibility has deteriorated to almost nothing.

There is really no better picture of what was about to happen to us when that medical exam room door closed. It was like suddenly flying into blizzard conditions, and when looking up from my instruments, suddenly seeing the ground with only seconds before impact, realizing there was no avoiding the crash.

Megan and I were expecting to hear good news, only to be overwhelmed by the pressure of more bad news. The death sentence we were about to receive was delivered with such urgency that only one with an equally grave diagnosis of mere weeks to live could fully grasp the dynamics of the moment.

Megan at this point was once again along for another crazy ride birthed out of my overconfidence when viewing the exit sign for Bethesda. What an extremely abbreviated decision-making process!

As the door closed, the doctors invited us to sit down. Being that it was a Friday afternoon, they cut right to the chase.

"I have looked at your scans, and they are . . ." began Dr. Malcus. Wait for it . . . I knew he was going to say it—impressive. He finished his thought and there it was, "IMPRESSIVE!"

I was thinking I had won the first round, and soon I would be excitedly sharing exactly how we were fighting the good fight with ten pounds of carrots a day, periodic fasting with colonics, immune-boosting injectables, enzymes, pure water, and the rest of our holistic strategy. As with many a wrestling match, just when you think you have the upper hand, in a blink of an eye, you are face down on the mat with sweat and spit in your eye wondering how you got there. His next words rocked our world.

"We cannot explain exactly why your cancer has not spread throughout your body in the past eight months, but what we can tell you is that you are losing this battle."

Really? Couldn't he have taken a breath after the first portion of the statement and let me explain why it hadn't spread through my body? Nope. He didn't. He fired the next shot in rapid-fire succession without taking a breath, and all I could do was stand there and absorb the shots. Meanwhile, the other two senior officers sat quietly and soberly as if they were viewing a dying man.

Megan sat there holding Grace Anne in her arms and feeling helpless as the doctors spoke. Tears built and quietly, slowly rolled down her cheeks. She prayed as I prepared for the battle. She knew I was going to fight. Grace Anne slept through the entire meeting, a gift of slumber that God granted us, as she slept unaware of the "three versus one the hard way" dog fight that would soon rage once the doctor came up for air.

Dr. Malcus continued from his opening barrage of bad news straight for the kill. He explained that my timing couldn't be better showing up in Bethesda and that we needed to get started on chemo treatments immediately. It was Friday, and he was so emphatic that this needed to start immediately that he offered to come in *Saturday* morning so that we did not have to wait until Monday for my first treatment.

Without skipping a beat, Dr. Malcus further explained the sense of urgency in no uncertain terms by painting a word picture of what I could expect to happen in the next thirty days if I left this Bethesda office again and continued our trip north without doing chemo. He could not be sure which of the following would happen first, but he assured me of what was in my immediate future.

"Captain Trombly, you will either be blind in your right eye or lose your nose at best." He paused for effect and then dropped the hammer. "But my greatest fear is that your tumor, which we can see has already penetrated the sinus cavity — an empty void space — will quickly fill with cancer cells and rapidly penetrate your brain." He expounded and made it clear that if my lymphoma reached the brain, my chances of survival diminished greatly.

Immediately my first rebuttal came to mind as I wanted to remind him that they were the ones who showed me data of only fifty other individuals with this type of cancer, none of whom had reached five years of remission. Time and time again I wanted to interrupt his barrage of bad news and cite the definitive zero percent chance of survival based on the results of their very own studies which they had provided the previous October. But I have learned over the years to temper my Bostonian sarcasm. Maybe a sign of maturity, or maybe I had just been away from my northern roots too long.

Dr. Malcus stressed that the tumor was much bigger in my most recent scan from a few weeks back than appeared on the February scan. It was February when I felt the bump in my jaw and believed my tumor had started growing back, and Dr. Ostergaard had ordered that CT in Pensacola. It had grown back during the three months after removing the first tumor at the dental clinic on Parris Island back in October. The aggressive cancer had continued its assault during those first few months Megan and I spent researching all our options.

As with any aerial engagement, the battles are fierce and quick. If you spend too long engaged with any one fighter, his friends will eventually join the fight, and you are going to face certain defeat. I may have looked outnumbered three to one, but Megan was praying and had my back as Grace Anne slept on. At worst, the odds were now three against two. Yet inspired again by seeing my Grace Anne in her mother's arms and knowing God had placed us on our path toward recovery I believed they were now outgunned! My decision to engage late on a Friday may have been ill-conceived, but our decision to continue fighting this cancer naturally most certainly was not. We had the knowledge to repel this malicious assault.

31| *The Darkest Day*

THERE was a brief silence as Dr. Malcus paused, and this was my moment. The office we were in resembled a briefing space, not unlike the place in my old squadron where we would discuss the mission prior to the flight and then debrief upon our return. I had been flying fighters for over three years and had been present for many excellently executed briefs. The mission commander or flight lead would take control of the briefing. This individual owned the room.

I knew what I had to do. There was a whiteboard in the room, and to my profound joy, my weapon of choice, a dry erase marker, rested on the ledge. I cleared a space on their board, with permission of course, and began to draw a graph to represent a timeline on the Y-axis, and the tumor's mass on the X-axis.

I began to draw this out with the precision of a seasoned WTI (Weapons Tactics Instructor) debriefing a recently completed ACM (Air Combat Maneuvering) also known as a BFM (Basic Fighter Maneuvering) training flight.

Basic Fighter Maneuvering is when we fly out and fight our fellow squadron mates one on one, "Mano a Mano." This adversary-for-the-day is usually one of your best friends, the guy whom you will trust with your life and who will entrust you with his when you fight a real enemy with real bullets and real missiles in a real aerial combat encounter.

To hone our skills, we do this type of training high above the ocean off the coast of the Carolinas in a military working area free of airline traffic. The loser frequently had to buy the winner a Coke and Snickers bars in order to refuel while in the debrief. Each engagement lasts only a matter of seconds, and then we do it again. Once in a while, the engagement may last up to a minute or two if we fight our way all the way down to the hard deck in a stalemate.

Had this session been an actual flight debriefing, the blue marker would have represented me, and the red marker would have represented the opposing aircraft. The lines drawn would have meticulously accounted for every turn and twisting climb and descent, each noted with Jedi accuracy along with a precisely detailed description of when and where every weapon shot was taken. Of course, I would have rather been debriefing an ACM training hop, but that was not my mission today.

I was now using my briefing/debriefing skills to reconstruct the past eight months of tumor activity. I specifically focused on the past four months from my February scan, when I had felt the tumor start re-growing, through the May scan which the doctors were calling impressive.

The whiteboard activity would have made my former squadron mates proud! Unfortunately, I only had one color marker. In the hands of a lesser pilot, that limitation could have been a problem, but I made do. On the left was a circle the size of a dime (obviously not to scale) representing the first scan in February. On the right further down the timeline was another circle the size of a quarter, representing the scan in May. I drew a straight line without a ruler, a skill developed building briefing boards for years of pilot training. It came to serve me well on this day.

As I prepared to deliver my best argument, I figured I would start with an easy victory, something we could all agree on. "Gentlemen, I may not be the smartest person in the room. I am certainly not a doctor, just a knuckle-dragging Marine fighter pilot. But I do know this to be true: two points do not determine a trend. Three points would be required to depict a trajectory definitively and accurately. Your argument is based on insufficient evidence for me to abort my current battle plan."

Thank God I actually passed advanced math in college. Finally, those hours spent plotting points and building graphs paid off.

"Gentlemen, I am fully aware that the tumor got bigger during the time-lapse from Point A to Point B, as is my doctor at NAS Pensacola. After all, he checks it every month, and I feel it every single day, multiple times a day. The scan yet to be taken will show it is now shrinking. I know it's shrinking. It started shrinking seven weeks after we instituted our natural battle plan after moving to Pensacola."

Trust me, it was many years after my cancer was gone that I finally stopped running my right index finger up and over my right jawbone to feel for the tumor's advance, subsequent retreat, and in the later years, to periodically ensure that it was not coming back. (Can you guess what I am about to do after I finish typing this sentence? Yep, exactly. And I am happy to report that there is nothing there today, either.)

During that year-long battle, I felt the tumor multiple times a day with my finger, and I ran my tongue over it, constantly checking the size and waiting for it to shrink with the patience of a cook watching a pot of water waiting for it to boil. I *knew* it was smaller and that it had started shrinking seven weeks after moving to Pensacola and instituting our natural battle plan. Unfortunately, without a third scan, I could not prove my argument any more than they could prove theirs. Unable to launch a winning missile shot in this argument, the best I could hope for was to last long enough to force a stalemate down on the deck.

The Bethesda doctors had a counter-argument, of course. As with any epic battle, there has to be some give and take, some glancing blows and direct hits. The briefing room filled with heated arguments going back and forth and neither side giving any ground. It was getting bloody.

I had defended with sound logic and was turning the corner for an offensive strike, but they hit me with an unexpected shot.

"Your tumor is not shrinking, Captain. It is just moving."

I gave up some ground when I didn't respond immediately. I didn't dare look at Megan. I had to maintain this valiant posture. I could not let Megan or the doctors know that the latest shot had landed right on target. I was stunned. I had already given up ground by not responding, and to have shown any emotion or to have flinched would have meant certain defeat under those conditions. Defeat not just in front of the doctors but defeat in my own confidence in our battle plan and in all we had done and were planning to do. Rattled but not defeated, my mind raced.

The doctors pulled hard on the controls and stole the angles I had given up as I relaxed my pull and eased up ever so briefly to gather my senses. They were coming around on my six, and I felt the searing impact of the next well-placed shot, "You can't feel the backside of the tumor. It is sliding into your sinus cavity so you only *think* it is shrinking."

Despite having no evidence to support this point without another scan, they planted the seeds that now had me doubting the past few months of effort. I was once again defensive but was quickly coming to my senses. After popping chaff and flares, the standard countermeasures when shot at by either a radar-guided or heat signature seeking missile, I was back on the offensive.

"OK, you could be right." I started in an attempt to lure them in closer and get them to ease up on their offensive measures. Then continuing, I found a way to neutralize the fight.

"Respectfully, Gentlemen, we won't know without a third scan.

I am willing to return in thirty days and take that scan, and if the image shows a downward trend..." Once again at the whiteboard with the dry erase marker, I drew a precise arcing swipe connecting not two, but now three circles in a downward, parabolic arcing motion.

I finished my thought " . . . then I continue on my faith walk. I continue to do what is working. However, if the tumor is larger . . ." I did not draw this circle to connect dots indicating a losing position at this point. It was my whiteboard and my marker, and I was certainly not about to depict my own demise, even on a two-dimensional graph. Just as there was power in words, I believed there to be power in images, and I would not draw my own defeat.

I gave the doctors as small a concession as I was willing, not sure I believed what I was saying. I felt that I had to give them something to consider while I maneuvered into a better position to launch my next shot and force them back from their posture of relentless engagement. I said, ". . . then we consider 'breaking glass in case of emergency.' At that point, maybe I would start the chemo, as we would finally have definitive evidence from the third scan that my plan is not working."

My efforts to fight for neutral footing in the fight appeared to be working. At least the doctors were not interrupting, and I continued to pull hard, gaining more angles to balance the fight. I did not wait for them to counter and fired my final two shots downrange.

"Gentlemen, when we started this briefing, you said you were surprised that my cancer had not spread throughout my body. In fact, after eight months we are well downrange of the two-year timeline to certain death you predicted when we left Bethesda. Your urgent argument to persuade me to start chemo the first week I was diagnosed has not demonstrated itself to be accurate."

I believed I had more than made up for lost angles and continued my offensive to launch my final missile.

"All that we have been doing with colonics, raw diet, and immune support has not only prevented cancer from spreading, but it's currently shrinking the single tumor in my jaw."

The bravado-filled doctors did not buy my perspective. That was OK. I was confident I had made my best argument. As a pilot I could only consider what I had to work with and, in the end, assess if I had executed my best fight and stood my ground. Yes, I had. I used what logic I had available to me, but of greater value was the unquestionable fact that I had lived with that tumor every single day, feeling it change size over the past five months. I knew beyond a shadow of a doubt that it had grown bigger after February's scan, but I also *knew* that now it was getting smaller.

The doctors, too, were holding on to their position that I was delusional and that in 30 days I would have passed the point of no return. One of us was right, and three of us were wrong. Only time would be able to prove this truth, and it was a risky gamble—a life and death game of chicken with the malignant tumor in my skull.

The battle of wills had raged for longer than a standard BFM set. I had come into this engagement looking for an easy win. Instead, I found myself out of maneuvers, out of emotional fuel, and neutralized on the deck in a two-circle flow cross circle from my opponent. We were just chasing each other's tails with whatever final shots and jabs we chose to unload, realizing neither side would concede or give ground. The time had come to key the mic and call "TERMINATE," disengaging from the fight.

The doctors strongly encouraged me to get a hotel room and connect with them first thing in the morning. Megan and I left the office, thanking them for their time on a busy Friday afternoon. We assured them we would get back to them with our decision.

I would never see any of those doctors again. I was pretty confident they never expected to see this Marine again either, but due to a much different outcome than we would experience.

Bad news which you expect to receive is bad news. Bad news whether true or false when expecting better news brings a deeper level of despair in an already desperate place.

I can honestly tell you that for those few minutes I was arguing our case with the doctors, I came alive! I was back. I was fighting, engaged in a meaningful fight for my life. The stakes were high, and I understood them completely.

Then, having fought my best, I retreated—not with words but in my mind. I found despair and doubt creeping in as the "what ifs" began to nag at me on the long, silent walk to the parking garage. This, my friend, was the lowest point of our valley. It was our darkest day.

"A cheerful heart is good medicine,
but a crushed spirit dries up the bones."
—PROVERBS 17:22 (NIV)

32| *Read You Loud and Clear*

I had climbed into a phone booth for a knife fight with one opponent who brought two friends, and I knew I would walk out bloody. Though I remained convinced I would emerge the victor, this encounter felt like anything but a win. Having stood my ground and not bought into the high-pressure pitch to start chemo first thing Saturday morning, I was emotionally and physically exhausted.

I may have appeared to have won a victory; I meant for my posture and words to give Megan and the doctors that impression. However, we had a long, lonely walk to the car ahead of us where my mind would walk through every turn and twist of the entire engagement a half dozen more times. Questions began to mount.

The enemy was creeping in again with doubt, the only weapon that still could bludgeon me if left unchecked.

We stepped out of the office and walked down the hallway to the waiting room. The lights and TV were off. No adult supervision in sight. Alex, Brianna, and Brad were sitting there with nothing but the light from the window illuminating the room, surrounded by guardian angels, no doubt, at least the ones that were not busy acting as my wingmen down the hall.

The children were no worse for the wear and just picked up their gear and stepped out into the hallway with us. We loaded up Grace Anne, who was still sleeping in the double stroller. But our children, like most, were intuitive; they just knew. Where I would expect banter and conversation about what had happened while their mom and I were in the office or frantic pleas from one who had to use the bathroom or was hungry or thirsty, there was no interaction. Instead, we all walked in absolute silence. Not a word was spoken between them and Megan and me. The children just walked quietly by our side down the empty hallways out into the parking garage.

What happened next, I am convinced, saved my life.

My mind was working overtime, and only God knew what doubts and anxieties were now running through Megan's mind. The two of us had arrived hours earlier with a sense of confidence and hope. We were sure of our path and confident we were winning and executing our plan with precision. Now because I had made a rash decision to show the conventional doctors our "impressive" progress, we were leaving in absolute shock at the words we had heard. With the Marine Corps Hymn echoing through my mind, as it always had whenever passing exits 148 and 150 for Quantico on Interstate 95 in Virginia, we proudly passed by Quantico, oblivious to how our confidence would soon be tested.

I could never have imagined that today was the day we would

experience the deepest, darkest recesses of the valley we were to walk. What if those doctors were right? What if in thirty days, I was beyond saving with conventional options? What if... THEN GOD!!

We made it to the parking lot, and six-year-old Brianna hopped right into the Suburban as Megan got Brad and Grace Anne situated in car seats. It was as if these young children understood the gravity of the moment and dutifully slid into their seatbelts and car seats without complaint. Alex, our oldest, helped me load the double stroller into the back before entering the vehicle and taking his seat directly behind the driver's seat.

Alex finally broke the deafening silence by sharing that while we were in the doctor's office, Brianna and Brad had been coloring, and he was reading his Bible. Alex had a children's Bible with lots of pictures, as you would expect an eight-year-old to have.

He said, "Dad there are lots of cool verses in the Bible, a lot of cool verses, but I circled this one. Proverbs 19:2 says 'enthusiasm without knowledge is not good. If you rush to make a decision you could make a mistake'" (Expanded Bible).

I looked across the cab of the truck, and Megan was staring at me as if to say with her eyes, "Did that just happen? Did our firstborn, our eight-year-old, strong-willed child *read* for almost an hour, and then *recite from memory* Proverbs 19:2?"

It was not lost on Megan and me that the energy level in the meeting was high. There was an "enthusiasm" about our arrival when the doctors saw us. And even more poignant was the high-pressure sales pitch to "start chemo before it is too late" that we were certainly not the first in such a position to receive. How many others had been told by the doctors that they would come in on a Saturday to start chemotherapy? Equally true was that the doctors who were so enthusiastically making this pitch had no *knowledge* of the alternative battle plan we were executing, nor what doors God had opened or was yet to open for us.

Sometimes the visit to the lowest point in the valley can last for a season, months, or even years. Other times the deepest darkest hours are just that, hours or days. This dark chapter ends with an exclamation point: A declarative sentence shared by an eight-year-old homeschooling boy who had struggled to learn to read and fought his mother on it every day for the previous three years! A verse of Scripture that was so clear-cut and dry and so applicable to the events of the day, though written thousands of years before, now ministered to our spirits, lifting them with an exclamation point!

> "Desire without knowledge is not good—
> how much more will hasty feet miss the way!"
> —Proverbs 19:2 (NIV)

God showed up in a very personal way for the third time in our battle to speak life into Megan and me. This time God spoke through Alex! Immediately, God's Spirit refreshed our spirits, assuring us that we were absolutely on the right path. The wisdom of Proverbs on the lips of our own son had dropped on us like a lead weight. Only minutes after enduring the hardest conversation on the absolute darkest day of our entire cancer battle, we were enveloped in a personal encounter with the God of the universe! God spoke, and we heard His voice through the tender heart of our son.

While we were engaged with the doctors, Alex was attentive to God's leading and then had the boldness to share the Scripture he read with us. My eight-year-old boy was my Wingman that day! He had the instincts of a fighter pilot at eight years old, and he fired a Scriptural truth with the precision of a laser-guided missile aimed by the Holy Spirit straight into my soul with Proverbs 19:2.

Alex, as our oldest, was the first child Megan attempted to homeschool. He was a strong-willed, type A personality. Stubborn did not begin to describe it. But there was more to the challenges Megan and Alex daily wrestled. Alex didn't so much choose not to learn to read, he struggled to learn and therefore rejected the process.

Megan had taken him to speech therapists and sought assistance. Feedback from professionals was that Alex had a learning challenge and would struggle with reading and academics throughout his childhood. As parents, we refused to accept such a prediction, but we could not argue with his apparent inability to read.

On this specific day, God performed a miracle, and the blinders came off as Alex read prolifically through his children's version of the Bible while we battled it out down the hall. The miracle of Alex reading that afternoon coupled with the pinpoint accuracy of the message God delivered through him that evening made my apparent rash decision to jump into the fray with Bethesda more than just a shortsighted, overconfident effort on my part. This tumultuous day proved to be a God-ordained, divine appointment. God miraculously used Alex to speak life over our family, something God had been preparing well before I saw the exit sign for Bethesda.

That supreme God-moment picked us up and allowed us to continue on our Faith Walk. God's Word strengthened us, giving us the courage not to give up on all that He had provided, not to turn back on all that He had prepared for us to accomplish.

I had rushed my decision to take an exit ramp earlier that afternoon. Megan and I confidently decided that taking a second exit ramp off the nutritional and natural path God had shown us would indeed be a mistake of its own. As you might have guessed, we did not go back on Saturday for chemotherapy.

God grabbed our hands on that profoundly dark day and kept us from turning onto an off-ramp, an exit that outside influences desperately argued for us to take. Instead, we absolutely needed to stay the course.

I believe God will guide you that way, too. Regardless of which Faith Walk God may have you take, if you are willing to "Dwell in the Shelter of the Most High" as we learned in Chapter 21, God will hold your hands. Remember Chaps' bookmark, my favorite passage of scripture, Psalm 91? Trust your Abba Father, friend, and never lose hope in His plan for you!

Trombly family picture on Boston trip to remove David's metal fillings with David at nearly his lowest weight of the cancer battle, having lost significant muscle mass and carrying little body fat (Left to right: David, Bradly, Megan, Grace Anne, Alex, and Brianna)

33 | EMCON

WE arrived at a hotel close to the National Naval Medical Center and grabbed a pizza to feed the children. Megan and I needed to call Dr. Schildwaechter to share with him our new concerns. As soon as the children were situated, we made the call.

"Dr. Schildwaechter, David and Megan Trombly here. We are in Bethesda for the evening and have a critical update. We also desperately need to ask you some questions. Do you have a few minutes to talk?"

We unpacked our entire discussion with the Bethesda doctors for close to thirty minutes over the phone with Dr. Schildwaechter. As he lived not too far from Washington D.C., he offered to meet us personally the next morning at McDonald's near the hospital to look at my CT scan himself before we drove to Boston. At sunrise, we packed the Suburban and checked out of the hotel before rendezvousing with Dr. Schildwaechter.

Our conversation with Dr. Schildwaechter reinforced what we already felt in our hearts: to follow God's audible encouragement to us through Alex "not to rush to a decision." By the end of our McDonald's rendezvous, we all believed that by turning down the chemo in October, we had effectively dodged a deadly warhead. To stop mid-course, retreating from our current Faith Walk out of fear on our part and lack of knowledge on Bethesda's part, would be catastrophic. Megan and I thanked Dr. Schildwaechter for his time to meet with us, grateful to finally hug this man who had been so instrumental in developing our natural battle plan. Dr. S. was a large man, and as he embraced us farewell, the love and sincerity of his heart and his mission enveloped us.

Late that evening, our family arrived at Sarah's and Bob's on the south side of Boston for our few weeks of vacation and my dental work. Eerily, something was oddly different after experiencing that nightmare with the Bethesda doctors and miraculously hearing God's voice from Proverbs on our darkest day.

Megan and I drove north with our confidence restored, thanks to God's intervention through Alex and Dr. Schildwaechter's wise counsel, reassured in our war plan's authenticity. We were still doing everything we had been doing with the juicing and the supplements. We maintained our daily programs and spent time praying and seeking God's wisdom daily as we had been, but something *felt* different. Something was definitely different, and we could not quite explain it to each other or anyone else. It was a mystery.

Despite God speaking loud and clear just days earlier when Megan and I were battle-worn and at the end of our rope—we now heard nothing. We felt nothing for days. We were both concerned, and I told Megan, "It feels like my prayers are bouncing off the ceiling and falling to the floor. Why isn't God leading? How are we to know the next step in this fight? Megan, it feels like we are in a spiritual EMCON!"

EMCON, Emissions Control or radio silence, is a status in which all fixed or mobile radio stations in an area are ordered to stop transmitting for reasons of safety or security. It is used in both training and combat environments to ensure the enemy cannot triangulate the signal source of a military unit or ship at sea. These EMCON procedures serve a purpose. For the military, it allows for force protection from a defensive perspective. As an offensive consideration, it allows for the element of surprise. Even a single cell phone on a ship at sea or a ground unit in the field can give away a tactical advantage at best or make a ship an easy target at worst.

Megan was experiencing the same disconnection. We talked about it. We prayed. We theorized. We asked God where He was and what He was doing. But nothing. We both engaged in some serious introspection and self-examination together and individually as we sought to determine if something of our own doing or some lack of obedience was blocking us spiritually. There was nothing. Though our faith was still strong, we felt shaken in a quietness that we had never before experienced.

During this emotional drought, this challenging place where we wondered where God was, we pressed on in faith doing what God had shown us thus far while we waited for what He was going to show us next. We had no contradictory orders to alter our flight path. We had a pretty clear course of action, and we planned to stick to it until we knew definitively we were supposed to alter course.

God had suddenly shown up in an incredibly personal and miraculous manner in that parking garage. But just as unexpectedly, He didn't seem to be leading. He didn't seem to be present. We weren't feeling His presence, only battling the fiery arrows of doubt.

A MOMENT
WITH MEGAN

This time was EMCON for me, too. I was overtired and overwhelmed, reeling with a roller coaster of emotions. God had just walked us through a very discouraging time at Bethesda. I felt relief when Alex spoke those life-giving words yet absolutely wrung out from overthinking and enduring the daily weight of waiting, not knowing, and longing to follow the Lord's leading.

The incredible uncertainty got to me, like when you want to know how the book ends, but you're only 30 pages into a 500-page book, and you can't look ahead. No definitive answer is hard, but no answer at all when we needed to know our next step was nearly paralyzing. I thought about growing up learning Bible verses and hymns but questioning why we needed to memorize them all. A teacher once said that those memory gems were for times when you didn't feel God there, and you just had to KNOW He was. This was that time for me.

Worship through music has been my strongest connection with God throughout my spiritual journey. The contemporary worship song, "Cornerstone" by Hillsong so vividly depicts this inability to see God in a dark place. The songwriter not only described the darkness in which we'd felt cloaked these weeks of spiritual EM-CON, but they also revealed the answer to what to do in this darkness. "Rest on His unchanging grace." God had not changed. His orders to step out on this Faith Walk had not been rescinded. With or without a *feeling* of His presence, we had to persist. We had to trust. We had to stay the course.

> "When darkness seems to hide His face, I rest on His unchanging grace. In every high and stormy gale,
> my anchor holds within the veil."
> —"CORNERSTONE" BY HILLSONG

The words of this song are so well written. "When darkness seems to hide His face..." "Seems" does not mean that something really is, but rather gives the impression or sensation that something is happening. The songwriter is driving home the point that God is not absent even when we sense that He is. Lyrics authors Edward Mote and Andrew Ehrenzeller provide a Scriptural directive to employ during EMCON: Rest, holding fast to our faith and remembering His unchanging grace. God is perfect and His promises cannot be broken. We can trust His faithfulness! Looking back and remembering His previous work in our lives assures us He will not fail us now despite what "seems" to be our present reality. Paul speaks to the promise of this very truth with joy and confidence even while writing from his prison cell.

> "Being confident of this, that he who began a good work in you will carry it on to completion until the day of Christ Jesus."
> —PHILIPPIANS 1:6 (NIV)

I remember from my childhood a great hymn of the faith, "My Anchor Holds" by William Martin, written in 1902. It also speaks to experiencing this darkness. Its lyrics encourage us that regardless of the storm or our inability to see God in the moment, He remains our anchor. He is still there and we can trust His silent moments.

> "Though the angry surges roll on my tempest-driven soul,
> I am peaceful, for I know, wildly though the winds may blow,
> I've an anchor safe and sure, that can evermore endure.

> *REFRAIN:*
> And it holds, my anchor holds: Blow your wildest, then, O gale,
> On my bark so small and frail; By His grace I shall not fail,
> For my anchor holds, my anchor holds.

> Troubles almost 'whelm the soul; griefs like billows o'er me roll;
> Tempters seek to lure astray; storms obscure the light of day:
> But in Christ I can be bold, I've an anchor that shall hold."
> —"MY ANCHOR HOLDS" by WILLIAM MARTIN

I have long since studied the Scriptures and sought out counsel to determine why God allows for this silence, this period of EMCON. I give credit to years of preaching and instruction from my pastor, Dr. Ted Traylor, for the following insights. I hope they enlighten and encourage you when you endure EMCON, maybe even at this very moment.

God's silence is not always a bad thing. It is real; it is biblical; it is common; and it has a purpose. Even the Old Testament Prophet Habakkuk, God's emissary, records his own experience of just such a period of silence.

> "How long, Lord, must I call for help, but you do not listen?
> Or cry out to you, 'Violence!' but you do not save?"
> —HABAKKUK 1:2 (NIV)

God's answer to Habakkuk was to wait: wait and see God do the unbelievable.

> "Look at the nations and watch—and be utterly amazed.
> For I am going to do something in your days that you would not
> believe, even if you were told."
> —HABAKKUK 1:5 (NIV)

In the silence, Megan and I had Scripture to turn to. Just as the words of these two great worship songs brought comfort and a reminder of God's faithfulness, Jesus set an example for us Himself quoting Psalms more than any other Scripture. Reading Psalm 91 daily reminded us of His promise for us, a habit we engaged from day one in the valley. Leaning into verses one and two gave direction during this dark period.

> "Whoever dwells in the shelter of the Most High
> will rest in the shadow of the Almighty.
> I will say of the Lord, "He is my refuge and my fortress,
> my God, in whom I trust."
> —PSALM 91: 1-2 (NIV)

To dwell in the shelter of the Most High invites all of us to savor our relationship with Christ. This offers so much more than just an initial conversion experience with Jesus. God wants us to mature in our faith and fearlessly walk in the dark.

Megan and I had to resist making ourselves the center of the problem or focusing on our discomfort and anxieties. Rather, we had to let go of the fear and completely put ourselves in the Lord's hands, allowing Him to be our refuge and our God, the One in whom we could and did trust.

Pastor Traylor shared in a recent sermon, "It is not just the rainbow after the rain that demonstrates God's faithfulness but also the stars in the dark of night." His point?

When the storm is over we can easily recognize God's hand in the successful resolution as the rainbow that fills the sky is unmistakable. However, in the darkness of night, we have to look up, not inward, to see the stars.

The timing and duration of this dark period wears on one's soul. But impeccable timing is one of God's hallmarks, as well as one of the hallmarks of an effective warrior. As a fighter pilot, my fellow air warriors and I must execute our mission with extreme planning and precision, being only one small component of a larger strike package. If we arrive too soon and enter the target area early, we may be struck by shrapnel from friendly exploding ordnance of our own pre-planned artillery barrage, specifically designed to force the enemy to take cover from the incoming shells and mortars, thereby providing protection for our airborne assault.

The timing error of just a few seconds too early means we can essentially shoot ourselves down. If we are a few seconds too late, the enemy is back on their feet and ready to engage us, increasing the risk of failure. One error can lead to us being shot down, or much worse, result in our Marines on the ground perishing because we failed to provide life-saving support.

Unlike a warrior off his timeline, God is always on time and on target. We just have to get used to the reality that it is all God's timing and not ours. God doesn't always lead us to the safest route forward but to the one where we will grow the most. Our Heavenly Father blesses us through answered prayers. This includes when His wise answers are not what we wanted to hear—even when we can't seem to hear the answers.

When God appears to have ordered an EMCON exercise for you, don't doubt Him. Trust Him. He is there, preparing the way for you, growing your faith. Stay the course He has set for you! Then don't be surprised when God suddenly ends your period of EM-

CON.

God broke our EMCON with a phone call from Switzerland! In a moment, we had two-way communications restored!

34 | *Two-Way Communications Restored*

TWO weeks into our Boston trip, we were still praying, yet EMCON remained. We had begun to feel that God wasn't hearing. Then, Dr. Liao to whom I had come for removal of my metal fillings began discussing his friend, Dr. Flechten. This US physician had moved to Switzerland to work at the Paracelsus Klinik, a biological medicine clinic.

After Dr. Liao had me take a significant amount of chlorella tablets to absorb any mercury flakes that I might accidentally swallow, he got busy removing all my metal fillings. He was ambitiously working all four quadrants in one day; so I was completely numbed with plenty of Novocaine. Over the next couple of hours, all my amalgam fillings were removed and replaced with composites.

When finished, Dr. Liao removed what appeared to be some kind of a spacesuit and respirator he wore to protect himself from the mercury vapors. Obviously, he had been doing all the talking and had been describing his friend's naturopathic work in the Switzerland clinic. Forgetting that I couldn't really talk at the moment, Dr. Liao decided to put me on the phone with Dr. Flechten. Really, I just needed to listen.

Dr. Flechten began scientifically describing many of the different treatments the clinic staff were effectively using. He carefully explained that none of them were designed to fight cancer but rather to strengthen the immune system. The goal was to strengthen the body's own battalion of fighting mechanisms, mobilizing the whole body to fight cancer the way it was designed to do. I was intrigued, and though I had many questions, all I could do was grunt and nod at Dr. Liao. Dr. Flechten conveyed that though there was a three to a four-month waiting list to get into the clinic, I should still fill out an application to put me in the queue.

Megan and I added the Swiss Klinik to our prayers, the prayers that in our minds still seemed to be stacking up on the floor going nowhere. More days went by. More prayer. Still no answer. Where was God? Megan and I revisited the same conversation and rehearsed our unanswered prayer, "Lord what would You have us to do next? We have done everything You have shown us. Is there a next step, or do we stand fast in all we have done thus far?" Over and over during this EMCON stage, we pressed the Lord to open the next door while keeping the faith. But it was getting harder.

Maybe you are experiencing a similar season of extended EMCON period, and you know exactly how we felt. The silence becomes deafening as you wait for further orders. How long will the eerie quiet last? Where is the enemy now? When will the General call the reinforcements in? EMCON is unnerving. You feel like you absolutely HAVE to do SOMETHING! Does headquarters still remember you are out here in no-man's-land just waiting to be captured or killed by the enemy? Then....

The phone rang at my parent's house early one morning. I was there alone as Megan had left to visit her parents. When I answered, it was Dr. Flechten from Switzerland!

"Hello, this is David."

"Hello, David. This is Dr. Flechten from Paracelsus."

"Sir! Great to hear from you!"

"I am calling with an opportunity. We just had a cancellation, and there is a full thirty-day window of treatments available to you if you want it. I'm calling you first as a favor to Dr. Liao."

"Thank you, Sir! And when is the opening?"

"You have to arrive in ten days if you want to take advantage of this opening."

"Sir, may I call my wife, Megan, and call you right back?"

"Absolutely, David, I'm here for a couple more hours."

I wasted no time as my fingers started dialing Megan at her sister's house, pulling her away from her visit with her parents.

"Megan, I just got a phone call from Dr. Flechten in Switzerland at the Klinik. If I can be there in ten days, they will take me for a month. I told him I needed to call you and discuss this first before making any commitment."

"Honey, that is amazing! It's, . . . well, it's a miracle!"

"I know. Do you think we need to pray about this? It's a huge decision."

Megan boldly and confidently responded. "David, we don't need to pray over this. God just answered our prayers. David, this is the answer. Go for it!"

In complete agreement with my wife, I told her I loved her, hung up, and called Dr. Flechten back immediately to accept the vacated spot.

Megan and I had been through a tough few weeks of wondering what God was doing. He had stood silent since His very profound manifestation in the Bethesda parking garage when Alex dropped the Proverbs 19:2 lifeline in our lap.

We did not understand God's EMCON procedures or purposes then or for years to come. Why would God be silent for so long? Relatively speaking, three weeks is not a long time. But under EMCON conditions, it seems like an eternity! We had felt His presence so clearly in the past, but during this extended darkness, feeling separated from Him was hard.

Megan and I never stopped praying. EMCON or not, we prayed and maintained our course. Because we did, it was easy to recognize God when He spoke again. As this miraculous Switzerland-answer appeared, we knew it was from God! Knowing that

God was once again clearly marking the path before us enabled us to confidently step out of the boat and walk on water, like Peter did with Jesus. It was incredibly reviving to feel He was with us once again. But the truth is that God never left us. We just didn't understand how He was working all things out for our good, growing us in our Faith Walk with Him.

> "And we know that in all things God works for the good of those who love him, who have been called according to his purpose."
> —ROMANS 8:28 (NIV)

This period of strengthening our faith was metaphorical. Our ability to walk in faith during the early months of our cancer battle paralleled the storm the disciples were riding out on the Sea of Galilee. It was dark, scary, and treacherous, yet they could reach over and touch the Lord's shoulder, wake Him, and ask for their miracle. He immediately directed the storm to be still. Like in our early months of this cancer War, the disciples saw the Lord and knew He was there and able to deliver them. Similarly, God's presence filled our hearts, our home, and our conversation. Every decision He anointed with peace, or we moved in another direction.

But when Jesus sent the disciples out on the Sea of Galilee alone while he stayed back onshore, that was an example of EMCON! Right in the middle of the storm, at the darkest point when they thought they were going to die, the disciples believed that they were alone, and total fear gripped them. Remember: *Jesus knew* a storm was coming and sent them anyway!

Suddenly, Jesus showed up walking on the water, affording them an opportunity to focus on their fear or focus on Him. Granted, they had never seen Jesus walk on water, but they weren't looking for Him, either. They were totally engulfed in their own terror. Then Peter recognized Jesus and called out to Him. Jesus' disciple Matthew recorded the story:

"'Lord, if it's you,' Peter replied, 'tell me to come to you on the water.' 'Come,' he said. Then Peter got down out of the boat, walked on the water and came toward Jesus. But when he saw the wind, he was afraid and, beginning to sink, cried out, 'Lord, save me!' Immediately Jesus reached out his hand and caught him. 'You of little faith,' he said, 'why did you doubt?' And when they climbed into the boat, the wind died down. Then those who were in the boat worshiped him, saying, 'Truly you are the Son of God.'"
—Matthew 14:28-33 (NIV)

Peter exercised his faith and walked on water while his eyes were fixed on Jesus. But when he took his eyes off Jesus and focused on the waves, Peter started to sink. What did Jesus say to him? Jesus asked him why he didn't *trust Him*. Convicting, isn't it?

During our weeks of EMCON, we endeavored to keep our eyes on Jesus or at least on all we knew He had been doing for us even when His face seemed hidden. We *chose* to remember the promise we had received that first day when I received my diagnosis. It was all we could do to keep from sinking into the deep.

Years later, we learned what happened in this quiet period when God went EMCON. God was preparing the way for us and strengthening our faith. Megan and I look back now and are grateful we walked through that dark period faithfully *hand in hand*. It was a period of growth for both of us together, synergistically. God was growing us closer together and closer to Him preparing us for ministry opportunities to come.

The lesson of EMCON is to trust in what God has already done when you can't see Him at the moment. There is *NEVER* anytime our Father leaves us! He does, however, sometimes ask us to wait, maintaining our worship, prayer, and actions with *child-like faith*. Then when the EMCON ends, you know it and are ready to move forward with clear directions from Him. Your environment may change; your *feelings* certainly will change. But God never changes,

295

and your mission with Him doesn't have to either.

Part Six
European Theater

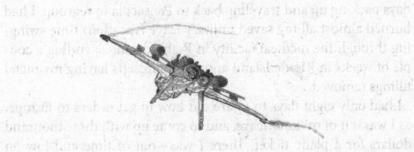

"Always bear in mind that your own resolution to succeed
is more important than any one thing."

—Abraham Lincoln,
16th President of the United States of America

35| *A New Set of Orders*

Our family now had a ten-day deadline for me to turn right back around and depart for Switzerland. We had already burned two days packing up and traveling back to Pensacola to regroup. I had burned almost all my saved military leave (vacation) time swinging through the medical facility in Bethesda and spending a couple of weeks in Rhode Island and Massachusetts having my metal fillings removed.

I had only eight days to figure out how to get orders to Europe, as I was out of military leave, and to come up with three thousand dollars for a plane ticket. There I was—out of time and low on money. That was right where God wanted me.

I went into work first thing on Monday morning and briefed my boss, Brett, our CRM Schoolhouse Officer in Charge (OIC), regarding the good news about the opening at the clinic. Brett had been a tremendous support and was fully on board when I told him I was hoping to spend thirty days away from work overseas. As I had burned up all my leave, my only other option was to get PTAD orders, Permissive Temporary Active Duty. PTAD orders would allow a military service member to be away from his or her appointed place of duty temporarily.

Wherever the PTAD orders sent you then becomes your new place of duty. PTAD essentially would allow me to go to the clinic in Europe as my official place of duty and continue to get my normal paycheck like I was at work. Sort of like civilian vacation pay or military leave pay, though not either. These types of orders do not cost the government anything. I still had to pay for my own plane ticket. There was no per diem because I wasn't told to go there by the military but rather permitted to go as I had asked to go for personal medical reasons.

After laying out my fully thought-out logistical plan, Brett immediately told me he would fully support it.

"*T-BONE*, I am completely on board. Go on down to the Command Deck and speak with the Skipper (the CO or Commanding Officer). Brief him and see if he will sign off on your ambitious idea."

It took me about three minutes to work my way down to the Command Suite. I left the second deck of Building 633 on Naval Air Station Pensacola and navigated my way down through the hallways where the API ground school classes were already in session for the day.

By the time I made it to the CO's Executive Assistant, she was waiting for me, and she walked me right into the Skipper's office. Brett had been busy in that few minutes, as he had already spoken with the CO and briefed him regarding my plan. Brett told the Skipper that he fully supported my desire to go to Switzerland to fight on in my cancer battle and that he had the manpower to cover my absence.

This meeting became another one of those moments when God went before me and incredibly blessed me with outstanding leaders. God once again allowed me to find great favor with both Brett as my OIC and with the Navy Captain running Naval Aviation Schools Command. Within just a few days I obtained a set of forty-day PTAD orders and my boss' approval to depart. All I needed now was a $3,000 plane ticket.

If you understood how rare it is to get a set of PTAD orders like that from a military command, then you would understand why I was fairly confident God was in control. If He could move the hearts of the leaders in my Chain of Command to essentially provide me a forty-day hall pass, He could certainly provide airfare. This was God we were talking about, and He was moving mountains on my behalf.

I took some time to share with the NASC CO what Switzerland was all about and why I believed it was the next door God had opened for me. The Captain had been fully briefed on my less-traveled path of natural and biological medicine when I first checked into his command. He knew I was on a raw diet, and he knew I was meeting with Dr. Ostergaard at the Naval Hospital on the first workday of every month.

The Skipper had been watching, and he, too, fully supported my natural efforts. I explained the different treatments I would be getting in Switzerland which I could not get here in the States. He had a couple of questions, more logistical and security-based than anything else. It wasn't long before I was out of his office and headed back to the second deck to thank Brett for setting me up for success with the big boss.

When I returned to the CRM Schoolhouse, the rest of the instructors had arrived for the workday. They asked questions about my weeks up in Boston and how my new fillings were feeling after all the work on my teeth. After a few minutes of small talk, Brett pulled me aside.

"*T-BONE*, go home, find a plane ticket, and pack."

"Brett, I can't thank you enough for the quick work of convincing the big boss to let me go away for a month, but I can't go home right now. The guys will be covering my classes next month already, and I'm here now. So I need to teach and pull my weight while I can, but thank you again."

Up in the CRM Schoolhouse, we taught Fleet Aviators how to become CRM instructors, and I taught some key classes. I had already had the past few weeks off in Boston using my annual vacation time, and as long as we had a class to teach, I wanted to do my part.

"*T-BONE*, I understand, but if you change your mind and think you need the hours to prepare for Switzerland, you can leave any time."

Brett's encouragement meant a lot, but I just couldn't leave. The Schoolhouse had students arriving in the morning, and I needed to be prepared. No one was going to teach my classes but me if I was in town, and I was for a few more days. My fellow instructors like Major Greg Butcher and Captain Jim Williams would have to cover for me in a couple of weeks during the August class; so it would not be acceptable to me to put my work on them and just be home all week surfing the internet searching for plane tickets. No, I could do that after hours.

The next morning the students rolled in. These were not newbies like the students downstairs in API. These were Fleet Aviators already winged with years of flying experience that were now instructors just as we were. Most were teaching in their respective Fleet Replacement Squadron or FRS. The FRS was the Schoolhouse for each and every type, model, and series of military aircraft currently flying in our Naval Aviation inventory.

When a newly winged Naval Aviator earns their Gold Wings and has them pinned to their uniform by a loved one, they also get a new set of orders. These orders send them directly to their FRS to learn how to fly their new weapon system. The students in our classroom every two weeks were FRS instructors themselves, and they were there to become Crew Resource Management experts. They then would go back to their squadrons and train other instructors to become CRM facilitators. But in order to be an FRS CRM Instructor, they had to spend a week with us first.

On that morning, God was at work. I happened to be back and teaching when I was not required to be, and *THOR*, one of my Marine Corps buddies from before flight school, was to be one of my students. *THOR* and I had been stashed Second Lieutenants together up at NAS Whiting Field in one of the helicopter training squadrons.

I guess you could say I had watched the movie *Platoon* too many times in college, because when I signed up to serve, I wanted to be a Huey pilot so that I could fly into hot landing zones (LZs), pull out wounded Marines, and save lives. It wasn't until I was at Officer Candidate School in Quantico that I found out the Air Force had taken over that job, and Marines didn't do Search and Rescue Medevac Flights like that anymore.

But that didn't stop me from asking to be stashed in a helicopter training squadron anyway while I waited for Flight School to start about a year after that butt chewing. I had come into the Corps wanting to fly helicopters, which was a shift from my childhood dreams of following in the footsteps of my Granddad, who had been a P-38 fighter pilot in World War II.

I married my high school sweetheart while in college. Our oldest child was a pleasant surprise showing up right after our first anniversary. Joining the Marine Corps a couple of years after college with a family and our second child on the way shifted my focus from having a twenty-year career to wanting to serve temporarily, and helicopters had the shortest commitment after flight school at the time.

But that rationale all changed when I flew my first aerobatics flight in primary flight school. I fell in love with being upside down, and you couldn't do that in a helicopter, at least not more than once. Formation flying and aerobatics sealed the deal for me. I had to fly fast. And I wanted to see the world the way God does, from up high and upside down. The extra few years of commitment were worth it to fly inverted.

Because of my initial desire to fly helicopters, I ended up working with *THOR* every day. We eventually went to flight school, where he flew helicopters while I went off to fly jets. Because the Marine Corps is small, we would cross paths again.

We did meet again years later out on a hill in a wooded training area in Australia. He was a Forward Air Controller, and I was working in the Fire Support Coordination Center for the CROC '99 joint military exercise with the Australian Army. You can imagine my surprise when from my tent on Sam Hill in the Shoalwater Bay Training Area in Queensland, I saw my old flight school buddy walking out of the woods with another young Marine who was his radio operator. *THOR* debriefed me and my Australian counterpart on the events of the day. After the debriefing, we caught up for a few moments, and then just like that, he disappeared just as he had appeared with the "Snake Eaters" out in the woods. I didn't see him again until this day when he walked into my classroom.

THOR was surprised to see me behind a desk, as I should have had at least one more year of flying in my first tour of duty in Beaufort. He raised his eyebrows and inquired, "What gives, brother?"

Trombly family trip to White Mountains, New Hampshire after removal of metal fillings with "Old Man of the Mountain" rock formation in the background

I proceeded to tell him about the past eight months of our Faith Walk. I briefly shared how God was moving mountains and about this great opportunity I had to go to Switzerland in a few days. I also confided that I needed to find that three thousand for a plane ticket. The class was starting soon; so we cut the stories short and got into the business of the day.

Happy children and happy dad on Trombly family trip to White Mountains,
New Hampshire after removal of metal fillings

36| *The Judge Called*

THE workday ended, and I hurried home to log onto my computer and wait for my dial-up internet to connect. That's right: this was June of 2001, and we still had dial-up.

If you don't know what that is, you are both incredibly blessed and also too young to get my references to Woodstock, which started on the day I was born. That's why I have left them out of this book. OK, I'll give you a quick tutorial on dial-up.

We old folks used to get our internet out of a phone line; so unless you had two phone lines coming to your home, you could not make or receive phone calls during the time you were online. I spent a few hours on the internet that afternoon and into the early evening trying to find the cheapest plane ticket to Zurich I could find. Every ticket was still over $3,000 and climbing in price as each day and each search passed, and I still hadn't come up with a plan.

I disconnected and took a break. I was finishing up the last of my carrot juice for the day when my phone rang. It was Jeff from Wisconsin. He was a great friend from college days and a former Army tanker. He, too, was married and had a large family that was getting even larger. For the past few months, Jeff had been sending us cash to pay a cleaning lady to take some of the load off Megan. With all Megan was doing to assist me with juicing and raw food preparations, she practically had a second job. Jeff was calling to check in on me. It was a habit he had developed months earlier.

Jeff was an entrepreneur who had recently been elected to sit as a District Judge. I shared the good news about the clinic and how there had been a last-minute cancellation affording me the window to go. Jeff was thrilled with the news, and being a former military man himself, he was impressed with the leadership I was serving under and their granting me the PTAD orders.

The conversation turned serious when I shared that I had only one obstacle left to get overseas—the plane ticket. The Judge was quiet and eventually said, "Brother, it is out of my price range, sorry."

"Judge, you and Cheryl have already done more than enough for us. I'd never ask you for more money. I'm just letting you know so you can pray for a quick resolution."

We continued to speak on this subject for some time. I walked him through the past few weeks' events, especially the miraculous past few days. We celebrated the doors God had been opening, and I finally summed it all up in one powerful statement of faith.

"Brother, God has this!" I told him with absolute confidence. "If

He can coordinate a cancellation in Switzerland and provide a set of no-cost orders allowing an active duty Marine to spend a month at the clinic, then the plane ticket is already taken care of."

Though I didn't know exactly *how* God would take care of it, I spoke it as if it was already done. This was not cocky showmanship or Marine bravado. This was an honest, deep-seated trust in what I knew God was doing.

Jeff was moved by this statement, and his voice trembled slightly as he expressed, "I'm proud of you, David. And to be honest, I'm amazed at your faith. I don't think I would have that kind of faith in your situation."

"Jeff, if you were in my situation, you would have the exact same faith I do, because the faith I have is not my own. This confidence, this knowing, this faith that it is already done is a gift from God. If you were in my situation, brother, you would have the same faith, because we serve the same God, and He loves us both the same."

"*T-BONE*, you have a point. I have to concur that God is definitely at work. I love you, Bro, and I will continue to pray."

Jeff had a heart of gold, and his call to encourage me had actually been mutually encouraging. This conversation was very memorable, and being he was an Army man whose emotions flowed more freely than mine, I thought I'd let the Judge down easy before he started crying. I initiated our manly salutations.

"Thanks for the call, brother. I'll keep you posted."

I hung up the phone and was about to release the receiver with my left hand when the phone rang. I was still grasping the phone; so I again lifted it off the cradle.

For those of you who are still wondering why I mentioned Woodstock, you may also be missing the point on this phone cradle thing and why it is significant.

Back at the turn of this century, most people still had phones *with cords*! That meant that the entire time I was talking to the Judge, I was stuck in my kitchen on a landline, not on a wireless phone or a cellphone. As I went to the wall to hang up the phone, *my hand was still gripping the receiver as it was dropping into the cradle when the phone suddenly rang.* In fact, it rang so quickly it startled me.

"Hello, this is David."

"*T-BONE*, is that you?"

"Yes, who is this?"

"Brother, this is *THOR*. What have you been doing all afternoon? I have been trying to call you for over three hours!"

"What do you think I've been doing all afternoon? I have been online searching for that plane ticket to Switzerland."

"Brother, you can stop searching! My fiancé works for Delta, and she has buddy passes she is willing to give you. All you need to do is pay about three hundred in taxes, and your plane ticket is free."

"*THOR*, you are a tool!"

That may have come across wrong at first, but I quickly explained to him that he was a tool of God's provision! I shared with him my previous conversation with Jeff. We spoke for a few more minutes and concluded the call with me once again sincerely thanking him. He would have the pass in a couple of days—plenty of time for me to use it to get to Switzerland after my classes wrapped up on Friday.

Now picture this: I placed the phone back in the cradle for a second time, and again without releasing the handle, picked it back up, and dialed the Judge. It was time to rock his world!

The phone began ringing, and now Jeff was the surprised one picking up the phone.

"Hello."

"Judge, *T-BONE* again. Do you remember that plane ticket I mentioned a few minutes ago? You know, the one God already provided and I just had to find?"

Jeff responded with a curious, "Yes."

"Brother, I had not even released my grip on the phone when, no kidding, it rang, and I immediately picked it up. It was my buddy *THOR*. He was calling to tell me his fiancé had gotten me a buddy pass, and I was going to Switzerland for three *hundred* dollars. Jeff, I am still holding the phone. I haven't let go of it since you called me earlier! Is that GOD or what? *I told you God had this!*"

It has been many years, and my memory of who started crying first may be a little foggy. But as it is my story, I am going to go on record and tell you that my Army brother started crying first. Of course, both being moved to tears by God's Spirit and overwhelmed with gratitude at what had just happened, I was right behind him. God was right there with us letting us know He was fully in charge. He was *completely* in control, and He was gifting me with a faith like I had never had before. God had so strongly put this truth of His sovereignty on my heart that I had been compelled to declare to the Judge, to myself, and to the spiritual realm all around us, "GOD HAS THIS!" And would you believe it? As soon as I hung up, God showed up with the plane ticket!

> "For where two or three are gathered together in my name,
> there am I in the midst of them."
> —MATTHEW 18:20 (KJV)

We may walk through the valley, our challenges in this life, with our spouse and immediate family, but few others accompany us through the entirety of the Faith Walk. This is what makes it our personal challenge. It is our burden to carry; however, God brings reinforcements. We are never truly alone, as God is always with us. Very often God as a loving Father will provide for a brief respite as a brother or a sister comes alongside to step in and walk with us for a mile on that journey through the valley and help carry the cross.

God did this for His own son, Jesus, as He made His way toward Calvary's hill and collapsed. Simon of Cyrene stepped in and carried the cross as Christ was unable to do so due to His utter exhaustion and the significant wounds from the beatings He had already withstood.

Megan and I were walking a valley, but our family and many friends, just like Jeff and his wife Cheryl, came alongside and walked with us. It seemed that at key moments when we needed them the most, God prompted them to provide relief and support. This time, it was *THOR* and his fiancé who stepped in and walked a mile with us. What a miraculous blessing!

Scripture speaks to this very concept of support and strength gained by walking through life together.

> "Two are better than one, because they have a good return for their labor: If either of them falls down, one can help the other up. But pity anyone who falls and has no one to help them up. Also, if two lie down together, they will keep warm. But how can one keep warm alone? Though one may be overpowered, two can defend themselves. A cord of three strands is not quickly broken."
> —ECCLESIASTES 4:9-12 (NIV)

The Judge and I struggled to compose ourselves as we celebrated what God had just accomplished. Now it was time to find Megan and tell her, too, how God had just shown up—again!

37 | *Deploying to Switzerland*

MEGAN was no more surprised by God's answer to this prayer than I was. We were walking out this path together, and God was holding us both close. From the dinner in that Bethesda restaurant almost ten months earlier until now, we had witnessed God's faithful provision. God provided all we ever needed at just the right time. He stretched us and grew us during those three weeks of EMCON in Boston. He was still there, ever-present, ever faithful, ever-growing our faith.

A MOMENT
WITH MEGAN

David deploying a month without me was something I had already experienced as the wife of a Marine Fighter Pilot. Being home alone with the kids was not going to be a new stress. What was different as David left, this time for Switzerland, was saying a very difficult goodbye. We had no guarantee he would do well there. We didn't even know if he would come back.

When he got the opportunity to go, I was relieved he would be under observable care by doctors and nurses that championed alternatives. I was relieved to get a break from preparing 96oz of juice every day and worrying about what veggies were going bad. I could finally breathe a little bit. Mixed feelings of some relief with some fear daily rippled through my heart. During that month, my sister, Sydni, came to spend some time with me and the kids. It was a reprieve from the norm of carrying everything. But that was the first and only time family would come visit Florida during this battle.

With Switzerland only a few days away, things began to happen quickly. That first Sunday our family was back home, I shared with my dear friend, Wayne Powell, about my sudden opportunity to go to Switzerland. Wayne worked the door as a greeter at our mega-church and had befriended me earlier in the year. Olive Baptist is a huge church, and Wayne was one of the first folks outside our Sunday School class that we were getting to know. He made Olive feel like family!

Wayne asked me if I would share my cancer challenge with the choir, of which he was a part, so they could pray for me. I agreed. That next Wednesday evening after work, I swung in as the choir prepared for rehearsal. Vernon Wayley, Olive's Minister of Music, shared a passage of Scripture, and then Wayne introduced me. Vernon allowed me a few minutes to share my need for prayer during the next month.

I quickly sketched out our story of fighting this rare bone cancer for almost ten months and how we were battling it naturally. I shared what little I knew about the Switzerland clinic expressing our excitement and gratitude for this treatment opportunity. I asked for the choir's prayers, and they prayed. I thanked them and left to continue my preparations.

This nearly one-hundred-person choir didn't say that they *would* pray; they *did* pray! Not just that Wednesday evening, but for the next month while I was away, they prayed. I know they prayed. I felt their prayers while overseas. What a powerful prayer team! Olive's choir and our Sunday school class, our church, our pastor, my entire family, Marines from Beaufort, our old church CBC in Beaufort, our childhood churches in Massachusetts, and even a little house church in Iwakuni, Japan that I'd attended a year earlier while deployed were all praying for our family and for my success in that Switzerland clinic!

It's hard to explain how you know and feel the prayers of hundreds of brothers and sisters, but if you have been there, you know exactly what I mean. It brings more than peace.

God supplied daily peace beyond human understanding from the beginning. This throng of people taking our cancer battle to the Throne brought an additional wave of serenity, supernatural power, and confidence that we desperately needed in my upcoming personal wilderness experience.

Wayne Powell did one more unexpected act of service. We had been in the church for almost eight months, and other than shaking the pastor's hand the Sunday we joined the church, we had not spent time with Pastor Traylor. Wayne and Vernon set up an appointment prior to my departure with the pastor in his office. We spoke about the trip, and then these three men prayed for this young and once stocky, but by now rather emaciated, Marine. The phenomenal prayer time with these men of God brought spirit-lifting encouragement that God knew I would need.

Megan now had the burden of taking care of our four little ones and a puppy while her husband stayed in a clinic thousands of miles away near the Swiss Alps. Respectively, we were both in places neither of us had ever been. My going through unknown treatments was one thing, but all of this happening overseas with a plethora of other unknowns was more than Megan or any wife should have to bear. But Megan and I together had jumped on this opportunity though we had very little prior knowledge or time to research what was to come. It was literally the next step in our Faith Walk and an obedient response to God's answer to our prayer that sent me to Switzerland.

Unlike the previous modalities that we had thoroughly vetted and researched, combing through the pros and cons and praying over each recommended weapon for this warfare, this directive was divinely spoken by God, ending the uncomfortable silence we were experiencing during those three lonely EMCON weeks in Boston.

This time we did not have *a decision to make,* but rather *a directive to obey,* as the play call came right at the line of scrimmage. We swiftly slapped our hands after that phone call from the clinic, broke the huddle, traveled from Boston to Florida, miraculously received PTAD orders, supernaturally bought a ticket, and put me on a plane all within ten days. I was going long for the "Hail Mary pass" for which we had been praying.

On our way to Pensacola Regional Airport, Megan and I made a pit stop at Lifeway Christian Book Store on Airport Boulevard. I had recently heard some inspiring music from the Christian band, Third Day. With time to spare and urging from the Holy Spirit, we stopped in and purchased Third Day's *Offerings* CD to take on my forty days of PTAD orders in Switzerland. I have often referred to this trip as my personal wilderness experience with God. In reality, it was me and God and the guys from Third Day. What an extraordinary adventure!

I had packed a half dozen CDs and my handheld CD player. Yes, that was a thing back then. Once on the flight out of Pensacola, I took the cellophane off that *Offerings* CD, popped it in the player, and never took it out for over thirty days. Memorizing those songs, I sang my heart out day in and day out. God sustained me during that wilderness experience, but Mac Powell and the guys in his band were my worship leaders and companions through it all.

I landed in Zurich, Switzerland late Saturday night, June 30, 2001. Having spent time in Japan the previous year, I quickly figured out the railway system. The short train ride from Zurich to St. Gallen was a picturesque transition from a booming metropolis to a historic European town as I sped toward my new fox hole to wage the next phase of my offensive battle plan.

An hour later, I was in St. Gallen looking for Christian, my host at the Hotel Shützengarten. Affiliated with the Paracelsus Klinik, the hotel was just a short walk up the hill from the Klinik which provided the patients some needed downtime with the distraction of beautiful scenery as we walked to and from our daily treatments. Located in the center of this storybook village, the Swiss Alps ski-chalet-style structure donned flower boxes in every window and ornate wood-crafting on the front and sides.

Christian took me to the quaint hotel boasting only half a dozen or more rooms. I unpacked what little I'd brought in my one-person room, complete with a window that opened to the garden. From my second-story room, I could look down into a small, landscaped oasis that my hosts, Christian and his wife Irene, had nurtured over the years. It was a beautiful arrangement of plants, bushes, flowers, and small trees with a winding path and some benches. It afforded patients a tranquil place to enjoy the beauty of nature between our treatments down the hill at the Klinik.

I shared this haven with six other patients, some with their families who accompanied them for their treatments.

Yes, in a whirlwind of miraculous events, I was in Switzerland. Only God could have given Megan and me the faith to accept this deployment about which we knew so little. Alone on this mountain near the base of the Alps, I was to fight my way back to health. This, per my PTAD orders, was my appointed place of duty for the next four weeks, my home for the month of July 2001. My forty-day wilderness experience with God had begun.

> "Nevertheless, He saved them for His name's sake,
> That He might make His mighty power known.
> He rebuked the Red Sea also, and it dried up;
> So He led them through the depths,
> As through the wilderness.
> He saved them from the hand of him who hated them,
> And redeemed them from the hand of the enemy.
> —PSALM 106:8-10 (NKJV)

38| *First SITREP from Fort Klinik*

WITH my bags unpacked, the local area explored, and excitement building, it was time to send word back home. I first wrote an email to Megan and then an email to all my friends and supporters praying around the globe. It was time for my first SITREP (Situation Report) detailing my reason for traveling to Switzerland and my great expectations for my time at "Fort Klinik."

Communication back to the States was through dial-up internet access via the one guest computer Christian had set-up in the second-floor hallway for the guests. Each day I had time to reach out and send Megan my love. We were on far different time schedules; so the responses were delayed.

Unpacking this story with you now, many years later, I thought it appropriate to share one of my SITREPS with you to give you a glimpse into my mindset during my first days at the Klinik and the gift of faith that God gave me during those difficult days. This was my first SITREP sent on Monday the 2nd of July 2001:

Subject: Hello from the ALPS!

Grüezi mitenand,

This is hello everyone. I am writing to you from Switzerland. I arrived on Saturday and will be staying through the 28th of this month for treatment at Paracelsus Klinik here in Tuefen. Many of you knew that I went to Bethesda for a follow-up in June. What I had not told you yet is that while the doctors there told me the cancer had not spread anywhere else, they were deeply concerned as the tumor in my jaw had grown and had entered the sinus cavity. This is obviously a bad development, and we are taking it seriously.

However, my doctors in Bethesda and I do not agree about when exactly the tumor grew. I believe that it grew before we started our natural battle plan and that it is actually shrinking. For that reason, I am not ready to give in to chemotherapy. I could already be well ahead of the cancer, and the chemo would only cause me to take a step back. This is why I have chosen to pursue the treatment available here in Switzerland.

My goal here is to rebuild my immune system, and that is this Klinik's goal, as well. The Klinik has a number of great doctors who treat chronic diseases with a whole-body approach. The first step is to detox, which will rebuild the body's immune system. I have my first consult today at 1330. After a couple of tests and consults, the doctors will give me a schedule for the rest of the month indicating what therapies I need and what time they will take place.

When I am not in the Klinik, i.e. Saturdays and Sundays, I plan to see Switzerland. However, after the long trip and jet lag, this first Saturday I slept and got up for dinner.

Sunday I walked to a village that was having a celebration for a mission organization called Helimission. For those of you who are not familiar with them, they are a mission aviation group stationed around the world that meets the needs of the local communities with relief support during natural disasters. After they have demonstrated the love of Christ, they are better able to tell them about what Christ did for them on the cross two thousand years ago.

This group was celebrating their thirtieth year of service and passing on the controls from the founder to his son. I met a couple of guys from LeTourneau University, my alma mater. One of them was my fraternity brother Jeff Hoebel, and the other was William Patterson, for all you L.U. guys out there. Small world!

I hope to take a train ride one Saturday all the way around the country and through the Alps. From my village, I can see a ridge that is not far away. The owners of the hotel where I am staying usually take the visitors on hikes each weekend and climb this ridge with those who are up to it at some point. The peak is at 9000' and is very steep. Talk about conquering your mountain! It would be a moral victory, one that can be accomplished in a day. The other mountain I am climbing to good health will take a bit longer, but it too shall be conquered!

All the visitors to the hotel are Klinik patients. It is like staying in a Ronald McDonald House with a breathtaking view. Most have a very positive attitude; a few others, not so good.

It is amazing how taking an affirmative role and following good logic can have a positive effect on your outlook. I know that the peace I have and the courage to take this step to come over here and pursue this type of alternative therapy comes from God. He has been faithful to me and my family throughout the past nine months and will continue to direct our path.

I cannot express with words the gratitude I have for the support we have received from all of you who are receiving this email. Many have helped us in so many ways. But all of you have been praying for us as a family, and that means more than anything else.

I believe that the level of confidence we have as we step out boldly and attack this disease is a direct reflection of the prayerful support you have offered. God honors the fervent prayers of His people, and that point is not lost on me or my family!

God bless all of you who are in this fight with us. I pray that He will reveal Himself to you through the love of Jesus Christ as He has to us daily!

I have shared with Megan many times how blessed we are to have friends like you. I consider myself a rich man as I think about the friends I have and their sincere concern for us. Megan and I are truly blessed!

I am heading for my first consult now. As I learn what is in store for me, I will keep all of you informed so that you can pray with us more effectively.

Fly safe, and for those who don't fly . . . buckle up.

In God's Hands,
David
Psalm 91

39| *Drills at Fort Klinik*

THE Paracelsus Klinik was founded in 1958 as a center for health and well-being based on the principles of natural healing. This biological and holistic medicine and dentistry center served as my foxhole for the next month. Dr. Rau, the primary doctor at the Paracelsus Klinik, was teaching back in the States when I arrived in Switzerland; so my primary biological medicine doctor was Dr. Flechten, the doctor to whom I had been referred by my biological dentist, Dr. Felix Liao. Dr. Flechten took the lead and did not disappoint, picking up almost immediately where we had left off on our phone consultation from Dr. Liao's dental office two weeks earlier.

On day one, Dr. Flechten thoroughly explained his comprehensive plan to support my body's ability to heal itself. His briefing meticulously detailed his comprehensive plan of attack using a multi-faceted, holistic approach to empower my own immune system to kill the enemy invaders—cancer cells. This philosophy diametrically opposed conventional methods, which focus on eliminating symptoms and the cancer with drugs, radiation, and surgery.

Dr. Flechten and I worked as a team during our consultations, employing a wonderful working relationship and trust. He and I developed a synergy comparable to that with which these diverse biological protocols worked in concert with each other. My immune system responded like a high-performance aircraft accel-

318

erating from idle to max power. There were a few key therapies with such kick and effectiveness that my immune system found itself in full afterburner for short periods of time. We were moving full speed ahead toward reversing deficiencies and recalibrating my body's God-given ability to heal. This foundational link encapsulated my reason for coming all the way to Switzerland: Here my medical team and I worked in agreement to build my immune system up, not knock it down. Conventional pharmaceutical treatment, focusing on cancer's symptoms rather than cancer's root cause, works in exactly the opposite manner, nearly annihilating the body's immune system—God's created powerful weapon in toxic warfare.

Following my initial consultation with Dr. Flechten, I had my first thermography scan. This imaging mapped each area of my body, detecting infrared heat markers. The bright red images depicted on the screen identified the underlying chemical and nervous system signals. From these scans, the doctors could see how well my body was functioning and thus determine on which body systems and locations to focus their time and attention with other treatments, such as Neural Therapy.

Neural Therapy, which also uses homeopathic medications, was more complex, less frequent, and had to be administered by my doctor rather than the nurses. This modality injects natural homeopathic medications directly into targeted nerve bundles through the use of very thin, hollow needles. These needles are inserted into key acupuncture points. My first Neural Therapy treatment was dispersed day one at the conclusion of my initial consultation with Dr. Flechten.

My first injection went directly into a large nerve bundle at the lower front portion of my neck as I was lying on my back with the doctor positioned directly above me. Placing his thumb just above the sternum, Dr. Flechten pressed hard into my neck to locate the nerve bundle he was targeting. Then slowly, he injected the medication filling the area near his thumb.

After removing the needle, Dr. Flechten released his thumb. Yet, I still felt the same pressure as if he were still pushing making it difficult to swallow. The homeopathic medication filling the nerve bundle and surrounding tissues generated the pressure. However, it gradually subsided as the targeted nerves absorbed the medications, and I could once again swallow with ease.

At the completion of this first injection into my neck, I immediately tried to sit back up. Dr. Flechten had turned his back and moved away from me to put up the needle. As he turned back to continue our dialog, his eyes widened, and he placed his hand on my shoulder and asked me to lie back down. Apparently, I had turned an interesting shade of green, and he feared I might get disoriented and fall off the examination table. After a few minutes, the room stopped spinning, and I was able to sit back up. My initiation into the biological medicine world had begun.

Neural Therapy treatments continued with one to two each week during my month-long stay. As the original Diffuse Large B-cell tumor had been in my right jawbone, Dr. Flechten targeted the right maxillary sinus for Neural Therapy multiple times. The volume of medication injected here seemed to be a little less than I had received on the first treatment to the nerve bundle in my neck. Dr. Flechten performed these injections by skillfully inserting an even thinner needle through the tiny cracks in the skull bone until it penetrated the sinus cavity.

The most interesting and dynamic of these Neural Therapy treatments came late in my time at Paracelsus. Dr. Flechten required me to sit in a chair as he stood over me holding the longest needle I had ever seen. You know, the kind used in movies that cause the pre-med students to faint as their professor pulls the monstrosity out of the drawer for a procedure. That's the one!

He told me to relax my jawbone and hold very still. That was easier said than done! But after weeks of learning to trust Dr. Flechten, I was calm and compliant. He inserted the needle near my temple in front of my ear and slowly plunged the mammoth instrument straight down into my jaw. He briefed me through the entire process. His calm explanation settled my nerves as he executed the procedure flawlessly.

Just as he finished explaining to me how he would easily know when to stop pushing because my jaw would immediately pop open when he reached the nerve, my jaw dropped uncommanded. He immediately injected the medication. My jaw felt stiff, making it a challenge to close my mouth for the next few hours while the homeopathic liquid took its time to absorb into the nerves and surrounding tissue.

Dr. Flechten and the Paracelsus team treated me with dignity and respect, answered every question I asked, and modified my treatments as the days progressed, all based on my body's physical responses and also on my feedback as to what I believed was having the most effect. He approved of replacing therapies I felt were less effective with the more robust ones, allowing me to maximize my time and funding while at the Klinik. An example of this teamwork between patient and doctor was his agreeing to remove all colonics from my program upon completion of my first one and my respectful feedback on the experience.

I expressed my belief that my seven-day fasting periods with two five-gallon colonics per day in my own bathroom at home were far more effective than the Klinik colonics for which I was scheduled throughout the month. The individual colonics inserted into my daily Klinik schedule while still eating, literally just helped to remove dinner from the night before. Because I had already implemented six months of productive colon cleanses before arriving in Switzerland, I knew my resources would be better spent on additional hyperthermia treatments, ozone therapy, or blood chelation.

It was both empowering and encouraging to be in a facility with doctors willing to modify treatments based on the individual needs of the cancer Warrior rather than blindly following the pre-determined regiment set forth by the cancer industry as if I existed on a factory conveyor belt without options or personal input. The Paracelsus Klinik became a refuge where I became an active participant in my healthcare surrounded by truly supportive staff, listening physicians, and like-minded cancer Warriors! I felt empowered as if I were the co-pilot rather than helplessly sitting in the back seat, unable to contribute to the decision-making process to determine our direction or destination.

Days at the Paracelsus Klinik incorporated little downtime as we busily moved from one scheduled treatment to the next. Each outpatient appointment transitioned from room to room, practitioner to practitioner. All the nurses spoke Swiss German; so I learned a few phrases to greet and thank them daily. Thankfully, the doctors spoke English. I could answer their questions in my own language, and they could answer mine.

A month was a good amount of time to be immersed in a language. I greeted my nurses regularly with "Guete Morge" and "Wie gohts?" to say "Good morning," and "How are you?" I learned not to say good morning in the afternoon or good afternoon in the evening. The staff appreciated my attempts to honor their language and culture, and I appreciated their bedside manner and skill.

Most of my therapies were with the nurses, not the doctors. Nurses administered my infusions of vitamin C, homeopathic remedies, and Ozone blood therapy. I had one of these treatments almost every day, cycling through the three in order to maximize the number I could do in this thirty-day battle in the European Theater. The nurses spaced these three infusions out in a strategic manner to strengthen my immune system. In addition to these tasks, nurses also facilitated my bi-weekly magnetic therapy.

Chelation of the blood to remove heavy metals to which I had been exposed through the vast amounts of immunizations during the first seven years of my military service and from my childhood was paramount. Dark Field Spectroscopy and Blood Drop tests allowed me to see how contaminated my blood was with heavy metals. Thus, chelation started very early in my treatment plan. Removing these metals allowed other therapies to be more effective.

Somewhere in the first few days, I was directed to undergo my first "colon hydrotherapy procedure," which was long for "colonic." However, I had already accomplished nearly sixty colonics before flying to Switzerland and had executed four full weeks of fasting to include two colonics a day. That's why I wanted to turn down the colonic appointment initially, but ultimately decided to do the first one for the learning experience.

What did I learn? I learned that one colonic at Paracelsus was more than enough for me, because my methods at home *while fasting* were far more effective. Upon sharing this revelation with Dr. Flechten, he canceled all future colonics for me and filled those therapy periods with vitamin C infusions or ozone treatments.

Over the course of those first few days, I learned that as the technical difficulty and the intimidation factor of any particular therapy increased, so did its apparent effectiveness. Though difficult for me, I had to learn to let go and trust my physicians, especially during the Neural Therapy sessions. I knew that my personality drives me and my profession requires me to be fully briefed and in control to the max extent possible. These new biological medicine therapies were a stretch for me to accept initially. But I knew that God had opened this door in a miraculous way, and I had to continue to step out in faith.

As my first week was coming to a close, I was about to undergo the second most uncomfortable experience of my cancer fight.

This would be second only to the bone marrow biopsy months before. It was long, hard, hot, and required a mental toughness that I had not been required to exercise since the biopsy itself. It would also be the one treatment which I asked Dr. Flechten to repeat more. The big gun in the armory was about to be employed!

40| *Lying Outside the Gates of Hell*

HAVING removed all my metal fillings back in Rhode Island, I truly anticipated smooth sailing though my time in Switzerland. What could be more challenging than having all your fillings removed and replaced—both top and bottom? Could there be something more invasive or uncomfortable? Yes!

I recognized that some therapies that might be a stretch for me to understand or even accept. Not having time to research protocols that might be introduced and performed immediately required faith—a trust that God had brought me here, and He had a plan.

I was walking in faith and trusting that this was where I was supposed to be, just as I had trusted for the past six months. Only now, things were moving so fast I truly had to walk totally by faith, not by sight. I could not read all there was to read on each of these modalities, and feeling uninformed was highly challenging. I worked hard to keep an open mind as new therapies were introduced and executed daily. Some I experienced once and never again. Others I realized were vital in this battle and grabbed my fascination. These became my staple. I worked through them with tenacity. *Hyperthermia* was the "missing" protocol I had been searching for but had not found in the States. You could say it was my unicorn, the reason I was in Switzerland!

Hyperthermia raises your core body temperature above 102 degrees Fahrenheit. Yes, even in Europe, they allow us Americans to describe our body temperatures in Fahrenheit, so accommodating. The treatment was expensive but worth every penny. The plan was to have four full-body hyperthermia treatments at the Klinik and to do localized hyperthermia back at the hotel each day on my own time. Christian and Irene had been gifted an Indiba machine from Dr. Rau for their Klinik patients to use back at the hotel for free each day. What generosity!

The tumor which had been removed in September the previous year was my ONLY tumor. It had grown back over the three months Megan and I had been researching alternative medicine options back in Beaufort. It had gotten larger than the first and was a serious concern. However, as I left for Switzerland, I was convinced it had been shrinking—an argument I made as forcefully as I could back in Bethesda less than a month earlier.

There was still a bump in my jawbone. The CT scan had shown penetration into the sinus cavity. Tumor cells were still in my jaw, and I finally had a SMART WEAPON I could use against the tumor itself at will! I was free to go into the dedicated hotel treatment room with the Indiba machine, fire it up, and blast the tumor with heat ANYTIME I wanted, and man how I wanted!

The machine was like a handheld iron that had attachable plates of different sizes. At the Klinik, the technicians taught me how to use the small plate, approximately the size of a quarter. I placed a dab of KY jelly on my cheek and also on the plate as it heated up. Once I felt the heat radiating from the plate, I would press the heated plate against the skin. I held the plate in place for a number of minutes while moving it slowly in a rotating manner to prevent the heat from getting too intense in any one spot and burning the skin. The KY Jelly kept my cheek from getting burned by the hot metal and transferred the heat deep into my jawbone.

This heat transfer created a "localized fever" deep beneath the area where the hot plate was placed. In my own hand, once even twice a day, I had a precision-guided munition… a smart weapon that could target the very tumor that had started me on my faith walk through this valley. My days had been numbered by my doctors back in Bethesda. Megan and I hadn't accepted that prognosis, and now I sat in a Swiss hotel room literally holding a deadly weapon against my enemy as the heat transferred deep into my jaw. The tumor's days were now numbered!

The handheld Indiba machine brought the offensive might of the Klinik therapies to Ground Zero—the tumor site. All the infusions and hyperoxygenation of the blood through the Ozone treatments along with everything that was given to me to hyper-stimulate my immune system could now come to bear on the target. As the local area in which this tumor had made its home was heated above 101 degrees Fahrenheit, the tumor cells could no longer sustain life and died off. While cancer cells do not have the programming to die off like normal cells, they are not as robust as healthy cells. Healthy cells can sustain temperatures up to 106 degrees Fahrenheit, but cancer cells die once heated above 101 degrees Fahrenheit. This, I believed, would be the end of the tumor cells in my jaw!

As the Indiba machine focused on the tumor site itself, the Hyperthermia Box back at Fort Klinik focused on the entire body. Once a week in a private room, I stripped down to nothing but a towel and climbed into a box-like cocoon made of a space blanket suspended over a Klinik bed. While lying there, the technician would insert a rectal thermometer which would monitor my core body temperature throughout and after the treatment.

A couple of hours later, this very same space blanket would then be collapsed and wrapped around me for almost another hour after the conclusion of the treatment. This blanket retained my body heat in order to ensure that the recently established whole-body fever took and lasted through the remainder of the day and well into the night every time I underwent this treatment. When the fever broke, not only would my shirt, shorts, and sheets be thoroughly soaked, but so would my mattress. Each and every time, I had to flip the mattress and change both my clothes and sheets to get a dry environment in which to go back to sleep. Despite the hours of discomfort, I valued these treatments, and I watched with interest the staff getting the room ready for them to begin.

Once prepped, the technician would build the box around me, placing a hand towel between my face and the heat lamp in the top of the box over my chest. This towel draped from the top of the box halfway down, keeping the brilliant lamp and direct heat off my face. The box was completely sealed except for a small opening directly above my eyes that allowed me to see just outside the box above me. I called that opening the chimney, as hot air rushed out but cold air never seemed to replace it. I was in an oven. Literally, I was in an oven designed to cook the human body, gradually raising my core body temperature from 103 to 104 degrees Fahrenheit.

This process took hours and was physically and mentally taxing. Once the light came on, the temperature came up, and the discomfort built. The heat was so intense that I felt as if I were lying outside the gates of Hell itself, completely boxed in.

There was no crying mercy and climbing out on my own. The technician turned on the box, sealed me up, and left. She only came back every fifteen minutes or so to check on the rate of temperature change and to see if my body had finally peaked. Then she left again as quickly as she came in. This happened a half dozen times per session. I lost track of time in the box. I even lost my sense of reality during my first treatment. As that heat built to a level I considered unbearable, I could only work mental exercises to cope. I had to focus on anything from reassuring myself that this heat, too, had to end at some point, to worshiping and thanking God for His gift of salvation and even the gift of this torturous technology.

I often spent this time praying for my best friends, some fellow

327

Marines who had not yet seen their need for forgiveness and God's gift of salvation. Hell to them was a storybook fantasy. I prayed, and even though tears were hard to come by while I was being baked, I wept over my friends who had no understanding of the fierce heat of Hell. The sense of urgency was as real as the heat I felt engulfing my body. I cried out for God to reach everyone that I hadn't reached and to touch their hearts so that none of them might experience the painful torture I was enduring at that moment.

I imagined myself lying a few feet from the gates of Hell itself. Never had I envisioned myself closer than I felt at this moment. The thought of getting hotter seemed impossible while still sustaining consciousness. It was as though I could see the gates and feel the heat, yet I could not move either toward or away from my position. It was torture, feeling as if I would surely perish if I were to move even a foot closer. There was neither refreshment nor relief.

All I could do was pray and thank God for my future. I asked Him to help my brothers not only believe in the reality of Hell but to recognize that Hell was never meant for them. I begged God to let them see that Hell is the destiny of every man without Christ due to man's disobedience in the Garden. However, God didn't create Hell for us but for His enemy, Satan, and the fallen angels who rebelled with him.

Hell is real, and Satan will be there paying his debt as promised in Scripture. Man does not have to experience Hell's intense fire because Christ already paid for our sins. We just need to repent and believe. *(In Chapter Thirteen, we discussed the Scriptures clearly defining the path to Heaven as provided by Christ's sacrifice and love.)*

Often the second time experiencing a difficult challenge can be even worse than the first due to the anxiety of anticipation. This was certainly true of my second bone marrow biopsy but not of the hyperthermia. After the first one, I prayed up and brought reinforcements to my remaining hyperthermia treatments. In fact, I even asked for a fifth treatment. Two in my final week! I got my game face on as I walked to the Klinik on my hyperthermia days. I envisioned the cancer cells in my jaw and any stray cancer cells that might be floating in my blood or lymph and pictured them dying and disappearing with each step I took toward the treatment room at the Klinik.

I got fired up for the staff to bring the heat. No, the discomfort wasn't any less intense, but I was playing the mental game at varsity levels now, and I knew how to pray and prepare. I also brought my friends, Mac Powell and the boys. I would wait until the staff turned on the light and then have the technician start my Third Day *Offerings* CD. Not only did I have a better sense of time progression based on the song playing and its place in the playlist, but even more powerful, the spirit of worship overpowered the discomfort! I could only imagine what the patients in the rooms next to me thought when they heard Mac and me rocking the house as loud as I could sing, with all the strength that I could muster in those exhausting conditions.

I will forever be grateful to the members of Third Day for their faithfulness to God in serving mankind with their gifts. They may never know this side of Heaven how they encouraged me daily and facilitated a spirit of worship in my darkest places. They led me to worship deeper and in ways I hadn't before this wilderness experience. To this day, I am transported back to the Hyperthermia room and the sweet spirit of worship in the hot box each time I hear "Who is This King." I am so thankful for the way Mac and the boys truly mustered up the strength and resolve in this Marine to fight on when things were the toughest.

Other cancer Warriors and their families often ask Megan and me about the protocols we chose to fight cancer. Rarely do people ask *why.* Rather they ask us about the *what* and the *how.* Another frequently asked question is which of all these treatments do we believe was the most important, or which was the most effective. After hundreds of conversations with fellow cancer Warriors, I truly understand why they ask this question.

We ALWAYS say that we cannot put any single treatment above another, or my raw diet above the defensive measures of water purification. I will personally, however, answer the question for you this way. For me, the mental edge of understanding the science and BELIEVING that what I was doing was killing cancer cells at a prolific rate is what ensured a successful treatment! I know for sure that this battle plan produced confidence and that my mental confidence was vital in assuring victory! The mind and emotions are key to survival. Buying into the prognosis of a two-year death sentence can just as easily become a self-fulfilling prophecy yielding an outcome of utter failure.

Educating ourselves about the importance of a healthy diet, pure water, and eliminating toxins was essential in developing confidence that our battle plan was an effective plan we could BELIEVE in. Yet this one incredibly intense treatment made the belief more palpable. The knowledge and understanding that cancer cells would die at these intense temperatures made this treatment, more than any other, the one that I would say accelerated my crossing the finish line.

And I was not the only person at the Klinik that needed to know about the mindset I took into each subsequent battle with the tumor and the hot box. I had my chance to share my impressions and convictions with my doctors.

After my second or third hyperthermia treatment, Dr. Flechten and a Klinik psychologist, Dr. Sigmund, asked me to share with them anything out of the ordinary. They were very specifically looking for me to recall any images, dreams, or inspirations revealed while in a feverish state in the box.

"David, you have undergone multiple hyperthermia treatments, and Dr. Sigmund and I are wondering if you would be willing to share with us what you recall about them. For example, do you think you ever lost consciousness in the box?" inquired Dr. Flechten.

"No, sir, I never lost consciousness," I reported.

"We have had some patients express that they found themselves in an altered state of mind while in this therapy. As you know, at the Klinik we believe emotional release and emotional healing are very much an integral part of one's war against cancer," commented Dr. Sigmund.

"Yes, sir. I must concur with your assumption on that," I nodded.

"What about any specific images, dreams, or inspirations? Do you recall anything like that while you were in a feverish state?"

"Gentlemen, I never fell asleep. I was far too uncomfortable to sleep. I did, however, have an experience I would be glad to share." I began as I took a deep breath, "Being in that box of sheer torture, I saw an image of HELL - not inside but just a vision of the gates of Hell. I was so HOT and so troubled by the thought of my friends encountering an even hotter heat than I could imagine bearing. So I prayed for friends that I knew had never trusted Christ. I wept while begging God to reveal Himself to my fellow Marine brothers."

"But David, how did you cope with such physical and mental pain? What did you do with that emotion?" asked Dr. Sigmund, who had taken over the conversation with sincere interest.

"Fighter pilots must develop a mental edge before we ever engage in battle. We are disciplined to bring our thoughts into captivity and compartmentalize them so that our mental energy can focus on the primary goal. We had a battle to win. But it had to be conquered one element or phase of training at a time."

"Before I left the hotel each day, I put all other thoughts and concerns aside. I deliberately focused on the coming treatment with resolve to GET THE MOST OUT OF THE MOMENT! I visualized the heat entering my body and at the cellular level destroying the cancer cells at a prolific rate. I saw myself being healed. Doctor, I expect VICTORY! I am no longer helpless, because I am no longer weaponless. Through you and your researched protocol, God is allowing me to fight this cancer battle more furiously than ever before, and not only in a physical manner but emotionally, mentally, even spiritually. Having that truthful mental picture helps me bear the intense furnace."

I paused and looked earnestly in their faces. I desired for both of them to understand that I was not alone and had supernatural strength while in the hot box.

"Gentlemen, even with this knowledge, because the hyperthermia treatment battles are long, I needed reinforcements. I called in Mac Powell and the boys to back me up. Their voices are the courageous spirits of the band Third Day. I sang with them with as much volume and strength as I could muster. They took me to a place of worship higher than the cancer battlefields." I smiled.

"Well, I guess that explains why someone was asking about the wailing, I mean singing, on Tuesday, Dr. Flechten," Dr. Sigmund almost chuckled, yet his face revealed that he understood the seriousness of the discussion.

"Gentlemen, seriously, God gave me victorious moments, working through the mental toughness drills before surrendering to the heat. He taught me how worship can overcome discomfort. In fact, I would like to ask that I be allowed to take a fifth treatment before I go home. There is no more effective treatment than this one, I believe, and I want to burn this tumor out completely before I leave."

Both doctors looked at me as if I possibly had spent too much time in the heat already. But they knew me well enough to know that I was sincere in my request and truly believed in this protocol.

"Warrior, I believe we can arrange that battlefield encounter one more time," replied Dr. Flechten softly. "Thank you for honestly sharing with us in this consultation. These images and stories help us, as we work with other battle-weary Warriors in understanding their emotional and mental state."

Dr. Flechten's point is critical. The importance of fellow squadron mates sharing Intel during a life or death scenario cannot be ignored. It is VITAL to the success of the mission!

41 | *My Shützengarten Squad*

THE Paracelsus Klinik at the time of my treatments was a relatively small Klinik compared to the large mega hospitals where I had been staged back in Bethesda and Boston. Spending a month at such a small facility meant that I crossed paths with the staff, doctors, and fellow cancer Warriors multiple times a day. While the staff, doctors, and innovative natural therapies were the reason people traveled all the way to Switzerland, there was another important element vital to each patient's battle.

That element was my fellow Warriors fighting disease! No soldier, and I do mean none. Not even a Marine wins wars by themselves. This fact has been proven over and over on military battlefields, but its significance has been sorely under-evaluated in our personal wars to regain health. Marines are known for never leaving anyone behind, including the wounded or dead. The power of the knowledge that every Marine in your squad has your back is irreplaceable! This same mental, emotional, and social force exists between Warriors fighting for their health. My Shützengarten Squad was no exception.

While there were a number of European clients, including many from Germany, that came in during the week for routine visits, the majority of the clients I met were from the United States. Almost all of them were staying with me at the Shützengarten atop the hill. There was a sweet couple from a great church in Kentucky, and the husband was fighting and winning his battle with Lymphoma. A college student fighting Lyme disease was in our squad. I met a wonderful Christian sister with whom I became fast friends as we greeted each other crossing paths in the Klinik.

I made another friend, also named David and from Boston, who was having miraculous results keeping ALS at bay with the help of Dr. Rau. *(Amyotrophic lateral sclerosis is a progressive neurodegenerative disease that affects nerve cells in the brain and spinal cord.)* Though ALS has no conventional cure, the Klinik had found a way to slow its progression significantly. David had been coming over regularly for a couple of years. His story was inspirational to me and everyone else at the Klinik. Comrades like these were a tremendous blessing! Together, we each walked through our respective valleys. The encouragement we received throughout the day passing by each other between appointments and again at night in the hotel was priceless!

When we finished our treatments, we were free to go. On some occasions, we were back at the hotel for lunch and finished for the day, but that was rare. More often than not, we were at the Klinik all day and missed lunch. Our evening agenda was dinner together, and then personal time in our rooms or in the small hotel library.

The library was full of alternative medicine books in all languages. Many of the books were gifts from former guests to Irene and Christian for their hospitality. I spent one evening reading the notes that others like me had left in the front covers of the books they gifted to the library. I saw heartwarming messages of thanks to their hosts and words of encouragement to any of us who might read them long after they were back in their home country and hopefully, healed.

I had an inspiration. I emailed Megan and asked her to find me a German-to-English leather-bound Bible I could give to my hosts, a Bible that could be left behind not just for Irene and Christian to have the Gospel, but for anyone who could read in either language. It took her some time, but Megan found one. It arrived a couple of weeks later, just in time for me to gift it before I left for home.

Christian and his wife, Irene, painstakingly prepared healthy meals during the week. These foods were all macrobiotic and alkaline, made to Dr. Rau's specifications as he was the lead biological doctor at the Paracelsus Klinik in Lustmühle, Switzerland. Besides the six families in the hotel, one other Klinik patient ate with us regularly in the hotel dining room. She, too, had come to the Klinik for a month of treatments like myself; however, she had her own apartment up the road.

Unlike the busy life we are all so used to leading back home, dinners at the Hotel Shützengarten were slow and relaxing. The slightly larger than normal dining space offset from the kitchen area was cozy and picturesque as the windows opened onto the street and the view of the village. The Warriors and families all agreed that was our favorite place to relax and regroup after a hard day. We would sit for a couple of hours and swap stories, enjoying the connections we were making.

There was not much to do afterward but write home, read, or sleep. Now sleep was paramount. Some days we came back absolutely exhausted as our bodies were using the therapies and waging a vicious war inside. Most of us knew by the time we had made our way to Switzerland how foundational sleep was to the healing process. Most of us turned in early each night, knowing that the more sleep we got the more ground we took in the daily fight to regain our health. A quick turn at the lone computer in the hallway and some great conversation were all that stood between us and our racks after dinner.

One evening, a couple of weeks into our stay, my new friend Steven and his wife sat across from me at dinner. Steven was also fighting a form of Lymphoma; so I asked him a question that had been on my mind for some time but had not been comfortable asking prior to this evening. Most of the American cancer Warriors were at the dinner table this evening, and we were fairly comfortable with each other as our daily conversations were always both encouraging and substantial. By now we were moving quickly from acquaintances with a cause to each other's personal support structure away from home. As friends all fighting health wars, we felt like a family bonding as we ate at least two meals a day together.

Steven was now fighting Lymphoma cancer for the second time. He had been in remission for a number of years, but when it came back, he chose to go 100% natural, as I did. His first fight had been with chemo treatments and radiation, an experience I had not endured having chosen to go all-natural from the start.

Familiar with the type of chemotherapy he had taken from my days of research during my staging process, I asked, "Steven, this is your second time battling this cancer. Were you completely conventional in your approach the first time?"

"That is correct. That was a few years ago."

"You have shared why you chose to go alternative and come here, but I am curious to know, which way is harder?"

"Which way?" he asked.

"Which path? Would you say that having to go through the side effects of the CHOP protocol is harder since you have to deal with nausea, with fingernails falling off, with hiccups, with diarrhea, with infections from low immune systems, with painful biopsies and drastic procedures? Or, is this natural path harder to walk, carefully obeying the strict diet, forcing down the gallons of nutritious juice, swallowing dozens if not hundreds of supplements, depriving yourself of every comfort food and holiday treat, enduring treatment after treatment at this Klinik, and taking the heat from the majority of people, including your friends and family, who think you are crazy?"

There was little delay in Steven's response, which was definitive.

"This way is much harder for me, David. It's great to not have the chemo's effects, but the discipline is hard. It's very hard."

Steven continued as we ate, sharing the challenges of taking all the supplements at the right time, the dietary restrictions, and the battle of the will to maintain the naturopathic approach while well-meaning friends, relatives, and health care professionals questioned the decisions he and his bride were making this time around.

"David, I miss comfort foods, and I am down quite a bit of weight," he added.

By now Steven's wife and the other cancer Warriors were not merely observing our conversation, but participating in our dialog.

"I completely understand the weight loss concern. During the past nine months of walking through this valley, I have lost more than thirty pounds," I expressed.

Back in Beaufort, I had broken one hundred and eighty pounds for the first time, as I was lifting heavy weights. All of us fighter pilots were.

When you fly jets, you lift heavy! You have to in order to build enough body mass to sustain the higher G forces your body experiences while flying the planes to their limits during our BFM training flights. Legs become a key muscle group, as pilots flex them during these maneuvers to prevent blood from pooling down in their lower extremities under high G, starving the brain of oxygen.

We were all in excellent shape back in Beaufort. Pilots had to be. Now, I was over thirty pounds lighter, and I had very little fat left to surrender at thirty-one years old.

The dinner crowd hung later than normal that evening as we had a robust discussion about conventional versus alternative modalities and mindsets. Steven had pricked a nerve when sharing about weight loss. Some of the folks had some grave concerns about the amount of weight loss they had already experienced.

In an effort to lighten the mood, I shared a story from a couple of months back, when four of my friends from MCAS Beaufort flew to Pensacola for a weekend BFM cross country. As I explained BFM and motioned with my hands, the conversation lightened, and my story served to entertain and distract at the same time.

My fellow Klinik squad members appreciated it when I shared that I knew why my friends were coming for a visit. They had all experienced similar interventions, when friends and/or family attempted to bring them back to the conventional options they had rejected.

For me, this intervention came almost seven months after diagnosis. No chemo. No radiation. I had moved from Beaufort to Pensacola, and all my friends knew was that I had rejected conventional treatments and was living on carrot juice. Word had gotten back to old squadron mates that I had lost *a lot* of weight. I knew that my health was a concern and a burden that they, too, were bearing. Their visit was truly appreciated and a pretty cool intervention attempt. Hey! How many of us get to say that a Division of Fighter Pilots flew into town to provide mutual support during a cancer fight? No doubt, I was blessed with great friends, and I sensed their genuine concern. I worked to set their minds at ease during the course of our dinner.

The five of us rendezvoused for dinner at McGuire's, our local Irish Pub. A historic landmark of Pensacola, it is famous for its great food and atmosphere. McGuire's routinely drew Naval Aviators returning to their roots in Pensacola, bringing back grey flying machines, and grabbing dinner. Generals, Admirals, politicians, and entertainers have all autographed pictures throughout this establishment. And by the way, if you ever visit McGuire's, be extra vigilant when seeking out the male and female restrooms. You'll understand what I mean after your first attempt.

Obviously, there wasn't much on the menu at a pub for me to eat while on my restrictive diet, but I would not let that make me miss this opportunity to reconnect with my brothers. I was excited to hang with four friends and talk flying. By the time we sat down to three steaks, one "garbage burger," and my salad, we had come to the meat of the matter, and the intervention began.

"*T-BONE*, we are worried," said *THUMPER*, the Marine I had just named my new puppy after.

"Worried, brother?"

"You have lost a lot of weight."

He was right, I had. At one point during their visit, I lifted my shirt, and we could count my ribs from the collar bone all the way down. I admitted that I looked like a POW wasting away. It was truly sobering, yet it was part of the process.

"Guys, it is normal to lose this much weight. Essentially, I only eat vegetables and fruit. I take in nothing but pure nutrition. No sugar or bulky foods to fatten me up. My body is fighting a disease, and it is using its reserves to take the battle to the enemy."

As I shared the story, I had a captive audience, not just the one in McGuire's having dinner with me all those weeks ago, but now my fellow cancer Warriors listening to this story here in the Shützengarten dining room. I was bringing home a point, one that I hoped would encourage those who were concerned about their weight loss.

I brought the story to its conclusion, letting them know that the four versus one intervention dinner had the exact opposite effect than expected. When I had finished eating my salad, three of the four Marines had not finished their meals, and the beer glasses were not empty, either. You just don't leave a McGuire's quality steak uneaten! These Marines were taking on board the intel I was serving up while I worked on my salad. At the end of the evening, my old squadron mate, *THUMPER*, confessed their plan to talk me into chemotherapy. But he admitted that he had been convinced of the logic, if not the wisdom, of my war plan!

"Keep doing what you're doing, brother," he conceded, and with that, dinner ended. Those warm beers went into the busboy's wash tub as we paid the tab, and the intervention was over. Mission accomplished!

42| *A Surprise Reinforcement at Fort Klinik*

SITTING like a family at dinner sharing stories with other Warriors and praying for each other was a daily occurrence, but it wasn't the only bonding opportunity. We as guests became like family, and the Shützengarten became our home away from home. A number of us identified ourselves as people of faith. It would have been hard not to embrace faith when walking in complete dependence on God, as we had to do while navigating our way through the valley of the shadow of death guided by God's peace. Experiencing God's presence in the dark places generated overwhelming gratitude. We couldn't help but express our feelings and share our gratitude with any who would listen—especially those in the valley with us. In spite of these circumstances bringing us together and the time we spent bonding that first weekend, we felt something was missing.

We had walked past an open church the first week—a beautiful church just a few hundred feet from our hotel and on the same side of the street. The small frame structure hundreds of years old with its large storybook front door was almost always open. We never saw a soul come or go, yet it was wide open like a tourist attraction or, dare I say, a museum. Eventually someone suggested we go to church together, even if we were the only ones there on the remaining Sundays.

View of the village hillside in Teufen, Switzerland

The next Sunday came, and excitedly yet cautiously our little group entered the church. We found it open yet empty once again, and so we ended up sitting in the first two rows by ourselves. Five to seven of us gathered there over the next three Sundays. It was our "home-away-from-home church." I hadn't found my singing voice yet; so I didn't volunteer to lead worship. Steven asked if I would be their Chaplain, as I had spoken so often of my faith. It was my first unofficial Chaplain job, and it was such a blessing to share with my brothers and sisters! Psalm 91 was an easy passage to start from that first Sunday, as it had been a daily source of blessing and strength for months!

Weekends were a time to get away from everything. Yes, literally everything– our hotel room, our hotel food, our Klinik, our disease–if even only for a day. Christian and Irene would force us out by not feeding us lunch or dinner on Saturday and Sunday. Because we had a tight crew, our hosts took us out on the town to restaurants instead. This experience was grand. I ate cooked food for the first time in eight months, and they told me that the French fries in Switzerland were actually healthy! So they made me order Papas Fritas, German for fried potato, on the weekends. They assured me it was the doctor's orders; so how could I refuse?

*Enjoying the countryside view during a weekend dinner
with David's Shützengarten Crew*

We enjoyed our weekend trips. Our second weekend, Christian and Irene took us from the village, which was high on the hillside, down into St. Gallen, the major city where our trains from Zurich had dropped us days earlier. We toured large cathedrals, which were also very empty. Yes, Christian and Irene made sure we had some fun and experienced the culture every weekend.

But still, we all longed for our families back home. I had long accepted that there was no way Megan could come. She had her hands tied up with our four children! Family reinforcements for me were not on the radar anywhere. But once again, God had other plans.

My brother, Carl, who serves as a police officer back in my Massachusetts hometown, chose to take some vacation time to join me in Switzerland. Carl had not been out of the police academy for even a year when he asked for leave to come to visit me. He spent a week with me, including my last weekend. What a memorable visit! Not just because we had never been anywhere like the storybook Swiss mountains together, but for a host of exciting experiences we would share, that neither of us would ever forget it!

One surprise for both of us was the fact that Carl ended up a patient of the Klinik his second day! His long flight over the Atlantic at a higher altitude and lower barometric pressure than was normal for his body had aggravated a persistent leg wound. When I brought Carl to spend the day with me at the Klinik, I introduced him to my personal doctor. Dr. Flechten noticed his discomfort and took him as a client for the day. Carl discovered that his painful leg was actually an infected abscess!

Dr. Flechten patched Carl up while I spent the morning getting cooked again in the hyperthermia lab. Carl spent more hours in the Klinik that day than I did, almost missing dinner. I left early as hyperthermia was my major treatment and as such was a one and done for the day event. I went back around lunch to sleep off the recently-induced fever until dinner. My Klinik family wondered where my brother was when I arrived for dinner without him. He, of course, became the topic of conversation that evening. He provided a humorous distraction upon his arrival at the hotel with a hole in his leg and a bottle of antibiotics.

The next day after leaving the Klinik, Carl and I took a long walk. I had a disposable camera, and I asked a local villager walking by to take a picture of the two of us. It turned out to be quite an interesting picture and one that has become my favorite picture of the two of us. Our backs were away from the hillside; so the picturesque background behind was the valley below. We each had a great smile, the kind which two mischievous brothers would have if caught in the act of stealing raw cookie dough just before dinner against mom's instruction.

David and his brother Carl walking on the hillside between treatments at the Paracelsus Klinik in Switzerland with David 40 pounds lighter since the start of his cancer battle

For the casual observer of this photo, these smiles masked the great challenges of the storm we were weathering as a family. I was so blessed to have him with me that week, the greatest week we ever spent together, and one for which I will forever be grateful. God knew my extended time away from home was having an effect on my morale. He sent in reinforcements just when I needed them.

Now as I look at that picture all these years later remembering fondly our time together, I am absolutely amazed at my size standing next to Carl. Though he has always been taller and skinnier than I am our entire adult life, in this photograph he's only taller. At the end of this chapter I'll share the words he wrote on the back of that picture, which I have kept on my desk for the past eighteen years. I don't want to give away the excitement to come.

Our third weekend at the Paracelsus Klinik, the weekend before

Carl's visit, our little Warrior group traveled by train to a destination about an hour away to climb a mountain in the Mini-Alps that make up the foothills along the Alpine Mountain Range. Most of us did not climb but rather took a gondola ride to the top and then walked down the path from the top back to the train station. It was spectacular! From the top, we could view all the way to the northeast corner of Switzerland and see into both Austria and Germany, as well as to the great lake, Lake Constance, which borders all three countries. It was an amazing day, and when Carl surprised me with his visit, I couldn't wait to show him this sight.

Carl and I separated from our Klinik group the following weekend. Carl's leg was better, and we decided to take a trip around the entire country on Saturday. Hopping on the train at the local train station, we bought a ticket that would take us all the way around Switzerland and get us back up to our little village by nightfall. Traveling southeast to start, we went up into the Alps, seeing a beautiful glacier from the train. It was the first glacier either of us had ever seen.

We enjoyed the view as we made our way around the country, only stopping to get off one time to eat lunch halfway through the trip in the southwest corner of the country. We grabbed lunch, and I found a Swiss jeweler. Megan and I were only weeks away from our ten-year wedding anniversary, and I found a beautifully crafted ring with small diamonds around it. I was going to surprise Megan with it upon my return a few days before our August 3rd anniversary.

Megan and I were married while we were both still in college. Her engagement ring, which she wears to this day, was humble yet beautiful. This anniversary ring would be a great complement to her humble diamond ring. I stepped back onto the train feeling like a conquering hero, excited to surprise Megan, who had been my rock and greatest supporter through this difficult year.

During our short stop in the city, Carl and I had lunch, found a bank to turn my American dollars into Swiss francs, and purchased Megan's ten-year anniversary gift. We had just enough time to get back on the train and make it back to the Klinik so as not to get trapped on the wrong side of Switzerland overnight. We enjoyed our relaxing journey back through Zurich, east to St. Gallen, and finally up to Teufen.

We were both trying to stay awake the last couple of hours as we were still wiped out from the past week's treatments. We reached the front door of the Shützengarten, climbed the stairs, and collapsed onto our racks half asleep before our heads hit our pillows. If that day's excursion was any indication of things to come, we would need our rest for tomorrow's adventure.

43| *"They Shall Mount Up with Wings like Eagles"*

SATURDAY had been an adventure in sightseeing and relaxation. Sunday was to be an experience on the *exact opposite* end of the adventure spectrum. Neither of us had any idea what we were about to experience as the memory of a lifetime awaited us.

Sunday morning came, and soon after our mini-church service with my Fort Klinik Squad of cancer Warriors, Carl and I went back to last weekend's mountain via the train from our village. We climbed to the top this time rather than taking the gondola. We were able to take in the Alpine sites over lunch and a German beer, once again per the doctor's orders, as German beer is not chemically aged like mass-produced American ones.

It was now recovery time: recovery not only from the hike up to 9000' but for me resurgence from my month of exhausting therapies, and for Carl, from the week of therapies he surprisingly found himself taking as well. As we enjoyed our lunch, I told Carl that the previous weekend the weather had been overcast but dry and we could see then, as we did this weekend, the lake, Germany, and Austria from the top. This Sunday was an incredibly sunny day with scattered cumulus clouds.

David and his paraglider pilot with view of the mountains and valley below preparing to strap into their two-man harness and fly

Lunch had been a sandwich at the little shop on top of this mountain. We sat in the shade and inquisitively watched as dozens of paragliders stepped off the gondolas and prepared for flight. Each would lay out a rig, unfold a parachute, strap into a harness, and gear up with painstaking precision. One after another after another, like the cyclic launching of fighter jets from the front end of an aircraft carrier in the execution of a preplanned strike, these paragliders launched themselves into the breezy afternoon sky. Paraglider after paraglider launched from a flat to a slightly descending field just below the peak where Carl and I were eating.

At one point, we left our seats to walk up to the rail on the far end of the peak protecting tourists from falling down a steep ledge. It dropped for thousands of feet, and below was a rapidly descending slope of pine trees. As we stood looking at all the flyers capturing updrafts and gliding down, time and time again, we detected one paraglider rapidly falling out of the sky beneath us. It seemed like an eternity, but it had only been a few seconds of free-fall before this jumper cut himself from his primary chute and deployed his reserve chute. He safely descended into the trees below following the successful deployment of the second chute. We looked at each other, said nothing, and went back to our sandwiches.

After this long, relaxing lunch and discussion about everything from the view, to whom my brother was dating, to our experiences serving communities and country (me in the Corps and he in the police force), it was time to head back down the mountain. I had a wild idea; so I excused myself and disappeared to the launch zone where the paragliders were setting up shop.

I had told Carl I would be right back, but I never returned. I was captivated by the conversation with these fellow aviators and totally lost track of time. Carl eventually found me, having paid for our lunches. I had not intentionally left him with the tab, but knew I needed to make it up to him.

The solution was right there in front of me! I introduced him to his pilot and told him I had found our way down the mountain! The look on his face was priceless, and if I had that picture, it is the one that would be sitting framed on my desk. Without question, it would easily be my all-time favorite.

Whether it was the conversation over lunch, the look in my eye when Carl saw my excitement to get to dance in the sky for the first time since my 17 October diagnosis nine months earlier, or just the fact that he couldn't show any sign of fear as a recent graduate of the police academy, but after his big brother said, "We are jumping!" he didn't say a word. I paid for the flying lessons. It was the least I could do since my all-consuming distraction with the paragliders had left Carl stuck paying our lunch bill!

Carl and I had dressed in shorts, T-shirts, and sneakers. We had no flight equipment; so the pilot radioed down and requested two jumpsuits and two helmets brought up from below. My anticipation and Carl's terror lasted only as long as it took one of their flight school crew to bring up the gear via the gondola. I was surprised at how quickly it arrived. I guess they were expediting it for fear that we might change our minds. NOPE! We were jumping today!

As we waited for the gear, I told my pilot that I flew fighters and I loved the aerobatics and dynamic maneuvering of dancing in the sky. He got excited; he knew that this was going to be a fun ride. He cautioned that while he was able to flip inverted forwards or sideways when soloing, he would not be able to do the same with me in that pure inverted position. Our weight could stop our rotation at the top, and we could fall down into the parachute. We would be entangled and unable to get free, which would terminate more than the adventure of the day. He did, however, promise to get me as close to a pure vertical position as he could as often as possible without putting us at risk.

David's brother, Carl with leg bandage,
harnessed up and ready to fly!

349

What was going through Carl's mind? He was still silent. Though showing no fear, he did not have the same smile brewing that I had. The gear arrived, and we dressed and split off with our instructors. I watched Carl connect to his pilot about fifty feet away from my set up. His pilot lifted the rigging lines and pulled the chute off the ground, allowing the breeze to inflate the rectangular-shaped parachute.

I never saw my brother run so fast as when his pilot said: "GO!" His skinny legs propelled his six-foot-tall body forward, yet they were moving faster than his pilot's legs. His legs were to the right, and the pilot's legs were to the left. Occasionally they kicked each other, momentarily slowing their forward progress. They moved farther and farther away from our position. The flat began to slope down toward the cliff, and they were still running. Still running. Still running! They disappeared from view. Other crews had gotten airborne much sooner, never going out of sight of our vantage point. Carl's and his pilot's helmets were now out of sight, and I could see only the top of their canopy. Just before it vanished as well, they reached liftoff. Though I had no idea how close they came to the ledge, needless to say, when it was my turn, I ran my heart out and as sideways as I could, never interfering with my pilot's legs. We launched in two-thirds the distance Carl had. We were flying!

> "But those who hope in the LORD will renew their strength.
> They will soar on wings like eagles
> They will run and not grow weary,
> They will walk and not be faint."
> —ISAIAH 40:31 (NIV)

We weren't just falling, no; we were flying! I had moments in the first few minutes when I could see Carl and his pilot. We never got too close, despite being in the sky over a fairly narrow valley in which dozens of airborne flyers were displaying their skillful maneuvers and flamboyantly-colored parachutes all at the same time.

What could have been a short glide to the bottom of the valley from the 9000' peak ultimately turned into more than thirty minutes of pure vertical adventure! After a few minutes of gentle gliding, my pilot and I worked our way underneath one of the closest cumulus clouds, immediately capturing the thermal updraft. This vertical energy that formed the clouds, to begin with, was still at work rapidly lifting us up like an airborne glass elevator with the most spectacular views.

David's brother, Carl, catches thermals while paragliding, lifting him above the highest peak

Carl captures a picture of David and his pilot on their way to the landing site

My smile was growing! And that smile would not go away for days after we landed. That smile was so huge that I cannot contain even now writing about this event years later!

The base of these individual cumulus clouds rested just a couple thousand feet above the mountain peak. Within minutes, I was at 11,000 feet looking down at the peak, the summit snack shack, and the launch zone. The view was spectacular. On more than one occasion, my pilot got us so close to the clouds riding the thermals up that we touched the ragged edge of the cloud's base just as he would maneuver out from underneath it and start our glide back toward the valley floor. They must have had similar Visual Flight Rules (VFR) for paragliders as we did for aircraft back in the States; so penetrating the cloud would have been both disorienting and ill-advised. I had come as close to cloud surfing as I had been in months, and I was in second heaven!

The rate at which we ascended was measured by a meter on the pilot's gear called a variometer or vario. Once we had a significant positive or negative rate of climb, it would beep. The greater our rate of climb in the thermal updraft, the higher the pitch. As our rate of climb decreased, so would the pitch of the variometer. This sound allowed us to find the strongest updrafts and to reach the base of the clouds.

Climbing and descending at rapid rates in a T-45 trainer as a student pilot was thrilling. Having a thrust-to-weight ratio of better than one to one in certain flight configurations in an afterburning F/A-18A with a General Electric F404-GE-400 engine was as close to playing astronaut as I had come.

Now, capturing rapid thermal updrafts, feeling the wind in my face, and having my body thrown with significant rates of turn and relatively low-end G forces while *outside the cockpit* were new, breathtaking experiences. My heart rate soared as we did!

My pilot kept his promise and brought me as close to over the top as he possibly dared. I truly felt as if we were completely up-side down looking straight down at the parachute and the ground below though we were not. He maintained positive G forces as he whipped us up one side and back down the other. We looked like a pendulum swinging full deflection left to right and back again as we executed these wingover maneuvers. Turn after turn, wingover after wingover, we carved up the sky over the valley as spectators on the ground enjoyed the death-defying maneuvers with us.

No doubt, my pilot was thrilled to have a fellow aviator as his passenger allowing him to push his limits, free of fear or airsick-ness. We both enjoyed this flight to the max! For those moments in the air, I was alive and free of any care in the world. Disease, treatments, diet plans, financial obligations—all of those concerns slipped away when we took to the air. I was flying again.

The memory of that flight is as powerful today as it was back then. Yes, I am trying to fight off this grin. Nope, never mind, can't fight it. I can never tell this story without smiling so much it al-most hurts. This was a ride of a lifetime, a flight that *seemed* like it would never end. The joy it still brings never did.

After the flight, Carl and I reclined against a bale of hay in the fields near our landing zone and just hung out for another couple of hours. I was enthralled watching the paragliders work the ther-mals, bend their chutes and bodies around tight turns, and execute daring maneuvers. Carl and I rested and sat quietly, taking it all in.

Long after we had landed and were still staring into the sky, with-out saying a word my brother grabbed my hand and placed it on his chest. Thirty minutes after our flight, his heart was still racing, and his heart rate said it all. He had either one amazing cardio experience or the terror ride of a lifetime on the way down —or possibly both.

I have since truly come to appreciate what Carl did for me that day. I needed that flight that day as much as I needed any one of the Klinik's powerful therapies or procedures. To this day, I have remained beyond grateful that Carl manned-up, put aside his fear, and just went for it with me.

He felt the same, as I perceived from what he wrote on the back of that photo we took on the side of the mountain that day.

Hey Bro,

Love this picture. Makes me look bigger than you. Maybe not bigger but definitely better looking. Had the best time of my life and almost died jumping off a mountain. What more could two of the luckiest guys in the world ask for? ...

Love ya man,
Carl

The story of that flight brought smiles to our friends' faces back at the hotel for the next few days. As my time with Carl came to a close, I was truly thankful for the moral support God graciously provided by sending my brother as a reinforcement in the fight. I expressed my deep gratitude to Carl for his precious time with me in Switzerland. He left for Massachusetts assuring me of his love and prayers while I remained at Fort Klinik.

44| *Offensive Mission Complete, Return to Base*

EARLY during the third week in Switzerland, I experienced something that I struggle even now to put into words. I can only call it a "knowing," a belief that the cancer was DEAD. I can't tell you definitively that it was dead at that moment; I just believed that it was and that I had won. Cancer had lost, and I was now in the bonus rounds at Fort Klinik just hyper-stimulating my immune system for the sake of regaining ground lost during the battle. Each day that I walked to the Klinik for treatments, it was as if I was taking a few more steps forward on the battlefield. Each day I was gaining ground, and I knew it. Confidence grew daily, as did my strength and my desire to bring back a part of my "old normal" that had been missing for some time.

I spoke with Dr. Flechten about this belief. I shared with him my theory that the cancer was dead and that my body was now in the process of eliminating the dead cancer cells.

"Dr. Flechten, these treatments the past two weeks are not my first exposure to alternative medicine. The diet, water, enzymes, and detoxes over the past six months have provided a foundation for us to build on here this month."

"Your dedication and discipline to this point has certainly given you a distinct advantage," he responded.

"Sir, I made a case to my doctors in Bethesda regarding the timing of the tumor's growth which they flatly dismissed as absurd. However, my assumption remains that the tumor had gotten larger faster and earlier in the year than the doctors in Bethesda believed and that it actually had begun shrinking as a result of our alternative medical protocol. I believe it is much smaller now. If my theory is correct, then wouldn't it also be possible, if not probable, that my tumor is already dead?"

I paused only for a moment and finished my argument as to why the tumor must be dead. "Dr. Flechten, if it actually started to shrink on its own without chemo or radiation, then it must be defeated and dying. These therapies at this point and for the rest of my stay should serve to clean out the dead cells in the tumor mass."

"David, I concur, and I have seen your body respond very well to every treatment thus far prescribed. I would caution you, however, that we cannot make that determination without definitive proof—specifically imagery from a CT or MRI."

"I understand, Sir. Do you do CT scans here?" I asked.

"Negative. I would have to set something up in the city, and it will be expensive, as it is not covered by insurance."

"Sir, I can get one through the military hospital back home quickly. Let's skip the scan for now as I am confident I can get one set up shortly after I return."

The conversation was incredibly encouraging to me. Dr. Flechten was open to my thoughts on already being cancer free, and that these whole body and localized hyperthermia treatments were helping the body *remove* the dead tumor rather than *kill* the tumor at this point. I asked him one last thing before our meeting ended. I asked to start exercising. He agreed it would be acceptable at this point and encouraged me to go for it!

So the CT scan was on hold, but after this consultation with Dr. Flechten, I started to do something I had not done in over six months. Deep within me grew a confidence I could not explain that the cancer was dead, and I began working out again. Physical training had stopped for me immediately upon diagnosis, as I did not want to break down muscle and create more free radicals through the oxidation process created by vigorous exercise. I knew that some people used exercise for stress relief with great benefit while fighting cancer, and others stayed away for the reason I mentioned. I chose to limit my PT to long walks every day with deep cleansing breaths to oxygenate the body without muscle breakdown.

If my immune system was back and firing on all cylinders, as it had to be to kill my cancer without chemo or radiation, then it was time to take my first steps on the road back to peak physical condition. I had some serious ground to make up. With a forty-pound weight loss and significant amounts of my muscle mass depleted, I started with simple pushups in my hotel room. I added slow jogs in the evenings on those nights I had the energy after therapy.

The climb up the mountain with Carl on my second visit rather than riding the gondola up was another victory and implementation of PT back into my daily regime. Not sure the jump with the paragliding organization "Flugshule Appenzell" counted as PT, but even so, it was healing even if only on an emotional and spiritual level!

After Carl left, I looked forward to my return home to Megan and the children even more. I finished my last few days of treatment and paid my last visit to the Klinik pharmacy, spending close to $1,000.00 on prescribed supplements, enzymes, and mistletoe injectables to bring home. Apparently I would have to declare more than Swiss chocolate as I went through customs.

Mistletoe is another one of the immune-boosting therapies I started at the Klinik and took home with me to continue for three months. All different types of natural mistletoe occur in nature. The type of tree on which the mistletoe grows affects its medicinal properties. I was given one specific for supporting the immune system in a blood-related cancer battle. I could administer this treatment, too, just like my injectable Canadian 714-X.

There was a small corner store just atop the hill and around the corner that sold Swiss chocolate—delightful chocolate bar souvenirs for friends and family, of course, as I was still sugar-free in my diet plan. Coming through customs on my return to the United States, the inspection officer would ask, "Do you have anything to declare?"

I planned ahead of time what I would tell the customs agent, "Yes, Sir I do. I declare that it is great to be home and healed and that I have three dozen Swiss chocolate bars in my bag!"

I made my rounds bidding farewell to my Shützengarten Squad, and then Christian took me down the hill to St. Gallen to board the train for Zurich. The flight home was long, but it started with a beautiful view of the Alps as the plane turned to climb up over thirty thousand feet. My anticipation to see Megan and the kids during my flight ended when my eyes met Megan's. Reuniting with my wife and Alex, Brianna, Brad, and Grace Anne brought me overwhelming joy. My fire team of little prayer Warriors hugged this victorious cancer Warrior returning from my Fort Klinik deployment like never before!

The embrace at the airport was long and strong. Megan had taken every step right beside me through this journey until I flew off to Switzerland. My amazing wife had homeschooled our older two and kept everything together at home, all with a four-year-old and a 16-month-old in tow. We'd had minimal contact during this deployment—just a few minutes on email each day. This past month had seemed much longer than it actually had been.

Cheers and shouts of joy from the children echoed down the airport corridor. "Welcome home, Daddy!"

Megan whispered, "Welcome home, David!"

Megan wanted to know all about the treatments on the drive home. The children mainly just wanted to know where we were going to dinner. However, they did love the story about jumping off the mountain with my brother. It must have left an impression on them, as my oldest son Alex accompanied his younger brother Brad skydiving on Brad's eighteenth birthday. It was Alex's second jump, as his first was tandem with an instructor celebrating his own eighteenth birthday. Flying was in the DNA from their great-grandfather on down.

Once we tucked the children in for the night, Megan and I sat up and unpacked our event-filled month apart. We spoke for hours about the therapies and the science, as Megan had researched and studied those topics for years before I was ever concerned about biological medicine. We shared story after story with excitement about my new friends, the food, the beautiful views, and my and Carl's trip around Switzerland—except for the ring. That surprise stayed safely hidden for a few more days until our anniversary.

With great excitement, I began sharing that just over halfway through the trip I'd had a shift in my thinking and how Dr. Flechten encouraged and supported my belief, although we didn't have any proof just yet.

"Megan, I am absolutely convinced that the cancer is dead!"

"Really! How?" she asked excitedly.

"Not sure how to explain it. But I just very confidently believe that what we did over there knocked it out completely."

"Did you get a scan?"

"No, Dr. Flechten offered one, but it was going to cost us thousands as I am not under their insurance. I will just get it done here."

Megan was concerned that getting the scan might be harder than I thought, reminding me of exactly what the doctors in Bethesda had said back in June.

"Dr. Malcus said they only do scans every six months. So how are you going to get another scan only two months since that meeting?"

"Considering all the treatments I experienced in the past thirty days, I can't imagine Bethesda wouldn't be at least a little bit interested to see if the protocol worked. They will grant the scan if not for any other reason than to prove I was wrong and to get me to finally agree to chemotherapy since they are so sure that what we are doing is foolish."

"I believe you, honey. I do! I know you are so in tune with what your body tells you. It would be great, though, to have them agree, too. If they document it, it would be an answer to prayer and a huge relief just to know for sure, once and for all, that it is gone."

"Understood, Sweetheart. I hear you, and I agree. Dr. Ostergaard would be able to make that happen with or without Bethesda's input, and I'm pretty sure he would be happy to schedule one. It is the first thing on my to-do-list now that I am home."

"So glad you went there."

"Me, too. Such an amazing adventure God took me on."

Yes, God had sealed in the deepest part of my being, my spirit, the assurance that the cancer was gone! Now I just needed documentation in my official medical records. So naturally, the only thing on my mind my first day back at work was scheduling a CT scan of the jaw and sinus area. I needed concrete proof of what I already knew was true. I contacted Dr. Ostergaard at Naval Hospital Pensacola for a referral, and he eagerly set it up. My scan was set for the 10th of August, just shy of two weeks after my return.

Megan and I celebrated our ten-year wedding anniversary on August 3rd at Flounders restaurant, a family favorite down on Pensacola Beach. We were seated indoors versus outdoors, which concerned me as I wanted the sunshine to show the splendor of her gift.

I distracted her with talk of my trip with Carl around the country, told her about a watch that Carl purchased, and then surprised her with the ring box that the shop had gift wrapped for me. As Megan opened the box and I saw the joy this gift brought her, I remembered how I had initially hesitated to make the purchase after having spent over sixteen thousand dollars on credit for the trip and therapies.

But knowing that I might never be back in Switzerland again, I had to take advantage of the moment and grab a gift that would mean something forever. A milestone gift for a milestone moment. I was confident that I was winning this war, and I had the rest of my life to pay off my medical bills. Why not buy this ring for my best friend and pay it off along the way as well? As Megan slipped the ring on behind her wedding ring and silently enjoyed its beauty, I realized I had made a great choice.

"Megan, you have been my best friend since high school and have given me the best ten years of my life. I know I would never have found this path nor had the courage to take it without your encouragement. I owe my life to you. Thank you for standing with me every day, preparing my juice, and doing months of research. I know we made the right choice, and I know that I made the right choice in asking you to marry me."

Megan loved the ring, which she wears to this day, probably wondering why she didn't get another one at year twenty. I guess we both should go back to Switzerland for a check-up, and I'll be sure to remedy that situation on our thirtieth.

PART SEVEN

THE DAY THE WORLD STOPPED TURNING

"Never be afraid to trust an unknown future
to a known God."

—CORRIE TEN BOOM,
Nazi Holocaust Survivor

45| *One War Ends as the Next War Begins*

MEGAN and I patiently waited for August 10th to arrive. For the next week, I took my salads, my glass pitcher with ninety-six ounces of carrot and green juice, and all my enzymes to work, just as I had done day in and day out at the CRM Schoolhouse for the previous eight months. Everything was on schedule, and my disciplined cancer protocol routines were all back on track. I was picking up right where I'd left off before flying to Europe. I even started another twenty-one-day cycle of 714-X. It was what I had done before my biological blitzkrieg in Switzerland, and Megan and I agreed that despite my optimistic confidence, there was nothing in my routine to change yet—at least not until the scans were completed and the results came back.

Work was enjoyable and a great distraction as I waited for August 10 to finally arrive. I shared class after class and story after story with my co-workers. I smiled uncontrollably every time I described my flight in the paraglider and the way it made me feel so alive with the wind in my face.

The long week had dragged on, but Friday, 10 August, finally arrived! I went in early that morning to take my scan. My cancer war had required a number of CT scans during my short time in Pensacola, and William, the technician, knew me by name. He, too, was from New England, and we'd built a quick and earnest rapport. Another family had come for a scan, and William asked me to let him run them through first. I agreed. I didn't realize why he did that until after my scan.

Mine was his last scan of the day. I explained how important this particular scan was to me and what I expected to find. Always friendly, William was a joy to spend time with, and today he took

364

extra time to let me bend his ear about all the Klinik treatments and my new-found confidence that the cancer was gone. He nodded in approval and smiled as I shared story after story. William remained professional, explaining that he could not tell me what he was seeing. That job was reserved for the trained radiologist, the only one allowed to interpret it. William was the only technician present. While he explained that it would be improper for him to say anything definitive about the images he was printing, he invited me behind the glass into his darkroom.

William let me tell my stories excitedly for the next few minutes and then stopped me with a wave of his hand. He said nothing as he looked at me and pointed to his computer screens just as they started to display the images of my right maxillary sinus. I stopped talking. Leaning in, I intently studied each and every image while he printed the scans for the radiologist.

William, who retired well over a decade ago and won't be in danger of his job over this revelation, silently obliged me by scrolling the slides as I asked him, clicking forward and backward through each individual slide, moving from front to back and then to the front again. Letting the other family go before me meant that William could give me all the time I wanted to review my scans. No doubt, he had planned to take his time with me today all along.

I had thoroughly studied my old scans the past few days before going in to avoid any surprises like we'd received at Bethesda in June. I knew what the tumor looked like and where it had been located. William knew that I knew, too. In an act of sheer friendship, he allowed me to see for myself what I would have to wait a few more days to hear officially:

The scan was CLEAN! There was no sign of a tumor in either my jawbone or in the sinus cavity itself. Not only was the tumor dead, but the therapies in Switzerland had also completely destroyed it, broken it down, and removed it from my body!

Dr. Ostergaard called me after reading the radiologist's official report to confirm early the following week.

"Captain Trombly, the radiologist submitted your report, and I am excited to tell you the CT scan of your head shows no sign of cancer! Congratulations, David. I am very happy for you."

"Thanks for the great news, sir, and thank you very much for making this scan happen so soon after my return."

"Happy to do it, David. Now I want you to know, I already called Bethesda to share this great news. Before we get too excited, they want dual confirmation."

"Commander, what exactly does that mean?"

"It simply means we have to wait a month to do an MRI. If the MRI confirms the results of the CT scan, then Bethesda will declare you cancer free."

My Bostonian smartass DNA was triggered, and my immediate response was, "Did they say a month or thirty days, Sir?"

"They said a month. Why?" Commander Ostergaard questioned.

"We are already halfway into August. Do we need to wait thirty days or just do an MRI anytime in September? I'm thinking September 1st if possible, Sir."

Doc and I had spent one day each month together every month for almost a year. We knew each other pretty well and mutually respected each other. Dr. Ostergaard was undoubtedly smiling through the phone as he assured me he would try to get the MRI scheduled as close to September 1st as he could.

Bethesda may have directed us to wait one more month to assure dual concurrence with an MRI before they would pronounce me cancer free, but personally, I already had my confirmation. During my third week on the mountain, I knew the cancer was dead, and this CT scan was dual concurrence enough for me.

Dr. Ostergaard indeed scheduled the MRI for Monday, September 3rd, the first workday of the month. I went into that scan with an air of confidence and an eagerness to know the results. I went to Naval Hospital Pensacola for the MRI as I had done for the CT scan, but a different technician performed the test, one who did not afford me the opportunity to view my scans like William had. This time, I had to wait. But with the MRI completed, I left expecting to hear something fairly quickly.

Once again, Megan and I waited with great anticipation for the results of yet another scan. Both of us were cautiously optimistic for great news from this last MRI, and we agreed that it would be prudent to wait for the official report before we shared what we already believed to be true with our friends and family.

Each day during that first week of September, I expected my phone to ring and for Dr. Ostergaard to be on the other end, ready to celebrate as we had in August. Tuesday, Wednesday, Thursday—no call. Friday came, and we thought surely we would hear something before noon. Then Megan and I and the children could celebrate the whole weekend! But Dr. Ostergaard did not call.

Remembering how the results of the CT scan had come within a couple of days, Megan and I had expected the MRI results to come just as quickly. When the results of the radiologist's report were finally available, they were sent not to Dr. Ostergaard, but directly to Bethesda for the oncologist to record the results into my official medical record. This processing alone took an extra week. Eagerness turned into anxiety as I wondered what could be holding up the results. Did the doctors see something? Could I be wrong? Could Bethesda be seeing something that only shows up on an MRI? The enemy was throwing fiery darts of doubt in my direction, intending to strap me on yet another emotional roller coaster ride. But as I continued to read and pray through Psalm 91, God maintained my peace.

Monday, seven days after my MRI scan in Pensacola, Bethesda placed an entry in my official medical record dated September 10,

2001. But I would have to endure more days of waiting before the news of my MRI results could reach Dr. Ostergaard and ultimately Megan and me, because the following day, two towers would fall in Manhattan and the Pentagon would be struck. American heroes like Todd Beamer, whose names should be in all future American History textbooks alongside Patrick Henry and George Washington, would overtake the doomed United Airlines Flight 93, dropping it short of its intended target into a vacant Pennsylvania field and sparing hundreds of lives on the ground.

Tuesday, September 11, it would seem as if the world temporarily stopped turning for many more people than just myself. The news of my test results would have to wait while we all struggled to get our bearings. Nearly every American had just witnessed the Pearl Harbor of our generation on national TV.

46| THAT *September Morning*

I had been on leave for a few days the previous week while Megan had flown to Boston to attend our niece, Melissa's, funeral and to support her sister. We had changed her plane ticket late in the week to give Megan and Sarah a couple more days together, as losing a child is a particularly tough moment for the family.

I coordinated with my boss, Brett Ulander to come to work a few hours late on Monday so the children and I could pick up Megan from the Pensacola airport. I thought about swinging by the hospital on our way home to see if there was any news. However, I decided not to bother Dr. Ostergaard, as I was sure his Monday morning would be busy. I was also quite confident he would call me as soon as he knew something, considering the importance of this news to our family.

Driving past the hospital moments later, we pulled into our

driveway. After giving Megan a little time to settle in, I headed to the base, again passing the hospital, resisting the urge to turn in and ask. Instead, I waited, but no call came from Doctor O by the close of business.

Tuesday morning dawned bright and clear, now eight days since my MRI, and we had heard nothing. Students would be arriving soon for their first day of our next Crew Resource Management Instructor Course. I left for work early with the intention to arrive well before the students. During my short commute, the decision pendulum of "to call or not to call" Dr. Ostergaard swung to its extremes. Confident he would call as soon as he knew yet growing impatient wondering if my results were sitting untouched on some desk, I decided to make the call in hopes that Dr. Ostergaard would push Bethesda for an answer.

First, I had to get to the office. I turned on the lights, put my carrot juice and salad in the fridge, and unpacked my personal flight helmet bag containing my water bottle, enzymes, and supplements. Each morning as I emptied that flight bag, I dreamed of pulling out my tattered old flight gloves and my camouflaged flight helmet instead of my healthy cancer modalities. I sat down at my desk to call Dr. Ostergaard. As I reached for my phone, Captain Scott *POLE* Vogt walked into my office with a big smile on his face. The call I had been agonizing over since climbing out of bed this morning was to be delayed a few more minutes.

POLE and I had gone through flight school together and lived in base housing back in Kingsville, Texas while we were students in the T-45 Advanced Jet Training Course. Megan had become fast friends with Scott's wife, Jenn, as they both were rearing children almost single-handedly while Scott and I were immersed in books and spending long nights preparing for the next day's training missions.

POLE and I had teamed up for our last phase of pilot training, which consisted of three reconnaissance "Road Recci" training flights at NAS Kingsville back in February 1997. We flew these last three flights as a section, or two-aircraft event, in which he and I flew one mile apart with one thousand feet of altitude separation and maneuvered tactically along the route. The positioning of our aircraft allowed us both to provide mutual support in defense of each other should we be attacked and to prosecute (attack) the targets of opportunity we encountered most effectively. We each flew the last flight solo with an instructor in a third T-45 high behind us observing our tactical maneuvering and ensuring our safe execution for those on the ground below, whom we were either motivating or startling along our route of flight.

This final flight concluded our time as Student Naval Aviators (SNAs), and we attacked it in an extremely motivated, gung-ho manner! Our briefing board was a piece of art with multicolored lines depicting our flight route and attack runs on key railway targets and weather radar installations. We built a fictional scenario about having to work our way into enemy territory flying a recon mission to locate a down pilot while identifying and prosecuting enemy targets as we found them. Our final flight went incredibly well, and *POLE* and I received our Gold Wings while wearing our Marine dress blues shortly after that last flight together.

Now four and a half years later, Scott walked into my office, and the reunion started. Happy for the distraction, I invited him to grab a seat on my couch, where we swapped stories of flying fast jets and coaching T-ball while the rest of the staff and students arrived. Excited for the week of classes with *POLE* in the room, I was eager to dive into what surely was going to be an incredibly enjoyable week. As we got right into catching up on what each other's families were doing and making dinner plans, I didn't pick up the phone before class. In fact, that phone call would not be made today at all, because *all* our lives were about to change.

I was sure this Tuesday morning would stick with me for a long time as I anticipated that after eight days, my MRI results would finally be delivered. I had no idea that the events about to unfold in the coming hours would make *everyone* remember that day. Yes, we all remember where we were *THAT* September morning, September 11, 2001.

The instructors and I were making our way into the main classroom behind our OIC, Lieutenant Commander Brett Ulander, to join our dozen CRMI students for Brett's introduction to our week-long course. As we were all making our way into the classroom with notebooks and coffee in hand, one of the students who had arrived right at the 0800 start time made a comment.

"Hey, I just heard on the radio that someone flew a plane into the World Trade Center."

This initial report our student relayed was limited at best. Nevertheless, Commander Ulander paused to listen to his captivating report and allowed us a few moments of discussion while making personal introductions to some of the students and reconnecting with friends from the fleet.

As aviators, we all speculated with a morbid sense of curiosity as to what might have happened. We settled on one of two options. Not knowing off-hand the weather in New York City at the time, some speculated that it might have been a small tour aircraft flying passengers around the Statue of Liberty that may have flown into low cloud ceilings and unwillingly flown into the tower. Others proposed that the pilot purposefully flew a light civilian aircraft into the tower in order to commit suicide in a dramatic fashion. All of us were intrigued by the news story, but as our workday needed to commence, we put the story out of our minds while Brett walked us through the plan for the week.

After briefly covering administrative issues like fire exits, restrooms, and parking lot do's and don'ts, Brett introduced the cur-

371

riculum, each of the instructors, and the courses we would be facilitating. Brett and the remaining instructors left the room, and I stepped up to teach our History of CRM course.

Our office spaces on the second floor were isolated from the rest of the Command. We did not have televisions in our offices, nor did we all have smartphones in our pockets back then with access to the twenty-four-hour news cycle. As we sat in our classroom on this beautiful Pensacola morning, we were oblivious to the initial overtures of war that were beginning to ring out over radio and television. Sequestered away in the classroom, we knew nothing of the first thirty minutes of this attack.

Brett returned to his office and turned on his portable radio. Our command was not allowed to stream twenty-four-hour news through our government-issued work computers due to bandwidth concerns; so Brett's radio was our only news source. Brett listened intently with a handful of our instructors as news of the crash ran like wildfire through the hallways and offices of the Naval Aviation Schools Command.

Captain Jim Williams, one of my fellow Schoolhouse instructors, moving quickly down the passageway intercepted me as I stepped out of the classroom for a moment to grab some water. I had just offered my students a five-minute break to hit the head and recharge their coffee mugs before continuing with class. I was hoping to learn more about the supposed aircraft accident and update the class upon my return.

"*T-BONE*, you need to come with me to Brett's office," he said gravely without breaking his stride.

"What's up, Jim?"

"It was an airliner that hit the North Tower of the World Trade Center, not a Cessna," he reported without missing a step. "And a second airliner hit the South Tower just as we started class."

"What? Seriously?" I interrupted.

372

"Dead serious, brother. We have all been in Brett's office listening to the radio, and only five minutes ago there was a report that the Pentagon was just hit either by an aircraft or a missile."

As Jim and I entered Brett's office, our brothers looked at us, speechless. The looks on their faces confirmed what I had already concluded from Jim's detail of the past hour's events. We were under attack. Someone had chosen this day to declare war on the American people and our way of life!

We huddled around the radio, which Brett had set up on the windowsill of his second-floor office window in order to get reception in the large stone building. This very same window on the west side of BLDG 633 offered a beautiful view of the Blue Angels practice each Tuesday and Wednesday mornings. I and other instructors would steal away to marvel at their precision aerobatics. On Blue's practice days, Brett's office became a great escape from our emails and courseware development work—the instructor's haven between classes.

David, Megan, and their four children with the 2001 Blue Angel Flight Demonstration Team on board NAS Pensacola, Florida

As we sat captivated by the unfolding story, we perceived no sights or sounds of the Blue Angels. The Blues had yet to take off, as it was only 0859 central time. Today, Brett's office would forever be etched into our memory while we heard the news reporter share the horror he was witnessing as the South Tower collapsed in upon itself.

We hung on every word as the reporter who had been calmly describing the flurry of activity outside the world Trade Center frantically attempted to describe the scene in the vicinity of the South Tower. The tower was collapsing down on the crowd below in a thunderous roar, creating a cloud of smoke that rushed through the streets, enveloping people, vehicles, and entire buildings, even obscuring the sun from sight. Realizing their peril, people were screaming and running for their lives.

Those watching downstairs on television also witnessed the images of the collapse captured live as Arron Brown, the CNN anchor, said these words:

"There has just been a huge explosion. We can see . . . "[13]

He stammered momentarily while taking it all in for himself at that moment, just as we all were watching the picture unfold before our eyes.

He continued, "Uh, a billowing smoke rising. And I can, I, I'll, I'll tell you that I can't see that second tower. But there was a cascade of sparks and fire and now this. It looks almost like a mushroom cloud explosion, this huge billowing smoke in the second tower. This was the second of the two towers hit."[14]

Pausing as if searching for words and straining to see the tower, he continued, and as he did his voice softened in pitch and slowed in pace. He concluded his report with a heaviness that carried into our living rooms, office spaces, and anywhere else Americans were watching at that moment.

"And I... you know I cannot see behind that smoke... But ... just look at that. That is about as frightening a scene as you will ever see."[15]

47 | *A Burning Fire Within*

OUR initial speculation from an hour earlier that the aircraft crashing into one of the towers at the World Trade Center might have been accidental evaporated with the second crash and the collapse of the South Tower. Each of us knew that we were under attack. The next war, *our war*, had commenced.

I left the office and headed for the classroom. One of the students was still making his way to the men's room as I intercepted him.

"En route to the head?" I asked

"Affirmative, *T-BONE*. I'll be quick."

"Hold it. You need to hear this," I said in a tone more direct and commanding than he was expecting or I had expected to deliver it.

I let him enter the room first, then I delivered to my fellow Warriors the peace-shattering details as straight forward and raw as I had received them.

"Gentlemen, there was a second crash just minutes after we started class this morning. The South Tower was struck and . . . just moments ago the instructors and I heard the news reporter's horrific live account of it completely collapsing. The Pentagon has also been hit either by an aircraft or a missile."

The room was silent. Rarely in a room of aviators has there been such deafening silence as each one of them processed and internalized the news.

I briefly delayed my next words, allowing the men a moment to take in the alarming news mentally and emotionally, just as I had needed a few moments ago. Then I unquestionably asserted, "We have been attacked."

There were no typical smartass quips or comments like those we had heard when class started upon receiving the first disjointed report. A somberness fell over the room that I had not felt in a public setting since the news of the Columbine High School shooting in April 1999. *THAT* April morning, I had walked into the Intel Office of VMFA-115 and stood silently with my Intel Gunnery Sergeant and the Corporal taking in the unfolding gruesome news report over live TV.

Helpless to do anything in those moments watching or listening to reports of school shootings, or on this day as the terrorists were striking us on our soil, our spirits were quickly suffocated, cloaked in quiet hopelessness which in time turns into embers of anger. Each and every Marine, Navy and Coast Guard Officer in my classroom knew that the remaining years of our military career would be dedicated to locating and destroying the enemy that attacked us.

Helplessness and hopelessness would shift to resolve and readiness over the coming hours, days, and weeks as Americans learned the name of our enemy and had time to process this watershed moment. The aviators around me had all volunteered to serve, and for years we had trained for the missions our leaders would soon ask us to perform with precision and excellence.

No doubt, each of my peers and my friends from former fighter squadrons along with these men in this room would have an opportunity to flex the mighty muscle of our military strength in the coming months and years. I could not be sure that I would have that opportunity to bring the fight to our new enemy in the same way that my grandfather had in World War II, as I was still waiting for the news of my MRI results. A fire burned inside, ever pushing my resolve to fight my way back into the cockpit. How long the battle would take, I didn't know.

What I did know was how to fight. The Corps had instilled that knowledge in me. The past year warring within my body against cancer had exercised it. Today an unnamed enemy challenged it, stoking the fire within. Never was I more committed to fighting whatever battles had to be fought to stay in uniform: to fly, to fight, to win! A voice interrupted my thoughts.

"*T-BONE*, is there a TV up here?"

This was the first thing I remember hearing anyone ask after delivering this grievous SITREP.

Snapping back to the classroom from my introspection, I responded.

"Negative, brother. There are only a few TVs throughout the building. The Quarterdeck at the main entrance is the only one we have access to."

It was apparent that the inability to see the news was a disappointment. I wanted to cut these students loose, but I needed to get word on what we were to do next before they ventured out on their own to learn more.

"Before you head off to find a TV, please hang tight for a few minutes and let me check with Commander Ulander to determine if we are expected to continue with training or if we are canceling the remaining classes for today—or for the week."

Students and instructors alike attempted to check internet feeds on staff computers and stopped in and out of Brett's office, listening to reports and then discussing in huddled groups what the impacts of these real-time attacks might mean. We instructors invited our students to use our office phones to contact their Commands to determine if they were needed to return back to their base and to call their families.

Commander Ulander received word that our class would be canceled at least for the day and that we would have more answers first thing in the morning.

There was no chance of our students getting their orders modified today and flying back to their respective bases. First of all, no one had a complete picture of what was happening. Secondly, no one could fly home, as everything had come to a total stand-still. The FAA had grounded all aircraft soon after the Twin Tow-ers were struck in an attempt to prevent any further attacks. Only military fighters policed the skies over Washington, D.C. and New York as Navy and Coast Guard helicopters supported the recovery efforts in New York City.

Brett released us from training.

"Go home and check in on your families. We will sort things out tomorrow morning."

I called Megan.

"Honey, are you home?"

"No, I'm headed there now. I have been at Everman's to restock the pantry. But David, I just heard the news on the radio! How bad is it?"

Everman's was the grocery store where we purchased almost all of the organic foods we had been using for my juicing since mov-ing to Pensacola. Since Megan had heard the news of the attack on the radio in the car, she knew there had been an attack on both the Pentagon and in New York City.

"Megan, please do not let the children see the reports. It is devas-tating. You should turn on the TV in our bedroom. And hey, Scott Vogt was in my class this morning. He is staying in base lodging. Mind if *POLE* spends the day with us through dinner while we figure out what all is going on?"

"Absolutely not. It will be great to see Scott again."

"Thanks, we will see you soon."

"OK. Love you, David. So glad I flew home yesterday."

Megan spoke as if the reality that she could have been on one of those flights this morning was just sinking in."

"Love you too, Honey! So glad you are home!"

POLE and I left the office and stopped by his room in the Bach-elor Officers' Quarters (BOQ). He quickly changed into some civilian clothes before we headed to my house. I asked him to grab his PT gear [shorts and a T-shirt] and go fasters [running shoes].

Listening to continuing news coverage on the radio as we drove back to my house just a few minutes north of the base, we learned that two of the four aircraft hijacked that morning had flown out of Boston Logan International Airport. I shared with Scott that Megan's older sister Sarah and her husband, who took us in that first couple weeks after my diagnosis, had just endured the tragedy of losing their daughter Melissa.

"Megan flew up to Boston for the funeral and stayed a couple of extra days to be with her sister, Sarah. *POLE*, she actually called me this weekend and asked if I would mind if she changed her ticket again and stayed another day."

"Understandable," he replied.

"Megan flew home yesterday. She wanted to stay another day or two. What if . . . "

I stopped speaking as the gravity of the possibility of how Megan could have been on one of those flights today humbled me. All I could do was pray to thank God for my Megan and pray for all those trapped in the North Tower, hoping they could escape quickly before it, too, might collapse.

I finally said it out loud, making it all the more real to me as I shared with *POLE*.

"I can't fathom the possibility. I thank God we decided she needed to be home yesterday since I had this class to start teaching today, or she might have been on one of those flights."

As we arrived at my home, we found the children helping mom unpack the groceries. With the little ones right there, we didn't speak of the attack as we walked in. Scott and Megan greeted each other with a warm hug that silently spoke of the trauma we were all feeling inside. I excused myself to get out of uniform and to turn on the bedroom TV.

Once we distracted the children, *POLE*, Megan, and I turned on the living room TV and stood in the middle of the room taking in the graphic footage of the aftermath at ground zero. We could not spend too much time watching the screen as it was hard to corral four little ones (including a toddler) for very long. But we saw what we needed to see, and I asked *POLE* to take a long run with me.

I had developed a perfect three-mile course from my front door through neighborhoods behind Naval Hospital Pensacola and back. This was the personal course I had just mapped out for light jogging to begin building my strength and cardio in preparation for my first Physical Fitness Test (PFT) since returning from Switzerland. I had been slowly increasing my pace over the past few weeks.

Today, there was no jog in either *POLE* or me. *WE RAN!* We burned up both calories and anger with every step. We did not say much but rather used the road and the silence to process what we had heard in the office and watched on my TV. In some small way, exercise helps you de-stress when you feel helpless, the emotion which gripped us both.

"*POLE* . . . I'm glad . . . you are here . . . brother."

I slipped the words in between fast, hard breaths, feeling the labor in my breathing and my heart pounding. My jogging routine had only been in place for five weeks since my first on a hill in Switzerland, after not having run in almost a year.

"Me too, *T-BONE!*" he acknowledged with relative ease.

"Someone... is going... to pay... for this!"

"Hell, ya!" he pragmatically affirmed.

"*POLE*... I want in... on this fight!" I declared, still struggling for breath with each step and every word.

"We will all get a chance to fight in this one, Bone. It's going to be big!" He assured me once again with relative ease as this warrior was in shape and ready to fight!

"Need them... to declare... me clean... so I can... get back... in the air... and join you!"

A MOMENT WITH MEGAN

When I married this amazing man, we were young and full of dreams. I watched him work so hard for his dream of flying the F18 and then lose that dream to cancer. But at least during our cancer war, the US had been at peace. But after THIS day, September 11, 2001—when our country needed him to go do what he had trained to do and couldn't—my heart broke for David. However, I must admit that I was thankful I didn't have to worry about him joining another battle so soon.

48 | *From Bended Knee to Standing Ready*

TUESDAY'S events caught us all with the ferocity of a pouncing lion. Wednesday we awoke with a burden which rested heavily on the soul of our country. The day ended quietly with the tranquility of a lamb. Thursday the FAA allowed most US airports to reopen and air travel to resume. News report after news report started to put the pieces and timeline of the attacks together. The shock we all felt on Tuesday had transitioned to sorrow and was working toward a fever pitch of anger and a rallying cry for justice.

As a nation, we regained our footing and our bearings, like a fighter in the ring after having his bell rung stumbles only briefly then steadies himself.

Friday morning, Americans that had spent most of that fateful week on bended knee praying for those who lost their lives, and their families continued to kneel when the President called for a National Day of Prayer and Remembrance.

That morning at the Washington National Cathedral, the President joined a number of religious leaders and clergy, including Reverend Billy Graham, who shared a profound and heartfelt statement. This honest and comforting answer to one of life's hardest questions remains the best I have heard. It's asked by people of all ages and religions and now the people of our great country were asking it again. Rev. Graham's apropos statement applies both to a nation in grief and to anyone who faces walking through the valley of the shadow of death. This seasoned man of God offered this wisdom to America and to the world as we watched,

"I've been asked hundreds of times in my life why God allows tragedy and suffering, I have to confess that I really do not know the answer, totally, even to my own satisfaction. I have to accept by faith that God is sovereign, and is a God of love and mercy and compassion in the midst of suffering."[16]

The President stepped into his role as *Encourager In Chief* and comforted the families who had lost loved ones with words of tenderness and faith.

"God's signs are not always the ones we look for. We learn in tragedy that his purposes are not always our own. Yet the prayers of private suffering, whether in our homes or in this great cathedral, are known and heard and understood.

There are prayers that help us last through the day or endure the night. There are prayers of friends and strangers that give us strength for the journey. And there are prayers that yield our will to a will greater than our own.

This world He created is of moral design. Grief and tragedy and hatred are only for a time. Goodness, remembrance, and love have no end. And the Lord of Life holds all who die, and all who mourn."[17]

Our President transitioned from *Encourager in Chief* to *Commander In Chief*, strengthening our resolve to act during his portion of the ceremony. It was clear that we would retaliate when he resolutely declared,

"Just three days removed from these events, Americans do not yet have the distance of history, but our responsibility to history is already clear, to answer these attacks and rid the world of evil."

"... This nation is peaceful, but fierce when stirred to anger. This conflict began on the timing and terms of others. It will end in a way and at an hour of our choosing."[18]

Two additional Presidential declarations on this day foreshadowed our coming response and resolve. Before heading to the memorial service, the Commander In Chief declared a national state of emergency and authorized the Pentagon to call up thousands of military reservists.

After the service, the President flew to New York City and toured the devastation by helicopter. Then touring the destruction in boots on the ground, he thanked first responders and rescue workers. The congregation of first responders cheered and chanted, "USA, USA . . . " as President George W. Bush delivered his now-famous "Bullhorn Speech." As first responders and volunteers burdened with the gruesome and heartbreaking task of digging out their friends and colleagues at Ground Zero struggled to hear, one cried out, "We can't hear you.

The Commander In Chief responded loudly with no hesitation,

"I can hear you. The rest of the world hears you . . . "[19]

Cheers and shouting erupted spontaneously as the President

started. He leaned into the crowd with bullhorn raised and attempted to continue but was drowned out by the continued shouting and applause. Moments later, he concluded his historic statement that rallied our Nation,

"And the people who knocked these buildings down will hear all of us soon!"[20]

The country knew at that moment we would see war. We were confident that in the days to come those responsible for this attack would pay for their cowardice.

As the President gave his speeches on September fourteenth—one from a cathedral of splendor and one from a platform of twisted steel and debris—we citizens began to rise up off our knees to stand ready to fight. Between the President's many speeches that Friday, I received the phone call I had been eagerly awaiting.

"Captain Trombly, I have great news!" Dr. Ostergaard started. "The results of your MRI confirm the findings of the August CT scan. You are officially cancer free!"

"Thank you, Sir!"

"You did it, David. Congratulations. I am very happy for you and Megan."

"Sir, thank you for helping us navigate our way through. We could not have done this without you."

"You and Megan found your cure! God provided your miracle, and your faith and discipline paid off." Dr. O's manner acknowledged our alternative efforts and dedication, yet firmly promulgated that God and God alone had delivered me.

"Doc, God opened every door. He showed us the way, and now we have a CURE to share with others," I said with an enthusiastic hope for others battling this modern-day plague.

More cautious in his tone now, Dr. Ostergaard stepped back from my use of the word "cure" so broadly. "David, you found a cure that worked for you. I am afraid we did not find a cure for everyone."

He continued, "There are very few patients who would approach the disease the way you and Megan did. You were a perfect patient, and you had Megan's full support. Not everyone has that level of family support. You also took complete ownership of the disease, and you were committed and disciplined in a way I rarely see." He added, "I wish all my patients were like you, but unfortunately far too many press me for a pill, a silver bullet that will solve whatever ails them. Few, if any would resolve to make the extreme lifestyle modifications you did."

The truth of his comment has continued to resonate in me even today as I was sitting in my barber's chair before heading to church all these years later. I viewed a total of four different pharmaceutical advertisements on the local news channel in the thirty minutes it took me to get my flat top.

I understood Dr. O's point and conceded only slightly. Ever the extreme optimist, I tried to encourage him with one last thought before we concluded our call.

"I understand, Sir, but maybe they just do not know that such an option exists. Now you and I have the ability to share this option to any who will listen."

"Maybe, David, I can only hope. Enjoy your weekend, and please give Megan my best. And call early next week to set up an appointment for us to discuss your periodic follow-up oncology requirements from Bethesda."

My personal cancer war was over and was officially documented as such on September 10 in Bethesda. But my notification, delayed due to the events of September 11, arrived Friday, September 14, via Dr. O's voice reconfirming the victory!

The next phase was battling with equal resolve my return to a Gun Squadron and my former cockpit as quickly as possible! That fire had been burning deep within me now for three full days. Our country's next war lay in front of me, and by my doctor's call and

by my Commander In Chief's speeches, I was filled with hope that
I would indeed have the chance to fight again.

386

PART EIGHT
FIGHTING
THE LONG WAR

"Wanting to win isn't enough.
You have to go through a process to improve.
That takes patience, perseverance, and intentionality."

—JOHN C. MAXWELL
New York Times *bestselling author,*
entrepreneur, and influencer

49| *One Year Ago Today!*

IT was absolutely appropriate for me to pass the good news of my healing along to all who had supported our family for the past year. I sent the email excerpts below on the one-year anniversary of my diagnosis in order to ensure we reached anyone who had not yet heard of last month's great report from the Bethesda oncologists. It also served as a request for continued prayer as Megan and I shifted our efforts from fighting cancer to fighting to fly!

> *From: David Trombly*
> *Date: October 17, 2001*
> *Subject: One Year Ago Today!*

17 OCTOBER, 2001

ONE YEAR AGO TODAY, I WAS DIAGNOSED WITH NON-HODGKINS LYMPHOMA. Most of you reading this today were aware of that diagnosis because you have followed our family's battle and progress throughout the past year. Your support came in many ways: friendship, financial help, and most importantly, through your prayers.

Your faithfulness to our friendship and my family over the past year is greatly appreciated and because of you and your love and support, I am able to share some great news.

My most recent test results are SUPER! A CAT scan in August and an MRI in late September show no indication of a tumor in my jaw. In addition, the CAT scan shows a healing trend, evidenced by new bone growth in the area destroyed by the tumor. My sinus cavity, which had been breached by the tumor, is now clear and showing signs of complete integrity. (This result is very important with regard to any future flying.) Last week's blood work was normal.

A week ago last Friday, I sat across from my military doctor here at the Pensacola Naval Hospital. For the first time, a conventional doctor (and more importantly one in uniform) told me I was cancer free and that he was going to state so in his report to the upcoming medical board.

THIS IS OBVIOUSLY A HUGE VICTORY FOR US!!!

Megan and I fully acknowledge God's hand in these events. We have shared consistently how God has been with us and our family through every step of the way. The ability to be disciplined enough to follow the therapies needed to beat this disease came from God, who strengthened me daily to be able to fight the fight one day at a time. The tremendous amount of PEACE that we as a family had DAILY most certainly came from God. The strength we had to go on day after day was surely a result of the prayers you offered and that God has honored!

The battle is not over. I will continue to take care of myself and eat much the way I had to do in order to get to this point. Some of the therapies I did require maintenance doses periodically. You can be sure that I will not be dropping my pack any time soon. We will not let up in our efforts to regain total health.

Many of you were concerned by our choice not to follow conventional 'Wisdom' regarding treatment. I understood and respected your concerns. In return, you tried to understand and respect our decisions.

In my case, we apparently made the right decisions. We firmly believed that we could beat this disease with nutrition and therapies designed to boost the immune system rather than with therapies that would have destroyed my immune system.

Bottom line: the two approaches spring from a difference of opinion. Conventional medicine treats the symptoms, while biological medicine seeks to determine the root causes and tackle the problem from a different, less damaging approach. I would encourage any of you who may face a similar battle in the future to take the time to explore your options before jumping into the conventional programs. However, I am certainly not saying to ignore *conventional medicine. I am saying that there is a place for both schools of thought.*

Nonetheless, I need to let you know that you will not hear about the programs I used from your doctor. Please call me should you get the same phone call I received a year ago today. I will stand with you, as you have stood with me. If there is any info or assistance Megan and I can provide to you at that time, you can count on it. Don't hesitate to call, email, or text us.

We are not out of the woods yet. The next two years are really big regarding 'remission.' The next big milestone to make after that is five years.

I have already set my sights on flying again. After patiently fighting one day at a time, I am now anxiously awaiting word on my future. I am preparing a report for the Physical Evaluation Board, which will meet next month to determine if I can continue in the Service. I am painstakingly documenting everything I did this past year in an attempt to convince the board that I am fit for duty and ready to fly!

This battle is more difficult for me than the last one. WHY? Cancer is too big to take on yourself. I had to rely on God, and that I did. His faithfulness and peace were tremendous. For this second War — the Battle to Fly, I have to focus consciously on the fact that God is STILL in control. He has given me my health back, and He can give me my flying status back, too, if He chooses.

Pray that I do not miss God's will and plan for me and my family by getting over-involved in this battle to save my career. I pray for patience, discernment, and the maturity to accept the forthcoming decisions as God's will and not my own. Achieving this mindset is easier said than done, but it is our desire and our plan to focus on His will.

I have shared my faith with many of you through this endeavor, and we have passed many verses back and forth as a source of encouragement for us all. I share this verse with you regardless of where you are in your relationship with God. We committed the cancer fight to the Lord one year ago. Today, we commit the Right to Fly Battle to Him and seek your prayer support once more. Consider this promise from Proverbs:

"Commit to the Lord whatever you do, and your plans will succeed."
—*Proverbs 16:3 (NIV New International Version, 1984 Edition)*

This verse and the Bible's promises I have shared over the past year are more than wise sayings or catchy inspirational phrases. They are the Words of God—promises from God to those who believe. Do not write them off as trite or outdated. The confidence and faith they inspired in us this past year were real because His Words are real. This triumph is much larger than my family. God is real. I experienced His presence and a deeper relationship with Him more than ever before in my life. I can honestly say to all of you that I thank God for this cancer and the past year's experiences and growth.

When you consider what Megan and I attempted to do and appear to have accomplished, do not think about us. Stop! Think about the God we have been trusting and pointing to each day the past year. Ask yourself the tough question about the condition of your relationship with HIM. I have never beaten any of you over the head with my Bible before, and I do not intend to start now. Instead, I simply share my desire to see you seize and hold the most important part of life, a relationship with Jesus Christ. And I am not referring to just another religion. I wish for you to celebrate not only my return to health but also the God who returned me to health. Christ came not only *"to give us life but to give us life more abundantly."* John 10:10 (NIV)

Many of you share my faith, while some do not. If God is not a major part of your life, or any part, seriously consider what you have witnessed the past year. Ask yourself, "Is it possible that there is a God who is capable of giving the kind of Faith, Confidence, Peace, and Blessings like David and Megan have received?"

I assure you: all of this was not Megan and me. It was God.

"Because he loves me," says the Lord, "I will rescue him; I WILL PROTECT HIM, FOR HE ACKNOWLEDGES MY NAME.
He will call on me, and I will answer him; I will be with him

> *in trouble, I will deliver him and honor him. With long life*
> *will I satisfy him and show him my salvation."*
> —Psalm 91: 14-16 (NIV)

Pray for continued healing and strength, for patience with the doctors, medical boards, and the military leadership as they make my career decisions. Pray for our family as we continue to seek God's will first. Most importantly, pray that God uses His victory in us to reach those who need Him.

Megan and I thank you for your prayerful support.

I THANK ALL OF YOU FOR YOUR FRIENDSHIP.

In God's loving hands,
David
Psalm 91

50| *Dreaming Beyond Personal Victory*

Stepping out of my personal cancer war onto new battlefields required different tactics but the same tenacity. The next battles were not going to be against cancer. Rather, I was going to begin a series of wrestling matches with the Naval Medical System that determines whether Marines and Sailors are fit for duty. Just like the previous fight, there was no definitive timeline and no one to reach out to who had fought these fights in the same manner as I would. The one constant I had was my unwavering belief that God had promised me victory on both counts. God had been with me every step of the way, whether Megan and I felt his presence or not, and we could attribute our first great victory only to His gifts and grace.

Bethesda could not explain my success. The doctors there had essentially issued my death certificate, leaving only the date to be filled in. Despite the cancer being cured without their treatments, all they could say was that it was a miracle. They would not concede that the naturopathic efforts Megan and I used had played any part in our ultimate victory. I could not have been happier to concur with my Bethesda team when they opted to declare that my cure had to be a *miracle*. If my doctors were going to give all the credit to God for His miracle, I had found the one piece of common ground we could agree on! It wasn't the first time God had interceded in my life or in the lives of His people.

"He said: "Listen, King Jehoshaphat and all who live in Judah and Jerusalem! This is what the Lord says to you: 'Do not be afraid or discouraged because of this vast army. For the battle is not yours, but God's. Tomorrow march down against them. They will be climbing up by the Pass of Ziz, and you will find them at the end of the gorge in the Desert of Jeruel. You will not need to fight in this battle; take your position, stand still, and see the victory of the Lord on your behalf, O Judah and Jerusalem, Fear not, and be not dismayed: tomorrow go out against them, and the LORD will be with you."

—2 CHRONICLES 20:15–17 (NIV)

"The Lord will fight for you, and you have only to be silent."

— EXODUS 14:14 (NIV)

The first board to consider my case was the local medical board at Naval Hospital Pensacola, which convened on December 10, 2001. LCDR Ostergaard, who was the Junior member, wrote the report. He was very complimentary toward me personally and the intensity with which I fought my diagnosis in an alternative manner. Only one other member, the Senior member, the Commanding Officer of the hospital joined LCDR Ostergaard. I had never met the hospital's Commanding Officer, a Navy Captain, because I had chosen not to go visit him a number of months earlier to report Dr. Bose, the Ear Nose and Throat (ENT) doctor who had professionally crossed the line with me. There were too many battles to fight, and I had to choose the best ones toward which to direct my energy and the vast reserve of goodwill I had developed with key individuals during the year-long cancer battle.

LCDR Ostergaard authored the report. Despite the positive comments regarding my attitude and efforts, the decision to return me to Full Duty status had to be referred to the Central Physical Evaluation Board (PEB) in Washington D.C. The following comment was from LCDR Ostergaard's write up from December 10, 2001:

"All clinical criteria currently available to include the MRI of the right maxilla seem to indicate that the patient is in remission from his non-Hodgkin's Lymphoma. Since there is no data available for this type of treatment, we cannot give estimates as to the likelihood that this remission will continue or to the likelihood that he will eventually be found to have a cure. It should be noted that the patient has absolutely no limitations physically at this point. He recently completed a Marine Corps Physical Fitness Test with a score of 294 out of 300. He is able to perform duties in his current position although of course, he is not in flight status at this time. Since there is no long-term data to determine the actual cure rate for his treatment program, it is difficult to estimate when or if he would ever be able to go back to complete unrestrictive active duty. Because of this fact, it is the opinion of the board that this patient's case be referred to the Physical Evaluation Board for final disposition in accordance with SECNAV (Secretary of the Navy) Instructions."

The Physical Evaluation Board would consist of a group of doctors I would never meet in person, as they were all stationed in Washington D.C. This panel would soon review my case to determine if I stayed on active duty. It was their job to make one of two decisions.

First, they could remove me from "Limited Duty Status," a designation that essentially started the day I was diagnosed in October of 2000. I was well into my second eight-month Limited Duty Period which prevented me from being deployed overseas while I wrestled cancer. Removing me from "Limited Duty Status" would immediately return me to a "Full Duty Status" making me deployable worldwide, but not yet eligible to fly. Their second option was to medically retire me based on their findings.

I anticipated that this Washington PEB would be seeking to medically retire me despite my having a fully-resolved medical condition completely substantiated with Bethesda's cancer-free findings. Despite Dr. O's comments and my having most recently performed a near-perfect Marine Corps Physical Fitness Test, I knew I faced an uphill fight. Having received a grave, rare bone cancer diagnosis combined with their lack of understanding of my holistic and biological medicine choices coupled with my refusal to follow any of the prescribed conventional treatments would make it hard for most medical doctors to return me to "Full Duty Status."

Looking at my decisions purely from their viewpoint, I could understand that many might question my judgment and judge me as stubbornly non-compliant. This response was predictable, considering I already had my judgment called into question. My interactions with Commander Briggends, my original Flight Surgeon at VMFA(AW)-332 onboard MCAS Beaufort, and Dr. Bose, the ENT specialist at Naval Hospital Pensacola, had enlightened me as to how many doctors were likely to view my decision-making ability. I could not afford to have this board make any unsubstantiated, career-ending assumptions. It was up to me to deliver proof that my decisions were sound and then let God soften their hearts and open their eyes. I had imminent work to do.

Immediately following my September 14 conversation with Dr. Ostergaard, I got busy putting together a binder almost one-inch thick full of our many months of research for the board at Naval Hospital Pensacola to be forwarded subsequently to the PEB in

D.C. Inside the black binder, I placed copies of the most powerful pieces of Intel Megan and I had uncovered from parasite, liver, and colon cleanses. I shared a few of the success stories many others had experienced with Essiac Tea along with raw and/or macrobiotic diets. Also included was an entire section on the treatments I'd received in Switzerland, which heavily focused on chelation treatments to remove the metals ingested from the immunizations I had received during and prior to my military service, and the power of the Hyperthermia treatment.

Leaving no stone unturned in our research to find a cure, I compiled a summary of the best-of-the-best data found under virtually every rock we overturned in our studies. Honestly, my intention was to overwhelm the board members with information on alternative medicine—information that I knew had not been included in their medical school education. Yet I had to maintain a balance in my approach. More was not necessarily better with this audience. Therefore, I limited myself to a single one-inch binder with a personal cover letter, despite the fact that I had a full filing cabinet of research at home. I knew that if the size of my package was too large, it might be summarily dismissed without ever being read.

When walking through the valley of the shadow of death, many of us have only enough energy, financial resources, and time to focus on reaching the other side. The road winds without prediction of what may be around the next switchback. The steep cliff faces envelop the Warrior on all sides, preventing him from seeing beyond the moment.

Having climbed out of that valley and experiencing our first victory as a family, Megan and I found that our view of the terrain changed dramatically. We could now see past just today, affording us a clearer view of the possibilities ahead. We saw a promising future not only in my returning to the cockpit, but also in thrusting us both into a ministry encouraging fellow cancer Warriors. Priceless were the valuable lessons learned and the source of hope we could be to so many others, based on the knowledge we had gained through the experience we had just endured and transcended.

With our first victory complete and with a greater vision for the future, I had two goals in mind while working with Megan to build this binder. My first goal was to ensure that the doctors on the board could in no way assert that my decisions were either irresponsible or based on wishful thinking or fear of conventional treatments. In order to set the hook and draw these doctors into the material I was putting forward to make my case, I inserted a number of key letters from my alternative doctors. Their endorsements and input were critically important for whatever Military Medical Boards might see this package. We wanted the board members to understand that Megan and I intensely researched our options and then made sound decisions based on our research and objective science. We did not blindly accept their medical textbook science, because the North American medical machine and the western cancer industry had not invested money in researching natural options the way many of us believe they should.

I'll let you as the reader decide why that might be. This book is to be an encouragement to those in the valley, not an indictment of the system we work within as cancer Warriors. Ralph W. Moss has done years of research and written much about the cancer industry which highlights these deep issues. In fact, *The Cancer Industry* is the title of one of his many works on the subject as a prior industry insider.

In an effort to help readers understand what these doctors would receive from me at the convening of each board I would face, I've included the enclosure list and cover letter from me to my very first PEB, which I sent with Dr. O's findings. Each subsequent board would receive the same enclosures with a fresh cover letter from me:

From: Captain David M. Trombly xxx xx xxxx USMC
To: Physical Evaluation Board
Subj: Physical Evaluation Board (PEB)

Encl: (1) Chronology of self-pursued therapies
      (2) Dr. Dietmer Schildwaechter, Sovereign Consultants International, Letter of 10 Dec 01
      (3) Curriculum Vitae of Dietmer Schildwaechter
      (4) Sovereign Consultants International, Cancer Profile & Immune Spectrum Blood Test Background Information and Results
      (5) Daily Schedule - Metabolic Supplementation Schedule - Enzyme Therapy from Dr. Schildwaechter
      (6) Explanation of 714X By Gaston Naessens
      (7) Felix K. Liao, D.D.S., M.A.G.D. Letter of 12 Oct 01
      (8) Dr. Xxxxx Xxxxx, Thermography USA, Inc. Letter of 4 Jun 01
      (9) Felix K. Liao, D.D.S., M.A.G.D. Letter of 3 Jun 01
      (10) Dr. Xxxxx X. Xxxxx, M.D. Letter of 20 Nov 01
      (11) Dr. Xxxxx Xxxxx, M.D. Integrated Medical Specialists Letter of 20 Nov 01
      (12) Dr. Xxxxx X. Xxxxx, M.D. Letter - A synopsis of Biological Medicine
      (13) Felix K. Liao, D.D.S. Letter - Naturopathic and Whole Person Dentistry
      (14) Article - The Grand Illusion of Chemotherapy - Ralph W. Moss
      (15) Paracelsus Klinik Lustmühle - Test Results, Civilian Labs, and explanations
      (16) Paracelsus Klinik Lustmühle - Mistletoe Injections for Cancer and Tumor Treatment

1. In conjunction with my doctor's dictation and my medical record, I respectfully submit to you the following information in order to help you

with your decision regarding my PEB. Enclosed is a brief explanation of Biological Medicine, the professional opinions of the civilian doctors I worked with over the past year, and other helpful pieces of information. Enclosures (1) through (16) are also attached for additional information.

2. I have gathered this information for you in the hopes that the information will help you to understand my choices and see the benefits of these therapies. I hope to further convince you of my complete recovery from the disease.

3. It is my humble request that you find me fit for duty. I desire to be found fit and then to pursue a waiver in order to regain flight status. Since 17 October 2000, I have diligently fought this disease with all of my resources. I have never wavered in my resolve to beat this disease and get back into the cockpit. On 15 October 2001, I ran my first PFT since before my diagnosis. I scored a 294. I consider this extremely valuable information. I was unable to perform at this level even five months earlier. I have worked tremendously hard over the past few months to rebuild after having lost thirty pounds and significant strength during the fight. This most recent PFT is evidence to me that having not done chemotherapy and radiation, I will be able to return to better health and full strength much sooner than if I had. I hope to have the opportunity to argue that very point to the waiver board as I seek to fly again sooner than would have been possible if I had chosen the conventional treatments.'

4. As with any fight, you must take things one step at a time. My first battle was cancer. Only now, after being in remission for months, can I in good conscience and great health take the fight to the next level. I need your support and recommendation to be placed in a full duty status so I can then pursue a waiver to fly.

5. As a result of the tragic events of 11 September 2001, I am more resolved than ever to retain the privilege to serve as a United States Marine

in capacity and level to which I have been trained.

6. *I deeply appreciate your time and ask your consideration of enclosures (1) - (16).*

David M. Trombly

My second and most noble goal was to positively impact whoever read what I submitted with the hope it would encourage them to have an open mind about these treatment options. An admitted, eternal optimist, I was and am still hopeful that as we tell our story, the system might be impacted positively and that change might take root for the betterment of our fellow cancer Warriors and their families to come! Megan and I prayerfully chose what information to include, hoping that our story of overcoming such a profoundly rare cancer one hundred percent naturally would positively impact the larger military and civilian medical establishments to look outside of themselves, even if only with a sliver of guarded optimism. Megan and I were hoping we could help to widen the aperture of these doctors to view biological and alternative options more favorably. In this desire, our battle would serve a purpose larger than my survival.

Even if the establishment only favorably considered these options for those they deemed to be well beyond their skill sets, a greater good would have been served. Our efforts to unpack all the research we had painstakingly uncovered might open doors to other health-minded communities, organizations, and alternative practitioners. Hopefully, these entities would then make this knowledge available to others encased within the walls of America's conventional hospitals and cancer facilities.

I'm a dreamer. Yet, I believe that dreams can come true and cultural changes can take place even within large, slow-to-adapt or-

400

ganizations.

Yes, just as I had experienced change and miracles within my own body, I dared to dream big dreams of flying again. Even more, I hoped to positively impact modern medicine and bring hope to hurting cancer Warriors who might hear our testimony. If the gift of flying was returned to me, I knew it would only be for a season. But to step into our future life's work as a couple was a dream worth pursuing. Encouraging these amazing cancer Warriors who each have their own inspirational stories is our audacious goal.

Dr. Ostergaard had responded that we had only found *my cure* not *the cure* when we spoke on the phone on September 14. In his December 10 memo above, he again used the word "cure." We realized the truthful assessment of our culture's approach to this plague. Megan and I certainly knew that we had not learned all there was to know about beating cancer. I was still hopeful that our research and ultimately God's victory gift would influence a larger audience.

My hope is that we will all come together one day soon and bring the best that each form of medicine has to offer to the front lines of this war—the very war that President Nixon declared back in 1971 as the "War on Cancer." This is the President's quote from his State of the Union Address to Congress, which eventually led to Congress passing the National Cancer Act of 1971.

"I will also ask for an appropriation of an extra $100 million to launch an intensive campaign to find a cure for cancer, and I will ask later for whatever additional funds can effectively be used. The time has come in America when the same kind of concentrated effort that split the atom and took man to the moon should be turned toward conquering this dread disease. Let us make a total national commitment to achieve this goal." —President Richard M. Nixon

51| *Divine Appointments*

WITH my Natural Medicine Protocol Binder, as I referred to it, completed and turned in, all I could do was wait for the Physical Evaluation Board's next convening. This was the first military board to which I would have to appeal located in Washington, D.C. During this time frame, I was scheduled for a medical disability retirement briefing at Naval Hospital Pensacola.

The purpose of this class was to learn about the procedures and paperwork for starting my separation from the Marine Corps with a medical retirement and how to receive disability benefits from the Veterans Administration. The board hadn't delivered its decision yet; however, I was still directed to go to a meeting that I felt was putting the cart well before the horse. Why had I bothered putting all that information together if the board's determination was a foregone negative conclusion?

My body was on time and in uniform in a proper professional military manner, but within my spirit was a reluctance as I entered the briefing room. A hospital administrator facilitated the class that lasted most of the morning. The room had no more than six or seven of us, some in civilian clothes. All the attendees were in one of two categories: either determined to be declared not medically qualified to remain on Active Duty and take a medical retirement, or like me, yet awaiting the board results and hoping to be reinstated.

After signing the roster that came around first thing in the morning, I respectfully yet resolutely refused to fill out or sign any additional forms. I was the senior military member present, at least in uniform, within the group and as such was sensitive to show the proper respect and deference to the individual conducting the class. Genuinely trying to avoid being disruptive, I quietly passed each form that was handed to me along to the next individual at the conference table. Eventually, however, the facilitator questioned me in front of the entire room.

"Captain, do you have a problem with cooperating in this class? I see you are not completing the required paperwork."

Again, trying to be sensitive not only to the job she needed to do but to the others who were actively dealing with the gravity of their own current medical conditions, I explained my reasoning.

"Ma'am, I mean no disrespect. A few months ago I was declared cancer free. I am hopeful that my Physical Evaluation Board, which is convening this week, will rule in my favor and reinstate me to Full Duty. This paperwork is all about *separating* from Active Duty. I respectfully refuse to complete this paperwork as a matter of principle."

"Captain, this class is for you to ease your transition. I am here to help you get your disability benefits when you separate. You are going to want this paperwork filled out correctly."

"Ma'am, I appreciate what you are doing here for all of us today. Please understand. I in no way mean to be difficult or make your day more challenging. I just can't concede defeat on this current battlefield that today, I have been required to advance upon. I don't think that I should be here, as my board results have not been determined, and the requirement to be in attendance today, in my opinion, is certainly premature."

I continued, "If it helps, let me share briefly that from the onset of my battle with cancer, I have refused to concede an inch of ground to this disease. When sent to Bethesda for staging, I absolutely refused to lie in my assigned bunk or stay in the hospital overnight as a helpless, inpatient victim of the diagnosis I had received. That was purely an effort to stand my ground and not concede an inch on that new battlefield where I found myself preparing to fight.

Neither that action nor today's is meant to be contrary or difficult. Please understand it is simply a matter of principle and not personal. We appreciate you trying to assist us here today, but I must respectfully decline to sign this paperwork until the board has made a decision."

There was no further push back from the proctor, and the class continued.

I considered just leaving after the next water break. Having made my comments, I realized that I was not going to get anything from this meeting, and I wanted to head back to my office to be productive. However, I could see that my story impacted a few attendees, as they nodded in agreement during my calm yet steadfast delivery. The words I had spoken seemed to encourage several individuals; so I stayed. Yearning to share more of my story, I hoped that my testimony might encourage them in some way.

One such individual was Jordan, a young Navy man who brought his wife to sign the paperwork, as he had been diagnosed with Lou Gehrig's disease (ALS) and was losing ground rapidly. ALS was the same disease my friend David from Boston was fighting in Switzerland. It was devastating to see how this couple was resigned to their predetermined end state of his diagnosis. Even today, though Lou Gehrig's disease is considered to have no medical cure, great progress has been made in biological medicine to slow its progress significantly. I witnessed it first-hand overseas. I wanted -- no, I *needed* -- to find a way to tell them David's story and connect them with the Paracelsus Klinik in Switzerland.

In the few hours we spent together, I worked to befriend Jordan and his wife, and at the end of the class I approached them as we exited the conference room. Briefly sharing in the hallway what little I knew about David's story and how he was currently finding great success overseas, I offered my contact information. They both appeared hopeful and gladly accepted my card. Unfortunately, I never heard from Jordan or his wife again. It was heartbreaking to think I may have had information that could extend his life, yet I felt powerless to impress the value of this GOOD NEWS on them.

I learned a valuable lesson from this early post-cancer encounter, and I mentally connected it to my own personal experiences from immediately after my diagnosis. Just as I sincerely wanted to help Jordan, people had genuinely wanted to help Megan and me, and so they bombarded us with information we just were not ready to receive. The endless amount of emails, calls, and packages in the mail with information and natural products became a significant source of additional stress on us during those first few weeks as we stammered to find balance in our new normal.

I realized quickly from my exchange with Jordan and his wife, coupled with their having not followed up, what I believe to be a universal reality. Megan and I have firmly continued to believe that unless an individual is searching and in the proper emotional state to receive helpful information, the effort to share it on our part may be nothing more than an added strain to a family in distress. Having experienced this situation many times ourselves from well-meaning individuals, we never wanted to copy that example and bring stress to anyone—only encouragement and hope. One wise adage has correctly counseled not to offer advice until you are asked. That proverb's application gave me something to ponder while I waited for the Physical Evaluation Board's decision.

52 | *Gaining Ground with Another Victory!*

As I left the hospital and went to my office for at least a half-day of work, I recognized that my morning had not been the waste of time I had expected it to be. I took a valuable lesson away from that meeting which has stayed with me to this day. Seeing individuals sign the administrative paperwork served as a metaphor of how so many people sign their health away with no expectation for a different outcome than what they have been told—simply because a medical expert had declared their fate via a terminal diagnosis. I knew then as I never had before that I had to share my story of God's miracle with any and all who would listen.

It wasn't long afterward that the results of the Physical Evaluation Board came back. Whether the board members were impressed as they read the binder we submitted or whether they were moved by the Spirit of God to give me a second chance, they did! Once again, Megan and I celebrated and recognized that God was going before us, providing the victories He had promised us! I was found to be fit for "Full Duty" as a worldwide, deployable Marine!

Shortly after September 11, I briefly visited our Training Squadron 86 Executive Officer, Lieutenant Colonel *BONEY* Orabona, informing him that Bethesda had officially documented in my medical records I was cancer free. I thought the good news would be a welcome change after all the bad news of the terrorist attacks we had endured the previous few days. In the very brief fly by meeting, we celebrated the victory, and I assured him I would return soon with news of when I could join the squadron and fly.

Frustratingly, it had been almost four months since that second meeting in September with LtCol Orabona. But now on a Friday afternoon in January with word that my second victory was secure, it was time to visit him for the third time. Only now he was no longer the Executive Officer. He was the boss. I had attended his Change of Command ceremony not long after my second visit. Now I made my way to the Commanding Officer's spaces to make my report to the new Skipper.

"Good afternoon, Colonel. Do you have a minute?" (Because it is customary in the Marine Corps to say Colonel when addressing either a Lieutenant Colonel or a full "Bird" Colonel with an Eagle on the collar, I addressed the Commanding Officer, who was still a Lieutenant Colonel, as Colonel.),

He looked up, and I could see the anticipation of good news on his face as I had only just delivered good news a few months back.

"Come on in, *T-BONE*. Have a seat."

"Thank you, Colonel." I continued, "I won't take too much of your time. I just wanted to stop in and give you a quick SITREP."

Seeing my smile that was untamable, he grinned and asked, "Good news, I presume?"

"Absolutely, Skipper! The Board results are back, and I have been successfully reinstated to Full Active Duty, avoiding the medical retirement they were threatening."

"That seemed simple enough. They must have liked the report you submitted," the Colonel teased, as I had shared with him in our last meeting how I planned to overwhelm the board members with the scientific approach.

I laughed. "Either that, or maybe they just couldn't argue with my challenge for them to step outside for a PFT. I offered to resign my commission and save them the trouble of holding the board if any of them could beat me."

The Colonel got a kick out of that and asked, "So how did you do on your last PFT?"

"294, Colonel! Better than my inventory PFT at The Basic School. Amazing how fast I can run being down almost thirty pounds, and that's after putting over ten pounds back on the last few months."

In no way had I offered to resign my commission, and the Skipper knew that was not a card I was willing to play with medical. But it was a tactical method for me to let him know I was eager to fly, no doubt back in shape, healthy, and ready to join his team.

The Skipper then asked what was still required before I could join the squadron and fly for him. Marine to Marine, he genuinely appreciated my fighting spirit. However, he had just taken over as the Commanding Officer, and as the boss, he had to ask a difficult question as military leaders often do. He had been truly supportive since my first visit almost exactly one year ago when I first moved to Pensacola and introduced myself. He wanted to hold a place on the squadron roster for me to fly for him, but he needed assurances that my optimism was not misplaced.

"*T-BONE*, congratulations on this recent victory. Any idea of the timeline before you will be able to fly with us?"

"Colonel, that is a fair question. Unfortunately, we are in uncharted waters, and I do not have a definitive answer. I was originally told that if I did not do the chemotherapy and radiation that was recommended by the Bethesda oncologist, I would be ineligible to fly even if somehow this cancer went away. This is a stipulation in the Navy's Medical Waiver Guide, but I intend to fight it and be the first to be granted a waiver despite rejecting conventional treatments."

"How certain are you that you will ever get your waiver to fly? Is this a realistic possibility to get the waiver? Or is this possibly an overreach of your great optimism, which has served you well so far? Might it be misplaced optimism with the steep Navy waiver requirements?"

LtCol Orabona understood, as do all Naval Aviators, the significant challenge of gaining a waiver once a pilot is declared NPQ (Not Physically Qualified). We both knew that no Naval Aviator beating cancer on 100% natural therapies while rejecting conventionally prescribed treatments had ever been granted a waiver back to flight status.

To our knowledge, no other pilot had ever fought and successfully beat cancer completely naturally while still on active duty. To have had such miraculous healing in less than a year afforded me the opportunity to avoid forced medical retirement. I was still on the team despite being benched, and now I wanted to get back into the game with every fiber of my being! I truly was blazing a new trail as a Naval Aviator and seeking the best counsel I could from Senior Military Leaders, Flight Surgeons, and fellow Prayer Warriors—all to help me navigate my way back into the cockpit.

The CO's question was reasonable, and I owed him the best guess I could offer. While I wrestled with decision-makers at NAMI (the Naval Aerospace Medical Institute), I did not want him to potentially pass on another aviator that could immediately be productive and support the squadron's mission while waiting for me for an indefinite period of time. Even if I had done everything the doctors asked me to do at Bethesda, the NAMI waiver guide stated that I had to be cancer free for two full years before I could fly again. That requirement created a window of opportunity that would arrive just weeks before his three-year orders would expire and he would relinquish command to his current Navy Executive Officer.

I could see the concern on his face, but before he could interject, I continued. "Sir, I know it is a long shot, but I'm two for two in the victory column, and I can promise you two things, Colonel. First, I am not going to quit till I get back in the air. Secondly, you will know immediately when I have any Intel to pass along regarding my progress. Thank you for wanting to give me a home here in VT-86. Your willingness to bring me on board has profoundly boosted my morale for the past eighteen months. You have personally emboldened my resolve to continue fighting to fly with the hope and promise of a squadron to call home. Again, thank you, Colonel."

For the moment, I had convinced LtCol Orabona to keep the faith, or maybe I had worked hard to convince us both. Regardless, I had truthfully assured him I would not stop fighting, and I left his office and began preparing for the next battle. I had to muster a groundswell of support from my Command and a number of the local doctors to pull it off. Launching my ground campaign, it was time to start knocking on doors. The first one was going to be my current Commanding Officer of MATSG-21, Colonel White, to whom nearly 5,000 Marines across Florida and Mississippi reported.

Returning to the cockpit would turn out to be a longer campaign than I expected, and I would need to rely on God for patience and learn to trust His timing. My ability to beat cancer had required a support team of elite biological doctors, friends, and Prayer Warriors. In the same manner, this next battle with the Special Board of Flight Surgeons would require some heavy hitters to go to bat for me if I even dreamed of having a shot at pulling off our next miracle. I was preparing to take on another large component of the Naval medicine machine. Grappling with this group of doctors to put me back in the air proved far more difficult than expected.

For just over a year, I had worked for Lieutenant Commander Brett Ulander as one of his CRM Instructors at Naval Aviation Schools Command (NASC). Brett's immediate boss was the Commanding Officer of NASC, Captain Craig *BADROD* Weideman. As a Navy Captain, he was equal in rank to Colonel White. However, Colonel White was responsible administratively for *all* the Marines aboard NAS Pensacola and NAS Meridian, Mississippi. Captain Weideman was operationally responsible for me and a handful of Marine instructors who taught classes within his command. Despite working for a Navy Lieutenant Commander within a Navy Command - NASC, I still belonged to the Marine Colonel, the Commanding Officer of Marine Aviation Training Support Group Twenty-One (MATSG-21), Colonel *JAWS* White.

53 | *Ask and You Will Receive*

COLONEL *JAWS* White was one of the more charismatic Marine Colonels I had ever met or served under. He said what he meant and meant what he said, and he oftentimes did so with a fair amount of color and expression. *JAWS* was a Marine's Marine and he took care of those within his command. His Marines loved him, and we would follow him to the gates of Hell and back. We always knew where we stood with Colonel White. If you stepped out of line, you knew it. But as quickly as he would tell you that you had screwed up, in a heartbeat, he would go to bat for you.

Colonel White had my back from the beginning. A fellow F/A-18 Aviator himself, he offered any assistance he could provide during my cancer battle. As the Commanding Officer of MATSG-21, he had fully supported the NASC Commanding Officer's efforts to provide me Permissive TAD orders to Switzerland months earlier. *JAWS* would soon become a major player in the efforts to get me flying again. I could not have asked for a better Commanding Officer going into the fight with the flight surgeons at NAMI (the Naval Aerospace Medical Institute).

In order to get an appointment with the Colonel, I had to get clearance from his gatekeeper, the Colonel's Executive Secretary, Mrs. Joan Hatch. Joan got me into the Colonel as often as I needed over the next year in order to brief him on each new victory or pending obstacle on my way back to the cockpit. I was just one of the many dozens of Marine Captains in Colonel White's Command. "Miss Joan," as I would address her on my periodic visits, quickly became one of my biggest fans, graciously cheering me throughout my efforts. She and her family have become lifelong friends. Moved by my story and a giving and nurturing personality, Miss Joan took a special interest in my case. If I needed to see the Colonel in order to give him a SITREP regarding my wrestling matches with the Navy, she made that appointment happen as quickly as possible.

Many years later, her grandson and my middle son, Brad, would play baseball and pitch on the same high school team. Joan and I would visit in the stands, fondly reminiscing over our long history together, while occasionally—no, frequently—complaining as parents and grandparents do about the coaches' decisions or the umpires' missed calls as our boys would drop a pitch right on the inside corner. To this very day, decades after our first introduction, each and every time I pass through the hallways of MATSG-21, I've made it a point to stop and give Miss Joan a hug and say thank you for her part in my career being resurrected!

Throughout my efforts to beat cancer and now in my battle with the waiver process, I had the full support of my Marine Corps leadership. This included not only my immediate chain of command, which included Colonel White and Captain *BADROD* of NASC, but also my former Commanding General of the 2nd Marine Aircraft Wing on the east coast, General William *SPIDER* Nyland.

General Nyland had since been promoted to serving as the Pentagon's top Marine Aviator, our Deputy Commandant of Aviation. But in 2001 while I was in Pensacola chugging carrot juice, he was the senior ranking officer in my extended chain of command. As Naval Aviators, we were all *SPIDER*'S Marines. *SPIDER* was the guest speaker at the MATSG-21 hosted Marine Corps Birthday Ball in November 2001, where friend and fellow Pensacola Marine Major Scott Roys reintroduced me to my former Commanding General during the party.

General Nyland listened as I succinctly described how my efforts to beat cancer holistically had worked out and included my month-long trip to Switzerland. I closed our conversation by sharing my heart's desire and deep motivation to fight my way back into a *HORNET* and give the terrorists who had attacked us Hell as soon as I could. The General congratulated me on my first and most important victory and directed me to keep him informed of my progress with returning to flight status.

The General spoke sincerely, "*T-BONE*, reach out if there is anything I can do to expedite your return to the cockpit."

Not long after my exchange with General Nyland at the Marine Corps Birthday Ball in November, the Physical Evaluation Board results had arrived. With the good news in hand, I stopped by to see Miss Joan and tell her everything. She informed me that the Colonel was in his office and that he would be glad to hear from me. When she inquired if he had a minute for me, the Colonel generously made time.

"Captain Trombly, I hear you have some good news," he stated while stepping from behind his desk to shake my hand and invite me to grab a seat. "How the Hell are you, Marine?"

"Outstanding, Colonel! Outstanding! I received word that I will not have to cash a medical retirement check every month and waste the government's money. Looks like I am just going to have to earn my check-in uniform for years to come."

"Now that is good news, Marine! We need to get you back into a fighter so you can go downrange, close with, and destroy the enemy."

Colonel White's phrase, "To close with and destroy the enemy" comes straight from Marine Corps doctrine. It is what we do as Marines. We go downrange, close the distance between us and our enemies, and yes, kill bad people and break things—permanently!

"You let me know what I can do to support the effort, Warrior!"

"Will do, Colonel. I will be visiting NAMI (Naval Aerospace Medicine Institute) in the coming days to take the next steps."

"Outstanding, Captain Trombly. Give 'em Hell!"

"Will do, Colonel. If I may, I could use a little guidance if you have a couple more minutes."

"Fire away, Marine."

"Thank you, Colonel. I had a few minutes to visit with General Nyland at the Birthday Ball. He remembered me as the Marine that was removed from Beaufort due to cancer when he was our Commanding General. He seemed tremendously thrilled when I told him that Bethesda declared me cancer free. He directed me to keep him informed of my progress moving forward. Colonel, my not being forced into a medical retirement seems to be a worthy update, but I am at a loss as to the proper manner in which to correspond with the top Aviation General in the Marine Corps. Do I just drop him an email with the details, Colonel?" I asked, not knowing what response to expect.

"*T-BONE*, General Nyland is *our* General, and he values *every* Marine. You are one of his Marines. If he says he wants to be updated, then he wants to hear from you. Absolutely drop him an email, Captain. He will remember you and will truly appreciate you keeping him in the loop."

"Thank you, Colonel. I will compose an email and send it as soon as I return to my office."

"Oh, and *T-BONE*, make it a very short email."

"Understood, Colonel. Thank you for your time today."

With that salutation, I left *JAWS*' office. I threw Miss Joan a huge smile and went directly to my office to find *SPIDER*'S email address at the Pentagon and send him the shortest email I had ever written with my SITREP on the board's results.

I let nothing distract me now that I had basically been ordered by my Colonel and our top General to send this good news.

414

-----Original Message-----

From: Trombly, David Capt-USMC
Sent: Thursday, January 31, 2002, 10:28 AM
To: nylandwl@hqmc.usmc.mil
Cc: whiteja@matsgfl.usmc.mil; Weideman, Craig CAPT-CO; Roys,
Scott MAJ
Subject: Current status of Captain David M. Trombly

General Nyland,

Sir, my wife and I were introduced to you at the Marine Corps Ball this
past year in Pensacola by Major Scott Roys and his wife. We spoke briefly about my battle and subsequent victory over cancer during the past
fifteen months. At the time I was awaiting a Physical Evaluation Board.
You requested that I keep you informed of my status. That is the purpose
of this email. This past Thursday I received word that the board found
me "Fit For Full Active Duty." That same day I scheduled a flight physical
for February 7th to be followed by six-month follow-up Cat Scans on the
14th. I expect good results from both and will be walking that information
to Mr. Fritz Koppy at NAMI as soon as I have them in my possession.
I am expecting to hear good news from NAMI as well. If all goes well I
could be flying by March, but I am not taking anything for granted until
I have a waiver in hand. There will be a large party at our home after
my first flight back in a jet. I'll be sure to invite you and Brenda. It will be
BYOOCJ (Bring your own organic carrot juice.)

The support I have received from both Colonel White and Captain
Weideman, the Commanding Officer of NASC has been outstanding this
past year. I would like to thank you for having taken a personal interest in
my case. Semper Fidelis.

Very Respectfully,
Capt David T-BONE *Trombly USMC*
USMC TACAIR CRM Program Manager

I proofread the email at least a half dozen times and deleted every extraneous word I could find before I hit send.

Stepping away from my desk to grab my next glass of carrot juice from my mini-fridge and check in with my coworkers, I returned to my desk a little over an hour later and heard the notification tone that I had just received a new email. The Deputy Commandant of Aviation had responded with,

From: Nyland LtGen William L
Sent: Thursday, January 31, 2002
To: Trombly, David CAPT-USMC
Subject: RE: Current status of Captain David M. Trombly

Dave,
This is absolutely terrific news - I could not be more pleased for you and for Marine Aviation. Please give my regards to your wife along with my congratulations on beating this together. I'll look forward to your party invitation and start saving carrot juice!! Fantastic news!!!

God Bless and Semper Fidelis,
SPIDER

Absolutely astonished the General himself had responded so quickly with a personal attaboy and not hours later via a message from his aide-de-camp, I shot back an immediate reply myself. The General was familiar with my cancer battle plan now; so I respond with:

General Nyland,

Thank you very much! Will do, and please know that there will always be an extra glass of chilled carrot juice available upon your return.

Semper Fi,
T-BONE

The miracle of healing and the comfort of peace from God Himself had brought unspeakable contentment and joy to Megan and me. Our victory also served to genuinely encourage all who had walked a mile or two, or those dear friends who walked twenty or more, with us through the valley. Six months passed slowly following the wonderful news of my complete victory over cancer and my subsequent reinstatement to full active duty status by the Physical Evaluation Board in Washington. It had been a period of celebration and a respite from the eleven-month battle we had endured. Yet there was a growing impatience within me with the medical flight waiver process.

After my two visits with Col *JAWS* White and LtCol *BONEY* Orabona, the Commanding Officer of Training Squadron 86, I made it a point to swing by NAMI to plead my case on a weekly basis. Week after week, I methodically and deliberately visited the office spaces in the NAMI building. I had sought orders to Pensacola after my diagnosis in order to be able to knock on NAMI's door relentlessly once cured and in an appropriate time frame to fight for a flight waiver. I personally believed my window of opportunity had finally opened. NAMI firmly disagreed, as it had in fact not even been 12 months, let alone the Medical Guide's two-year requirement to be considered for the decisive waiver.

So with you: Now is your time of grief, but I will see you again and
you will rejoice, and no one will take away your joy. In that day you will
no longer ask me anything. Very truly I tell you, my Father will give
you whatever you ask in my name. Until now you have not asked for
anything in my name. Ask and you will receive,
and your joy will be complete.
—JOHN 16:22-24 (NIV)

NAMI routinely encouraged me to come back after twenty-four
months. I would, of course, wait a week and stop back in for a
friendly visit, making the argument each time to whoever would
be willing to listen that the minimal two-year remission requirement from the waiver guide should not apply to me. I was not in
remission. I had been fully CURED!

Now if I had gone through chemotherapy and radiation, then I
could understand the need to refer to my newly found cancer free
state as remission. I would have also agreed that a wait of two years
should be required as I would need that time to rebuild my immune system. Cancer could get knocked down but not necessarily
knocked out completely, and then it would take some time to return in a significant enough amount to appear on a medical scan.

Unfortunately, in many of those instances, it does come back—
with a vengeance! Undergoing chemo and radiation not only
shrinks the cancer but also knocks down the cancer Warrior's immune system. If the immune system is not able to rebound quickly enough, it is not there to prevent resurging cancer from overwhelming the body completely.

Because I had not received any conventional treatments of chemo and radiation, I argued respectfully yet tenaciously that I was
truly cured and that the two-year wait for returning to the cockpit
should be waived. I could not get anyone to listen to my argument,
as I had no formal medical background and no way to prove what
seemed to be common sense to me and others who assisted me

within biological medicine circles. It was time to bring in some horsepower. I needed to stop by and get some advice from Miss Joan.

"Good morning, Miss Joan. How is the family?" I started.

"Wonderful. Thank you for asking. How are Miss Megan and your little ones?" She greeted me with her famous smile and her ever-engaging joyful demeanor.

"The family is doing great. We are blessed, and we know it."

"Yes, you are. YES, YOU ARE!" she repeated nodding her head. "How can the Colonel and I assist you today, Captain?"

"Ma'am, you read my mind. I am having a little trouble getting the Navy to entertain my request to get back in the sky. In fact, I'm having a hard time getting anyone to have a serious conversation with me at all."

"Well, I think the Colonel might be able to make a phone call and help you with that. Let me see if he has a minute for you."

Moments later as Miss Joan stepped back out of *JAWS'* office I heard, "*T-BONE*, come on in."

The Colonel was up and headed my way as I stepped into his office, and he motioned me to sit in one of the two chairs stationed just in front of his desk. Colonel White sat next to me and said, "What seems to be the trouble over there in NAMI-land."

"Colonel, I hate to bother you as I know how many Marines you are responsible for, but after weeks of knocking on doors, I am getting ZERO traction with anyone at NAMI. I know I have a case to be made and should not have to sit for two solid years. NAMI's waiver guide in no way references any of the methods I used to beat cancer, and as such, the requirements to wait for two years should not apply to me. I believe I have expended all my ammo and am in need of some O-6 level horsepower to get in the door."

I had just referenced the Colonel's military pay grade of O-6, and with some trepidation I waited for his response. To my delight, he concurred.

"Makes perfect sense to me. Why waste your talent on the ground if we can get you into the fight sooner? I'll make a few calls, and Miss Joan will let you know when we have some news."

"Thank you very much, Colonel. I greatly appreciate your time and effort on my behalf." And that quick, I was out the door and back in Miss Joan's space.

"I guess I will be waiting to hear back from you, Ma'am. Have a great week."

"You too, Captain. Keep your chin up. It's all going to work out," she said confidently, as if she already knew the powers of persuasion *JAWS* wielded in his sphere of influence.

54| *Invitations "TWO" Fly*

WHILE waiting for word from Colonel *JAWS* White, I reached out to my former Executive Officer of VMFA-115 back in Beaufort, LtCol Bruce *NOTSO* Bright. *NOTSO* had just been selected to be the next Commanding Officer of VMFA-212, the Lancers in Iwakuni, Japan, and he would be taking Command in a few months. My best chance at getting back into an F/A-18 and seeing combat with Marines whom I had come up through the ranks and served with in my two previous gun squadrons had arrived. I contacted *NOTSO* to congratulate him.

"Good day, 'XO,' *T-BONE* here." Though Lieutenant Colonel Bright was no longer my Executive Officer, I addressed him as such as a term of endearment from our time serving together. "Just wanted to congratulate you on your selection for Command."

"Thank you, Devil Dog. I appreciate the call. How are you doing with that cancer fight?" he asked.

NOTSO was still the Beaufort XO when I attended our Silver

Eagle's reunion with my former squadron mates featuring guest speaker General Joe Foss just days after my diagnosis. *NOTSO* was not yet aware that I had beaten both the disease and the Navy's efforts to medically retire me.

"Sir, I am Full Duty worldwide deployable! Currently fighting to get NAMI to give me the time of day to argue for a waiver so I can get back in the air."

"Congratulations, *T-BONE*, and our congrats to Megan, as well. How is the family doing?"

We spoke for a while about our drop-dead gorgeous wives—his redhead and my brunette; how we were so tremendously blessed; and what our children were up to. We even took a few moments to talk about his Harley Davidson and my 1952 Chevy pick-up truck. Then it happened.

"*T-BONE*, I take Command in a few months. You get your waiver, and I will get you back into the *HORNET* flying for me, Marine."

"Thank you, Colonel. I had hoped you would be willing to have me. Your invitation means the world, Sir. I will continue to beat on NAMI's door until they say yes."

Wow! I now had two open invitations to fly from two Commanding Officers from two different squadrons, both fellow Marine F/A-18 Aviators. Due to the graciousness of the Colonel back at Headquarters Marine Corps (HQMC) in Quantico who was in charge of providing orders for all Aviation Captains, I already had flight orders to Pensacola from almost two years earlier. As a result, all I needed was a waiver from the Navy, and I could serve either as a flight instructor right here in Pensacola or as a warfighter stationed in Japan.

Having two Commanding Officers requesting me by name abundantly boosted my spirits! Once cleared to fly, my first stop would be to get directly into a training aircraft at VT-86 within just a matter of days right here at NAS Pensacola. Once I'd been airborne, current, and qualified as an aviator here, it would be much easier for HQMC to order me back to a *HORNET* squadron (specifically VMFA-212 in Iwakuni, Japan) once NOTSO became the Commanding Officer.

I was extremely optimistic. The Marine Corps was coming through for me in every way. Nothing was preventing me from joining America's newest fight except the Navy, which I was very hopeful would soon say, "Yes."

Two victories under my belt, and now two squadron Commanding Officers offering me a home at the same time! I saw my opportunity to fly and to fight on the horizon. There was no doubt I would be able to get into the fight that had already begun in Afghanistan. It couldn't be too much longer before I could get off the bench and join my fellow Warriors on the field of battle! Or could it?

"Listen to advice and accept discipline, and at the end you will be counted among the wise. Many are the plans in a person's heart, but it is the LORD's purpose that prevails."
—PROVERBS 19:20-21 (NIV)

Colonel White wasted no time reaching out to the Commanding Officer of Naval Aerospace Medical Institute (NAMI), Navy Captain Tegwich. Colonel White personally requested I be looked at for issuing an early waiver. Captain Tegwich considered the Colonel's request, and she agreed to set a date for me to stand before the board and make my argument.

I was directed to go in for an annual flight physical, which I knew would result in my being told that I was NPQ. But this requisite formality had to be completed before I could initiate the appeal process. I eagerly scheduled my first flight physical since the cancer fight at the Branch Medical Clinic aboard NAS Pensacola in March. The Flight Surgeon found me to be in great health, yet he had to issue me my NPQ (Not Physically Qualified) to fly paper-work due to the Waiver Guide's edict that Marines diagnosed with cancer could not fly until granted a waiver. The prior diagnosis forever condemned me to be classified as Not Physically Qualified yet still eligible for a waiver. Handing me back my medical record and Downing Chit, he wished me well in my efforts to acquire a waiver from NAMI.

My evaluations were set to begin Monday, May 13, 2002. This was going to be a full medical workup as if I was a brand new flight student arriving for the first time. The doctors would check nearly every system within my body with any required scans that might not have already been accomplished as part of my six-month on-cology follow-up at Naval Hospital Pensacola. Following this full week of evaluations, the board would convene at 1300 on Friday, May 17.

Hours of effort had gone into the binder I had previously pre-pared for the Physical Evaluation Board back in January. With nothing new to add to its contents, my research preparations for this second board appearance were already complete. I eagerly submitted the invaluable binder once again to be reviewed by a second group of doctors.

Along with double-checking the paperwork prep, I had faithfully hit the gym and was now eight months into rebuilding and restor-ing the muscle mass I had lost the previous year. I had put on a few more pounds of muscle and was quickly regaining my strength with the assistance of a fellow F/A-18 Aviator and friend, Major *TONTO* Ardese.

A fast friendship had developed with *TONTO*, whom I consid-ered to be the strongest, most hard-core Marine in the School-house. I asked if he would be my workout partner. Of American Indian descent, *TONTO* always wore a poultice around his neck under his flight suit, one his grandmother had given him. He shared with me his heritage and his family's beliefs as we swapped stories about our experiences with holistic medicine. At one workout session, I detailed my experiences with the hyperthermia treatments in Switzerland. He countered with his experience as a young man with the Native American sweat boxes. *TONTO* invited me to join him and his family sometime in the future, an invitation I still hope to accept once we reconnect in our retirement.

When *TONTO* and I started working out together, he could bench over 300 pounds. At five foot nine inches tall and having lost thirty pounds from my pre-cancer weight of 175 pounds, I could only push a 45-pound bar during my first week's bench presses. (It is still hard to believe all these years later that I lost so much muscle mass during the battle for my life.)

TONTO, a great leader of Marines, offered zero patience for young students who did not bring their best to the training environment. His high standards went on to serve him well, as he would command a Marine Aircraft Group as a Colonel during his career. *TONTO* did, however, exhibit incredible patience with me in the weight room, faithfully working with me for over a year. Our work paid off! Before our last workout together just prior to his orders out of Pensacola, *TONTO* spotted me bench pressing two hundred and fifty pounds — only a few pounds light of my pre-cancer all-time best!

Having reintroduced fish and chicken to my diet, I was getting stronger each week. *TONTO* and I used a personalized software workout program specifically developed for the Blue Angels by a Naval Aviation physiologist. The designers built this program to build muscle mass rapidly for the purpose of sustaining the significant G-loading the Blue Angels endure each flight during their spectacular demonstrations.

The Blue Angels do not wear the G-suit which fighter pilots are required to wear in-flight; so muscle mass is extremely critical for both their success and safety. The G-suit assists fighter pilots in preventing blood from pooling in our lower extremities while under excessive G-loading. When pilots pull hard on the control stick deflecting the elevator and turning the aircraft sharply, this increases the G-loading on both the aircraft and the pilot. A high-speed turn of more than seven Gs forces our skeletal and muscular system to support seven times our body weight. Therefore, a two-hundred-pound fighter pilot would experience the weight of fourteen hundred pounds of pressure on his body.

The heart is not designed to force blood to the brain under such extreme conditions; so we employ an anti-G straining maneuver to force the blood to remain in the brain. Doing so prevents a loss of consciousness. As fighter pilots, we must tighten all of the muscles in our legs, our glutes, and our core while deliberately restricting our breathing to very quick, deep breaths.

We must employ a breathing cycle which consists of taking a very quick, forceful breath, holding it for three seconds, forcing out all the air in our lungs, and very rapidly inhaling another breath to begin the cycle again. The pilot must maintain this cycle for however long the G loading lasts, or we are going to take a nap and lose control of our aircraft. This muscle-flexing and controlled breathing prevents excessive blood flow into the legs, allowing the pilot to remain conscious and effective throughout the extreme maneuvers.

As May 13 approached, I was growing in confidence. With *TONTO*'s assistance, I was also growing stronger in preparation for the physical demands of flight. My speed was back in my legs. My overall fitness was excellent, and my upper body strength was more than good enough to max perform our annual Marine Corps Physical Fitness Test (PFT). Able to pull more than 20 pull-ups, I ran a near-perfect Marine Corps Physical Fitness Test, dropping only six points. I wasn't where I wanted to be or where I had been years earlier, but I knew one thing. I was in better shape than most every doctor that was going to be evaluating me and voting on whether I should or should not be returned to flight status. I was eager to get the evaluation process started. All I could do now was to continue to train and rebuild my body, pray, and wait for my appointment at NAMI.

Cancer free and growing in strength every day!

After completing my medical and physical evaluations, it was time to face a room full of voting doctors and state my case. This Special Board of Flight Surgeons would review my record, confirm my scans, hear oral presentations from Dr. Ristretto and then from me, then vote. This board consisted of all available flight surgeons from the three local NAS Pensacola flight training squadrons, the six squadrons from NAS Whiting Field, the Naval Aviation Schools Command's senior flight surgeon (my personal flight surgeon), and the designated Naval Flight Surgeons on staff at the Naval Aerospace Medical Institute (NAMI). Located right down the road from my office on NAS Pensacola, NAMI was where the hearing would take place.

Because my form of cancer had not been considered before, nor had anyone stood before such a group having rejected all recommended treatments from the military medical community, this presentation drew a packed house. I was crossing the "Line of Departure" and entering "Enemy Territory." I would soon learn that this territory was robust with doctors predetermined to vote against me even before the proceedings began.

These thirty-one flight surgeons held the authority to reinstate me to flight status. Conversely, this board could keep me from joining my brothers and sisters back in Beaufort, who were all anticipating Persian Gulf deployments. These Marines were joining the efforts to bring justice to the terrorist organization and their governments — the enemy that had to be fought. The fire inside tormented me. *I knew I needed to be there.*

Flying authorization indeed had to be earned. I remained intent on proving I was both physically fit to remain on active duty and also qualified to exercise flight privileges again. If these doctors were going to keep me grounded, they had a fight on their hands. I intended to prove that my luck did not cure my cancer. Rather, the well-informed, decisive actions Megan and I had taken combined with God's sovereign hand had brought healing.

The data I believed this board needed to make this decision came from the thoroughly researched facts Megan and I acquired during the cancer battle, and I delivered it in the same well-organized report I had previously shared with the January Board in D.C. I had given this package to Navy Lieutenant Commander Ristretto, the NAMI Internal Medicine doctor who was appointed to represent me at the NAMI hearing.

Colonel White had convinced Captain Tegwich to start proceedings on my behalf as quickly as possible. In just a matter of weeks, I would stand before the Board with whom I had been seeking an audience for months. With the hard work of rehabilitation complete, I was ready to fight. In my thinking, this Special Board of Flight Surgeons had to see the truth in order for God's promise to me in Captain Morgan's office to be fulfilled. As such, I was confident that victory was only a week away, unaware that a traitor had infiltrated a strategic position in the forthcoming appearance before the board.

PART NINE

FIRST DEFEAT

"Failure is not a one-time event;
it's how you deal with life along the way.
Until you breathe your last breath, you're still in the process,
and there is still time to turn things around for the better."

—JOHN MAXWELL,
New York Times Bestselling Author,
Entrepreneur, and Influencer

55| *Repeating a Vetted War Plan*

I had not forgotten what God had promised me when Captain Morgan shared my diagnosis. As I shook his hand that first day of my journey, I declared to him what God had declared to me in my heart. "Captain, a strong will to win is second only to a deep faith in God. I have both. I will not only beat this disease, but I will FLY again!"

The day Captain Morgan told me that the tumor he'd removed was malignant tissue, I was *grounded*. My flight status changed indefinitely from PQ (Physically Qualified) to NPQ (Not Physically Qualified. There are a lot of three-letter acronyms that strike fear in people, such as FBI, CIA, KGB, and of course, IRS. Only one steals the joy and shatters the confidence of any Naval Aviator—NPQ! Having been NPQ for just shy of two years and cancer free for less than one, I was days away from making my presentation to the doctors who could reverse that label. It was time to fight again! Coming off a tremendous victory over cancer and remembering God's promise, I was confidently optimistic that the next victory was around the corner. This fighter pilot would FLY again!

Even as Megan and I had celebrated victory over cancer months earlier, we knew there were more battles ahead. Just as we needed an emotional and physical reprieve from combat, so did our Prayer Warriors. Having given them a break from January to May, it was time to reenlist support as we rolled up our sleeves to fight once more. This second engagement with the military medical system, if victorious, would once again provide me the privilege to fly. This second fight was going to be an extended engagement, and for me to emerge victoriously would be equally as miraculous.

I realized God had provided the first victory, and it would be God who would be the victor again. He honored and answered the prayers of hundreds of our friends.

> "Therefore confess your sins to each other and pray for each other so that you may be healed. The prayer of a righteous person is powerful and effective."
> —JAMES 5:16 (NIV)

Prayer had been a key weapon of our warfare. Why change the strategy now? If it ain't broke; don't fix it. So I dusted off our original War Plan and sent the following message to all our wingmen requesting prayer as we prepared for the NAMI battle. This SITREP contained a little surprise. God had provided another great blessing on top of my healing, and it was time to share the good news with everyone while calling our friends to battle with us.

I sent my next SITREP (Situation Report) on Saturday, May 11, 2002:

From: David Trombly
Date: May 11, 2002 at 6:33:27 PM CDT
Subject: Our Next Challenge

Dear Friends and Family,

Megan and I are again sending out a long overdue update to all of our friends and family. The timing of this one is critical as we are challenging all of you to take some time to pray for us this coming week.

All of you have been such an integral part of our success this past year and a half. Megan and I sincerely believe and have shared with you numerous times how strongly we feel that your prayers have given us the strength to stand strong and possess a peace that passes all understanding—a peace that can only come from God.

431

Your faithfulness to our family and the love and sacrifices that you have given for us is overwhelming.

Today we come to you humbly requesting your support again. Monday morning at 0700, I will start a week-long medical evaluation. This will be done here in Pensacola by the Special Board of Flight Surgeons. These doctors will spend the week doing every kind of test they deem necessary to determine if I will be returned to flight status. There will be the standard eye, ear, and heart exams, and I may get the old Dr. Jelly finger routine. (Those of you with flight experience, or are over forty or have too much time on your hands, you know what I mean.) I may do a pressure chamber and certainly a psychiatric evaluation. I know many of you that I have worked with in the past are interested in the results of that test. Basically, I will be going through the most thorough physical evaluation I've had since the cancer staging at Bethesda almost 19 months ago.

We are all well. All systems are functioning and I have regained my weight and my strength from before the diagnosis. In fact, I am stronger and faster than I have been in 6 years. As a matter of fact, to prove that all systems are functioning, I want to share that Megan is pregnant with number 5. This child is truly a miracle. We believe to be a special blessing; God's way of saying 'Well done, you did it right.'

Had we gone through with chemo this would have been impossible. We certainly would not have taken any measures to provide for future children with our size family. We kind of look at this new child the way Noah probably looked at the Rainbow after the flood.

A PROMISE OF THINGS TO COME!!

Anyway, we will keep you all informed of the progress of our family and of this week's Board results.

God has opened every door so far to see me reinstated to flying. He healed the disease, put it on the hearts of the Medical Board in DC to reinstate me to full active duty in January, and He too has this in His hands. Some days I get anxious over the results to come and what I might do if they say no. But when I look back over all that God has brought us through the past two-plus years, I can't help but realize that He is in control.

I have done my part boldly seeking to fulfill what I see to be my duty—to return to flight status. We put this matter in God's hands asking Him for peace to get through the next few days.

Please pass our request and our best wishes and sincere thanks to your Church Families and to all the others who have been supporting us in prayer so faithfully this past year.

Megan and I love all of you and are indebted to you for your prayers, time, efforts, sacrifices and friendship. Keep seeking Him, as we endeavor to do the same.

In God's Hands,
David and Megan
Psalm 91

A MOMENT WITH MEGAN

Oh, this email! David and I were so, so excited that our prayers were answered! Finally—no cancer! Finally, our family could get back to balance and life as it was before cancer. Yet while I knew that God was good all the time, I had unanswered questions.

David was spending time in the gym and continuing to eat/drink the things I prepared daily, and our children were ending another year of homeschool. But I was tired and dreaming of the day I would get back to being able to focus on my fitness.

Before David's diagnosis, I restricted myself to an 80%raw and 20% cooked diet and worked out two hours a day. But when the cancer battle began, I forgot to take care of myself. I forgot the value of that time and those particular foods that helped me manage my stress. I laid down my life's health to help the man I loved. However, the stress mounted over the year. I ate on the run and gained weight. In short, I felt myself getting weaker as David was getting stronger.

My health was in fact quite the opposite of David's. So this amazing news of another child evoked very different reactions in the two of us. What gave me pause wasn't the baby . . . for our son, Noah, I am forever grateful. It was the timing; it was the thought that I couldn't do any more. I was past being done; I was overdone: completely depleted and exhausted.

Megan with little Noah, the fifth child,
both a blessing and a promise!

I had four young children whose schooling I needed to catch up on, who needed their one-on-one time and their individual needs met. And what about me? When was I supposed to rest? Who was going to take care of me? Yes, for me as mom and caretaker, though we were rejoicing at David's miraculous health milestones and news of a new baby, my body was weeping.

> *I had to learn that life doesn't stop just because we fight a battle.*
> *And I realized that it was God's mercy and blessing that gifted our*
> *family with a new life, in fact two more lives! But looking back, I*
> *should have prioritized time for me to take care of myself along the*
> *journey. So if you are the caretaker, set up the time to take care of*
> *yourself.*

As our friends prayed, I prepared to appear at the upcoming Special Board of Flight Surgeons review. The doctor who would be my advocate and who put together all the data to brief this august crowd of medical professionals was my Internal Medicine doctor at NAMI, Lieutenant Commander Ristretto.

Lieutenant Commander Ristretto and I had spent countless hours together over the previous couple of weeks preparing for this historic day at NAMI. He had taken my case after my reinstatement to full Active Duty by the previous panel of judges. Then the January Physical Evaluation Board and Captain Tegwich agreed to initiate the waiver process early upon Colonel White's request.

Lieutenant Commander Ristretto directed my follow-up for additional CT scans of my head and abdomen as well as an X-ray of my lungs. He coordinated my appointments within NAMI for my ears and eyes and even scheduled me for a psychological evaluation.

My time with the NAMI psychiatrist was entertaining, and I recognized the two Army Flight Surgeon students who had come over to my home to interview me sitting on the psychologist's couch as I entered his office. There was a third Army Captain sitting along the back wall behind the doctor. I stood in the doorway of this tiny room filled with Army Flight Surgeon trainees of the same rank as me and realized the only seat left was the one immediately to the doctor's left in the corner. The psychologist was at his desk, his back to the hallway. He did not see me about to enter the room.

The Army doctors all looked up at me with a rather serious demeanor as if pre-briefed by this senior officer that this was to be a professional and serious meeting. Not thrilled about walking into a four-doctor interview, I had to take immediate control of the room.

"Doc, there are a couple of female army docs on your leather sofa. Now how am I supposed to lie naked on your couch and bare my soul?"

Both of the Army Captains I knew laughed out loud, breaking the tension. They had come to know Megan and me a fair bit over dinner at our house recently. The other Captain wasn't sure what to make of me. He just stared straight-faced at me. More than likely, he was thinking that I needed to revisit my annual training requirements because I'd said "naked" in a public setting (and you just can't say things like that in today's military). He would get over it.

Without turning or looking away from his computer, my interviewer simply questioned me with one word, "Marine?"

"Yes, Sir!" I said confidently.

"There is nothing wrong with this one. He is as normal as they come. You are dismissed," he joked.

I just stood there for a moment with a confident smile, quite pleased with my initial entry. Grinning like the cat who had just successfully swallowed a canary, I knew I had made a good first impression with three out of the four in the room, one being the senior evaluator. I was off to a great start.

"You're still here?" the psychiatrist asked rhetorically. "Glutton for punishment, I see. Have a seat. Let's see what dark secrets we can learn about you today."

The evaluation was brief. He asked about my time at Bethesda, drilling down specifically on the type and location of the cancer diagnosis. Many of the answers he was seeking were in my record already. I gathered he was just determining if I understood the significance of this Special Board of Flight Surgeons. There was nothing too memorable about the event, other than my entry and exit from the room, and in no time I was dismissed for real.

"I find you to be about as normal as any Marine Fighter Pilot gets. Thanks for stopping in, Captain Trombly. Godspeed with the board."

"Thank you, Sir. I appreciate your time."

I dropped a friendly head nod back to my new friends on the sofa. "I'll see you at the board next week. Vote for me," I said, smiling as I made my exit.

56| *Unraveling in the Situation Room*

WITH all interviews, scans, blood work, and functional evaluations finally completed, I was ready for the big day. I entered the room and was invited to sit on the front row in the first seat closest to the small table where the president of this Special Board of Flight Surgeons, Navy Captain Tegwich, sat. Captain Tegwich was the Commanding Officer of NAMI, and in the end, she would become one of my most supportive allies within the Navy medical system with regards to my efforts to get back to flight duty.

Once Lieutenant Commander Ristretto received a head nod from Captain Tegwich to begin, he stepped to the podium to proceed. My day in court had finally arrived, and I was ready for a third victory!

Lieutenant Commander Ristretto and I had painstakingly walked through my research binder while preparing for these boards. As we walked through the material, I was confident that he was reviewing the documents looking for material to support my arguments for returning to flight status.

His introduction and detailed layout of my diagnosis was straight-forward if not clinical in nature, but I was completely blindsided by the words he spoke only minutes into his presentation.

"Madam President, Esteemed Colleagues: While Captain Trombly is currently clear of any sign of cancer as indicated by his CT scans and MRI, it is my recommendation this board should *not* grant a flight waiver at this time." He continued as if what he had already said was not condemning enough. "While the traditional waiver approval would begin no sooner than two years from the start of remission and we are well inside the two-year window, I do not recommend that there be a waiver even in two years."

His line of reasoning painted me as an irresponsible and foolish individual. "Should Captain Trombly still be cancer free as the two-year window opens, the facts will not change that Captain Trombly chose to do his own research and develop his own plan to fight cancer with unproven, unscientific methods, needlessly risking his life to avoid the chemotherapy and radiation that Bethesda direct-ed. This level of arrogance and unwillingness to take on the wise and educated counsel of his military doctors in order to pursue unproven methods speaks far louder than the MRI and CT scan results." Condescension and judgment dripped from every word.

"Are we not responsible for all aviators that Captain Trombly could fly with or around? Are we not charged with the solemn re-sponsibility to ensure that an aviator with a proven record for poor decision-making ability be kept out of the air, despite his physical condition being clean for the past many months?"

This man was supposed to be my personal advocate! I'd shared everything I had done with him. I trusted him as if he were Dr. Ostergaard, whom I had invited to attend my board as a character reference should something like this happen. I was so glad that Dr. O was there and that he did indeed get to speak for a brief moment on my behalf. Unfortunately, that positive endorsement was delivered after I was invited to leave the room for the deliberation portion of the board.

I was unsure of the ROE (Rules Of Engagement). Was I able to fire this guy like a court-appointed attorney? It quickly became apparent that he did not work for me, was not my advocate, but rather was serving in the exact role of his job title, the NAMI Internal Medicine specialist. He represented NAMI. At no time did he represent me, nor was he working to build a case for me to fly again. All the data I had delivered, the conversations and explanations of why I chose to do these treatments and avoid chemotherapy he skillfully used to make an argument against my ever flying in the military again, never mind after two years in remission.

I was mad... mad as a hornet. Shocked and betrayed, I felt my blood rapidly evacuating the vessels in my face, yielding me both physically and emotionally frozen. My hopes of flying drained from my spirit the way Caesar's blood drained from his veins as his most trusted advisor, Brutus, stabbed him in the back. I knew I had antagonists in the room who were not going to support my efforts to return to the skies. However, I did not know until that lethal blow struck on this grand stage that LCDR Ristretto was not the trusted ally I had believed him to be.

Soon, hoping to win over enough of the younger flight surgeons to win my case, I would take the few brief minutes afforded me to make my argument. Fortunately, I had a prepared statement; so I did not have to develop my response under this crushing stress.

This wasn't the first time my circumstances had demanded a cool head while under tremendous pressure. Instantly I was back in the cockpit on that dark and stormy Texas night where I ultimately earned my call-sign, *T-BONE*. Just as in that chaos I had to professionally execute my emergency procedures without panic to survive the night, I had to maintain my bearing as my Benedict

Arnold manipulated the conference room to survive the day. It was again time to follow that age old advice we all learn as young aviators from our sage experienced flight instructors: "SOUND COOL, BE COOL."

This tried-and-true principle is quite simple. When you stay calm and *sound cool* over the radio, you will *be cool* in the cockpit in the midst of the crisis—in this case, the emotional chaos I was now processing as I awaited my career-defining moment.

Once Lieutenant Commander Ristretto concluded his presentation and delivered his findings that I ought not to be returned to flight status, the president of the board offered me the floor. I maintained my composure despite my intense anger and sense of betrayal over the treachery of my advocate and spoke briefly, reading from the following prepared statement:

"Captain Tegwich, Members of the Board: Thank you for this opportunity to speak. Doctor Ostergaard, thank you for coming. I would like to personally thank you — the voting members for taking the time to be here when you could have been flying or catching up on other pressing issues you have been tasked with.

Nineteen months ago today, OCT 17, 2000, I received word of my disease as well as the greatest challenge I would have to face up to and including today. That's right — even today. THE LAST YEAR AND A HALF HAS BEEN ABOUT PREPARING FOR TODAY. FOR ME, TODAY IS GAME DAY AND IT IS MY INTENTION TO HIT THE BALL OUT OF THE PARK!

Everything I have done for the past 19 months has been carefully researched, and faithfully and diligently executed for the express purpose of literally living to see this day and have this opportunity to say these words. The goals of these endeavors were two-fold: Longevity via cure of my disease and reinstatement to flight status as a SERVICE GROUP I NAVAL AVIATOR.

440

It has been explained to me that after my statement you will deliberate over my case and render a decision that will determine what future I have as a Naval Aviator if at all.

I realize after spending a week at NAMI that you will have questions, concerns and no doubt a spirited debate about my choices of modalities chosen and my decision process after I leave this room.

It is my intention in the next few minutes to answer some of those questions and eliminate some of the fair and appropriate concerns. In doing so I hope to make it easier for you to grant me a waiver to Service Group I.

I stated in my introduction that all I have done was carefully chosen in order to beat my disease PRIMARILY, and to PRESERVE my ability to fly single piloted training and tactical jet aircraft for the Marine Corps! I believed then that in order to accomplish both I had to find a way to side-step the possible debilitating side effects of chemo and radiation that MAY have saved my life, but very likely could have caused irreversible damage to my heart, other vital organs, and even my eyes, thus preventing me from ever flying jet aircraft again.

MAKE NO MISTAKE, ladies and gentlemen, my PRIMARY goal and continued priority is longevity, to be here for many years with the woman of my dreams — a very supportive wife whom I could not have beat this disease without. I have my fifth child coming and my children need a father. I would never allow my flying or desire to fly to get in the way of my family or allow me to lose sight of my priorities. You can rest assured that my health comes first and I would immediately inform my flight surgeon of any abnormality as soon as I became aware of it. My integrity on this issue cannot be questioned. I refer you to the inch-thick packet of research I compiled for the PEB and NAMI 6 months ago. In it, I carefully documented all I have done to include the self-medicating with natural immune boosters not recognized by the FDA. Why would I share that unless I had every intention of demonstrating my forthrightness regardless of the cost? Let no one question my integrity on this issue!

My greatest priority is my faith and relationship with God above all else.

We may not come to an agreement today on why I am cancer free at this time. As I understand it, that is not the debate of the day. However, I believe we can all agree that only God knows and I am very comfortable in giving Him all the credit and Glory for this victory.

Next, come my wife and children and that has been pointed out to you already. Then and only then comes the duty to my country through service as a Marine Officer.

My flight status is not just a privilege that I wish to enjoy again in the future. No, I see it as a fulfillment of my oath, my duty for the past year and today and for as long as it takes is to aggressively fight on the ground for my flight status to be reinstated.

The Marine Corps invested a significant portion of limited funds to train me to be a single piloted tactical aviator. It is my responsibility to fulfill, at a minimum, my contractual obligation to faithfully carry out my duties by expending every ounce of energy and every resource to regain my health, rebuild my strength and G-tolerance and to regain my flight status. The former I have accomplished, only one task remains.

Whether I eat, rest, push weights, gut out sit-ups, run, man a classroom podium, travel to inspect the CRM programs of the Fleet Replacement Squadrons around the country, or stand a duty; I HAVE ONE THING IN MIND, REINSTATEMENT TO A SERVICE GROUP I FLIGHT STATUS.

By this point, it should be obvious to you that my desire here is for Service group I alone. I understand that a Service Group II may still allow me to instruct in the T-2. I have orders to fly down here and have the invitation of the future CO of VT-86 to execute those orders in his squadron as an augment instructor while I continue to serve as the Marine Corps Crew Resource Management expert for the Navy's CRM program.

LtCol Orabona is aware of my current diet and Cleansing plans to take place every six months for a week. As an augment I would not be flying during that week, as I have to teach academics one week of every month anyway. The bottom line is this: a Service Group III Waiver would not accomplish my mission and would force me into a C-12 or C-130. I have no desire to perform such duties or to take my experience to the airlines. I want to fly the T-2 for the next two years, and get promoted after the convening of this September's Majors Board in which I am more likely to be promoted if I am flying. At the conclusion of those orders, my commitment will be satisfied. My options at that point are many and will have to be carefully explored with the needs of my family taking precedence. If the war is raging and the Air Force is not stealing all the action, and the Marine Corps is involved as we should be, I will continue to fight to get back to the F/A-18. Otherwise, I plan to pursue Test Pilot School after flight instructing and building my hours to a level that would be acceptable for my admission. Another option at that time is to join the reserve squadron to be built down here and to continue training this country's future warriors. Regardless of which of the three choices I take, all require an SG I Waiver.

In conclusion, I would ask you to consider the events of this past week to include the Memorial Day events we all attended. As you consider the seriousness of the job we undertake in Naval Aviation, the responsibility you have in holding the keys to these aircraft and to the dreams, aspirations, and call to duty of the men and women you see and support each day—today that would include me—please remember that each one of us does this because it is a love and a calling not a job. I would not have fought this hard for 19 months for a paycheck or any job, but for my dream, my calling, my sense of duty.

I chose this job because my grandfather before me was a fighter pilot during WWII. He died just before the end of the war. I know that I honor him and other heroes of the past in my chosen career path. It is what I have always wanted to do.

Four months ago I faced a Physical Evaluation Board (PEB). According to my doctors, it would result in an almost certain Medical retirement. That may have been a quick 40-50 Grand that I could have used to pay all my medical bills with, but it was not what I wanted. I was forced to sit through a DTAP class with 14 people who were getting forced out of the military. Some of them had minor medical issues, one man had ALS and was convinced he would be dead in 18 months. I was a healthy 32-year-old who no more wanted to sit in that class than I wanted to sit at home and watch the events of Sept 11th and following unfold as friends of mine in VMFA-25l flew sorties off the USS Theodore Roosevelt night after night fighting this new and very real war on terror. Imagine for a moment the frustration I felt and continue to feel not being able to fly or be called up to fly by a potential CO despite my health and fitness level today. Today I may be able to run a 294 Marine PFT, but that won't get me airborne. Only you can remove that frustration and hand me back the keys to my career.

Saku Koivu, Captain of the Montreal Canadians hockey team, and Mario Lemuix, both overcomers of Non-Hodgkin's and Hodgkin's disease respectively fought for their lives and then were afforded the opportunity to pursue their dreams to earn the Stanley Cup, hockey's greatest prize. Lance Armstrong fought first for his family and then for the opportunity to make history three times at the Tour de France.

I now have my health and my aspirations. My prize is the lofty goal of service to my country as a Naval Aviator in a single piloted aircraft. I ask you, what better goal or career could I pursue than the last?

I ask you to return me to my place among the warriors, training America's future warriors today, and eventually if required or called to lead those warriors tomorrow.

Captain Tegwich, unless someone has a question for me I have finished pleading my case to the best of my ability. I very respectfully thank you, the board, and the voting members for your patience and careful consideration on my behalf.

Semper Fidelis

Despite the proper use of the term remission from the conventional point of view, I never used it in my prepared comments.

444

Even in the Navy's building at my own hearing, I refused to use the word remission.

I believed I should be reinstated, having less than a 1% chance of incapacitation from the disease which was now gone as per the very waiver guide requirement from which we were to make our informed decision. By *Navy doctor* standards, I was cancer free and remained cancer free. Not choosing the establishment's methods for treatment was not a medical reason to keep me grounded, but an emotional one. I had no heart valve damage, cataracts, or organ damage as caused by the side effects of chemotherapy that would preclude me from flying.

My robust immune system, now stronger than before my cancer diagnosis, having zero chemotherapy or radiation side effects that would further ground me, should have been the ultimate determining factor. The two-year post-treatment delay before issuing a waiver should not have applied in my case.

After making the calmest and most thoughtful and purely scientific argument I could, based on the data I thought the board members would receive, I did make one emotional plea but kept it focused on Memorial Day and a sense of duty, pointing them to my grandfather's service.

"Ladies and Gentlemen, I must tell you that after sharing my heart, thoughts, concerns, and decision-making processes with him, I am truly shocked by Dr. Ristretto's recommendation. It is apparent that he has taken this information and used it to argue that my judgment cannot be trusted. I believe that your psychologist found me to be of sound mind. Furthermore, the Marine Corps has trusted me as a leader of Marines."

I could only pray now that the board members would make their decision solely based on whether the science had demonstrated my physical condition as medically worthy for reinstatement to flying status. I could only pray they would not allow their deliberation to degenerate into a debate between alternative medicine versus conventional medicine. I feared that if this hearing became a referendum on biological and alternative medicine, then all my time would have been wasted.

I was directed to wait in the waiting area in front of the building. I found a seat and sat quietly, eyes closed, tuning out the conversations and noise of the waiting area. There were very few individuals left when I stepped out of the board room, and within the hour, the front of the building cleared out. I spent the next hour and a half alone—waiting.

I thought about some of my most memorable flights and dreamed about my first flight back in a slick jet, dancing around the clouds and breaking the sound barrier just because I could! My thoughts quickly returned to the ground and all the trips that Megan and I had taken up and down the eastern seaboard pursuing therapies and knowledge. Overwhelmed with gratitude, I thought about this godly woman who had stood by me from day one and helped me survive to be able to fight that day's battle for my career. I wanted so badly to bring Megan some great news!

The longer I waited, the less hopeful I became, anticipating that just as I feared, the discussion had degraded into a debate over alternative versus conventional medicine. If so, I merely awaited bad news, as even today, two decades later, no aviator could win that debate with this audience.

57| *From Crushing Defeat to D.C. Bound*

MY repeated prayer when I was first excused from the boardroom into the waiting area was centered on getting the votes. Repeatedly I prayed, "Please, Father, get me the votes that will put me back up in the air." As time passed and my confidence waned in this board's ability not to degrade into a full-on, heated debate over my choices instead of the desired topic of my current state of wellness, my prayer slowly changed.

I stopped asking for votes and favor with the doctors. I stopped pleading for this moment to be the moment of victory. Instead, I began just talking with God, my Heavenly Father. Sitting still, I became thankful and began slowly letting go . . . of the outcome of this board.

"Thank you, Lord! Thank you for your victory over this cancer! Thank you that I still have my jawbone and all my original teeth. Thank you, Father, for the strength that is returning to my body! Father, I am so grateful for what you have already provided—my cure!"

Believing God had promised both the cure and the flying to be returned to me, I relaxed and waited with a greater sense of peace than I had when I started my vigil in the waiting area. I knew what God had promised. I just had no idea when it would happen or what I was to do next if the doctors inside indeed said "No."

Maybe Dr. Ostergaard could capture a few more votes. Only he, my trusted friend and greatest cheerleader within the military medical community over the past year, remained in the board-room with the platform to fight a whole platoon of his peers for me. If given the opportunity to speak, maybe Dr. Ostergaard could enlighten the audience on my true character. Perhaps he could bring one or two more board members to my camp if they recognized that I was not irrational or irresponsible, as Dr. Ristretto had so effectively yet inaccurately portrayed me to be.

In addition to Dr. Ostergaard, who graciously accepted my invitation to attend, I only knew for sure that I had two additional allies—the two Army Flight Surgeon Trainees who had come over to my home months earlier and interviewed Megan and me. They were intrigued when they heard I was trying to return to flight status and learned our amazing story of this rare bone cancer in the skull disappearing without conventional therapy. They had spent that evening with Megan and me and were fully supportive of my quest to return to flying, and they would have voted for me if they were eligible. But they were still trainees with the Navy.

These same two Army flight surgeons did, however, invite me to San Antonio months later to share my testimony in front of over two hundred Navy, Army, and Air Force Flight Surgeons and military physicians at the Aerospace Medical Association's (AsMA) Annual Scientific Meeting. It was an honor to tell these doctors that God healed me and to encourage them to listen to their patients and not summarily dismiss them when they sincerely asked about alternative options.

Finally, a young flight surgeon stepped out and found me in the waiting area, inviting me back into the proceedings. He wore a poker face, and I could not read any clues from him as we walked back to the meeting room. The president of the board invited me to the front of the room and reported the results of the vote.

"Captain Trombly, at this time this Special Board of Flight surgeons has voted not to reinstate you via a waiver for Non-Hodgkin's Lymphoma by a vote of 19-12. That being said, you do have the right to appeal this decision to Admiral Hart's office at BUMED in Washington, D.C. via a Senior Board of flight surgeons. Do you have any questions or comments for the board?"

Recognizing it would do no good to question them on their decision at the conclusion of their proceedings, I simply panned the room looking at each member. I offered a sincere thank you for their effort to give me the fairest look possible under the circumstances. I am sure those who voted for me *knew* what I was saying. As to those who didn't, it would have gone over their heads anyway. After twenty minutes waiting in the foyer, I knew that my fears had been realized and the discussion had digressed. It was never about returning a cured Marine back to the cockpit, but about how I found my cure. This decision was a crushing defeat and one I had hoped to avoid by imploring the board members in my prepared statement not to fixate on the methodology but on the man.

A number of the younger doctors made their way to the front of the room to pass their regrets that the vote had not gone my way. Meanwhile, their older colleagues exited swiftly. More than one flight surgeon encouraged me to keep fighting and assured me that I had their vote if I returned next year to try again.

After the last encouraging doctor left, the president of the board asked me to take a seat. She was gracious and apologetic as she began.

"Captain Trombly, you handled yourself very well today, and you made me and your fellow Marines proud. I think you know what happened in here this afternoon, don't you?"

"Yes, Ma'am. I am pretty confident that after the initial debate in which no one could have argued about me being truly cancer-free, the discussion went off the rails despite my respectful request that it not do so. I would wager a month's salary that the older flight surgeons who outnumbered the younger made it less about a highly trained fighter pilot returning to the cockpit and more about the very thing I requested not be their focus—alternative versus conventional medicine."

"You are exactly right. Your case was lost in the first half hour. Then the discussion continued for over two hours in a very interesting, and you may be interested to know, heated debate. Many young flight surgeons believed you should be reinstated and maintained that position throughout the agitated discussions. Unfortunately, you were four flight surgeons short of a victory, with a very consistent divide between the old school and the younger doctors."

"Ma'am, I appreciate your time to inform me of this," I said, assuming my time with Captain Tegwich was over.

"I have more, Captain Trombly. As the president of the board, I feel it is my duty to tell you that you did not get a fair shake today, and I recommend that you appeal to Admiral Hart's office. If you choose to do so, you will go to Washington, D.C. and appeal this decision in front of a panel of five Navy Captains and one Marine Line Officer. They are the only body that has the authority to overturn this decision. Or you may wait and try again here in twelve months.

"Thank you for the information, Captain Tegwich, and for facilitating as fair of a hearing as could have been afforded me, considering the volatility of this topic in our culture today. I will most certainly seek to appeal with Admiral Hart's office once the results are published."

I shook Captain Tegwich's hand and excused myself. I had lost the battle that day. It was my first significant setback since that dark day in Bethesda. But just as we drove north from Bethesda bloodied from that battle yet confident victory lay ahead, I pulled out of the NAMI parking lot confident that Captain Tegwich had given me the best COA (Course of Action) to win the war.

A MOMENT
WITH MEGAN

By now, you know David is the eternal optimist! I knew David would champion this one glimmer of hope that Captain Tegwich gave him to appeal all the way to Washington, D.C. I was not worried about his career, just hopeful that for David's sake, God would grant him the victory.

The board findings were officially signed by Board President Captain Tegwich, on June 10 and made available to me exactly one week after the board concluded on June 17, 2002. I read the executive summary and the detailed findings from LCDR Ristretto *multiple times* as righteous indignation stoked a fire within me.

After copying and filing the original report in my filing cabinet at home, I liberally marked up the duplicate copy. I circled any comment with which I took issue via a red highlighter. Between the lines, between the paragraphs, and in the margins, I printed counter-arguments to LCDR Ristretto's assertions. Beside every bogus assumption or false declaration neatly typed in black ink, I angrily scribbled my counterpoints in blue.

In order to stand before five Navy Captains and one Marine Lieutenant Colonel in Washington and counter the forceful indictment levied by LCDR Ristretto regarding my judgment and decision-making ability, I certainly needed something stronger than my personal rebuttal scribbled in the margins of the Pensacola Board's report. It was time to visit both Colonel *JAWS* White and Captain *BADROD* Weideman to muster some firepower to attach to my formal request for an appeal.

JAWS and *BADROD* each afforded me a sit-down, an opportunity for me to walk them through the Special Board's findings and my personal rebuttal. Both Senior Officers drafted a First Endorsement Letter to Admiral Hart highly recommending my return to flight status and requesting my appeal to the Senior Board be granted at the earliest possible opportunity.

In addition to his powerful endorsement letter to Admiral Hart in D.C., Colonel White generously arranged for my upcoming annual FITREP, the yearly fitness report performance evaluation that all non-commissioned and commissioned military officers receive, — to be written by Captain *BADROD* Weideman and reviewed by

451

JAWS himself.

This was an unprecedented offer. Rather than having LCDR Brett Ulander write my FITREP as an O-4 and have it reviewed by Major *DOC* Knell as an O-4, I was going to have my next FITREP written by two O-6's! Having a Navy Captain and a Marine Colonel draft and sign an exemplary FITREP for me as a Marine Captain, O-3, was unprecedented. It most assuredly would make a statement!

This offer definitively not only opened the door to D.C. but also afforded me my next promotion to Major a year later, despite my having spent a couple of years medically grounded. Significant time out of the cockpit often becomes a career-ending event. The loyalty-forging support *JAWS* provided at the start of every board I had to face also provided support for my next promotion.

The FITREP from *BADROD* and *JAWS* was extraordinary — one of the top two highest-graded fitness reports of my career. The month also brought me a nomination for the 2002 Naval Aviation Schools Command's General Roy S. Geiger Instructor of the Year award. That honor wasn't awarded until 2003; however, this year's nomination served me well on my FITREP. It helped accomplish the task of dispelling the damaging character issues put forth by LCDR Ristretto. Colonel *JAWS* White and Captain *BADROD* Weideman's exemplary comments combined with the Instructor of the Year nomination and other accomplishments working under LCDR Ulander's mentorship provided the justification for my senior leaders to flex their Command muscle and endorse me as fiercely as they did.

The success I was having physically in my reconditioning with *TONTO* along with the favor I was finding with my senior military leadership in *JAWS* and *BADROD* only emboldened my saber-rattling with the medical boards. Any documented push back by a medical professional that departed even slightly from a purely medical assessment or crossed the line toward character assassination was met with the full force of my own defense and dual letters of support from my O-6 level senior leadership.

The Marine Corps fully supported my efforts, as did the Navy Command I was serving. Only some in the Medical Corps offered condemnation. I had a united front going into the Senior Board of Flight Surgeons' hearing, while the medical community had a fractured defense with some supporting me and others opposing. Ultimately, the decision came down to Admiral Hart's team of five Navy Captains and one Marine Lieutenant Colonel.

Little did I know that just as I had an unknown *enemy* in my camp stepping into the Special Board of Flight Surgeons, an unknown *ally* waited to support me upon my arrival in D.C.!

PART TEN

FINAL VICTORY

"God has His part, or margin in everything, that's where prayer comes in. . . . We've got to get not only the chaplains but every man in the Third Army to pray. We must ask God to stop these rains."

The force of 250,000 troops did pray,
and God changed the weather.

—**GENERAL GEORGE S. PATTON,**
U.S. Army Commanding General in the European and
Mediterranean Theatres during World War II

58| *"Too Close for Missiles! Switching to Guns!"*

LCDR Ristretto had made this fight personal in more ways than one. It was one thing to elicit every pertinent detail he needed out of me by drawing me in close and leading me to think he was my advocate. It was something completely different to surprise me with the use of our private conversations and twist them to sink my efforts during the medical board. It was even more demoralizing and unappreciated to insert numerous assumptions into his official report for Admiral Hart's team—many of which were completely unfounded at worst or painted only half the picture at best. As a former dog-fighting aviator, I was itching for a fight, now in more ways than one. Losing the board by such a close vote, I needed a phone booth to climb into with a dedicated adversary for a knife fight. I rolled up my sleeves and grabbed my weapons of choice—my red highlighter and blue pen—and proceeded to dismantle my opponent's slanderous report. I may have lost the previous medical board battle, but I had been given the opportunity to get in the last word via this appeal process.

LCDR Ristretto's report was received and finalized in Washington D.C. The cover letter was signed by one of Admiral Hart's Staff Captains from the Navy's Bureau of Medicine and then addressed to the Commandant of the Marine Corps. A copy of this report was permanently attached to my medical record as well. It stated:

"Captain Trombly has a history of a recurrent Non-Hodgkin's Lymphoma in the right maxilla. He declined traditional therapy (radiation and chemotherapy) and pursued non-traditional therapy. Currently, he follows a macrobiotic diet which includes an every six month, week-long "cleansing" fast and twice-daily high-colonic therapy. A Physical Evaluation Board dated 17 Jan 02 found him fit to continue on active duty. The Poor prognosis for his cancer, coupled with the lack of scientific studies to support the effectiveness of his alternative therapy, and the metabolic effects of his ongoing treatments deem this a safety of flight risk."

I had no opportunity to rebut the official results of the Special Board before Admiral Hart received, accepted, forwarded them to my ultimate boss, and permanently inserted them into my medical record. Before I started deconstructing Dr. Ristretto's report, I had to deal with this cover letter to the Commandant. Therefore, the first shot in my rebuttal read as follows:

"In response to BUMED's assertion that there is a lack of scientific studies, I contend that I cannot control what the FDA and pharmaceutical companies chose to support through clinical trials. The 714X I self-administered is categorized as an immuno-modulator health product aiming to both support a weak immune system or to slow down an overactive one. It intends to restore the body's immune defenses without side effects. Additionally, Dr. Naessens shared with me himself that 714-X was having great success in a double blind study before it was abruptly halted once Dana Farber Cancer Institute realized it was a natural product from Dr. Naessens and not from mainstream pharmaceutical establishments."

LCDR Ristretto conveniently categorized the seven aeromedical concerns the board deliberated thus pulling back the curtain for me to see what the board's ultimate focus had been. Halfway through his report under the title Aeromedical Concerns, he listed:

The Board deliberated on multiple issues regarding aeromedical concerns of Captain Trombly's diagnosis and treatment. The topics discussed were:

Capt Trombly's priorities regarding flying versus survival

The degree to which we can rely on Capt Trombly to report symptoms and abstain from treatment regimens which the Board felt would be incompatible with flying

The degree to which Capt Trombly's lifestyle changes have pervaded throughout all areas of his life and whether or not those changes would interfere with his deployability, safety, and reliability

The risk of metastatic complications

The opinion of the consulting oncologist

Whether or not Capt Trombly's case actually represented significant enough of a variation from either other similar cases or from other pilots in general to warrant an exception to our current policy of waiting five years before returning to flight duties once diagnosed with lymphoma.

While Capt Trombly stated to the Board that his number one priority was survival, his actions did not actually reflect this. He chose to forego traditional treatments with good evidence for high cure rates in lieu of CAM (Complementary and Alternative Medicine) methods with no evidence of a cure... Patients treated with chemotherapy have indeed been waived at less than five years. We have no information regarding patients who did not undergo treatment in our database. So while Capt Trombly states he is more interested in survival than in returning to flying his actions taken from the time of his diagnosis are those of a person more focused on flying than on the survival implications of not utilizing conventional treatment methods. He also based his decision on no data since there was no inquiry regarding return to flight status without treatment.

My counter-arguments were legibly drafted in the white space around this paragraph.

"My integrity is above question—I have held nothing back! I have consistently maintained that survival is my first priority. These comments border on slander and demonstrate ignorance by fellow officers who have taken the same oath that I have."

"The reason there is 'No Data' in your database is because I am the first Naval Aviator to have this rare bone cancer; and therefore, the first to go 100% Biological. Additionally, I was willing to reject a medical disability discharge to continue to serve!"

On the following page, the most damning of all Dr. Ristretto's allegations were laid out in black and white:

"The Board discussed Capt Trombly's ability to make good judgments and whether or not that may be a factor in recommending a waiver to return to flight status. The question posed to the Board was whether or not the reasonable person, faced with Capt Trombly's diagnosis would be expected to make the same decisions regarding treatments as Capt Trombly. The Board discussed this with the knowledge that Capt Trombly had credible medical sources providing both counseling and peer-reviewed literature support of conventional chemotherapy. The Board also had been provided a thorough review of the propaganda provided by the CAM practitioners "supporting" their techniques… Presented with both sets of material Capt Trombly chose the non-supported writings of the alternative practitioners over the well-established medical therapies. None of the literature was peer-reviewed nor published in any medical journal."

Here Dr. Ristretto labeled the very report I had built for the Physical Evaluation Board and had then resubmitted to the Special Board as "propaganda" rather than as recognized science. This line alone spoke volumes to the demonstrated bias and closed-minded reception of Megan's and my research that had permeated the boardroom on that important day. Dr. Ristretto continued his assault:

"Given this body of evidence the Board was instructed to use their own individual judgment to decide on whether or not a "reasonable person" decision was made in this case and to factor that decision into their individual vote for waiver recommendation in Capt Trombly's case. The underlying principle being that we rely on our fighter pilots to make reasonable judgments every day while flying and potentially dropping live ordnance on targets in and around populated areas. If Capt Trombly's decisions regarding his own healthcare were unreasonable, especially with the wealth of information he was provided then can we trust his judgments in a combat situation where he must make decisions with significantly less information?"

My response was righteously indignant, as what was obvious to me and the president of the board at the conclusion of the Special Board now appeared clearly in the text before me. The comment about none of my supporting material being peer-reviewed or in medical journals was severely disingenuous, as medical professionals know that most medical journals refuse to print alternative material due to the stranglehold the pharmaceutical companies have on testing and conventional medicine as a whole. I responded:

"TOO MUCH TO COMMENT ON! My judgment is being questioned by a very educated professional body which is making huge assumptions without having taken the time to study all I have done with regards to nutrition. The honest professional doctors I have worked with have admitted weakness in nutritional training while in medical school and no time to read up on these issues as doctors due to an excessive workload demand. I respect their honesty and point this out as a causal factor in our inability to see eye to eye on any nutritional benefits. This is unfortunate."

I continued on the right-side margin with:

"There are no medical facts in this argument, only close-minded opinion regarding my integrity and my judgment. This Board was unable to see my current level of health and my discipline or my sense of duty. This is extremely disappointing!"

This back and forth with each argument against my future flying, followed by my counterarguments in the margins, continued for all eight pages of Dr. Ristretto's report. My closing rebuttal at the bottom of LCDR Ristretto's report was as follows:

"It appears to me that the Board dismissed my statements, minimized my integrity and extensively deliberated issues pertaining to my judgment (that of a fellow commissioned officer) rather than deliberating the true aeromedical facts. Despite the misguided discussion, I only missed victory by four votes. Encouraged by this moral victory in such an obviously hostile environment, I request an open and honest debate with both myself and my Biological Doctor present. I am confident of my judgment and decision-making ability and my integrity as is my current Command and CO."

On a positive note, the ear nose and throat doctor who assisted LCDR Ristretto in writing a portion of the final report actually typed:

"Approximately 13 days after the surgery, he was called back to the clinic by the oral surgeon and was informed that the lesion was Non-Hodgkin's lymphoma. He immediately grounded himself, and visited his flight surgeon, who arranged for him to have a consultation at NNMC Bethesda."

He also reported that I had reached out to a third conventional hospital, Johns Hopkins, for advice. I was able to use these two lines written by the ENT doctor in the report to argue that my ultimate motive was personal survival rather than a misplaced desire to fly.

The third and final doctor to weigh in on the board findings was a full-bird Navy Captain who had interviewed me for my psychological assessment. He wrote regarding his interview with me:

"He was alert and fully oriented. Memory and cognition were clinically intact. Judgment and insight were unimpaired."

The psychologist's summary and conclusion section included:

"Though he was not formally psychiatrically evaluated at the time (of diagnosis), there is no evidence from present evaluation to suggest that he was not competent to make the choice he made. His adaptation to the diagnosis, treatment, and aeromedical consequences of these is considered to have been normal, and not indicative of any disqualifying psychopathology."

In the margins of the report by his summary paragraph I wrote in bold print:

"This should reflect on my judgment and decision-making ability. A question to the Board — Did the voting members take a serious look at the psychologist's evaluation? They should have let the Psychologist evaluate my judgment, not LCDR Ristretto!"

Having strategically placed my rebuttal comments throughout the margins of the report, my preparations were complete. The time had come to call up the Prayer Warriors to prep the battlefield in D.C.

Below I've included a portion of the email I forwarded to our friends and family announcing both the third and final medical board review, and the good news that our fifth child was going to be another boy!

From: *David Trombly*
Date: *August 17, 2002 at 8:49:25 PM CDT*
Subject: *I am going to the Big Game (Washington DC)*

Dear Friends, Family, and Fellow Warriors,

It has again been a few months since I last sent you an update, as I try to send one only before or after a major event. Now is such a time.

I wish to share two pieces of great news. First, Megan and I found out on Monday that number five due Nov 2nd is going to be a boy! That's right, somehow this very symmetrical guy was blessed with a perfectly symmetrical birth order of Boy-Girl-Boy-Girl-Boy. I asked Megan if we should test the system and perfectly balance it out with one more girl next year. I won't tell you what happened next.

The baby appears to be growing fine and is healthy. Please pray for Megan and the baby as they check to see that all is well for the continued safe development of the fifth member of our hockey team.

The second piece of good news is that my one-year cancer follow-up found me in top shape with no signs of cancer, both from the military-medical tests and the German blood tests I continue to do. My military doctors, as well as my alternative doctors, remain very encouraged by these continued cancer-free reports.

It is undeniable that our choice to follow alternative, homeopathic, and biological medicine was a tremendous success. We thank all of you for your love for us and the sacrifices you made over the past two years. So many of you spent countless hours praying for us. Now once again, we ask you to pray. This battle has been two-fold since day one of my diagnosis: first to beat the disease, and second to be reinstated to flight status. God has brought about miraculous healing through the knowledge He has given us and the discernment to make the tough decisions.

I have fought for my flight status for almost as many months as I fought for my life. During the last year, I put back on 20 pounds, worked out 5

463

to 6 days a week, and rebuilt my strength to where it had been and more. My fitness level has not been this high since I joined the Marine Corps.

But despite my good health reports, I find myself engaged in a major struggle to convince the Navy's medical community to allow me to fly. The fact is that they do not understand my chosen nutritional programs and immune system boosting therapies, and as a result, they have sorely misconstrued my motives. In this stage of our cancer war, I've had my judgment questioned, my decision-making capabilities scrutinized, and my integrity blatantly dismissed.

My main focus has always been to be here for my family. I desired above all to beat my disease, form a strong team with my wife, and rear my children—the whole team! I always prayed for God to salvage my career and reinstate my flying privileges, but never at the expense of my health and longevity. Many doctors have falsely reasoned that I refused chemo and radiation because their damage to major organs would forever take me out of the cockpit. Therefore, I have had to aggressively argue with the conventional doctors that I made my choices first in the best interest of regaining my health and only secondly in the desire to remain a healthy, highly trained pilot to fly for the Corps. Convincing the Navy medical establishment that my approaches were not unreasonable or illogical remains a huge land mine I must circumnavigate. Certainly, I concede that my approaches were uncommon, but they're rare partly because nutrition and biological medicine are not common knowledge in our fast-paced western culture. Discovering alternatives takes research, and that takes time and discipline. I had the time after suddenly being grounded, and God granted the discernment and the discipline for me to face the challenges ahead one day at a time.

Many of the principles I applied have been around longer than more recent conventional philosophy or the advent of synthetic pharmaceuticals. I have maintained a healthy respect for my doctors and a working relationship with them despite my choice to pursue other approaches.

Unfortunately, those Navy doctors who are deciding my fate don't know me or the tremendous amount of research Megan and I did. Some of my military doctors reacted automatically with anger at having their protocol questioned, and they have therefore interpreted my actions as selfish, irresponsible, unwise, and without integrity. Despite the fact that these alternative programs and principles have worked and have been studied by other physicians and other cultures for generations, those over me have dismissed the data as 'propaganda.'

Yes: this second, even tougher, War involves convincing the medical establishment that what I have learned and aggressively implemented not only worked but also offers a viable option and solution for others going forward.

My heart's desire is threefold. First, I want to share with everyone the reality of God. There is no more important purpose in life than to find Him and share Him with others.

Second, I want to share the truth that is out there about nutrition and alternative medicine. I don't think there could be two more pointed or controversial subjects to champion and worth fighting for. Both are worthy of a lifelong pursuit.

Finally, I want to fly again for the Marine Corps. Though resuming life as a pilot would be a dream, two out of three desires fulfilled would not be bad. That may be where God is calling us, but I have one more shot at that third goal. I am not afraid to ask for all three, and that is where all of you come in.

On Monday morning from 0800-1100, I will stand before the Senior Medical Board of Flight Surgeons of the United States Navy in Washington, D.C. I have been given the privilege to argue my case once more, this time at the highest level in Naval medicine.

I am sure that I will again have to defend my integrity. The mission remains: to convince the board that my decision-making process was not flawed or misguided and that my judgment is sound and unselfish. To aid in the presentation, I thank God my civilian biological doctor has offered to stand with me before the medical board to rebut the conventional view and theories of the established medical bureaucracy. He has over 50 years of conventional and alternative wisdom working for him, more than any Navy personnel on the board. It is my prayer that we will be victorious in this endeavor.

I am confident in my argument and am comforted to know that my fate and career rest ultimately in God's hands, as did my health. God's will shall be accomplished.

> *"The king's heart is like channels of water in the hand of the Lord;*
> *He turns it wherever He wishes."*
> — *Proverbs 21:1 (NIV)*

If however, we are not victorious, it is my prayer that I would have the maturity to accept God's will and move in whatever direction He would have me go. He is bigger than cancer; He is surely bigger than this small challenge before me now (Psalm 91).

I cannot imagine not flying again, but I am willing to accept whatever God has for us to do next. I will share the results of this board with you next week. Until then, thank you in advance for your efforts and prayers. Megan and I are beyond grateful for all you have done and love you all.

"Do you not know? Have you not heard? The Lord is the everlasting God, the Creator of the ends of the earth. He will not grow tired or weary, and His understanding no one can fathom. He gives strength to the weary and increases the power of the weak. Even youths grow tired and weary and young men stumble and fall. But those who hope in the Lord will renew their strength. They will soar like eagles; they will run and not grow weary, they will walk and not be faint."—Isaiah 40:28-31 (NIV)

In God's hands,
David
Psalm 91

59| *A New Wingman for D.C.*

ACCOMPANYING my aggressively thorough yet respectful rebuttal letter to Admiral Hart was a copy of the previously-developed package of sixteen enclosures I had sent to the previous three medical boards.

The cover letter for my Senior Board of Flight Surgeons request was addressed to BUMED 02, Admiral Hart MC, USN. It contained only a single line below the Subject line:

From: Captain David M. Trombly, xxx xx xxxx
To: BUMED 02, Steven Admiral Hart, MC, USN

Subj: Request for Senior Board of Flight Surgeons; CASE OF CAPTAIN DAVID M. TROMBLY XXX XX XXXX/7523 USMC

1. I very respectfully request reconsideration for a waiver by the Senior Board of Flight Surgeons.

DAVID M. TROMBLY

Unlike I had in my cover letters for the previous boards, I chose to limit what the board heard from me initially. Allowing my leaders to speak on my behalf upfront, I held my comments in reserve for the back of the package just before my enclosures. Following the cover letter, the first four letters lauded four wildly supportive and powerfully impactful statements of endorsement written by Captain *BADROD* Weideman and Colonel *JAWS* White. Once my annual FITREP was completed by these gracious leaders, I also forwarded it for the board's consideration. Shortly after receipt of my request and the submission of my FITREP, the doors to D.C. finally opened!

With the date of the Senior Board set for Monday, August 19, 2002, I immediately contacted Dr. Schildwaechter, who lived just outside Washington, D.C.

"Good evening, Dr. Schildwaechter. Am I reaching you at a good time, Sir?"

"Oh yes, Captain *Trommmmmbly,*" he said, drawing out my last name as he often did with his strong German accent. "Wonderful! Wonderful to hear from you!"

"Thank you, Sir. It is great to hear your voice, too. I am calling with very good news and word of an opportunity that would allow us to spend a little time together up in D.C."

"Ah, that would be a pleasure, Captain!"

Dr. Schildwaechter, now well into his seventies, had served the U.S. Air Force in Bitburg, Germany in the late 1950s. He often spoke of his time supporting the 12th Air Force at the 36th Tactical USAF Hospital. His pride in supporting our military members never waned, and he almost always addressed me by my rank, despite my junior officer status. I enjoyed his accent and his compassion that came through loud and clear as we spoke. I found myself smiling when we conversed no matter the topic. I knew what I was about to share would motivate him like nothing else in our previous discussions.

"Dr. Schildwaechter, as you know it has been almost a year since that August CT scan showed that the tumor was gone when I returned from Switzerland. It has taken a year to battle my way through three medical boards. Good news, Sir! I have been granted an audience with the Admiral's team in D.C. in a couple of weeks. I get to present my case and refute the findings of the last board with Dr. Ristretto that I sent you a couple of months ago."

"Captain *Trommmbly,*" he replied, drawing out my name with his strong German accent which always brought a smile to my face, "Very good! Very good! This is great news! I would like to see you."

"Doctor Schildwaechter, I would be honored if you would agree to be my advocate and speak for me at this board. I will be grossly outnumbered by very senior military officers. In fact, all five are Navy Captains and seasoned medical professionals. I thought I did well against the 31 doctors I went toe to toe with here in Pensacola back in May, but I am greatly outgunned in this coming fight. These five doctors, all heavy hitters, work directly for the Admiral running the entire Navy's Bureau of Medicine."

"This is the big game, Sir, and with you speaking for me, I am convinced they will overturn the lower board's decision. More importantly, I truly believe they will listen to you. I think we have a shot at taking my story and what God did in my body with your protocols to open doors in the military medical community. We want to afford others the opportunity to succeed in their health battles and their careers. Maybe we can do that if we win this!"

I had made an offer that touched him on both a personal and professional level. Dr. S had served as a full faculty member at the University of Pennsylvania School of Medicine's Department of Preventative Medicine and Public Health from 1963—1970. As a teaching doctor, he had been shaping the industry, and in those years his focus had been early cancer detection, the epidemiology of cancer, and special cervical cancer studies. While at the university, he also worked directly with the National Institute of Health (NIH) on multiple issues, including cancer and a tuberculosis screening, changing the way the United States screens cancer to this day.

Dr. Schildwaechter was being offered an opportunity to get back in front of today's doctors that worked side by side with Bethesda and the National Institutes of Health. Not only had his fifty-plus years of experience saved my life and possibly my career, but at

469

this board, he would also influence the Navy's top military medical decision-makers.

"Captain, I would be honored. What a generous offer you make. When is the board?

"The date is set for Monday morning August 19, 2002. I fly up on Sunday and can meet you Monday morning. We can head in together through security on my ID card."

"I will work to clear my schedule and get back to you shortly, my friend."

"Thank you, Dr. Schildwaechter. I have prepared my rebuttal and will be sure to forward you a copy of my argument as well as my binder of research I have been forwarding to each medical board. I look forward to hearing from you, Sir."

Over the year that Megan and I worked with Dr. Schildwaechter, we had only seen him in person once following our darkest day in Bethesda. The brief visit sealed our decision to keep the faith and stay the course. Most of our monthly conversations over the phone were for him to review my blood work from Germany and to hear my progress report. The majority of the time, Megan and I interacted with Kerstin, Dr. S's daughter in Vero Beach, Florida. As with her father, each month we spoke over the phone with her to order my next batch of Biotics Research Company's bovine-based enzymes, which were the backbone of Dr. Schildwaechter's program for me. I did not meet Kerstin personally until after we beat cancer as a team.

Dr. Schildwaechter indeed captured this opportunity and quickly let me know he would be there. I did not know at the time that August 19 was also Kerstin's birthday, the one day each year she saw her busy father. Not only did Dr. Schildwaechter graciously give us his valuable time, but he also sacrificed his annual visit with his daughter, allowing us to storm the halls of medicine side by side!

Only my second time visiting Dr. Schildwaechter in person, I looked forward to sitting beside a man of his character and professional stature. This appearance granted us a rare platform. Much more important than simply arguing for a pilot to put on a helmet and flight gloves and go tear up the atmosphere for a few more years, we could contend the "system!"

This D.C. engagement did not involve fighting for my life but fighting for my career, a totally different battle. My last D.C. engagement had flown me into Andrews Air Force Base with *PUDGE* on my wing. For this D.C. engagement, I enlisted a new wingman. The fight did not entail a simulated ACM engagement, but the real deal. This was the final stop in my fight to return to the cockpit.

The desired "Yes" vote from this board meant I might get a chance to fight alongside *PUDGE* and my other brothers and sisters again in the F/A-18! And I hoped *PUDGE* had been practicing, because I was coming back with a vengeance. A "No" vote from this board meant I was looking at trying to reinvent myself, going to law school or leaving the Marine Corps altogether.

I arrived in D.C. on Saturday and checked into a room at Fort Myer in Arlington, Virginia adjacent to Arlington National Cemetery. After checking into my room, I headed up to catch a view from the hilltop of our Nation's capital, admire the sunset, and pray for victory in the next morning's battle at the Marine Corps' War Memorial. People often call this memorial the Iwo Jima Memorial; however, it honors all Marines who have given their lives to our country since November 10, 1775.

Monday morning, August 19, 2002, arrived, as did Dr. Schildwaechter. We parked his car near the Navy's Bureau of Medicine, driving my rental car to the security gate. We arrived early and were offered fresh coffee and water while waiting in the boardroom for the board members to gather. The atmosphere immediately felt less formal and uptight than the previous Pensacola Medical Board.

Dr. Schildwaechter and I visited during the drive in and in the boardroom as we waited.

"Sir, thank you for being here."

"It is my honor, Captain! You have given me an opportunity to share things on one of the highest medical platforms of the land. I never dreamed we could reach this plateau. I do not know if I will ever be afforded such a rare opportunity again."

"Dr. Schildwaechter, this would not end in victory without you. It is my intention to argue one key point at the start that is not medically related in any way, but rather of professional and personal nature. Once the board has heard my heart, I will introduce you as my civilian doctor and the architect of our alternative battle plan. Once I turn the time over to you, Sir, I will not speak again unless directly asked a question by either you or the board members. This day and this room are yours for as long as they will let you speak. I trust you completely with this moment, just as I trusted you with my life. Please feel free to say anything God puts on your heart."

"This is a good plan, Captain. Thank you. I am ready!"

60| *"You Have the Lead on the Right, Sir!"*

DR. SCHILDWAECHTER and I waited only briefly before all five Navy Medical Corps Captains entered the room in working khaki uniforms. I just smiled when the sixth and final officer walked through the door and delivered half a smile, complete with a head nod. The Senior Board of Flight Surgeons is entirely comprised of Navy Medical Officers. But when their decisions impact the career of a Marine Line Officer, the Board also requires a more senior Line Officer from the Marine Corps to be a voting member.

To my great surprise, in walked Lieutenant Colonel *SPIT* Avaz, USMC, in his Service Charlie uniform, the Corps' equivalent to the Navy Khaki uniform. I, too, was in Service Charlies, and Dr. Schildwaechter had donned a suit. Despite the formal dress and us standing to greet the board members as they arrived, this board was far different than I was expecting. The format was far less formal as we took our seats together around a conference table and the conversation started.

"Good morning, Captain Trombly. Good morning Dr. 'Schildvector.' Did I say that correctly, Sir?" the Captain asked Dr. S.

"Yes, yes, quite right, Captain," Dr. S. replied.

"I am Captain Goodspeed, and I believe, Captain Trombly, that you know our guest at the end of the table, LtCol Avaz?"

"Good morning, Captain Goodspeed, Captains, and yes, I do know LtCol Avaz. Great to see you again, Sir." *SPIT* nodded and fully smiled my way this time. Without giving away too much, he conveyed enough to let me know that I was among friends.

SPIT had been my first boss when I finished pilot training and qualified in the F/A-18. When I checked into VMFA-115 in Beaufort, I was blessed with the opportunity to work for *SPIT* as his Airframe and Ejection Seat Shop OIC. *SPIT* was the Aircraft Maintenance Officer, and as such, he wrote my very first observed FITNESS report in the Marine Corps. Of the hundreds of officers on staff at HQMC, the one selected to represent the Marine Corps to ensure I received a fair hearing was my very first boss! God was smiling on me!

SPIT had been promoted to LtCol after he left VMFA-115, Then he landed a staff job at Headquarters United States Marine Corps (HQMC) working for Colonel *CUBBY* Barraclough. I later learned about the candid conversation between those two men before this board convened.

"*SPIT*, I need you to attend a hearing for an unusual case involving a Marine *HORNET* pilot. Captain Trombly was diagnosed with terminal cancer, and basically, the man beat it. Now he wants the keys to his jet back."

"*CUBBY*, I'm honored to represent the Corps at this hearing. But I must inform you, Sir, that I do know Captain Trombly personally. I have the highest regard for his commitment to the Marines and his integrity and talent as a leader. I wonder if it would not be a conflict of interest to be a voting member of this board, having been his former Reporting Senior."

"*SPIT*, I appreciate your candor and integrity. But I trust your judgment, or I wouldn't have asked you to go." The Colonel then emphatically added, "Hell, from what I hear, that Marine could use an ally."

CUBBY had given his order. For me, it was divine intervention. Obviously not known to me at the time, I learned about the pre-Board discussion *SPIT* and *CUBBY* had held a year later from *CUBBY* himself when he relieved *JAWS* of Command as the new MATSG-21 Commanding Officer in Pensacola. This proved another blessing for me, as *CUBBY* already knew my story through *SPIT* before he became my CO. *CUBBY* fully supported me with the same intensity that *JAWS* had during his Command tour.

"Well gentlemen, we have a lot of ground to cover today; so let's get started." Captain Goodspeed began. "Captain Trombly, would you like to start by introducing us to your guest today and providing us with an opening statement or asking any questions you might have."

"Thank you, Captain Goodspeed. Gentlemen, *SPIT,* thank you for your time today and for your attention and consideration of our arguments for my reinstatement as a Service Group One (SG I) Naval Aviator and my return to the F/A-18. I am truly blessed to have beaten my rare cancer in the short time that I did, and I could not have done that without the guidance of the man to my right. It is an honor to introduce you to Dr. Dietmer Schildwaechter."

"Involved in medicine since 1940, Dr. Schildwaechter proffers

474

over 50 years of medical experience, both as a professor of conventional medicine at the University of Pennsylvania and as a counselor in alternative medicine. This man opened the door for my wife and me to gain great naturopathic knowledge and to apply his research base in our cancer victory."

"Gentlemen, I made a passionate plea speaking on my own behalf at the previous board in Pensacola. But considering we are sitting here today, neither my deliberate tact and tempered professionalism nor my explanations of the alternative methods I pursued were enough to sway the audience there. I ended up four votes short of victory. With only six of you here today, coming up four votes short again would be catastrophic; so I give you Dr. Schildwaechter, who has graciously offered his time and expertise to detail our protocol, which he developed, and the science behind it. I would be happy to answer any questions you have during these proceedings. But I request that Dr. Schildwaechter speak as the medical expert regarding biological and alternative modalities on my behalf if the board is accepting of such a request."

"That is perfectly acceptable, Captain Trombly."

"Thank you, Captain Goodspeed."

I turned and smiled at Dr. S., knowing that the second portion of our mission was in good hands, but I had one more request. I felt that these next few minutes were key to my success. Even if Dr. S. should absolutely WOW the board members, the question of my character and judgment had to be addressed first.

"Gentlemen, if I may, I would like to address one issue before we turn to the medical conversation. It is the question raised by LCDR Ristretto in his official findings published in the after-action report from the Special Board of Flight Surgeons on May 13, 2002. I have forwarded a detailed rebuttal of his write up to you, specifically addressing each instance in which I found either an error in his account of our cancer battle protocol or an improper assumption regarding my judgment."

"With this report and rebuttal already submitted to you, and in an effort to avoid a further 'He-said-He-said' back and forth, I offer the official assessment of my professional and personal abilities by submitting my most recent FITREP written by Captain *BADROD* Weideman of Naval Aviation Schools Command and signed by the Reviewing Officer Colonel *JAWS* White, the Commanding Officer of MATSG-21."

I took a breath as I prepared to argue the value this FITREP report brought. The positive endorsement from the officers who wrote my FITREP would go a long way to disputing the slanderous assumptions of my judgment and decision-making ability by some of the voting members as well as LCDR Ristretto, the author of the previous board's decisions.

However, before I could speak, Captain Goodspeed interrupted.

"Captain Trombly, first let me commend you on your bearing and poise in your opening remarks. I will take that FITREP for our review, but I would like to assure you from the start that you have nothing to prove, although your concerns were warranted and recognized by this governing body. We have had the opportunity to thoroughly review the read-ahead you provided as did LtCol Avaz. We also had the privilege to speak with LtCol Avaz earlier. You may rest assured he has fully vouched for your character, work ethic, and judgment—none of which are in question with this board."

"We are here to learn about your chosen methods and to determine if there is a reason to put you back in the air earlier than the waiver guide currently stipulates. Your treatment choices and the success of those choices are not only respected by this body but, quite frankly, we are very intrigued by them. Please set your mind at ease. You will receive a fair and impartial decision from BUMED at the conclusion of our review."

I slid my Fitness Report across the table while looking Captain Goodspeed in the eye and smiling. "Thank you very much, Captain. With that input, Sir, my work here is done."

Smiling confidently, I looked to my right at Dr. Schildwaechter. I reached up with my left hand and tapped my forehead twice, pointing at Dr. S. with a firm knife-hand and announced, "Dr. Schildwaechter, you have the lead on the right, Sir!"

When flying formation, pilots use the double-tap to their helmet followed by the pointed knife-hand signal to pass the flight leadership role from one aircraft to the other. This action transfers tactical leadership of the flight to the other crew if they accept it with a knife-hand pointing forward signal of their own. The former flight leader becomes the wingman, and the former wingman becomes the tactical leader in control of the mission. When the two aircraft are separated by a distance in a more tactical environment where hand signals are unable to be seen, the crew will pass the tactical control of the flight to the other aircraft via the radio.

I passed Dr. S the lead of my defense in the same manner I would have transferred it to *SPIT* or he would have transferred it to me when we were flying together back in Beaufort's VMFA-115.

At the Special Board of Flight Surgeons in May, I'd delivered a four-page statement which I thought was respectful and well thought out. I had hoped that Dr. Ostergaard would be given the opportunity to speak for me. He was afforded an opportunity to say a few words, but not being a flight surgeon, he was not able to vote for me. He also demonstrated great respect to his colleagues, fully understanding his role and theirs. It was not his place to champion my cause, specifically not the natural and biological medical methods. He was a great wingman that day. He truly had my back, but he was never in a position to take the lead and fight the fight against the 31 voting members.

Dr. Ostergaard remained my top ally in the military medical system and stood by me month after month. As a brother in faith, he prayed for me continually. He allowed me to ask tough questions and even allowed for debate of the medical theories during our monthly visits. Each and every month throughout our cancer war and follow-up visits after I was cured, Dr. Ostergaard made it a point to have his medical students do the preliminary workups. He would ask me to share my cancer victory story with them. He could make that call because he was in charge of their mentorship as the director of the Family Practice Department.

Other than Dr. Ostergaard, the next most influential military medical staff member that showed me the respect and support I needed to get my career back on track was the OIC of NAMI herself, Captain Tegwich. Because of her, I knew I could appeal. Both of these great military officers and doctors exhibited a respectful and kind manner for which I will forever be grateful.

Dr. S. had certainly been the most influential physician throughout my cancer fight, and now he sat to my right. I watched as he detailed his life's work and laid the foundation for the biological arguments he would soon diligently and carefully lay out before the BUMED staff. Dr. S. now had the controls, and he owned the room for the next three hours.

61 | *On Time and On Target*

ALL Five Captains listened intently for the first fifteen to twenty minutes as Dr. Schildwaechter laid a brief historical foundation and set the tone in the room. *SPIT* and I sat diagonally and farthest apart from one another, as I sat closest to Captain Goodspeed. *SPIT* and I sat motionless and took in the sights as Dr. S. drew the board in with each story. Quickly, the doctors began utilizing the legal pads and pens in the center of the conference table, feverishly scribing notes. Dr. S. did not take a breath for over an hour.

His discussion points were exactly what were needed to convince these senior doctors. Every story, study, and experience he shared significantly impacted these doctors, and they were eating everything up. *SPIT* and I sat there recognizing that every shot he took at convincing them was on target. The timing of this board of inquiry was perfect. If we had brought Dr. Schildwaechter to Pensacola to meet with the more junior physicians that voted back in May, it might have had positive results. But he could have created an even more robust and adversarial environment, resulting in an even larger loss of votes.

These five members of Admiral Hart's staff, however, were exactly the professionals to whom a physician of Dr. Schildwaechter's caliber should be presenting. It was God's timing. Dr. Schildwaechter's lifetime of experience resonated with these men of decision and influence in the military medical system, and it was all on my behalf. I could not help but wonder if it could make a difference well beyond the decision they would make about me today. I sat quietly praying that it would do exactly that for the sake of those who would follow a path like mine.

During the second hour, the stories of his conventional experience and his biological medicine research and successes transitioned to my story and the protocols Dr. S. had prescribed for me. I was the first of his patients to go on a fully raw diet and to work with the nutritionist from Canada that he and his daughter had recently started to recommend. Other than the diet, the various protocols he recommended for me were the same that he had used on hundreds of other cancer Warriors. He detailed my successes and stated that my recovery and cure came faster than previous clients. He believed it was due to the implementation of the raw diet with the enzyme protocol.

In time we came to the conclusion of the program description and rolled directly into questions and answers from the doctors. Not one inquiry came to me, but the board members peppered Dr. Schildwaechter with questions. Dr. S. responded with a flood of valuable intel for a third hour. Time stood still. *SPIT* and I had front-row seats as I sat quietly praying for what I believed would be the beginning of a more favorable view of alternative medicine within the military medical community. Such a future truly seemed possible as the climate in the room offered a far more positive, open discussion than the one in Pensacola. The Captains' questions were sincere and truly inquisitive, not condescending nor meant as a means to an end. These men voraciously sought knowledge, and Dr. S. brilliantly afforded them more than two notepads of Intel a piece.

We took a break after the long discussion, and Captain Goodspeed invited Dr. S and me to make ourselves at home in the board's break room while they reconvened. We sat for just over an hour as the Captains and *SPIT* deliberated. This time, the long delay gave me hope, not despair. These doctors were seriously considering putting me back in the air, despite my not following the Bethesda oncologists' protocol. A victory would be a historic reversal of the published print in the flight waiver guide itself.

One by one, the Captains stepped out, shook our hands, and genuinely thanked Dr. S. for his time and for sharing his wealth of knowledge. Individually, they'd each experienced Dr. S. the way I had the past two years.

No doubt, they were not expecting to meet this caliber of a physician or such a well-spoken and knowledgeable expert in his field. This was not some crazy medicine man or snake oil salesman; as alternative doctors so frequently are portrayed on the internet Quakwatch sites. This man was an icon in biological medicine like Dr. Rau from the Paracelsus Klinik in Switzerland. To bring a parallel from our military world, these five doctors had sat in conference with a biological medicine General and walked away seriously considering his arguments.

Captain Goodspeed stepped out to brief Dr. S. and me.

"Gentlemen, it is impossible for us to give you a final decision today. Dr. Schildwaechter has given us far more information to research than we could possibly run down in one afternoon."

Dr. S. smiled, and I nodded, acknowledging this truthful situation.

"Captain Trombly, have patience with us. We must do our due diligence in this matter. It will take several weeks for our investigation to be completed. I assure you, Captain, we will be doing the research specifically to be able to refute the waiver guide's published requirement to sit for two full years before getting airborne again."

"I am truly grateful, Sir," I humbly acknowledged while hoping for some more concrete indication of their verdict.

"Captain, though I cannot give you a final ruling today, I do feel comfortable telling you that every board member voted positively to reinstate you to flight status."

My choice to use alternative measures had not prevented me from ever flying military again! We had VICTORY!

A MOMENT
WITH MEGAN

Every time David left to challenge a board or even meet with his doctor for follow ups, I waited with such a worrisome heaviness. He needed to fly again, but I had no idea if such a thing was even

possible. I wanted him to have his dream back—that dream that cancer had robbed from him and which he now had a glimmer of hope to get back. When he finally called to tell me they said he would most likely win his wings back, I was totally elated! He needed to get back in the air. The man I married had a boyhood dream that I wanted so badly to see him chase again.

LtCol *SPIT* Avaz loitered for a few extra moments after Captain Goodspeed departed in order to pay his respects to Dr. S. and thank him for helping me regain my health. We caught up briefly before he had to rush back to the start of his HQMC work week, no doubt having a day's worth of emails to dig out when he reached his office. *SPIT* and I swapped numbers so we could reconnect later that day and stay in touch.

Dr. Schildwaechter and I left together, and I dropped him off at his vehicle before heading to the airport to turn in my rental car. The two of us stepped from the car and said our farewells. I promised him I would let him know the board results as soon as I received them. I hugged this larger-than-life figure whom I had come to love and respect and to whom I now owed both my life and my future flying career as well. Over the past three years, I had come to cherish him like an adopted grandfather.

This would be the last time that I would stand beside Dr. Schildwaechter until the day I stood over his casket at his funeral just a few short years later. His daughter Kerstin and Megan and I were close friends, and Megan and I had been referring many fellow cancer Warriors to her father until he passed away. Kerstin offered me the great honor of delivering the eulogy of this giant of a man. It was the ultimate honor to have been asked by Kerstin not only to attend but also to wear my dress blue uniform, as the family had such high regard for the American military. Dr. Schildwaechter touched the lives of tens of thousands in his lifetime, and as one of the many lives he impacted, I was humbled to be singled out to share in this precious celebration of life with his family and friends. That privilege has remained one of the greatest honors of my life.

I left Washington, D.C. with no concrete answer—only the encouraging brief from Captain Goodspeed. It was hard to detail that hope to our Prayer Warrior support team, but I endeavored to do just that with this email upon my return.

Hey guys,

I am back in P'cola. I got back late last night. I wanted to give a quick note to catch you up. First let me say thanks for the prayers, support and encouraging emails.

I do not have an answer yet. After three hours of discussion, the board deliberated for over an hour then adjourned until next week. The board members wanted to do some more research.

My experience was great. The board was extremely receptive to the arguments Dr. Schildwaechter made. The character issues were dismissed in the first few minutes, and so he and I were able to spend all our time discussing the medical facts alone!

I am very happy with the professional treatment I received, and regardless of the outcome, I know that at a minimum I received a fair shake. Of course, I am always optimistic and holding out for the big victory, but then I always do. God has been great to Megan and me and has blessed us greatly in the past two years.

Again, I can reach for the sky, yet regardless of the outcome, I win. I have my health, a message to share with others who are struggling with their health, and my family, including our future son on the way. I have seen God move in ways I hadn't before in the lives of our family and our friends!

I have nothing to complain about. Thanks for your prayers. I will send you the results when I get them.

In God's hands,
 David
 Psalm 91

PART ELEVEN

FREE TO FLY

"The secret of my success is that I always
managed to live to fly another day."

— General Chuck Yeager, USAF
First Pilot to Break the Sound Barrier in Level Flight

62| *Victory through Compromise*

THE results came as promised, and in less than 30 days. I was going back to the cockpit; it was the "when" that disappointed me. The news brought mixed emotions as the chance to fly with VT-86 in the next year officially evaporated when BUMED signed the correspondence below and submitted it to the Commandant of the Marine Corps.

My fight was finished. The verdict was final with the correspondence signed on the anniversary of the terrorist attacks the previous year. It was now time to put down the red highlighters and blue ballpoint pens, the weapons of my warfare for the past many months. It was time to rest and be at peace with the verdict the Senior Board had reached.

11 SEP 2002

From: Deputy Chief, Fleet Operations Support (M3F)
To: Commandant, U.S. Marine Corps

Subj: SENIOR BOARD OF FLIGHT SURGEONS ICO CAPTAIN DAVID M. TROMBLY, USMC, XXX-XX-XXXX

Ref: (a) NAMI ltr 6120 Ser 326/0138 of 10 Jun 02
   (b) Manual of the Medical Department (NAVMED P-117)

Per reference (a), CAPT Trombly was found by a Special Board of Flight Surgeons to be Not Physically Qualified but Aeronautically Adaptable for all Duties in Flying with waiver not recommended. In accordance with reference (b), a request was made for his case to be reviewed by a Senior

Board of Flight Surgeons at the Bureau of Medicine and Surgery. The Senior Board met on 19 AUG 2002.

Recommendations of the Senior Board of Flight Surgeons:

*Having thoroughly reviewed all of the factors presented in this case, it
is the opinion of the Senior Board of Flight Surgeons that CAPT Trombly be given a waiver to SGIII until 2 years post-remission at which time
he may be considered for a waiver to SGI.   Any recurrence of the
lymphoma or any return to oral or injectable forms of treatment (enzyme
therapy, 714-X, mistletoe, standard chemotherapy, or other therapy not
expressly approved by Navy Aeromedical Policy) will result in permanent
disqualification for flight.*

*Any questions regarding this decision may be directed to CAPT Dwight
Fulton, Director of Aerospace Medicine (M3F8), at (202) 762-xxxx or
DSN 762-xxxx.*

W. V. MUSTACHE

Copy: CO, NASCCO, MATSG OIC, NAMI

It was time to make one more visit to LtCol *BONEY* Orabona,
the Commanding Officer of VT-86, and give him the final verdict,
both the goods and the "others."

KNOCK, KNOCK, KNOCK: the three raps on the Commanding officer's hatch reverberated. "Good afternoon, Skipper. Do you
have a minute for an eternal optimist?"

"Welcome, *T-BONE*! What is the news? I gather you have returned victorious from D.C.?"

"Colonel, I have. However, the historic reinstatement back into
the cockpit has a stipulation. I have been reinstated to SGIII as of
the conclusion of the Senior Board. This is one day short of one

full year prior to what the Waiver Guide required; so that is a huge victory."

"Congratulations, Marine! You made history!"

"Yes Colonel, I sure did."

LtCol *BONEY* Orabona was gracious and encouraging. He knew me well enough to hear the disappointment in my voice, despite my saying all the right things. He recognized quickly my faux victorious demeanor as I stood in his office overlooking the flight line full of training jets. I knew I was not going to grasp the controls of a jet with my left and right hand for another year, and as that reality was settling in, *BONEY* probed my thoughts.

"If I understand the Service Groups, SG III keeps you from flying the F/A-18 as well as our T-2's. Training students make it a single piloted platform."

"That is correct, Colonel. I talked to my monitor, who is a C-130 pilot, and he offered to get me redesignated and over to the C-130 schoolhouse. I already turned that option down, Sir. No disrespect to my brothers and sisters in other communities, but I have no desire to be redesignated away from my jet community to go to the C-130 or helicopter community as a SGIII Aviator. By the time I could get orders from Pensacola and over to train in the C-130 and reach my first squadron, the next twelve months would have come and gone. I could just as easily be headed back to the F/A-18 refresher course and be on my way back to Beaufort or Iwakuni, Japan anyway."

"My plan is to wait out this next year right here in Pensacola at the CRM Schoolhouse and travel the country doing the CRM inspections. With my SGIII awarded, I can now do the flight inspection portion and get some flight time as soon as I schedule a day in the swimming pool and get a few blindfolded upside trips in the helicopter dunker. It will be great to be able to get in the air again. With our upcoming inspection schedule, I should be able to get into a half a dozen or more different aircraft I never would have flown in otherwise. I'll make the most of the time, Skipper, while I wait for my SGIII to automatically transition to SGI on September 10 of next year."

"*T-BONE*, I know you want to be here. I want you here, too. If the SGI is as automatic a paperwork drill as you say it is, then you should be eligible to come and fly with me this time next year. That will be a couple of months before my Change of Command. Keep your head up, and know that you will be flying for VT-86 next September."

"Colonel, you have been more than patient and encouraging. Thank you. It will be an honor to serve in your Command, even if only for a couple of months."

I left his office with the next year to consider and reflect on just how blessed I was to have had both promises from God fulfilled. My two Wars were now over, and the bonus promise of a cockpit at VT-86 during *BONEY*'s tenure as CO was secure.

After fighting daily for exactly two years, the battle plan for healing was complete. The battle plan for returning to the cockpit was also complete. It was time to rest. It was an order—not from HQMC, not from *SPIDER*, or *JAWS*, or *BONEY*, but from God Himself.

I now had to find new peace waiting on the ground for another year while my friends departed on combat tours. It was now time for me to rest and be at peace with the decision made by the Navy to keep this Marine out of the jet and out of the fight for at least twelve more months.

Walking in this peace was harder to find than the peace Megan and I had fighting cancer. And I am convinced that was purely because I did not seek God's peace daily on my knees. I still wanted to fight. I wanted to fight in the air.

Each of my sons has asked me at one point in their development from boy to man, "Dad, wasn't it hard to train to become a fighter pilot, and then not be able to join the fight because of cancer even though you beat it?"

My answer was that for a couple of years I did not have rest or peace about it like we had as a family during the two years prior. Although that is the truth, it is not something I am proud to admit. I was frustrated, and I held onto the frustration for a couple of years before I finally made peace with God that His path for me was perfect. I had to accept the path of being an instructor in the support role rather than being on the pointy end of the spear of our National Defense.

I have since found peace in being the support that is able to help the greatest aviators in the world become just that: Naval Aviators. Though my hand may not grip the stick and throttle of the fighter jet I once pressed to its limits while testing my own, my hand proudly grasps the base of the spear that thrusts the pointy end forward toward the enemy. I am there providing knowledge and skill sets, transferring the collective confidence of the Warriors who have trained and fought before them so that they might execute their mission with excellence and return home.

63 | *Back in an F/A-18!*

AFTER not being allowed to fly for the past two years, LCDR Ulander offered to send me on any CRM inspection trips around the country that I wanted to volunteer to take. Over the next year, I traveled for every inspection except one as either the primary or secondary inspector, depending on the community. For the TACAIR (jet) community, I took the lead. For the Helicopter or Propeller Platforms, I was the wingman. LCDR Ulander's offer got me into the air multiple times.

One of the first CRM inspection trips took me to Hawaii to inspect the CH-53D Marine Helicopter Heavy Lift platform. The inspection took only half a day, and my group had hoped to fly out over the north side, launching from MCAS Kaneohe Bay. However, we were unable to get a flight as the CH-53Ds were having maintenance issues, and the base did not have a helicopter it could spare to fly us that morning.

Due to our newly-found free time, I was once again able to get up to the Punch Bowl Cemetery and visit my grandfather's grave for the third time. I paid my respects and shared my grandfather's service story with my wingman, Major James *OGRE* Day. After visiting the Punchbowl, *OGRE* and I took a drive up to the North Shore taking the long way around the island, then settled back on Waikiki Beach. *OGRE* purchased an umbrella drink and watched with amusement as I took my second surfing lesson in Hawaii.

T-BONE *and Major* OGRE *Day in Hawaii relaxing after surfing*

Soon after the Hawaii trip, we prepared for our west coast CRM inspection trip in late February of 2003. This was a multiple base trip that required us to go to NAS Lemoore, California to inspect the Navy's F/A-18 CRM programs and then drive over to TOP GUN in Fallon, Nevada. My traveling partner this time was LCDR John *COMA* Souma who had an F/A-14 background.

The two of us started in Lemoore, California to inspect the legacy F/A-18 A/B/C/Ds and the Super *HORNET* F/A-18 E/Fs respective Fleet Replacement Squadrons, which were brand new at the time. We inspected both squadrons over the course of the morning and then had the afternoon to fly. Being a Navy officer, *COMA* flew the Super *HORNET*. Being a Marine, I flew with VFA-125, the Rough Raiders, in a legacy F/A-18B equipped with a rare control stick in the back seat!

The Legacy *HORNET* flight instructor that took me flying had completed Advance Pilot training with me, and we had not seen each other in years. Recognizing me, Navy LT Lightstone got us switched from a two at Delta model into an older two-seat F/A-18B and invited me to fly with him. I shared my cancer victory with him and let him know I was absolutely pumped to get to fly my very first flight in an F/A-18 with an old friend!

This was not a dedicated CRM inspection flight. This was a student training mission with a solo Nugget in the second aircraft. The mission today was a two-ship simulated weapon delivery flight at one of the bombing ranges in the valley on the other side of the Sierra Nevada mountain chain.

On February 19, 2003, exactly 855 days after my last flight in my F/A-18D, I strapped into the backseat of the instructor's F/A-18. Only the kick of acceleration we felt matched the rush of adrenaline I felt as LT Lightstone went to MAX power, and we started our roll down the runway. The student, as the wingman, took off five seconds behind us and joined us on our right side a little low. As soon as we broke through the numerous low level stratiform cloud layers in California's Central Valley, the instructor directed the student to take a tactical position in Combat Spread with a swift hand

492

motion in the canopy. Combat Spread, the tactical wingman's position, placed the Nugget one mile off our right wing and stepped him up 1000 feet above us as we climbed.

As the student aggressively yet smoothly banked to the right to reach the one-mile Combat Spread position, LT Lightstone generously offered me the controls, "*T-BONE*, you have the controls."

"I have the controls!"

"You have the controls."

I maintained our climb attitude until we reached our pre-briefed cruising altitude to transit safely over the mountains to our weapons range. We performed our FENCE checks—an administrative check of our aircraft engines, Flight Management Systems (FMS), and tactical check of our weapon systems. The student immediately reported that his HUD (Heads-Up Display was inoperative.

"*CRYPTO* Flight, *CRYPTO TWO* is negative HUD."

"*CRYPTO TWO* confirm. Your HUD is INOP?" the instructor inquired as I continued to fly.

"Affirmative, Sir. Multiple cycles and No Joy. I am unable to execute a weapons release profile."

"Copy that *CRYPTO TWO* . . . Standby."

Without a HUD in the student's aircraft, he was unable to see the weapons delivery information that the targeting system provided the pilot; so we had to cancel the training mission. Rather than take the controls and fly us back to base, the instructor came over the ICS (intercom system) and asked me what I would like to do.

"*T-BONE*, seems the American taxpayers just bought you a full bag of gas. How shall we burn it?" The student's equipment failure became an hour-long refresher course for me in three-dimensional maneuvering. Yep! Just like riding a bike!

"Let's see what kind of hands your STUD has. (STUD is an affectionate term that flight instructors use for students.) How about we do a little tail chase over the tops of these mountains? I haven't had a 'Guns Kill' in over two years!"

"Tail chase it is," he relayed over the ICS to me. Then he keyed the MIC and transmitted over the tactical frequency, directing his student to go to max power for our initial setup. We set a hard deck for our maneuvering and climbed up out of the valley and over the tops of the mountains.

I chased the Nugget around the sky, scoring a couple of quality kill shots. We each got a thorough workout while max performing the jets a few times. My G-tolerance had waned just a bit after having lost significant weight and the muscle mass from my pre-cancer days. Not having pulled Gs in a couple of years, I was very grateful for the months of preparation in the gym with *TONTO* for this first flight back in a *HORNET*. It would serve me well again as I would soon climb back into the cockpit for a flight-suit-drenching F-5 workout the next morning.

COMA and I departed Lemoore swapping stories of pulling Gs and breaking the sound barrier, smiling tirelessly as we embellished liberally about our first flight stories back in tactical fighters. We arrived in Reno to spend the night before heading out very early the next morning for NAS Fallon to inspect the TOP GUN CRM program.

Following our inspection of their paperwork, we had a short meeting with their Commanding Officer for the out brief. *COMA* and I were both jet guys and itching to fly for the second day in a row. We had both fought against F-5s before but never had been able to fly one. The Skipper offered to get us both up for about thirty minutes each. We jumped at the chance to strap into the back seat of one of the TOP GUN aggressor F-5s and go tear up the sky. I was beyond grateful to have a second opportunity to do some dynamic maneuvering and feel the Gs again!

I suited up and grabbed a puke bag just in case. Having not flown in a couple of years, I knew that the likelihood of my losing it on this flight was pretty high. However, it pleased me to find that I did not need the bag on either this flight or on my first flight back in the *HORNET*!

Despite only flying for thirty minutes, I had the best time. That pure joy was worth every pound of jet fuel we burned. There I was—making fossil fuels transform into the sound of freedom. I was proud that I could actually practice what I was preaching in the air. But more importantly, the other pilot and I were about to experience something that made the thirty-minute flight mission *essential* to our inspection and a wise investment of taxpayer dollars.

The F-5 is dynamically unstable, and the takeoff requires diligent adherence to the rotation and climb-out speed. The landing itself is even more critical, because as we approach the airport and transition to gear and flaps down, we fly dangerously close to the aircraft's stall speed.

The TOP GUN pilot appreciated my F/A-18 experience and let me tear up the sky up high but would not even consider allowing me the controls from the back seat for take-off or landing. I told him that his judgment in itself would have earned a passing grade for his decision making.

Once we reached altitude shortly after takeoff, the TOP GUN instructor passed me the controls of the jet and told me the sky was the limit. I had twenty minutes to bend the jet around the sky and give myself a workout.

"*T-BONE*, you have the controls."

"I have the controls!"

"You have the controls. Enjoy the ride. You are cleared hot for any maneuver your heart desires."

"Any maneuver?" I asked mischievously, already starting a gradual pull up, preparing to roll inverted rapidly and pull straight back on the control stick toward the pure vertical and straight down for the initiation of a Split-S.

"Anything but a Split-S, brother. We need to set Take/Off flaps for that maneuver, or we would end up on the desert floor below, unable to make the required turn radius."

I lowered the nose just as gradually as I had raised it and set the flaps to T/O while stating, "That was an excellent use of communication and assertiveness. You definitely pass the check ride portion of our inspection this year. I was seconds away from rolling inverted and pulling!"

As the cold sweat dissipated that had broken out as I was about to initiate the maneuver with my flaps fully up, I verbally confirmed the flaps were now set for T/O with this salty veteran aggressor pilot. With the proper flap setting, I pulled the nose up again, this time to ten degrees, rolled us onto our back, and gently eased the power back to IDLE. Once inverted I pulled the nose of the jet around this descending vertical turn with the force required to not only avoid the ground but also to maximize our turn performance. I was ready for the job interview. The next fifteen minutes flew by—literally! Before I knew it, the flight ended with sweat soaking my flight suit. *COMA* and I left Fallon and returned to Reno, Nevada again for some chow before boarding our flight back to Pensacola.

My next chance to fly came two months later in Meridian, Mississippi with one of my first Fleet Squadron brothers from VMFA-115, *THUMPER*. Yes, the very same *THUMPER* whose name I had given to my little cancer Warrior puppy pal, who was no longer flying *HORNET*s but was an instructor at TRAINING AIR WING ONE.

The five Training Commands that produce Naval Aviators were required to undergo the same thorough CRM inspections as the Fleet Replacement Squadrons. This requirement once again provided an opportunity for me to fly the T-45 for which I had been an instructor for almost a year after I had earned my Wings of Gold in 1997. So on April 23, 2003 I was able to fly three flights in the T-45. *THUMPER* took me up on the first flight of the day for what was going to be his student's second ACM training flight. Of course, I was in the back seat of *THUMPER*'s jet, but I was smiling as I flew and fought against this young hungry Student Naval Aviator.

The second event was a more advanced ACM-12 event, and my next instructor co-pilot also gave me another thirty minutes on the flight controls flying administratively back to base after allowing me to fight a couple of aerial engagements with his student.

At the end of the day, I had flown a total of three and a half hours on three separate missions, and almost an hour and a half of that time I was at the controls. Flying and instructing, even if vicariously through the actual instructor once in the debrief, I was in heaven! I was only months away from my promised return to the cockpit as an instructor myself, and the five flights in these jets the past few months only fueled the fire. The season of fighting for a return to flight status was over. The time to wait patiently for my SGI waiver was almost over as well.

I patiently and joyously stayed busy in the API and CRM classrooms, mentoring each new class with our two-hour CRM introduction. Through the summer I would escape the classroom a couple of times a month to fly with my future squadron, VT-86. *BONEY* had offered any empty back seat flight I was able to break away from my day job to exploit. A number of my fleet brothers were full-time instructors at VT-86, and they periodically called me to let me know when they had the rare and coveted empty back seat following a student or flight surgeon cancellation.

LT Nate *DISH* Dishman, an F-14 pilot, called me one morning and told me he had an empty back seat as his student had just canceled for a medical reason. *DISH* was flying as a dedicated wingman on a WEAPONS LOW LEVEL for the remaining student. This was my first low-level flight since returning to flying, and sharing a cockpit with *DISH* left an impression. He had a passion for flying and teaching. We hit our simulated target area on time and executed an aggressive simulated attack on the target. After the victorious flight, we executed an expeditious rendezvous, join up, and climb up to altitude for our return to base.

It was sexy, and that is all I will put in print! I learned a lot from this flight with *DISH* that I carried into my teaching style a few months later. These low-level weapons flights would soon become the mainstay of my scheduled flights once I joined the squadron.

September 10, 2003 finally arrived, and just as Captain Goodspeed had promised, I was automatically awarded an upgraded waiver to Service Group I (SGI) by the Navy's Bureau of Medicine. That information took two weeks to work through both Navy and Marine Corps administrative channels. Once processed by Headquarters Marine Corps, I could finally fly a single-piloted aircraft. On the 24th of September 2003, the official paperwork from the Commandant of the Marine Corps reached me, providing me with my requalification to fly again. On this day, I became the first Marine Aviator to survive my rare bone cancer successfully using 100% alternative medicine methods and also to be returned to official flight status. This culmination of two years of effort to return to flying brought to fruition the second of God's promises to me on that first day in Captain Morgan's office— final victory! I was more than ready to check into VT-86 as a part-time flight instructor and tear up the sky once more.

64| *Inverted over Pensacola Beach*

I arrived back at *BONEY*'s office for the fifth and final time touting my waiver like a VT-86 rushee trying to join a fraternity.

"Skipper, I am ready to start the instructor training syllabus on your order! Looking forward to serving you as an associate instructor, Sir."

"Associate? I don't want you part time. Why not come over here and fly full time? You have paid your dues behind a desk. If you want to fly here, the job is yours—full time."

"Absolutely! Thank you, Skipper. I wasn't aware that was an option. Let me speak to my new OIC at the CRM shop, and I will get with the Operations Officer to set up my ground school classes."

My friend and former boss LCDR Ulander had just retired as I hit my two-year cancer-free window and upgraded my waiver, allowing me to fly single piloted in a trainer. The new OIC was immediately concerned when I walked in and asked him to release me to fly full time.

"*T-BONE*, I am just getting here, and we have had a tremendous turnover. Everybody, including me, is new to the shop. You are the only source of continuity during my initial spool up. Please give me 90 days with you in the saddle before you leave the shop."

We negotiated, and I pushed back respectfully.

"Sir, I fully understand your concern, and I am more than happy to return to support the efforts if you are ever short a man. But with three years out of the cockpit, I am itching to get back in the air. I need to get through the training syllabus before the new Monitor at HQMC comes looking for me. How about I start the training syllabus next week but remain on your staff for 60 days before reporting into VT-86 full time?"

"*T-BONE*, I can live with that. You deserve to be flying after all that Brett told me you have had to overcome the past couple of years while working for him. I know it has been a long time, and I appreciate you giving me the extra weeks."

The T-2 Ground School was short as the aircraft systems were

1950s technology. The instructor flight syllabus was only a few flights and then a checkride. The T-2 Buckeye was a simple aircraft to start up and fly. This jet's rush of power proved worthy of the three-year wait. The T-2 provided the power and mechanics to do maneuvers that are prohibited in most tactical jet fighters, like spins. In my first three flights back in the air, I did as many as I could handle without having to break out the puke bag. For almost three years I'd worked in Building 633, onboard NAS Pensacola. Finally, I was back in the air inverted over Pensacola Beach turning and burning spin after spin, looking down on that tiny little Building 633 from high above. It was well worth the wait!

A flight student in 1995, 1stLt Trombly, Megan, Alex, and Brianna with T-2 BUCKEYE in the background

I was only three flights into my training syllabus, and sure enough, HQMC caught up with me as I returned from my instructor training flight. The Operations Officer, who had taken me on board his staff when I checked in, told me that I had received a call from Quantico while flying. My heart dropped, and I knew that I was about to get the news that it was time for me to get new orders as I had been on base for three years.

"Here goes nothing," I thought as I dialed the number back to Quantico.

"Captain Trombly, Major *ICEBERG* Tanglewood here. I am calling to congratulate you on your selection to major and to let you know you are an upcoming summertime mover."

"Good afternoon, Major. Thank you for the good news on my promotion, Sir. But I believe there is a mistake regarding my timing for new orders."

"No mistake, Captain. You have been there for almost three years, and you will be moving in the summer."

"Major, I received two-year orders following my completion of the Flight Instructor Training Unit (FITU), and I am three flights into it with a check-ride set for the end of the week. I should be good to go for another two years."

"Why the hell are you just starting the FITU now, Marine?" the Major asked, clearly agitated.

"Sir, I was diagnosed with cancer just over three years ago, and the previous monitor provided me two-year flying orders to be executed after beating the disease and securing my flight status. I have been fighting for three years to save my life and my career. I am finally flying as of this week and couldn't be more blessed."

"I hate to break it to you, Captain Trombly, but your time is up in Pensacola, and I will be moving you."

"My orders clearly state 'two years after FITU, Major."

"Captain, I am the Major's monitor, and with your coming promotion, that means I determine when and where you go next. I can cancel those orders upon your promotion to Major, and I will."

"OK, Sir. If that is the way it has to be. I would like to return to MCAS Beaufort with my family."

"Captain, let me explain what becoming a Major is all about. You have reached middle management, and it is time for you to fill a staff officer billet. You will not be getting orders back to Beaufort." The Major came off the top rope and was pulling no punches. This entire conversation was aggravating me to a new level. I was trying to work with the major, but nothing was working.

"Major Tanglewood, I have just spent three solid years not flying. I did my staff tour as a Captain. I am respectfully requesting orders back to an F/A-18 squadron on either the east or west coast, or to VMFA-212 in Japan where the Commanding Officer is willing to ask for me by name."

"Captain, cancer or no cancer, you have spent the last three years in an aviator's paradise. You are moving, and you are not going to be flying."

The respectful approach did not impact the Major. No! Tact and respect did not move this monitor an inch. This Major had clearly 'drunk the Kool-Aid,' as we say, when he checked into his staff role regarding how the needs of the Marine Corps come first. Major Tanglewood needed a more robust push back from one fighter pilot to another.

"Major, I have fought and beat cancer, and then I fought NAMI and BUMED as well and won. Now that I am sitting in the cockpit, I do not plan to leave it. I will not be taking another set of orders. The reserves are hiring, and if HQMC is not willing to place me in a cockpit after I relentlessly fought my way back from a two-year death sentence, then I'll just drop my letter of resignation. I'll join the reserves and become a reserve flight instructor. I'll be dropping my resignation letter as my ten-year commitment will be completed in February, only three months away. If you have a change of heart and are willing to reconsider chopping me a set of orders back to a *HORNET,* you have my number, Sir."

It was a bold and dangerous approach, but *ICEBERG* had painted me into a corner. The only card I had to play was the end of contract resignation. I played it and hung up the phone.

502

"How'd that go?" asked the Operations Officer.

I shook my head, "Don't put me on tomorrow's schedule just yet, brother. Looks like I am going to need to get a minute with the Skipper before I climb back into an aircraft!"

The Skipper was in with the Executive Officer, a Navy Commander. The door was open, and I knocked on the hatch. "Skipper, do you have a moment?"

"*T-BONE*, come on in."

"Good afternoon XO." I greeted the XO appropriately but then engaged the Commanding officer again. "Skipper, I just received a call from the monitor at HQMC. He congratulated me on my selection to Major and then told me I was moving in a matter of months. I do not want to move but agreed to take orders back to the *HORNET,* which is my end goal. But he held the party line and confirmed it was a non-flying staff tour for three years following my non-flying three years here in Pensacola."

"I just hung up with him and led him to believe I was going to drop my resignation letter for the reserves. Honestly, Colonel, I have no intention of resigning. I would just like to fly here for a few more months to reach the 1000-hour milestone making me eligible for the Reserves option if I need to play that card. I am hoping to outlive this monitor's time in D.C. and find his replacement a little more sympathetic to my desire to fly after being grounded three years."

"I feel a little uneasy telling him I plan to quit when in reality, my loyalty to *SPIDER, JAWS,* and *CUBBY* drives me to stay in an effort to honor their loyalty and support to me over the past three years. I don't feel I owe HQMC anything, as I faithfully executed my previous orders. But I do feel a sense of loyalty to these leaders and a need to somehow pay them back for saving my career."

"*T-BONE,* if you chose to join the reserves, I am sure they would be honored to hire you on your first application."

"Thank you, Skipper, for the vote of confidence. But I need you to unequivocally know, Sir, I am not ready to quit and will take orders whenever *ICEBERG* finally catches up with me. My threat to drop my resignation was spontaneous. I only threatened it in order to buy some time. It is my desire to fly and reach the 1000 hours and hopefully fly below *ICEBERG*'s radar until his replacement shows up. Hopefully, he will be more reasonable."

"This may come across as disingenuous or disloyal to the Corps, but I am here and have already flown three training flights. Before I waste any more training dollars, I need you to know my intentions and confirm that you are OK with my plan. If you are willing to allow me to finish the last few training flights, despite the likelihood I may be snatched up in less than six months, I will continue. I would like to stay and fly for you. But if you think I am cheating the Corps in some way, I will call him back and take whatever orders he declares now, in order not to waste your resources."

The Commanding officer made it clear he was fine with my flying for as long as I could and that he supported my line of reasoning. Another Skipper might not have been so understanding, but *BONEY* knew my three-year history, having been on base for as long as I had.

Looking at the XO, he asked, "Commander, it will be your squadron in a few weeks. I shall defer to you as the incoming Commanding Officer. Do you mind having *T-BONE* fly below the radar here for the next few months?"

The XO responded, "Not at all. Give 'em Hell, *T-BONE*. Glad you are here, and hope you get a *HORNET* when the dust settles."

"Thank you, Gentlemen. I shall schedule my next event." And with that, I did not think about *ICEBERG* for almost five months.

65| *Calling ICEBERG's Bluff*

ONCE again, I returned from a morning flight to find a yellow Post-it note on my computer at my desk in the Operations Department. I looked over at the OPSO, and he just smiled. He didn't have to say a word. I just smiled back, took a deep breath, and called *ICEBERG*.

BONEY had promoted me to Major, standing by the P-40 in the Naval Aviation Museum just before his Change of Command. *ICEBERG* and I were both Majors now; so this call was going to have a different *tone*.

"Manpower Division, Aviation Major Monitor, Major Tanglewood, how may I help you?"

"*ICEBERG. T-BONE* returning your call from Pensacola. How can I be of assistance today?"

"*T-BONE*, you promised me a resignation letter. I have yet to see it. What is the story?"

"You know, *ICEBERG*, I have been flying two flights a day every day and just have not found time between flights to draft that resignation letter the last few months." I dropped that grenade in his tent to test the waters, and I was not at all surprised by the reaction I received.

"Well, Marine, you pulled one over on me, I'll grant you that. But here is how this is going to play out moving forward. You have 24 hours to submit your letter of resignation. If it is not in the system by then, I am going to draft you the most God-awful set of orders to the worst location I can think of."

Not shocked at all by *ICEBERG's* reaction and certainly choosing my next words carefully, all I could do now was be forthright and honest. I had just reached my goal of 1000 hours and was now eligible to return to the reserve force one day in the future.

"*ICEBERG*, I'm not quite ready to resign yet. I have had a number of great leaders stand with me as I fought my way back into the cockpit. And at the moment, the only thing preventing me from flying is you and your stubborn quest to keep me grounded. I'll take whatever orders you have, Devil Dog. Give me your WORST, because I plan to give the Corps at least three more years of my BEST! One more set of orders out of loyalty to the great leaders who have stood by me seems a small price to pay for their efforts. So where am I going?"

It was dead silent. *ICEBERG's* reputation preceded him. I knew that if he wanted to jam me into a hole unaccompanied, he not only could but would. I wasn't bluffing; so all I could hope now was that he had been. I gather he knew I was serious, because he did not test my resolve. He simply picked up the conversation by being as forthright as I had just been, which was refreshing.

"*T-BONE*, I do not have any Major billets left," he stated flatly. He had been fishing for my resignation letter in order to clear his slate of movers as he prepared to leave his current job and get promoted. "I have moved everyone, and you are the only one left."

"*ICEBERG*, if there are no jobs left for this year, why are we having this conversation? You will have your replacement soon, and there will be a new slate in a few months. Can't you place an asterisk by my name noting that I am the first Marine to ship out next year? Let me work out a set of orders with him. My chances of flying would go up dramatically, and that is all I have been fighting for the past three years."

"I can't do that, *T-BONE*," he said, his tone softening.

We both had slowly come down from DEFCON TWO and were talking like reasonable Marines troubleshooting a problem in the cockpit.

"*T-BONE*, where are you from, where would you like to live? Give me a location, and I will see what is out there and get back to you later today."

"Thank you, *ICEBERG*. I appreciate your willingness to work with me. How about Beaufort, San Diego, or Iwakuni?"

"*T-BONE*, you are not going to fly. I just can't get you refreshed and back into a cockpit this year. You have to fly a desk again."

"*ICEBERG*, how about a C-12 on one of those bases? I can fly as an MCAS pilot for the Command and fight my way back into an F/A-18 from there."

Disappointed in his responses but recognizing that he was actually working with me, I told him, "My wife and I are from Boston. Do you have anything up north?"

"That is doubtful, *T-BONE*. Let me get with my boss and see what we can come up with."

ICEBERG's boss and my new Executive Officer LtCol Baxter spoke, and after having removed the two pit bulls from the fight, they soon found neutral ground. I returned from my second flight of the day, and the XO invited me into his office. I knew it was not going to be to my liking when he asked me to close the door and have a seat.

When the boss asks you to close the door and stand at a position of attention in front of his desk, it is going to be short term pain that you can get over. When you are invited to sit down, it is likely going to be news you did not want to hear, and that is exactly what I got.

"So what did you do to piss *ICEBERG* off, *T-BONE*?" he asked.

"I pretty much told him how I had beat cancer, NAMI, BUMED, and would beat him, too . . . in not so many words."

"This guy has his sights on you, and he has powerful allies to include the first General Officer in his chain of command. That's right, his General knows you by name, and in this instance, that doesn't help you. Despite me pleading with his Colonel that you

507

are one of my top producers in the squadron and sharing a portion of your inspirational story, you *ARE* moving this summer. But I have good news. His boss offered two unfilled LtCol billets, and they can place a newly promoted Major into either one. You can either go to Quantico to help build the new Marine Corps Museum or go to Newport, Rhode Island to serve on staff in the basement as a War Gaming Department Subject Matter Expert. Your choice. You can discuss it tonight with Megan, and I can call the colonel tomorrow."

Megan and I discussed our options and requested Rhode Island, as our families were all in New England with her mother's health failing. This situation proved to be a godsend, as our children were able to spend the next few months with their grandmother before she passed.

I had fought for three years to get into VT-86. In the end, I was able to fly from December 2002 to August 2003. These were an amazing nine months of flying the T-2 on mostly low-level weapons flights including a few outstanding spin flights and some cross-country trips for instrument training along the way. I never took for granted a single flight with my students. I had come to realize that all of us as pilots should enjoy every flight as if it could be our last, because we just never know.

Megan and I packed up the family and moved in August of 2004, only two weeks before Hurricane Ivan tore through Pensacola. We watched the destruction we were spared on national news, praying for our close friends who were digging out.

Shortly after our arrival in Newport, Rhode Island, the Boston Red Sox won the World Series for the first time in 86 years. Again, three years later, they were World Champions. Thanks to *ICEBERG*, I enjoyed local Boston sports radio on my commute to and from the Naval War College as the Red Sox and Patriots twice earned World Championships during that four year set of orders.

It was a great time to be in New England as a fan.

Exactly four years later, in August of 2008, I finally did drop my resignation letter to leave active-duty, returning to Pensacola as a Marine Corps Reserve Flight Instructor Pilot. I spent the next eleven years flying the T-6A and the T-6B as a Marine Reservist. In that time, I was also privileged to recruit dozens of great Americans to join the reserve team when their active duty opportunities ended, just as I had.

Serving the Marines of the 4th Marine Aircraft Wing for my eleven Reserve years proved an outstanding way to complete my career. NAS Pensacola's MATSG-42 (Marine Aviation Training Support Group Forty-Two) was both my first and my final home in the Marine Corps Reserve, with a couple of years on the Wing Staff down in New Orleans in between. I will never be able to adequately thank all the great leaders with whom, and for whom, I served during those amazing years of flying and leading Marines within the Reserve Component.

To have those years—healthy years, flying years—fulfilled both of God's promises beyond my wildest dreams. In time, I got over not being able to serve in combat in the *HORNET*. I eventually came to peace with that dream deferred, realizing that much of what happened was a result of dealing with monitors and budgets, and those career influencers were well out of my control. Despite being out of my hands, I realized that nothing was outside of God's hands. I knew I served and flew in the exact capacity that He had chosen for me to serve. Following a two-year death sentence, how could I question my God while flying in any capacity in uniform years after my '*expiration date*' had come and long since gone?

Every time I am honored to stand before a brand-new class of Student Naval Aviators sitting in one of my classes, I share with them that I know that I am truly the most blessed individual, having been able to fly with and teach the next generation of America's

Best and Brightest in the T-6B at NAS Whiting Field.

*David's son, Alex, flies around a growing cumulus cloud in the training area
prior to initiating aerobatic maneuvers*

God truly has blessed me beyond my wildest flying dreams with more than eleven years of military flying after cancer. As if that was not enough, God had one last surprise—an exclamation point—as my career was coming to a close.

66| *Final Flight; Not the Final Chapter*

IN preparation to close this journal, I share the link below. Indulge me for one final Marine Corps memory, and join me on my last flight in a military aircraft. Don't join just me. Also join my oldest son, Alex. He is the last Marine Corps student with whom I had the privilege to fly as I prepared to take my uniform off for the last time and step into the next mission God has for this Warrior. Yes, God is faithful, and sharing this testimony with you is our way of being faithful with HIS-story!

Grounded and Cured

http://bit.ly/T-BonesFinalFlight

The link above is to video coverage of LtCol David Trombly's final flight in the Marine Corps with 2ndLt Alex H. Trombly, USMC on Friday, June 21, 2019. Below is the written transcript of the above WEAR News Report.

After 25 years of service in the United States Marine Corps, Lieutenant Colonel David Trombly flew for the last time at NAS Whiting Field in Santa Rosa County.

These flights are almost always done solo, but Friday morning there were two pilots. It was one last flight for LtCol Trombly, but just the beginning for Marine Student Naval Aviator Alex Trombly. Father and son who doubled as teacher and student took on the skies together.

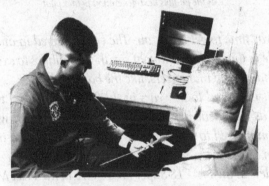

2ndLt Trombly briefing Lt Col Trombly on the
finer points of aerobatic maneuvers.

First order of business before take-off was a briefing where pilots go over flight details and weather. This time around, student Trombly briefed his father. From there, the two suited up.

"I'm still faster than these young guys. Let's see how he's doing," noted LtCol Trombly.

On his final flight, Lt Col Trombly prays over Alex, his son, while walking to the aircraft as 2ndLt Trombly takes on his father and great grandfather's legacy as the family's next-generation fighter pilot.

Then it was time to get in the air. The two strapped in and flew for an hour. While in the sky, father taught son the techniques to execute some of the more challenging maneuvers, like the barrel roll.

This flight is an end to 25 years in the Marine Corps. LtCol Trombly started off as a student in the T-37 primary jet trainer, which he flew when he volunteered to be one of the first four Marines to train with the Air Force in 1994.

Then he flew in the F/A- 18 Super HORNET in the Fleet Marine Forces and he also beat a rare form of bone cancer. After that battle, he served as an instructor and reservist flyer.

"I've got to give God all the credit; I shouldn't even be here. Got 18 extra years and a lot of bonus flights," said LtCol Trombly.

*Victory! God's promise of returning to flight status
both fulfilled and now completed!*

The duo was welcomed by family, friends, and other servicemen. The two Marines also got doused with a big bucket of water, a tradition, and celebration.

LtCol Trombly says out of all the hours he's spent in the sky, this one was by far the best.

"It was an opportunity to get out there, get airborne. Thank God for the day, airplane, memory, the fact that I'm here 18 years later cancer free. That he's got a dad, I had a career and that I had that moment. I wouldn't have done it any other way," he said.

*2ndLt Alex Trombly reliving highlights of the flight as his father,
Lt Col Trombly hangs on every word*

513

His son is following his lead. He has just a few more flights to go before getting his wings. From there, Trombly hopes to fly jets just like his dad.

"I never would have said I'm going to follow in my dad's footsteps. It just kind of happened that way," Trombly said smiling.

Faithful Wingman Alex hugs his father as T-BONE *receives the traditional 'wetting down' after his final flight as a Marine.*

And what would a father-son flight between two Marines be without a little bit of competition? The two joked about maneuver performance.

"We were going toe to toe on some maneuvers. I'd say I beat you on the barrel roll. Of course, I'll say I beat you on something," said LtCol Trombly.

"I'd say I beat you on just about everything," his son responded.

—WEAR Channel 3 News,
Pensacola, Florida, 21, June 2019

Thank you for taking this final flight with me—the exclamation point at the end of a career God promised to restore.

T-BONE *and son, Alex, can't stop smiling after their aerobatic competition
ending one career and beginning another*

A MOMENT
WITH MEGAN

*This flight is still surreal to me. It represents so many battles for
both these men. That little boy I raised, who struggled to read, was
now pursuing his dream to fly like his dad. And the man I love
who I had watched fight so many battles to be here for this very
moment, was ending his. It was the most bittersweet moment!
Proud Mom, absolutely, yet I was saddened at the same exact time,
watching my husband end this career he fought so hard to pursue. This moment could only happen within a certain time frame.
Things in both these men's lives had to align for this very moment
to happen! It was yet another very special day in our lives when we
could only proclaim, "But God!"*

We remain humbled and grateful that you allowed Megan and me to share with you an inside look at the challenges and triumphs of our cancer war. It is our prayer that in your Wars and Battles, you, too, will feel your burdens lifted as God pours out His peace on you and your family. This is the message we eagerly seek to share with each and every cancer Warrior with whom we are blessed to walk.

"Come to me, all you who are weary and burdened, and I will give you rest. Take my yoke upon you and learn from me, for I am gentle and humble in heart, and you will find rest for your souls. For my yoke is easy and my burden is light."
—MATTHEW 11:28-30 (NIV)

"And the peace of God, which transcends all understanding, will guard your hearts and your minds in Christ Jesus."
—PHILIPPIANS 4:7 (NIV)

Retired LtCol David Trombly with youngest son, Noah, at Naval Aviation Museum in Pensacola

Volumes of memories could be shared in countless more books capturing the blessings our family has shared together—moments that would have been lost without God's intervention, His healing hand, His choice to restore me. But allow us to share a brief glimpse of the joys and blessings we did not miss out on as a result of God's miracle:

Noah and Morgan, who were born in the first few years after receiving the news that I was cured, by far are our most priceless blessing, a reward for choosing biological medicine. Our home, no matter where we have been stationed or chosen to live, has been full of activity with healthy children and far too many animals, all bringing joy and purpose to our lives.

Our rewards encompass Megan's mothering and homeschooling six children and the two of us being together at home most nights and weekends, even as I walked out the blessing of finishing a twenty-five-year career in uniform. The thought that Megan might have reared only our first four children, Alex, Brianna, Brad, and Grace Anne alone as a grieving widow is unfathomable to me today.

(Left to right) LtCol Trombly's daughter Morgan (14); CWO4 Hershel WOODY Williams, USMC and last surviving Battle of Iwo Jima Medal of Honor recipient; Master Gunnery Sergeant Bob Rivera with whom LtCol Trombly served; LtCol Trombly's daughter Grace Anne (20); and LtCol Trombly

Watching our children grow up both physically and spiritually and seeing each of them impact the world around them is our greatest blessing and joy this side of Heaven. Launching our older four children as they spread their wings and fly away to chase their dreams, we champion them and look forward to celebrating their victories just as they celebrated ours. As they marry and start their families, I wait with great anticipation for the opportunity to cherish our grandchildren, holding them in my arms rather than looking down from Heaven above.

Close your eyes, and imagine the moments that God did not allow to be stolen by this plague. Join me for a moment at our table for chaotic family meals, board games, and holiday festivities now complete with in-laws celebrating as two families unite in support and love, watching our married children start their journeys together with both our blessings and God's.

*David celebrating at the highest point in Africa, the peak of Kilimanjaro, in
2019 with his Pensacola Ice Flyers' team colors*

Quietly take in and appreciate, as Megan and I have, every silent sunset together. Kneel with me and shout out to our Lord and Savior, thanking Him with a broken voice and little breath at nineteen thousand feet in absolute, pitch, predawn darkness only a thousand feet from summiting Mount Kilimanjaro. Join me on bended knees, arms raised high and tears streaming, praising my God who saved me from certain death to give me the coming view as dawn draws near on the eastern horizon of Africa's highest pinnacle.

Yes, God bountifully fulfilled every promise he made in Captain Morgan's office! His first was that I would win the cancer war. I did, and enjoyed countless more blessings than I could describe in this treatise.

God also bountifully kept His second promise He made that day. I did indeed fly again. I served in uniform leading Marines, Navy, and Coast Guard Officers and flew three more flight instructor tours for a total of eleven more years in the cockpit as an instructor to the greatest military pilots and navigators in the world.

Immediately after his final flight, Lt Col Trombly shares the moment with his wife, Megan, and their children: (from left to right) Brianna, Morgan, Megan, Lt Col Trombly, Alex and his wife April, Grace Anne, Noah, and Brad

God faithfully kept those personal promises to me and more, just as He keeps every promise in Scripture He has made to all who believe in Him. God is faithful beyond our wildest dreams! I have been granted many bonus years to continue dating my high school sweetheart, to rear our six amazing children, and to tackle the next chapter God has opened in this life with my best friend. Yes, even during our dark weeks of EMCON, God divinely prepared Megan and me to fulfill our life's work together as a couple, walking out a ministry as reinforcements to fellow cancer Warriors.

> "I will extol thee, O LORD; for thou hast lifted me up, and hast not made my foes to rejoice over me. O Lord my God, I cried unto thee, and thou hast healed me."
> — PSALM 30:1-2 (KJV)

Megan and I, along with our children—Alex and his wife April, Brianna, Brad and his bride Jenn, Grace Anne, Noah, and Morgan—found our way out of our valley to victory over cancer. For almost 20 years, our children have supported Megan and me in our work of ministering to fellow cancer Warriors. Our heart's greatest desire is to share a path to God's peace for these precious families walking through their personal valleys. Helping our new friends learn of Christ's gift of salvation and His unexplainable peace brings us more joy and sense of purpose than we can describe.

This book ends here with our acknowledgment that God graciously granted every success we have achieved so far. But this is not the end of our story. It is the beginning. If you have walked through the valley and emerged victoriously on the other side, YOUR story does not end there any more than did ours. Sharing YOUR struggles and victories with others brings purpose and passion to life after tragedy, challenge, and heartache. Those around you desperately need the peace you experience. YOUR testimony points others to that peace found in Christ.

"To give his people the knowledge of salvation through the forgive-

ness of their sins, because of the tender mercy of our God, by which
the rising sun will come to us from heaven to shine on those
living in darkness and in the shadow of death,
to guide our feet into the path of peace."
—Luke 1:77–79 (NIV)

EPILOGUE

A MOMENT WITH MEGAN

Dear Caretaker:

I want you to know that you have what it takes to take care of your loved one. Things in life have prepared you for this moment. There will be times when you don't know where the money is coming from to keep going and times when you don't think you have the strength to carry on. But just work like it all depends on you and pray because you know it all depends on God.

And please take time for self-care. Take a moment to breathe, a moment to cry, and a moment to walk away. When your job of caretaker is over, you will still need to live the life you were meant to live. You want to be healthy yourself to have strength for the next chapter of your life. And the person you are taking care of wants that for you, too.

The hardest part is doing all these things you feel God has put in your path to do, with no guarantee of the results you're hoping to see in the end. The enemies of doubt and the fear will come desperately trying to take away the peace that passes all understanding. So guard your heart and your mind. The days get long and hard, but God is an awesome Father. He will meet you in the middle of the night, in the middle of your tears, and when you have no strength for tomorrow. So Friend, take care of YOU, too. It's the best gift you can give to the one you're fighting for.

God bless,
Megan
Fellow Warrior,

Peace is the opposite of fear. Peace—true peace that springs forth from deep within your soul—comes from God. Fear—the enemy's greatest weapon—is not from God, as our young Brad shared so adorably when he quoted 2 Timothy 1:7 during our early weeks as cancer Warriors. Life's greatest fears can be neutralized when our salvation and position in Christ are secure. When God's peace and assurance dismantle Satan's nuclear option of fear, our enemy is forced to shift gears. Satan must use other weapons from his arsenal to try to distract and destroy us.

The enemy's new weapons? Confusion and indecision.

After two decades of coming alongside cancer Warriors following their diagnoses, we experience this recurring drill. During the initial weeks following their diagnoses, cancer Warriors are caught off guard, just as Megan and I were. If this news is your first earth-shattering, life-altering experience, it may well ambush you, too.

Don't be defeated by these overwhelming moments of shock and awe the enemy unleashes with uncanny precision. Know that you are not alone in your experience. If your eternity is secure, then fear has no grip. Therefore, the enemy wastes no time assaulting you on that front but rather quickly reaches deep into his quiver for the flaming arrows of indecision and confusion. We pray that reading about our family's cancer war will assist you in deflecting those fiery darts and embolden you to take up a commanding position to fight YOUR fight and walk out YOUR faith to find victory over the enemy.

The redeeming, saving, healing work of Christ's shed blood on the cross is all any of us needs for salvation. There is nothing we can do to earn that position and relationship with God other than accept His free gift. However, we are privileged and empowered to engage in the spiritual battles which are all around us. When we share our testimony, we influence and affect the fight, and we know that the ultimate victory is ours! My friend, in Revelation 12 God declares that YOU can have a part in defeating Satan himself by sharing YOUR testimony.

> "Then I heard a loud voice in heaven say: 'Now have come the salvation and the power and the kingdom of our God, and the authority of his Messiah. For the accuser of our brothers and sisters, who accuses them before our God day and night, has been hurled down. They triumphed over him [Satan] by the blood of the Lamb and by the word of their testimony."
> —REVELATION 12:10-11 (NIV)

While this is THE END of this portion of one cancer Warrior's testimony of faithful healing and reinstatement to flight status in our nation's service, we hope it will encourage YOU on YOUR journey. No matter what type of valley you may be walking through or what challenge you may face head-on in the future, may this be only THE BEGINNING of YOUR walk in God's peace!

To learn more about us and to find additional information for yourself and others walking through their valley, visit www.groundedandcured.com.

Together in God's Hands, my friend!

SEMPER FI,
T-BONE | Psalm 91

Endnotes

1. Joseph Price, Coronaries Cholesterol Chlorine, Pyramid Health: Canada, 1977, https://www.bonanza.com/listings/Coronaries-Cholesterol-Chlorine-by-Joseph-Price-Pyramid-V2544-1977-Paperback-/830366086?goog_pla=1&gpid=293946777986&keyword=&goog_pla=1&pos=&ad_type=pla&gclid=Cj0KCQiA9P__BRC0ARIsAEZ6irhw6p-FrsnjrFTfqhX_GJkEQIdb-1f3e4TAdk-gBQod1Zf-FpJqnq4aAkK-cEALw_wcB

2. SciNews, "Scientists Categorize Earth as a 'Toxic Planet'" Phys.org, February 7, 2017 https://phys.org/news/2017-02-scientists-categorize-earth-toxic-planet.html

3. H S Brown, D R Bishop, C A Rowan, "The role of skin absorption as a route of exposure for volatile organic compounds (VOCs) in drinking water", May 1984, PubMed.gov, https://pubmed.ncbi.nlm.nih.gov/6711723/

4. Martin Fox, Healthy Water for a Longer Life, Dunway Foundation, 1984 https://www.amazon.com/Healthy-water-longer-life-Martin/dp/B0006YRXT6

5, Lono Kahuna Kupua Ho'ala, Don't Drink the Water: The Essential Guide to Our Contaminated Water and What You Can Do About It, Lotus Press: WI, 2003, https://www.barnesandnoble.com/w/dont-drink-the-water-lono-kahuna-kupua-hoa-la/1112848757

6. Chlorine Free Products Association, "Medical Hazards of Chlorine," http://www.chlorinefreeproducts.org/Medical_Hazards_of_Chlorine.php

7. Joshua Bote, "Can You Get Cancer from Tap Water? New Study Says Even 'Safe' Drinking Water Poses Risk", USA Today, September 19, 2019, https://www.usatoday.com/story/news/health/2019/09/19/your-tap-water-safe-study-claims-cancer-risk-even-safe-water/2350072001/

8. SydneyEvans, ChrisCampbell, Olga V.Naidenko, "Cumulative risk analysis of carcinogenic contaminants in United States drinking water", Heliyon, Vol. 5 Issue 9, September 2019, https://www.sciencedirect.com/science/article/pii/S2405844019359742

9. "The tip of the iceberg: Chemical contamination in the Arctic," Executive Summary, World Wildlife Fund International Arctic Programme Detox Campaign, February 2005, https://wwfint.awsassets.panda.org/downloads/the_tip_of_the_iceberg___full_report.pdf

10. Roger Masters, "STUDY FINDS CORRELATION BETWEEN FLUORIDES IN WATER AND LEAD LEVELS", Dartmouth News Press Release, August 31, 1999, http://www.fluoridation.com/lead.htm

11. Wikipedia s.v. "714-X", accessed 1/18/2021, https://en.wikipedia.org/wiki/714-X

12. *Miracle* Quotes (2004), Movie Quotes, accessed 1/18/2021, https://www.moviequotes.com/s-movie/miracle/

13. Arron Brown, CNN anchor, live news coverage, September 11, 2001.

14. Arron Brown, CNN anchor, live news coverage, September 11, 2001.

15. Arron Brown, CNN anchor, live news coverage, September 11, 2001.

16. Billy Graham, Speaking for the National Day of Prayer and Remembrance, September 14, 2001, https://memorial.billygraham.org/in-his-own-words/.

17. President George W. Bush, "President's Remarks at National Day of Prayer and Remembrance," The National Cathedral, Washington, D.C., The White House, September 14, 2001 georgewbush-whitehouse.archives.gov>20010914-2

18. Ibid.

19. George W. Bush, "Bullhorn Address to Ground Zero Rescue Workers," New York City, New York, September 14, 2001, https://www.americanrhetoric.com/speeches/gwbush911groundzerobullhorn.htm

20. Ibid.

Appendix of Scriptures
by Chapter and Principle

I. First Contact with the Enemy

Chapter 4 - Weaponless
    Philippians 4:7 (New English Translation) Peace
    Philippians 4:7 (New International Version) Peace
    Ephesians 6:10-20 (New International Version)
        God's Armor for Spiritual Battle

Chapter 5 - Check Six
    1 Peter 1:6 (New International Version) Rejoicing
        in Trials

Chapter 6 - The Green Goo and Second Timothy, Too
    2 Timothy 1:7 (King James Version) Spirit of Fear
        not from God
    Proverbs 17:22 (King James Version) Joy - Good
        Medicine

II. Bethesda Battlefield

Chapter 7 - That's Not My Bunk
    Luke 6:45 (New King James Version) Good Man's
        Heart
    1 Chronicles 11:22-25 (King James Version)
        Benaiah's Character

531

God's Promise of Rest
Philippians 4:7 (New International Version) Peace
Psalm 30:1-2 (King James Version) God's Exaltation
and Healing
Luke 1:77–79 (New International Version)
Testimonies Point to God's Peace

Epilogue
Revelation 12:10-11 (New International Version)
Decisive Victory

Glossary of Military Acronyms, Terms, and Organizations

ACM – Air Combat Maneuvering - Air combat maneuvering is the tactical art of moving, turning, and/or situating one's fighter aircraft in order to attain a position from which an attack can be made on another aircraft. Air combat maneuvers rely on offensive and defensive basic fighter maneuvering to gain an advantage over an aerial opponent.

ACT – Air Crew Training - Precursor to Naval Aviation's Crew Resource Management program. The initial program used by Naval Aviators to teach leadership skills for use in the cockpit to increase mission effectiveness and crew coordination.

AOR – Area of Responsibility - A geographic region assigned to Combatant Commanders used to define an area with specific geographic boundaries for Command and Control purposes.

API – Aviation Preflight Indoctrination - Initial military training system which includes classroom academics, water survival, and physical fitness evaluation before Student Naval Aviators start flight training.

BFM – Basic Fighter Maneuvering - tactical movements performed by fighter aircraft during air combat maneuvering, to gain a positional advantage over the opponent.

Bingo Bug - A pilot selected preplanned low fuel warning which is monitored by an aircraft's fuel system alerting the pilot that it is time to knock off the current mission and return to base with the remaining fuel in order to land with proper emergency fuel reserves.

Blitzkrieg – German term literally meaning "lightning war," a word representing a multi-pronged military tactic calculated to create psychological shock and resultant disorganization in enemy forces through the employment of surprise, speed, and superiority in presence and firepower

BLUF – Bottom Line Up Front - Commonly used acronym in military correspondence delivering the primary point early in the correspondence to save the reader time as a courtesy.

BOQ – Bachelor's Officer Quarters - Military version of a basic hotel on base.

Break Turn – Standard Military entry into the landing pattern at both military and civilian airfields which allows tactical aircraft to approach at higher airspeeds. The direct entry and the extra airspeed provide for a safer entry due to a lower Angle Of Attack allowing for better forward visibility as well as maneuverability for the military pilot.

BRU-14/A –bomb racks attached to the F/A-18 for the suspension and release of conventional and special weapons/stores up to 2,200 pounds.

Call Signs - Military nicknames. Aviators receive call signs more often than not for some mistake they made during the execution of their job. TORCH, for example, would be assigned to a pilot who ruined an engine due to an engine fire or over temp on start. *T-BONE* might have something to do with cow tipping . . . further explained in a forthcoming book. For the purpose of identifying military members' call signs within the storyline, they have been set in ALL CAPS and *italicized* for ease of recognition.

CHAPS – An endearing nickname Marines and Sailors use to refer to all the Chaplains they come to know and respect

Combat Spread – The most basic of maneuvers used prior to engagement. A pair of attacking aircraft will separate, often by a distance of one mile horizontal by 1500 feet vertical.

CRM – Crew Resource Management - The effective use of all available resources by individuals, crews, and teams to safely and efficiently accomplish the mission or task. CRM also refers to identifying and managing the conditions that lead to error.

DIFDEN Orders – Non-Flying Orders formally referred to as Duty Involving Flying - Denied - A duty assignment where an aviation officer is assigned duty in a flying status not involving flying.

DIFOP Orders – Flying orders formally referred to as Duty Involving Flying - Operational. A duty assignment involving flying while in training for an aeronautical designation or while assigned to an operational flying billet.

F/A-18 – The McDonnell Douglas F/A-18 *HORNET* is a twin-engine, supersonic, all-weather, carrier-capable, multirole combat jet, designed as both a fighter and attack aircraft.

FAC – Forward Air Control is the provision of guidance to Close

Air Support (CAS) aircraft intended to ensure that their attack hits the intended target and does not injure friendly troops. This task is carried out by a Forward Air Controller (FAC) who is an aviator serving alongside ground forces.

FENCE Checks – An administrative check of our aircrafts' engines and Flight Management Systems (FMS), and tactical check of our weapon systems. FENCE check is an acronym we used to set up our systems and switches going into then out of hostile territory— or the military operations area for a training mission.

FMF – Fleet Marine Force -The United States Fleet Marine Forces are combined general and special purpose forces within the United States Department of the Navy that are designed in engaging offensive amphibious or expeditionary warfare and defensive maritime employment. The Fleet Marine Forces provide the National Command Authority with a responsive force that can conduct operations in any spectrum of conflict around the globe.

Guns Kill – Terminology indicating a successful aerial engagement concluded with a kill shot from the victorious aircraft's machine gun as opposed to a missile shot.

HUD – Heads-Up Display - is a means of presenting information to the pilot in the line of their external forward vision which projects key flight instrument data onto a small 'see-through' screen positioned just in front of the pilot's line of sight looking ahead out of the aircraft.

INOP – Inoperative

ICS – Intercom System

Instrument Flight Rules – Federal Aviation Administration [FAA] published rules that govern aircraft that fly in IMC, or Instrument Meteorological Conditions. In general terms, instrument flying means flying in the clouds.

MAG-31 – Marine Aircraft Group Thirty-One is located aboard Marine Corps Air Station Beaufort, SC. It was the home to seven USMC F/A-18 squadrons during the author's tour of duty to include his first squadron VMFA-115 the Silver Eagles and his second squadron VMFA(AW)-332 the Moonlighters.

MATSG-21 – Marine Aviation Training Support Group Twenty-One, the Command onboard Naval Air Station Pensacola where all Marine Student Naval Aviators start their pilot training.

NAMI – Naval Aerospace Medical Institute. The branch of the Navy's Bureau of Medicine responsible for providing flight clearances and waivers to Naval Aviators.

NFO – Naval Flight Officer - Non-piloting aviator who serves as a navigator or Weapon Systems Operator (WSO) in Navy and Marine Corps aircraft.

No Joy – In military aviation, a term indicating that no visual confirmation of another aircraft either friend or foe has been made.

Nuggets – A traditional reference in Naval Aviation to a new pilot or WSO joining the squadron directly from the training squadron.

OCS – Officer Candidate School - Initial military training and commissioning source for military officers who did not commission through a Service Academy or ROTC program.

OIC – Officer In Charge - The commissioned Officer In Charge of a military department or unit who is not screened for command position but rather appointed by a more senior commander he or she reports to.

Quantico – Home of the Marine Corps Combat Development Command – MCCDC in Quantico, Virginia.

Recaged – to reset one's attitude indicator to the horizon during the preflight checks. As used by the author it applies to the author himself regaining perspective.

ROE – Rules of Engagement - The internal rules or directives among military forces (including individuals) that define the circumstances, conditions, degree, and manner in which the use of force, or actions which might be construed as provocative, may be applied. (Pulled from Wikipedia)

Skipper – A common, yet respectful, reference to the Commanding Officer or CO of a flying squadron

STUD – An affectionate term that flight instructors use for students

Tail chase – Formation flight training exercise utilized to demonstrate how the use of lead, lag, and pure pursuit by the wingman pursuing the flight lead during high-G, dynamic maneuvering are the basics principles of how flight paths relate to each other.

TBS – The Basic School - The six-month Marine officer training program to train and educate newly commissioned or appointed officers in the high standards of professional knowledge, esprit-de-corps, and leadership to prepare them for duty as company grade officers in the operating forces, with particular emphasis on the duties, responsibilities, and warfighting skills required of a rifle platoon commander.

TRARON Eighty-Six (VT-86) - Advanced Naval Flight Officer training squadron located onboard Naval Air Station Pensacola, Florida.

Up Chit – Official medical document signed by a qualified medical professional utilized to indicate the named aircrew member is now medically cleared and recommended for duties involving flight.

VMFA-115 – Marine Fighter Attack Squadron One Fifteen, known as the Silver Eagles – Single-seat F/A-18A Fighter Squadron within MAG-31, 2nd Marine Aircraft Wing and the author's first Gun Squadron.

VMFA(AW)-332 - Marine All Weather Fighter Squadron, known as the Moonlighters – Two-seat F/A-18D Fighter Squadron within MAG-31, 2nd Marine Aircraft Wing. This squadron was composed of maintenance, ordnance, operational enlisted Marines, and Warrant Officers. The officers included Aviation Maintenance Officers and both pilots and back seat Weapon System Operators referred to as WSOs. This was the author's second Gun Squadron.

ACKNOWLEDGMENTS

Thanks be to God from whom all blessings flow, and so many blessings flowed over the course of our family's walk through the valley. God's blessing began by providing the best family any Warrior could ever ask for in my wife, Megan, and our children: Alex, Brianna, Brad, Grace Anne, Noah, and Morgan. Thanks beyond words to each of our parents and all of our siblings and extended family who prayed over us in the Garrity's driveway (Megan's oldest sister and her husband) and anointed me with oils only a few days after my diagnosis. A very special thank you to another of Megan's sisters and her husband, the MacKinnons, who housed us during our time in New England and watched over our children while Megan and I were in Bethesda. Thank you, family.

Megan and I wish to thank our friends around the country who stood by us and provided timely support to meet our family's daily needs and some critical financial ones. While there are too many to name, I must recall a few that God used to bless us.

Thank you to my college fraternity brother Dave and his wife Debbie who dropped a thousand dollar check in the mail from Alaska. It arrived many days later, but only one day after we made a payment that dropped our checking account to $990 in the red. Their generosity met a critical financial need in God's perfect timing. God used many others to minister to us financially, through meal preparation and other household chores, and encouraging us with words and prayers. To thank everyone adequately between the covers of this book would be impossible.

During the publishing process, Megan and I contacted most of the characters in this book to thank them once again and honor them for their support, sacrifice, and belief in Megan and me on our faith walk. Additionally, there are other public figures mentioned who have provided blessing and comfort with their words, actions, or songs whom I have yet to meet and thank. Words cannot express how deeply we appreciate their work, and we pray for the opportunity to meet and thank them personally in time. Others, like Billy Graham, we will have to wait to thank until reaching the other side.

The protagonists know who they are. They have received our gratitude, and we will always hold them in the highest esteem. The antagonists, too, are appreciated for the part they played in our journey. Without the various forms of opposition and pressure that they brought, our flightpath would have been very different. They brought the challenges that required us to question, research, and daily execute our plan.

There are military leaders: Commanding officers, my Commanding General, and others in Marine Corps and Navy leadership who fought to ensure my success in both my fight to live and my fight to fly. Our story would have certainly been far different without their unwavering support. To my band of brothers and sisters in uniform who stood by us and prayed us through, thank you.

A special thank you to the pastors and military chaplains who spoke life and shared truths with us in preparation for battle, during the battle, and for years after the battle that have helped us grow, appreciate the challenges we faced, and find purpose in the pain. Pastor Carl Broggi of Community Bible Church in Beaufort provided deep scriptural teaching over the two years prior to my diagnosis and prayed with Megan and me before our Beaufort departure. Pastor Ted Traylor of Olive Baptist Church in Pensacola prayed over me at a key transition point, and his leadership strengthened and encouraged our family through the valley and for many years following. Pastor Jerry Martel of Grace Gospel Church in Swansea, Massachusetts, helped birth the idea of sharing our testimony in the form of a book. He planted that seed during a sermon, sharing this thought based on a quote by A.W. Tozer. "What we think immediately after we get news of terminal cancer defines us. What we think immediately after we hear the Word of God defines our walk with Him." In that moment I made this note in my Bible: "Write a book and key in on what I said and felt in response to my diagnosis that first day, as those words defined the Battle and how both my family and I walked it out in faith."

While the seed to write this book was planted in that church service, it was watered and nurtured by the consistent gentle nudges and the occasionally bold challenges of friends and fellow cancer Warriors to put in print all that God had miraculously provided. This included the fervent prayers of one who would become my editor, Ms. Delia McLeod. Our paths crossed shortly after I received my cure, and her son-in-law received his terminal diagnosis with only three months to live. Years later after our move back to Pensacola, God brought us together again. Delia shared that she had been praying for 17 years that we would share our testimony in print and offered to help us begin writing a book. Thank you, Delia, for your support and encouragement to put pen to paper, or rather, fingers to the keyboard. Grounded and Cured would not exist today without you. Your prayers, your pen, your eraser, and your love greased the gears of productivity. Your connection with the powerful publishing duo of Robbie and Sharilyn Grayson has led not only to a publishing success but a lifelong friendship.

A special thank you to General *SPIDER* Nyland, Colonel and Mrs. David Guardanapo, Jack Siler, Brian Friedl, Todd Hatfield, Andrea and Rachel Duncan, Dr. Jim Bob Haggerton, Kristy Christian, and Verick Burchfield, who graciously read the manuscript. These godly men and women provided encouragement and meaningful insight from a reader's perspective. Thank you for your time and wisdom, my friends!

Thank you to the doctors, both conventional and alternative, who went the extra mile and opened doors, like Dr. Dietmer Schildwaechter from Germany. This former oncologist who transitioned to biological medicine, along with the assistance of his daughter, Kerstin, started us on our natural battle plan and provided weekly course corrections as we navigated our way to a cure. Without Dr. Schildwaechter and Kerstin, we would not have found the other members of our biological and alternative medical team whose wise counsel, directive guidance, and hopeful encouragement allowed me to cross the finish line without chemotherapy, radiation, or cancer surgery. Dr. S. was my quarterback, guiding the offensive attack. He has my eternal gratitude. Thank you, Dr. S. On the conventional side, my military primary care manager, Dr. Cary Ostergaard, prayed for me and monitored and coordinated all conventional tests, scans, and communication with Bethesda while also caring for Megan and our children during this chapter of our lives. Words cannot express how compassionate and open-minded he was, as he worked with our unique circumstances. I do not believe any other conventional practitioner would have supported our faith walk and methods as much as Dr. Ostergaard. He and his staff at Navy Hospital Pensacola were amazing. Thank you, Dr. O.

The strength that Megan and I found in our vast support coalition has continued driving us to share our testimony on stage and in churches, assemblies, and support groups, but most effectively in living rooms. Thank you, Sue Best, for setting the example and for empowering others. You will always have our deepest love and admiration for opening your home and heart, allowing us to see your feet of clay as you shared your triumphs and struggles. Thank you to Sue and William and their son, Billy Best, who blazed a trail capturing national headlines as a seventeen-year-old pursuing alternative treatments to find his cure! Thank you, Best family, for embracing our family and encouraging us to think outside the box.

Finally, thank you, reader, the one who picked up this book. What a special privilege to walk into battle beside you. May you find strength to win your victory within these pages. We are thankful to have met you again on this end of the tarmac at this treatise's finish line. Be encouraged in your journey, and may you triumphantly fly!

Semper Fi,
David & Megan

About the Author

LtCol David "T-Bone" Trombly retired in 2019 after serving our nation for 25 years. As required by an F/A-18 *HORNET* pilot, withstanding 7Gs sets the tone of David's never-quit warrior mentality, something in which Marines take pride. Successfully returning from his first overseas deployment followed shortly afterward by a terminal cancer diagnosis, David's primary mission changed. He was to fight in a different war back home than his fellow Warriors who were engaged overseas in the War on Terror. Victory upon victory, cancer cured, and back in the air, David flight instructed for three more tours of duty. His military career culminated in training Student Naval Aviators and first tour Flight Instructors as the Reserve Senior Marine at Naval Air Station Whiting Field in Milton, FL. For his final flight as an Active Duty Marine, he proudly shared the cockpit with his very last student and fellow Marine: his oldest son, 2ndLt Alex Trombly.

In the prime of his career, David Trombly received the shocking news that he had a rare terminal cancer, a Primary Lymphoma of Bone, from which there had never been a military survivor. With this knowledge, he and his wife, Megan, embarked upon the difficult research of alternative biological medical treatments. This propelled them into a battle not only for David's life but also for his military career. Journey with David and Megan through ambushes, EMCON, and reconnaissance missions all the way to Washington D.C.'s highest military medical court in this exciting, true story of courage and peace as told in the pages of GROUNDED AND CURED.

David and Megan needed a fighting spirit to pioneer ground-breaking holistic and alternative medical strategies, but they had something even more powerful. A peace that passes all understanding undergirded them to withstand the traumatic cancer battle they fought. Their own life experiences and God-given discipline yielded not only an education for themselves but for others. Since David's cancer-free proclamation in 2001, the couple have encouraged hundreds of families battling cancer. Among their continued weaponry for quality health, quality water ranks near the top. And T-BONE doesn't hold back in telling it like it is when it comes to the nationwide challenge we face with poor water quality and toxicity. (Click on the Water" link on the homepage of www.groundedandcured.com)

David and Megan's greatest prayer is that through their efforts in educating others, many will find victory in the journey that they are called to walk. Whether a broken relationship, PTSD, job loss, depression, injustice, a deadly diagnosis, or the loss of someone dear, they hope that *Grounded and Cured* will deliver a powerful message of peace and hope for their valley. A published author and sought-after motivational speaker, David also serves as Chaplain for Pensacola's professional Hockey Team—the Pensacola Ice Flyers, Chaplain for the Cpl J.R. Spears Det 066 Marine Corps League, and Chaplain for the Pensacola Gold Star and Surviving Families CONNECT Organization (GSSFC). He and his wife, Megan, have six children and reside in the Pensacola, Florida area.

CONTACT US

To contact David Trombly, to coordinate a speaking engagement, or to secure additional information regarding David and Megan's alternative cancer battle plan, visit:
www.groundedandcured.com